THE B·E·S·T COMPANIES FOR W·O·M·E·N

Baila Zeitz, Ph.D. Lorraine Dusky

SIMON AND SCHUSTER

New York London Toronto Sydney Tokyo

Simon and Schuster
Simon & Schuster Building
Rockefeller Center
1230 Avenue of the Americas
New York, New York 10020

Designed by Kathy Kikkert

Manufactured in the United States of America

10 9 8 7 6 5 4 3 2 1

Library of Congress Cataloging-in-Publication Data
Zeitz, Baila.
 The best companies for women / Baila Zeitz and Lorraine Dusky.
  p. cm.
 Includes index.
 1. Women—Employment—United States—Case studies. 2. Career
development—United States—Case studies. 3. Corporations—United
States—Case studies. 4. Business enterprises—United States—Case
studies. I. Dusky, Lorraine. II. Title.
HD6095.Z45 1988
331.4'2'0973—dc19   88-6706   CIP
ISBN 0-671-60741-3

To the memory of my mother and father,
Tillie and David Weinstein
—B. Z.

To Judy Klemesrud,
who stood for what this book is all about: equality
—L. D.

CONTENTS

THE QUIET REVOLUTION

According to the latest figures:

> 38 percent of all accountants are women.
>
> 30 percent of all computer systems analysts are women.
>
> 33 percent of MBA candidates are women, with the percentage rising to 50 percent at Harvard, Yale and Stanford business schools.
>
> 20 percent of engineering students are women, and at MIT, 38 percent of the class of 1990 are women.

In 1970, 16 percent of managers in industry were women. In 1987, it was 35 percent. The number is likely to grow. More than half of all undergraduates today are women, and the vast majority are expected to join the work force in the first few years after college.

But regardless of these numbers, it is not all sweetness and light for working women. Sexual discrimination and sexual harassment on the job continue to be problems in some companies, as do the difficulties of combining a career and family. Women still have a long way to go before they reach the top. In 1985, of 1,362 senior corporate executives surveyed by Korn/Ferry International, an executive search firm, only 29—2 percent—were women. Of the 12,000 directorships in America's top companies, only 4 percent are held by women. And those women who do reach senior management pay an enormous personal price. Whereas 90 percent of male executives are married, only 41 percent of female executives are; 28 percent have never been married.

Are women being paid like the men in their respective new fields? No. How bad is the discrepancy? It depends on how you slice it. For years, the comparative wage averaged 59 cents on the dollar, rising gradually to 68 cents in 1987. The best news is that women 21–24 years of age now earn 86 cents on the dollar, and women aged 25–34 earn 78 cents. But women in their thirties, forties and fifties lag far behind men. If only total figures are considered, women college graduates who work full-time, year round, are earning on a par with male high school dropouts. Optimistic economists predict that women will average 74 cents on the dollar by the year 2000. That's appalling. At the upper reaches, the news is no better. Another executive search firm, Heidrick & Struggles, found that women at the vice presidential level and above earn 42 percent less than their male counterparts. This was in 1987.

Clearly, women in some industries fare better than in others. And within an industry, women in some companies fare better than in others. The key question is: which industries and which companies? We wrote this book to answer that question.

HOW WE DID THE RESEARCH

To identify those companies that were best for women, we went to the sources most likely to know where women are doing well. In May 1985, we sent letters to 76 executive recruiters, 72 professional women's groups and 15 researchers with specialized knowledge in this field. We explained that we were looking for companies that excel in one or more areas we considered important:

Recruiting and hiring of women
Opportunities for promotion
Pay
Commitment to equality
Flexibility for parenting needs
A strong policy on sexual harassment

The total number of companies nominated was 198; some were nominated many times.

In August 1985, we sent a six-page questionnaire to the heads of the human resource divisions of all the companies nominated, along with a letter describing the purpose of the book. We asked for specific information on the policies and practices of the companies in the following areas:

Recruitment
Hiring
Programs aimed at promoting women
Handling of sexual discrimination and sexual harassment
Training programs on sexual harassment
Thinking on rectifying inequality of pay
Flexitime
Maternity benefits
Paternity benefits
Adoption benefits
Sick leave for family illness
Leave without pay, position assured

On-site child care

Subsidies for child care

Resource referral directory for child care facilities

Cafeteria-style approach to benefits (various options from which to
choose)

Part-time work for managers and professionals

Policies on employing couples

We also asked several questions originally posed in the 1980–81 Zeitz study, *Corporations and Two Career Families: Directions for the Future*, published by Catalyst, to learn whether attitudes had changed during the five years since that study was done. Finally, we asked about numbers of employees, the percentage of employees who are women, the number of employees who are considered upper management and the percentage of those who are women. We also asked for numbers of women in specific job titles. As we did this phase of the research, the names of other good companies surfaced, and we also contacted them. In all, we contacted 213 companies.

Some companies refused to participate. The reasons generally fell into one of these categories: a pending takeover or restructuring would change them drastically, and policies and practices (as well as numbers) were in flux; some stated flatly that they were not a good company for women; others said they didn't want to reveal the kind of information we were asking for; some said they didn't want to be bothered; and some didn't want to reveal their shortcomings.

In all, 81 companies—38 percent—responded to our survey. From those 81, we made our final selection of companies to be visited. Companies were eliminated because they were not good enough, they were too small in an industry already represented, or they were bought out and absorbed by other corporations as we did the research.

After analyzing the hard data, we visited 55 companies to interview on site the women who worked there. Policies are important, but how do they affect the women working at a company? Is a company as good as its reputation? Or better? If there is a strongly worded policy on sexual harassment, is it taken seriously? How are offenders treated? What happens to women who take three-month maternity leaves? Do they get their old jobs back or are they shunted off to the side and not taken seriously anymore? Is there a glass ceiling? At what level? Are men and women really being paid equitably?

One of us visited at least the corporate headquarters, and sometimes other locations, of each company. We got a feel for the go-go pace on the PepsiCo campus, the gentility of a Herman Miller factory, the excitement in the middle of the night at a Federal Express Hub. We talked to a minimum of six women and up to 15 at each company.

We talked to engineers, lawyers, psychologists, accountants, general managers, vice presidents, directors, attorneys, plant managers, sales representatives and regional managers. We talked to MBAs and Ph.D.s and to women who had come up through the ranks with high school diplomas to senior management positions, some earning degrees as they rose, some not. We talked to single women, married women, divorced women, parents married and single, mothers of infants, mothers of teenagers and widows. We talked to women who have their eye on the CEO slot and women who had made hard decisions about how much they're willing to give up for their careers. We talked to many smart, talented and honest women and came away with hundreds of stories about the diverse ways they are confronting the obstacles that women face in their careers and home lives. Their words sometimes contradicted, sometimes confirmed what their companies had said about themselves and their policies toward women.

Three companies were dropped during this phase; Johnson & Johnson and Control Data because the women were not positive enough about their chances for advancement to meet our standards (see explanation following profiles) and a third, Arbor House, because it was merged with William Morrow & Company during the research and writing.

Ultimately, our final selection was based on a combination of benefits, policies and practices, along with the personal experiences of women working for a company, which carried more weight than what the companies said about themselves or had in their handbooks. We believe the companies profiled here offer the best opportunities and most amenable workplaces for women. A supplemental list of companies we recommend but did not profile for a number of reasons is at the end of the book.

HOW TO USE THIS BOOK

The Best Companies for Women is meant for women at every stage of their careers: college women who are starting the job search; women with established careers who are ready for a geographic move, a within-industry move or perhaps a complete career change; women who have left the work force for personal or family reasons and are now ready to return. Career selection and change involve many factors, some personal, some professional. *The Best Companies for Women* provides an important piece of the puzzle for every woman contemplating a new job or a new career or a move to a new location. And if you are unhappy with your present job but haven't verbalized what's wrong, this book may help you make an informed decision as to whether you should stay where you are or begin looking elsewhere.

The companies appear in the book in alphabetical order. Following the name of the company is a brief summary of salient facts and company policies:

▲ Number of employees; percentage of female employees
▲ Revenues
▲ Recruiting and hiring of women
▲ Promotion of women
▲ Number of women in upper management;* number on boards of directors
▲ How the company addresses sexual discrimination

*Upper management is defined differently in different industries; it can't be done solely by title. A female vice president is rare in manufacturing, quite common in banking. Most often, it's defined by grade level, and people above a certain level are eligible for executive compensation packages. We always give you the number of people who are considered upper management, as well as the percentage of those who are women. The smaller the absolute number, the better. We are wary of companies, no matter how large, that told us their percentage of women on a large base. As we will note repeatedly, women in the early stages of management are doing quite well in many companies. When a company gives you percentages of women based on several thousand managers, you can be sure that they are less proud of the percentage at the very top.

▲ How the company addresses sexual harassment
▲ Flexibility of company on pregnancy, parenting
▲ Benefits
▲ Major employment centers
▲ Address and phone number of corporate headquarters

The profile that follows each of these brief summaries presents a comprehensive picture of what it is like for a woman to work in that company—most often in the words of the women who do. Their experiences will give you an insight into company policies and the corporate culture that you will not hear from the director of human resources or read in company literature. These profiles tell you what to expect not only if you apply for a job there, but also what will happen if you get it. What are your opportunities for additional training, advancement, equality of pay and responsibility? Are opportunities better in some areas of the company than others? Will sexual discrimination or harassment be a problem? Will the company discourage you from combining career and family? What are your chances for a meaningful, long-term career?

Reading these profiles will widen your awareness of your range of options. Good career counselors invariably tell you to talk to people who are already doing the work you think you might like to do. These profiles provide exactly that kind of information.

In the chapters that follow the company profiles, we have compared the policies and performances of these companies and discussed trends in the workplace that will profoundly affect women at every stage of their careers. You will hear from men as well as women, for in all but rare cases, it is still men who dominate the corporate culture and determine its policies toward women. You will also find advice on how to make a realistic and rewarding career choice and, just as important, what you can, and often must, do to avoid the pitfalls and take advantage of the opportunities that will make whatever career you choose pay off for you.

Reading these profiles and comparisons for women, you'll discover the truth about the real world of career women. Most of them are *not* headed for the CEO's office. Neither are most men. Most of them get both pleasure and grief from their careers. They pursue careers for the same reasons men do: for the money, the satisfaction, the recognition—usually in that order. They know the glass ceiling exists. They also know that progress is possible, more possible in some industries than in others, more possible in some companies than in others. They love their work, but they want other satisfactions too—families, community involvement, personal time. They know there are trade-offs. And yet they are committed to their work. They are in it for the long haul.

The women we talked to inject a healthy dose of reality, of humor, of "let's get on with it" to the problems and the satisfactions of the workplace. They represent a broad spectrum of talents, interests, career opportunities, goals and dreams. They are where you want to be. The women we talked to are talking to you.

PROFILES OF THE
BEST COMPANIES
FOR WOMEN

AMERICAN EXPRESS/ SHEARSON LEHMAN HUTTON

A MULTINATIONAL CONGLOMERATE IN FINANCIAL SERVICES

▲ EMPLOYEES: 57,400 (in the United States); approximately 60 percent are women. We focused on the corporate staff, Travel Related Services (TRS) and Shearson Lehman Hutton.

▲ REVENUES: $14.7 billion; income in 1986 of over $1 billion.

▲ The financial services industry is one that attracts women, and American Express has responded in kind. Since 1977 it has vigorously recruited and hired women, particularly at the entry level for professionals. AmEx did not release the number of women in senior management; however, of the 23 corporate officers of the holding company, 5 — 22 percent — are women. Two women sit on the 20-member board of directors.

▲ At Shearson Lehman Hutton, approximately 3 percent (7 women out of 225) of senior management is female. One of the 16-member board of directors is female.

▲ The company has a number of programs for entry-level and middle management employees: job posting, management development seminars and a thorough review process, as well as intern programs that include approximately 50 percent women.

▲ Sexual discrimination allegations are handled through an informal hearing, and the current CEO has issued a strong statement denouncing harassment. The women we interviewed do not believe that inequality of pay exists at the company.

▲ Maternity disability leave for normal childbirth is eight paid weeks for employees of Travel Related Services and the holding company. All employees of both these companies may take 12 weeks of unpaid leave for family care with job guaranteed; thus, a new mother could tack on four unpaid weeks to her disability leave. At Shearson Lehman Hutton, the maternity policy is 13 weeks. The company provides a resource and referral service for child care in many locations and has flexible benefits.

▲ Major employment centers: New York City (all companies): 17,000 (slightly more than half are at Shearson Lehman Hutton); Phoenix: 3,000 (TRS); Ft. Lauderdale: 4,000 (TRS); Salt Lake City:

1,700 (TRS); other major facilities are in Chicago, Boston and Atlanta, and there are smaller offices throughout the United States. Shearson Lehman Hutton's major locations outside New York City are: Boston: 2,700; Chicago: 1,600; Atlanta: 750; and there are smaller facilities throughout the United States.

AMERICAN EXPRESS
COMPANY
American Express Tower
World Financial Center
New York, NY 10285
(212) 640-2000

SHEARSON LEHMAN
HUTTON INC.
American Express Tower
World Financial Center
New York, NY 10285
(212) 298-2000

If the words competitive, aggressive and political used to describe a company excite rather than scare you and finance is your game, American Express may have more than a card for you. It might have a job.

And while the executive washroom was virtually a men's room as little as five years ago, today women are emerging at the highest ranks with titles such as senior and executive in front of the vice president on their blue-and-white business cards. The change is so recent, however, that when the executive gym for the new American Express Tower in Manhattan's financial district was designed, it featured a minuscule locker room for women. When senior women said, ahem, *Don't you think there's going to be more of us?* there was a resounding—if somewhat red-faced, one imagines—"Of course! You can have three toilets and four showers! Of course!" Equal facilities for men and women were installed.

That wasn't the way when Lehman Brothers built a lavish new gym not long before the financial house became a part of the American Express umbrella. The gym had no women's locker room because, as one woman put it, "They couldn't imagine that there would ever be a woman senior enough to use it." Once Lehman was acquired by AmEx, women were eligible, and a few brave female souls now use the gym and men's locker room with the aid of large, thick towels.

Locker room politics aside, the big push for women at AmEx came with the ascendency of James D. Robinson III to the position of CEO in 1977. "I believe he has no sex bias," says Rennie Roberts, head of human resources at AmEx and a senior vice president. "If you can do the job, he doesn't care if you are male or female. Now there are other pockets of the organization where that attitude is not as strongly felt, but he's always asking the CEOs [of the subsidiaries], 'Where are the *senior* women?' I don't mean to imply it's all sweetness and light. I don't mean there isn't more to do, but overall it's really an open environment. Whoever can do the job can do it, male or female." Roberts herself is an example of that policy. Although human resources, an expanded version of personnel, tends to be a woman's ghetto in industry, very few women make it to the top job, particularly in large corporations. In early 1986 Roberts was one of three such women who headed the human resources departments for *Fortune* 500 companies.

Women from the Travel Related Services (TRS) subsidiary, which accounts for the AmEx credit card and travelers checks businesses, agree that it is not sex but the bottom line that counts—up to a point. One vice president says it's possible to cut through the bureaucracy if you know the right people or have a good idea. "If you can present your idea well—and presentation counts for a lot—you can sell your idea and get the support you need and very little difference is paid to whether you're male or female," she says, adding that such fair play wasn't the case before Robinson's personality was strongly felt. "Go back five, seven years and I'd have to say the attitudes were almost hopeless then." Since that time, she says, "Management has very consciously promoted and pushed women—and I'm one of the chief beneficiaries of that." Getting to the next level, senior vice president, is a harder nut to crack since the competition is so keen.

However, she is one of the lucky ones who wasn't promoted before she was ready. A few who were found themselves unceremoniously fired. Although the company gave them a generous package and office space while they looked for a new position, no effort was made to hide the fact that they had been canned and that lack of experience was the issue. "At American Express you can rise quickly, get a lot of experience early on, but if you don't cut it in a year, you are vulnerable," says Paula Saint-Amour, a vice president in finance at TRS. "They pay you well and give you responsibility, but you are pressured to make the numbers."

You had better be fairly light-footed and flexible to keep up, as the current management style involves quick changes to stay abreast of the market. What you're learning today may not be what you're doing in six months.

And you're not likely to get a lot of help. Executives—even junior executives—are expected to take the job and run with it. The company does not spend a lot of time training anybody. "We hope we've put the right person in the right job to seize the opportunity and get the support where you find it," says Rennie Roberts. Even in one of the management training programs (which are now approximately half women), you are held responsible for what you actually accomplish. The program gives people jobs with hands-on experience in a number of different areas. Saint-Amour's background is typical. In 13 years, she's had nine jobs; another vice president has had six jobs in seven years. "It's a very good training ground if you spend ten or twelve years at the company," Saint-Amour adds, particularly because it's not difficult to move from one division to another. Lawyers go into marketing, marketing people move to operations and so on, at both entry and high levels.

While the pressure is great, so are the rewards. Money is only one. "What's exciting to me is that I'm working for a corporation that's on the cutting edge of the financial services revolution," says Rennie Roberts. "American Express is making the industry into what it's going to be. If you're into that and want to be part of it, working here can really be a thrill. In my job, I'm involved with the top management of the company on a number of important issues, like executive compensation and senior management succession. That's very heady stuff."

Another high-ranking woman finds the same excitement one of the great appeals of her job. Stephanie Joseph, associate general counsel for the holding company, is responsible for buying millions of dollars of outside legal time. "I call up, and I represent American Express. That's very important— I have instant access to the best legal minds in the country and I love it."

Part of the fun undoubtedly stems from the growth pattern that AmEx has aggressively set for itself in recent years. Quickly and not so quietly it has become a multinational conglomerate in the financial and travel services industries. Assembled under the AmEx corporate roof are four major companies: TRS, American Express Bank, Ltd., Shearson Lehman Hutton and IDS Financial Services. Additionally, AmEx owns a major interest in Fireman's Fund Insurance Companies. A 50 percent interest in Warner Communications resulted in a loss of more than half of the company's $175 million investment in the early eighties before AmEx found a way out.

Overall, AmEx's earnings look extremely healthy, according to *Financial World*, primarily due to the consistent performance of TRS, which accounted for more than half of the company's $610 million profits in 1984. More than 20 million people don't leave home without their cards, green, gold and, since 1985, platinum. The last is available only to people who charge more than $10,000 annually, and AmEx charges you $250 each year for the privilege. What does it get you? Instant membership in exclusive clubs around the world, for starters. By the mid-eighties cardholders were charging more than $47 billion annually, with AmEx collecting an average of 5 percent.

Rapid growth naturally requires a lot of bodies. "If you're willing to work hard and have some skills, there's a job for you," says Roberts. "We are in need of people to meet the challenges as they come, and because the industry is always changing, the challenges are always coming. You get a tremendous opportunity to test yourself and do some things in ways you wouldn't get in other parts of American business."

Now that the talent pool is roughly half women, finding the best—of either sex—makes good business sense. "The difference in the financial services industry is the people you have," Roberts goes on. "The money is all there. The question is, 'Do you have the people who can develop the products, package and deliver them, and do it fast and do it right?' If we're to keep a competitive edge, why should we cut ourselves off from half of who's out there?" Roberts and her staff track the women to make sure they don't get lost in the bureaucratic maze in dead-end jobs and are promoted when they are ready and a job is available. "We are committed to women, we are pushing them into the pipeline and they have been succeeding."

While the rise to the senior level may have slowed somewhat from when inexperienced women were given the opportunity to fail, it does mean that the women who are promoted now are every bit as seasoned and ready as the men to move to senior positions. An extensive annual management review process which includes several hundred employees results in a lengthy dossier on each employee, and it is reviewed two levels above your own. The process continues all the way up through the vice chairman level. A good report is apparently a must if you're to rise. And it helps to have a mentor pulling you along.

While nobody's claiming that life is a picnic for *anyone* at a high-stakes place like AmEx, the company attempts to get the message across through its advertising campaigns that it's at least as friendly to women as to men. Some ads have been specifically aimed at women, not only to suggest that a woman use *her* card to pick up *their* dinner tab, but to serve as subtle recruiting aids. Women at other companies looking to move up watch television and read magazines too. And women are, after all, a major block of consumers.

Like many other large corporations, in-house consumer advocates are now helping to shape practices and policies that directly affect the consumer, and American Express has the distinction of having the most visible of such new professionals in the person of Meredith M. Fernstrom. She is widely quoted in the financial press and has held several leadership positions with consumer affairs groups and professional organizations. "Now more than ever," reads a line from an AmEx consumer affairs booklet, "staying competitive requires that our products and policies be continually fine-tuned to respond to the changing consumer environment." Fernstrom, a senior vice president, has been at her present job since 1982. She was in her late thirties when she got it.

Not surprisingly, the highly charged atmosphere attracts ambitious women willing to work long hours, women who, if they have children, have child care under control. Live-in nannies are the norm for mothers with young children. Youngsters are tolerated in the office on *weekends* or just before the holiday break. A company-paid counseling and referral service helps parents find adequate child care. Maternity leave is treated as a medical disability. A woman might use vacation time to prolong her paid leave, which is eight weeks, longer if complications arise.

Her job will be held for eight weeks (Shearson Lehman holds it for 13); after that it's up to the boss, and there are no guarantees. However, the company will make every effort to try to find other positions for mothers who want absences longer than their jobs can wait. That's not the issue with many women, as they tend to hide their pregnancies until they no longer can and come back sooner rather than later. Not surprisingly, the higher the level, the easier it is to have a job on hold. Stephanie Joseph was offered a promotion when she was seven months pregnant. "They let it be my decision," she says, "whether I wanted to take on the added responsibility at that time. The point is, I was given the opportunity to get that job when I was pregnant." Joseph bit. Medical complications with her pregnancy required that she be out for four months. The job was waiting when she returned.

Abby Kohnstamm had a somewhat similar experience. She was promoted to the vice president level at TRS during her maternity leave, having made it clear to her superiors beforehand that she, with full-time help, wasn't going to be on the phone or running home all the time.

Another woman didn't reveal her pregnancy until late in the game because she felt it was important to be perceived as a person who had the ability to provide leadership and direction, and she didn't want the men who worked for her to feel that she was distracted. However, once she 'fessed up, she found a pleasant acceptance. "Men with children in particular warmed up to me—they could relate to me as a family person."

Sexual harassment appears to be a nonissue these days. When it was a topic on people's minds back in the early eighties, Robinson issued a formal statement denouncing it, making supervisors responsible for seeing that it does not exist and telling employees with complaints to discuss the situation with the personnel department without fear of reprisal.

At Shearson Lehman Hutton, women don't find the atmosphere so amiable. The Lehman partners, particularly, who joined AmEx in 1984, were not accustomed to dealing with women as equals. Most Wall Street firms aren't. One woman calls the situation just plain "lousy" for females. "They may be one of the better places on Wall Street, but they don't get high marks in my book," she says. "They don't want women in senior positions." The acquisition of Hutton is so recent that its impact cannot be measured as this book goes to press.

Another woman with a responsible job—and an assistant as well as a secretary—tells of being ignored by one of the Shearson Lehman Hutton managers during a meeting, even though her boss had made it clear that the manager would have to deal with her. Later he insulted her by demeaning her position. Fortunately, she was able to laugh in his face since he could not affect her directly. Except for irritations like that, she is confident that she has not been held back or discriminated against because she is female. Nor does she have difficulty with the innuendos in the banter that accompanies everyday dealings but does admit that "being married is a comfort" and may make such joking easier to tolerate.

It may also reduce the amount. Single women say they feel they are more likely to be targets of sexual harassment than their married counterparts are. And because nothing is said as blatantly as "You have to sleep with me to get ahead," women have to find their own ways of handling it as well as enduring being called "dear" and "honey" by men several years their junior. "Sexual harassment is not rampant, but it exists," says one woman, "and I'd have to say that women feel uncomfortable talking about it, even with each other."

What the men may find unsettling is that the women at the upper echelons at Shearson Lehman Hutton are breaking new ground into what was once an all-male preserve. Women in senior management can be counted on the fingers of one hand. One of them, Barbara Dixon, an executive vice president, says that she sees attitudes changing as the world changes. "Younger men are less hung up in dealing with women as their equals— they've been brushing their teeth next to them in the dorm, not driving five hours on a weekend to spend some time together," she says, "and the women who are coming up now are going to have it a lot easier." Dixon also sees the attitudes of older men change as their daughters get older. "They are beginning to think about how they want their daughters treated and what kind of opportunities they want them to have, and all of a sudden they deal with you on a more open and interesting basis."

Dixon had a somewhat different experience when she was a broker, a job in which success and respect are determined solely by sales volume. "The rules are very simple as a broker," she says. "If you're good, you're recognized. I didn't come up against anything any man wouldn't. You make your money and you talk to your clients, and that's that."

Although American Express would only reveal the number of high-ranking women in the holding company and not in TRS, it is clear that women are mainstream in entry-level and middle management. Approximately half of the people hired just out of college or business school are women; at management training seminars, women are represented in proportion to the number of women filling those slots. Their pay is equal to the men's. They are getting jobs in increasing numbers in operations, usually the last male dominion at most companies and the surest route to the top. Up to the vice president level, women talk of going to meetings where fully half those present are females.

Then the going gets tougher. The ratio of female to male thins out drastically. Meetings are now likely to have five women sprinkled among 90 men;

and at the senior and executive VP level, there are only a few. Yet they are there, offering hope and providing role models to the women below. Women do wonder, nevertheless, if their chances are truly equal with a man's, particularly if he's black. They say that minorities are getting the push these days, not women. "If I were a black, I'd be a senior vice president, not just a vice president," comments one woman. She talks of chucking it in and starting up her own business or running a smaller company. In any case, she doesn't want to be at AmEx still fighting it out in five years. This is a woman who will probably be in the work force for the next 25 years.

Company women generally agree it is possible to become a working vice president without a whole lot of problems, but after that, it gets difficult. "If it's between you and several other people and everything is equal, and the president of a division is making a choice, he'll probably choose someone he feels comfortable with—someone who plays golf and smokes cigars, someone he can relate to in the washroom, and we can't go to those meetings," says one woman. Pointing out that a lot of business gets done on the golf course and in the bars, she adds that she has heard of one high-level woman who is learning to play golf in order not to be locked out of those meetings. "We can drink the brandy, but the cigars are rather tough," she jokes before turning serious: "The company may be committed at some level to having women in the upper echelons, but the company doesn't dictate who is hired."

Stephanie Joseph knows that her sex was definitely a question before she got the promotion that put her right near the top. "Senior management was asked if they would be comfortable with me as a woman," she recalls. "Maybe they wondered if I'd be tough enough, or if I'd be difficult to work with because I'm a woman. My being a woman definitely added another dimension to my promotion."

She got it anyway. William Fargo, who ran the company at the turn of the century, is probably squirming in his grave. He once wrote this terse message: "When the day comes that American Express Company has to hire a female employee, it will close its doors." Not bloody likely.

But old policies from established companies die hard. This is the company that ran the macho Pony Express, after all. With a huge number of senior, experienced men vying for the places at the top of the AmEx corporate pyramid, the competition is fierce. Women wonder if they have to be barracudas to make it. If you're going to stay for the duration, you had better be good, and tough, and it would help to find a friend higher up who can pull you along.

And don't expect the culture to change overnight. Rennie Roberts believes that enough women are making it at the director (one step below VP) and VP level that it will happen. She points out that only in the mid-seventies did large numbers of talented women become available, and that it takes 15 or 20 years for these women to rise, just as it does for their male counterparts. She is encouraged by the open attitudes of younger men. And she finds the women impatient. "The thing I worry about is women who think it's going to happen overnight. It's not."

AMERICAN TELEPHONE & TELEGRAPH

NO LONGER MA BELL, BUT STILL THE LARGEST TELEPHONE COMPANY IN THE WORLD

▲ EMPLOYEES: 300,000; approximately 47 percent are women.

▲ SALES: $34.1 billion, down slightly from the previous year.

▲ AT&T is concerned about recruiting, hiring and promoting women, and does a fine job at entry levels. They recruit at all graduate business and technical schools and conduct prerecruiting programs such as information nights and career fairs. The company searches out professional organizations such as The Society of Women Engineers, National Black MBA and Society of Hispanic Engineers. In addition to in-house developmental programs and tuition reimbursement, the company has a number of high-potential and succession planning programs. They sponsor executive education programs at the top business school campuses as well as graduate programs in engineering and computer sciences.

▲ At upper levels the news is not so good. 3.1 percent of the 753 employees considered upper management—fifth level (director) and above—are women. Of the very top 131 senior managers, 3 percent are women. Of the 19 members on the board of directors, 2 are women.

▲ In addition to the standard disability for maternity leave, new parents can take up to six months unpaid leave, with like job guaranteed on return. The company allows flexible work hours, flexible workplaces, and part-time work for professionals and managers. A host of alternative provisions for child care are currently under review. AT&T provides super medical, dental and pension benefits. The company also makes a point of buying services and supplies from minorities and women to the tune of half a million dollars' worth a day, or $180 million a year.

▲ Charges of sexual discrimination are handled by informal complaint through supervisors or through EEO. Occasionally, charges

> may lead to a lawsuit. The company implemented a training program on sexual harassment in 1987.
>
> ▲ The company feels it has adequately addressed equality of pay by examining job descriptions and assigning point values.
>
> ▲ Major employment centers: New York City: 10,000; New Jersey (Morristown, Berkeley Heights, Basking Ridge, Short Hills): 50,000; offices in all major U.S. cities.
>
> ▲ American Transtech, in Jacksonville, Fla., employs 3,000 people.
>
> **AMERICAN TELEPHONE & TELEGRAPH**
> 550 Madison Avenue
> New York, NY 10022
> (212) 605-5500

"People were supportive of me just like they were of any other individual. I didn't have to worry so much about whether or not I was a woman."—Nancy Dreicer, vice president of American Transtech, an AT&T subsidiary.

"American Transtech doesn't look like anything I have heard about in the old Bell system. Take the organization that I am part of and ask, how long it will take before women are truly equal? I would say never."—A staff manager at AT&T Communications.

Although we consistently found that women's experiences within a company can vary widely, depending almost entirely on the attitude of their bosses, from no other company did we hear such divergent views as we did from the women at AT&T. In some pockets of the company, women are doing splendidly. Dreicer, for instance, is one level below the man who runs the 3,000-member American Transtech, a rung she shares with four other men. And Dreicer has managed to do this as well as raise two young sons. But in other places within AT&T—unhappily in more places—women aiming for the top have a much harder time. A company that needed the weight of law before it began to hire women at the same levels as their male counterparts is not likely to be able to turn attitudes around in a decade, no matter how hard it tries. Old ideas die hard, and sometimes they don't die at all until the old guard leaves and is replaced by fresh new faces, managers who believe that women can do the job as well as men.

So, what else is new? AT&T is not alone in this respect.

But in spite of lingering sexism, there is good news at AT&T. Officially the company is committed to moving women up the pipeline and into senior management. Women and minorities have an equal shot with men at getting hired right out of college. Salaries for these jobs are scrupulously equitable and, depending on the employee's skills, start in the low to mid-twenties. (Most jobs available now are in technical and marketing areas.) Farther up the ranks, the company sends women as well as men to Harvard, MIT and Dartmouth for executive training programs. It's possible to get a wide range of experiences within the company, moving from staff to line jobs, from one function to another. And while it may be more difficult for a woman than a man to become a vice president, it is possible. Five women out of a total of approximately 130 senior management people had the title in the spring of 1987. Women and minorities who might make officer material are tracked by the company in an effort to see that they get the experience they need and don't get lost. How successful the plan is remains uncertain. Although the restructuring brought about by the 1984 divestiture is still under way, causing turmoil and confusion, reorganization has its benefits. With every reorganization, new opportunities open up—*if* you play your cards right and keep your enthusiasm from flagging.

But that can be difficult in these unsettling times, when whole departments and armies of people have been laid off, and more layoffs are on the way. At divestiture in 1984, the company had some 375,000 employees; at the end of 1986, their numbers were down to 300,000. Pin your star to the wrong person, and you can be left in the dark when he or she disappears. Be in the wrong business, and you could find your division collapsed or sold. AT&T no longer sells car telephones, for instance, and a few years back even considered getting out of what comes to mind when the phone company is mentioned—residential telephones. That division was saved when it slashed costs and increased profitability. How strong AT&T's computer business is remains an open question, and doubts that the company will stay in that hotly competitive field began hurting sales late in 1986. In recent years the company's profits have remained flat and barely cover its $1.20 dividend. Revenues declined slightly in 1986 to $34.09 billion, the first such decline since 1933. The major problem was a loss in revenues from telephone rentals, as more people now buy their equipment rather than rent it; the loss was made up somewhat by an increase of long distance revenues. For the rest of the eighties, analysts predict, the company will be mired in sluggish earnings and little or no revenue growth.

These problems make the company unattractive not just for women, but for anybody. However, official policy has strongly influenced attitudes because, in a sense, it has had to: AT&T has lived through a court-ordered consent decree, signed in 1973, which put the company under the gun as far as the hiring and advancement of women and minorities were concerned. Consequently, even though the company is going through troubled times (although no one's suggesting that the phone company is about to go under), women stand a reasonable chance here.

Women can be heartened, furthermore, by the outlook of Charles Marshall, executive vice president for administration and external affairs, who became vice chairman in 1986. In him, women at the company sense a strong commitment to their advancement. "Individuals make all the difference," says Peggy Sieghardt, division manager for equal opportunity at corporate headquarters, whom we interviewed in 1986. "With Chuck Marshall as vice chairman, you will see changes occurring in this company faster than if we just waited for them to happen." One piece of concrete evidence is the relatively recent policy that Equal Employment Opportunity (EEO) concerns be on every manager's list of objectives, which are reviewed quarterly.

Nor is Marshall the only equality-minded boss in the company. Carole Spurrier, a division manager of AT&T Technology Systems in Washington, D.C., says her boss is "the kind of person who takes talent where he can get it and as a result is wonderful for women in his organization." After listening to women at the New Jersey headquarters say they are sometimes treated like "pet rocks" at meetings, Spurrier comments, "I don't find being the only woman at my level or the only woman at meetings a hindrance. It is an enhancement because you have such visibility."

Still another woman who is upbeat about the company is vice president Paula Gavin, who supervises operator services, a division that employs some 40,000 people. According to Gavin, being a woman at AT&T now is enviable: "There is the opportunity to be just a little different and bring diversity to the work environment." In other words, women don't all have to come out of the same cookie cutter. The way AT&T men do, we hasten to add.

Gavin began her career at the company some 20 years ago, took transfers to sites throughout the country, and gained experience in operations and marketing before her promotion to officer in 1986, back in the same division she had started in as a first-level manager in 1967. Most of Gavin's jobs were in results-oriented fields where success or failure was very clear, a factor she believes contributed to her success. A good bottom line knows no sex.

As in many other companies, however, the Paula Gavins are the exception. At a senior management meeting in 1986, out of more than 800 people present, only about 25 were women. The great majority of these 25—75 percent was one woman's estimate—were attorneys and doctors, who qualified because they were professionals rather than in actual managerial positions. Many women said that while some of their sex slipped through, the real ceiling for women is at the division manager level where, by and large, one is a manager of people and not making policy. "While you have some input, you're more involved in the successful implementation of policies that have been established by men."

And it is men who install the ceiling. They are unable to acknowledge that a woman's abilities may be different in execution, but not in results. One woman who was a trainer in company workshops on male-female issues reports that executives who have not worked with women as equals can relate to them only as wives, daughters and secretaries—in other words, in subservient roles. What she called an "internal screen" obscures their ability to see the skills and attributes of women the way they read men's. The situation is worst in divisions such as operations where managers come from the blue collar ranks with set ideas about where a woman's place is. It is not at the desk alongside theirs.

One woman who has cracked the division-level barrier in a technical area said that in one job she had it was *verboten* for a male peer to lunch with her to share information because the other men told him they would lock him out if he continued to do so. Luckily, the fellow turned out to be a prince and continued to feed her information that would help her do her job. How did he do it? By telephone.

In other departments, men who have been friends for years, who socialize on weekends with their wives, who play golf and go out for drinks after work protect one another in the face of impending layoffs. "I see executives protecting individuals that I would argue are less competent than others," said one woman. "They find jobs—or they create them—for their friends. If this much protection is needed, they probably shouldn't be around in the first place." Most women don't have these kinds of long-standing friendships with enough people in high places because there are few women in high places. Only slightly more than 3 percent of senior management are female.

One woman who is in a position to help others is Dana Becker, a director who has made the move from a technical job to a marketing one. Becker found that the year she spent at MIT on a Sloan fellowship, paid for by the company, eased the way for her. "It was a real shock to be sought after by managers who had only heard about me from others, rather than have to sell myself and reestablish my credentials." Another woman found the Sloan fellowship the ticket to being a member of the right club: "When there was a convocation three years later, some of those who had also gone to the program came up and said, 'Are you going? Do you want to go in the corporate jet?' and I'm thinking, this is all right."

For women at the senior management level, sexual harassment is not an issue, but women farther down the line are not so fortunate. While the machinery is in place for a woman to complain, company women said not only that the charges were difficult to bring but that the offender probably wouldn't be dealt with harshly. The higher up he is, the more problematic it is to complain. One woman was urged by friends at AT&T to seek help from a therapist rather than report someone. He was a senior executive, and the woman justifiably believed that it would be her word against his and she would lose. Company women are angry that known offenders are quietly transferred instead of exposed and fired. If they are later fired for another infraction, their termination may omit any mention of sexual harassment, although it is on their record; however, management says that people have been dismissed for harassment. Yet the message isn't out. In short, AT&T's response on sexual harassment has been extremely weak, and when we interviewed them, the women felt abandoned. (In 1987 an attempt was being made to turn matters around, and an all-day program on harassment for managers was making the rounds and being presented to small groups within the company.)

At American Transtech, it's a different story altogether. If a man turns out to be a mailroom pincher or worse, he can expect to be quickly canned. American Transtech, like the woman said, is unlike anything else within AT&T. The Jacksonville-based subsidiary provides shareholder and stock transfer services to AT&T and other companies.

Other pockets of the company can also be especially good for women— the Washington, D.C., operation comes to mind—but what is good today may be different by the time you are reading this due to the constant restructuring AT&T is undergoing. So much depends on the individual running the show. Women looking for jobs here need to ask pertinent questions of the person they would be working for to make sure that he or she has a modern approach not only to women in business but as an overall management style.

If you are stuck in a bad job, savvy political skills may help you maneuver your way to a different area and a better boss. You would be wise to disguise your reasons for a transfer rather than flat-out state that your boss is a chauvinist. Although it is difficult to move out of an organization and into another in today's environment, that doesn't mean you won't be able to change areas within that organization. And if you're good, the company will make every effort to find you a job if your husband is transferred to another city and you're going to follow. With a company this big, his transfer doesn't mean you have to start all over again.

Flexibility for parenting is not well tolerated generally, unless you are blessed with an understanding boss. If you expect to rise, your clear-cut priority must be your job, as it must be for any man. Dreicer, naturally, says it's different at American Transtech and that she has all the flexibility she needs. But then, she's a VP at a company with a corporate culture all its own.

The standard leave for childbirth is six paid weeks; you can take up to six months' unpaid leave and be guaranteed a job of like status and pay. Some women in lower and middle management jobs they don't particularly like, or who work for chauvinistic bosses, take the leave and hope for a new job when they come back. Since few positions can wait six months for anyone, and at lower management levels there are a lot of jobs, the women usually get their wish.

All AT&T employees enjoy superb benefits—something the telephone company is known for—and the pay, as we said, is good. At the upper reaches of middle management you can be bringing home $90,000. Tuition reimbursement will pay for outside schooling—including that MBA and Sloan fellowship—and when you're finished, you'll be looked at in a new light and find more job opportunities open to you.

Job qualifications include a liking for rules and a high tolerance for bureaucracy. Policies that seem to have been set down at the beginning of time remain in force simply because they are policy. Implementing the policies, which have more to do with form rather than content, take up a lot of otherwise productive time. A corporate paranoia akin to the FBI's is evident. While perhaps a dozen or so companies had a company watchdog sit in on all the interviews, AT&T was the only company that insisted on taping the interviews. If you understand this kind of mentality, you won't have a problem at AT&T. Question it, and you'll be better off elsewhere.

Good pay, then, but limited opportunities at the top. An official commitment to affirmative action, but a bureaucratic mentality. A still fuzzy message on sexual harassment but lots of flexibility in a rapidly changing structure. AT&T is a very mixed bag.

Yet in spite of its shortcomings, Carole Spurrier remains enthusiastic about her employer: "We might not be able to make it to the office of chairman, but if we look at the kinds of jobs that we have, a number of us are in positions of authority. We run fairly large organizations. If we look at the salaries we make, they compare favorably to what else is out there. In a small business, we might be the chief operating officer. I am pleased with the kind of opportunities we have, and I believe things are only going to get better."

AVON

THE WORLD'S LARGEST MANUFACTURER OF BEAUTY PRODUCTS

▲ EMPLOYEES: 15,400; 69 percent are women.

▲ REVENUES: Close to $2.9 billion in 1986 for the entire corporation. Worldwide, beauty products and jewelry accounted for $2.23 billion, up 11 percent, while domestic sales increased 8 percent to $1.2 billion.

▲ Avon Products is a company concerned with recruiting, hiring and promoting women. They conduct an annual human resources review with the corporate management committee, and they focus on the promotability of women and minorities. The company selects one or two women a year for the Simmons Business Certificate program. Independent contractors (sales reps) get strong training and development, with promotion to district manager possible.

▲ Of the 270 employees considered upper management, 60—22 percent—are women, including one executive vice president, one senior vice president and 10 vice presidents. Three of the 12 members of the board of directors are female.

▲ In addition to the standard maternity disability leave, mothers can take up to three months' unpaid leave, position assured. Flexibility of time and place are handled on a case-by-case basis, and the women interviewed reported that their bosses were unusually accommodating.

▲ The company is committed to rectifying pay inequity. To do so, it examines what other companies are doing, reevaluates individual job descriptions and makes grade level adjustments, where necessary.

▲ Charges of sexual discrimination are handled informally on an individual basis; sexual harassment complaints are handled in a similar manner. There is no training program on sexual harassment, but the women interviewed asserted that harassment is not a problem.

▲ Major employment centers: New York (Manhattan, Rye and Suffern): 1,580; Newark, Del.: 1,060; Atlanta: 970; Norton Grove, Ill.: 830; Pasadena, Calif.: 810; Springdale, Ohio: 780. Manufacturing facilities are located in Suffern, Springdale and Norton Grove. The sales force in 1987 was 375,000 independent contractors across the country.

AVON PRODUCTS, INC.
9 West 57th Street
New York, NY 10019
(212) 546-6015

It's hard to talk about Avon at all without a wait-and-see attitude. Will the world's biggest beauty concern, which has always relied on door-to-door direct selling, be able to keep up with its customer? Is she at home? Or is she at the mall, picking up a tube of somebody else's lipstick at the drugstore on her way home from work? Is she buying bath beads from the supermarket? Will the company's foray into the hotly competitive market of department stores, where it is represented at the perfume counter, be enough to offset the uncertain future of direct sales?

Are a sharpened sales force and up-to-date marketing techniques enough to turn around a company that seemingly ignored—or at least grossly miscalculated—the impact of women leaving the home for the workplace? Sixty percent of all U.S. women work outside the home.

The company began a disastrous downhill slide in 1979. Stock fell from a high of $140 a share in 1973 to an embarrassing $25 a share in 1983, when Hicks Waldron was called in to be CEO and save the empire. A turnaround doesn't happen overnight, and it didn't here. The sales force began to drop, down to 375,000, where it is today, or 65,000 fewer Avon ladies than were ringing doorbells in 1982. In 1985 the company lost $59.9 million. At one point the stock dropped to under $18 a share.

But in 1986 Waldron announced that the worst was over, the company was indeed turning around. Avon finished the year with close to $2.9 billion in sales, a 17 percent increase over 1985, and earnings of $158.7 million. While the number of sales reps has stabilized at 375,000, training and motivation have increased individual sales. No matter if the company is in the midst of transition, it is still selling a lot of lipstick—and since 1971, costume jewelry as well—with sales figures that make many a competitor envious. Avon is still the world's largest cosmetic company with sales in more than 50 countries.

Yet analysts remain skeptical. The core business is still lackluster. Toiletries, fragrance and cosmetics account for 70 percent of the company's sales (and 80 percent of its profits), and almost half of these are made door-to-door. It's hard to get over the skepticism that anything or anyone can put the oomph back into direct sales. The future could lie in selling at the office, where fully a fifth of all Avon sales now take place, or direct mail sales, which Avon is doing in its clothing lines (James River Traders, Brights Creek and Avon Fashions), but as we go to press there are no plans for these.

But Avon is diversifying. Its health care services division includes Foster Medical Care, a medical equipment rental subsidiary (again, the company's slowness to respond to market changes cost dearly in 1986); Mediplex Group, Inc., which operates nursing homes, alcohol and drug abuse treatment centers and a psychiatric hospital; and Retirement Inns of America. Those divisions, operated as wholly owned subsidiaries, have been acquired in the last few years. Their senior management is heavily male dominated.

But Avon's beauty business is something else. It's one of those rare companies where it's possible to achieve a high-ranking post, as well as a gorgeous office with a view of the Empire State Building, and still have a family. Nobody says it's easy, but nobody says it's impossible the way they do elsewhere. First, however, you have to pass a test. "You're looked at very carefully those first few months—are you going to be leaving every day at four o'clock, are you going to be asking for a lot of time off?" says one woman. "If you pass the test, if your performance doesn't slip, then you can be promoted." And promoted women are.

Siri Marshall, the vice president of legal affairs, who reports to the general counsel, has a daughter who will be 6 this year. Marshall manages both the domestic and international staff of lawyers, 13 in all. A veteran of a big New York City law firm, she says she loves her job not only because it is more diverse than the work for a legal firm, but also because Avon is a fabulous place to be a woman. "I've always felt comfortable," she says, "I don't have to be something I'm not." Marshall, who wore a pale pink print dress the day of the interview, is a very feminine woman. If she has an aggressive personality in business, it somehow recedes when the work stops.

Marshall found that although the law firm where she used to work was more prestigious than Avon (and after graduating from Harvard University and Yale Law, it seemed like the natural progression), she became disaffected after a few years. "It was so technical I sometimes felt like a machine. When I left I wanted a child, and I could not envision myself at a law firm with a child. I may work just as many hours now as I did before, but here it's different."

Corporate legal staffs have changed in the last decade from small operations that did little more than farm out the work to law firms. Now they are more likely to be competent departments where much of the nuts-and-bolts work is actually done. And many women, such as Marshall, find these jobs more compatible with their lives than a job at a law firm would be. The atmosphere is likely to be less combative, the sexism less defeating, the culture more conducive to work and motherhood. But, Marshall cautions, you have to find the right company. "And Hicks Waldron has made Avon the right company," she says. "They told me there would be challenges and this was an upbeat environment, and I've never for a second regretted my move."

The challenges weren't quite the ones Marshall anticipated, as she joined before Avon paid heed to the exodus of women from the home to the workplace, but the work has been enormously satisfying. Marshall is responsible for seeing not only that legal documents and plans are drafted, but that they are implemented. "You're not just a good lawyer here, you have to get things done," is how she characterizes it. "It's much more intangible, you have to understand the company, understand the people and be able to win them over. It calls on more diverse skills. I've grown tremendously as a person."

While she is still something of an anomaly in the corporate hierarchy, Marshall has found a way to use her motherhood to her advantage: talking about her daughter and husband helps point up that she's a family person just like her male peers. But she says she never uses family situations as a reason to ask for time off, and she doesn't blink when she has to travel overseas.

Another mother, this one with two children, is vice president Gail Blanke, who heads communications for Avon Products. When we spoke in 1986, her eldest child was 11, her youngest, 4. "Over those 11 years there has been a growing sensitivity to the fact that not only the women but also the men have to have a well-balanced life," she says. "Before, senior men might have made the statement that they would never take the time to drive their daughter to college. Now they would."

Blanke recalls that when she was pregnant the first time, she was told in no uncertain terms by a man who's no longer with the company that he would not make one single allowance for her. Once, near the end of her pregnancy, when they were walking on the street, he refused to slow his normally quick gait and left her stranded in traffic. He telephoned her with business as usual an hour and a half after she came home from the hospital. "It was a super macho attitude that made no allowances for anything," Blanke recalls. Happily, that kind of attitude is all but dead.

While officially the company does not have flexible hours, many, if not most, division heads and supervisors are unusually understanding. Corporate policy is generous too. It allows for a three-month leave of absence following the maternity disability period; your job—not a similar job—will be held for you, and your benefits will be paid. On the job, the hours are not normally brutal. Most people are gone by 6 P.M. It is assumed that the work gets done. "If I want to go to the first day of nursery school, I go," says Madeline Accardi, a group product director for the jewelry business. "Everything is on a one-to-one basis with your boss, and you can usually work it out. But you could run into a boss who is totally rigid."

Even in the midst of Avon's restructuring, such a boss would seem to be a misfit. This is a company where everybody is *nice*. They are polite. They are upbeat. Even when you are presenting bad news, it is best to smile. While it is now permissible to disagree with somebody's presentation or criticize their suggestions at a meeting, in the old days even such standard operating procedures in most businesses was not only discouraged, it was simply not done. "We were so involved in the Avon style, the substance was ignored," says one woman. "If you made a presentation and there were questions or challenges, you had failed." And the Avon style? Friendly, positive, high energy. Well groomed. Not heavily ethnic anything. Italians, Jews, blacks should be assimilated. Like the Avon lady.

Some of this gentility is gone and has, of necessity, been replaced with a more confrontational style and a questioning attitude, but overly aggressive types still will not fit in. This politeness has to take partial blame for Avon's being so slow to see what was happening in the marketplace. It's as if everybody had been wearing a smile button every day, while walls were caving in. Nobody wanted to be the bearer of bad news. By 1983 the bad news became impossible to ignore and Hicks Waldron came in as CEO to, in plain English, goose the business. Under Waldron, some of this has changed. Some of the new management team Waldron brought in are not schooled in the old Avon style, yet they haven't changed the overall picture. Generally, when people speak up and criticize, they do it politely. Disagreements begin with, "Good point. But . . . what about . . . ?"

Accardi, who is responsible for $350 million in jewelry sales, knows that she's in a hot seat. If her business doesn't grow, she'll be out. "We are all competing for who's going to be in the front of the [Avon] book, who's going to get the premium," she says, "but it happens on a frank, open basis, much more than it did five years ago. Compared to other places I've been, it is still not vicious, and I don't feel like I'm getting stabbed in the back or lied to. It's a healthy competition."

In such a polite atmosphere, sexual harassment doesn't take root. When it has been uncovered, the gentleman has been shown the door . . . the Avon way. Because a flat-out firing would cause so much difficulty for his family, a financial cushion is normally included with the pink slip. However, the message is very clear: do it and you're out.

You would expect that women would be listened to at meetings here, and you would be right. After all, women executives do know what product points are likely to be a plus with the customer, and the assumption that women know what they are talking about is carried over to other aspects of business. Only *infrequently* are women's ideas ignored until they pop out of the mouth of a male a few moments later and are then credited to him. However, now that talent is at more of a premium, any lingering sexism is being winnowed away by the need to have the best person in the job. Consequently, nobody knows where the glass ceiling is at Avon.

Phyllis Davis became a group vice president back in 1977, way ahead of when most other corporations were promoting women to such high levels, and is one of the few veterans left from the previous management. When the national sales manager was replaced in a shake-up, Davis, who had a good track record but no sales experience, was the one given the job. National sales manager in a company with approximately 375,000 sales representatives is a critical spot, make no mistake. Is Davis a real candidate for the top job in the beauty division? Some say yes, some are skeptical that any woman will be given a shot at it in the next 10 years.

While Waldron brought in a new corporate management team, only one of them, Cam Starrett, was female, and she heads up the department of human resources. Others point out that while the numbers of women in senior management in the beauty division are good (seven out of 35 vice presidents are women) nearly all, like Starrett, are in staff jobs, not the line positions that take you to the top. But no matter what happens next, Avon's record to date is excellent on the issue of women in management.

If the beauty business appeals and the Avon style comes to you naturally, you'll do best getting your feet wet in business elsewhere for a few years and then joining. Very little recruiting is done on college campuses, and there is little career pathing other than what you make for yourself. Formal training programs were just being initiated in 1987. It's possible to be transferred to other divisions to gain wide experience, but you'll have to speak up and ask. The women say their salaries compare favorably with those of the competition, and that in the last couple of years an attempt has been made to redress any salary inequities based on sex.

The offices are the kind young women from out of town dream of. They are squarely in midtown Manhattan, right off Fifth Avenue on 57th Street. With lots of glass, burled wood and taupe carpeting, they are sleek without being slick. The cafeteria is comfortable and democratic. Although smaller dining rooms can be reserved for meetings, everybody not at a lunch meeting eats at the same 27th-floor cafeteria, which has a view of Central Park. Some of the corporate offices share the same view from a higher floor. The Plaza Hotel is a block away; Bergdorf Goodman is next door.

All this and a corporate culture just as appealing. It's not the eat-'em-alive atmosphere that gives some Manhattan companies a hard edge. Here the job is done—and today there is no coasting—but it's done with a certain gentility. Doris Day in her heyday of Nice Girl in the Big Town would have fit right in.

Wall Street may be giving the company mixed reviews right now, but Wall Street has been known to be wrong. As far as women are concerned, the vote is already in.

BARRIOS TECHNOLOGY

AN AEROSPACE COMPANY THAT
OFFERS SUPPORT SERVICES TO NASA

▲ EMPLOYEES: 270; slightly more than 50 percent are women.

▲ SALES: $11 million in fiscal 1987; projected for fiscal 1988: $15 million

▲ Barrios is a company started and partly owned by a woman, and the company is concerned with recruiting, hiring and promoting women, as well as minorities. All job openings are posted, and employees are encouraged to apply for transfers. A large selection of training courses is offered to upgrade skills; 69 percent of the 52 people currently enrolled in management training classes are female. The company uses a participative performance appraisal.

▲ Of the 25 upper management people, nine—36 percent—are women, including the president, a vice president and a general manager. Barrios also has a professional ladder with grade levels equal to those of managers. Of the 35 highest-ranking people in that group, six—17 percent—are women. In this privately owned company, two of the seven members of the board of directors are female.

▲ Barrios offers a range of flexible options for parents. In addition to standard maternity disability leave, women may take up to three months' unpaid leave, position assured on return. The company offers flexible working hours, flexible workplaces and part-time possibilities for managers and professionals. The flexible benefits options include up to $6,000 pretax dollars allocated to child care. Employees may take sick leave for family illness.

▲ Barrios is committed to equality of pay for women, and individual job descriptions are reevaluated.

▲ Charges of sexual harassment are handled by both informal and formal procedures. The company offers a program on harassment for all employees. The women interviewed commented that charges are handled swiftly and with punch.

▲ Major employment centers: Clear Lake City, Tex.: 250. By the spring of 1988, Barrios expects to have approximately 90 people in Washington, D.C., as well as additional personnel at military bases and space installations throughout the country.

BARRIOS TECHNOLOGY, INC.
1331 Gemini
Houston, TX 77058
(713) 480-1889

They call her Emy, and you can't help thinking of her as a grandmother, as long as you imagine a grandmother with manicured red fingernails and running a $15 million aerospace business. She will be 62 in March 1988.

When she was in her fifties and a business manager at Kentron International, Emyré Barrios Robinson was preparing cost proposals and financial reports for National Aeronautics and Space Administration contracts. When NASA began to earmark contracts for small businesses, Robinson submitted her own proposals with a group of engineers, six men and one woman. Together they beat out four other competitors. Robinson was in business. And she owned 51 percent of it; the engineers divided up the remaining 49 percent.

"I started this company at 54," she jokes. "Me, an old Mexican woman without a technical background." The statement somewhat colors the truth. She comes from a patrician, if poor, Mexican family and grew up in El Paso. Her father was a doctor who practiced in Ciudad, Juárez. A great-granduncle was once the president of Mexico. When she was 45, she went back to school and finished a degree she had abandoned at 19. She has been married for 29 years to an engineer for an aerospace company.

But those credentials didn't help when it came to getting that first contract. This was based strictly on what she could do for NASA. The task was to provide paraengineers—people who are technically skilled but do not have degrees, much like paramedics—who could take over some of the routine calculations of the space shuttle's test flights, relatively mundane tasks that were being done by engineers. It was like having a heart surgeon remove splinters. Using paraengineers for simple tasks would save NASA millions. But there were no paraengineers ready. The proposal Robinson put together was to find the people interested in the work, train them and get them on the job at the Johnson Space Station. There was no shortage of people wanting to sign on. Barrios graduated its first class in early 1981.

Since then, Barrios Technology has won contracts for instrument calibration and repair services for the Johnson Space Center, program support for the space stations, managing and coordinating data accumulated on station design, and supplying administrative assistants versed in aerospace technology. The number of people who work at Barrios goes up and down, depending on whether or not they've won or lost a contract bid. Late in 1987 the number was close to 300, and more jobs in the Washington, D.C., area appeared to be on the horizon as some of the work from the Johnson Space Center in Houston was being transferred to the nation's capital. Barrios was going along and had plans to open an office in nearby Reston, Virginia, where approximately 90 people would be based.

"It's opened a whole new career for people who've never imagined working in the space program," says Robinson. "A lot of people we've gotten have been clerking at Sears or flipping hamburgers at McDonald's."

Michelle Moore was already working in the industry, but doing very basic, simple copying of flowcharts and code sheets, when she heard about the opportunity to be trained for something better at Barrios. After passing a simple mathematics aptitude test, she was accepted and jumped at the chance to enter the training, even though, at $4.58 an hour, it meant she had to take a cut in pay. "I could never have had the type of opportunity I've had here anywhere else—part of it has to do with Barrios being a small company, part of it has to do with Emy's philosophy," she says. "She likes to be able to give people a chance. She basically believes the best people for the job are the ones who try the hardest, and that as long as you give them enough direction, they will be an asset to the company no matter what you ask them to do."

Moore, with little over a year of college, now makes around $32,000. "I don't think this could have happened anywhere else. I don't think I would have had an opportunity in a high-growth company anywhere else, especially not having a degree." When Moore was given the opportunity to go to another company that subsequently got a contract for flight design calculations, she turned down the offer even though it would have meant a pay increase of approximately 20 percent. And she is not the only one who did.

Kay Hoffman, who was a schoolteacher for 12 years, made the same decision. Hoffman, now 44, says she knew what she wanted from a company when she decided to stay at Barrios: "At a small company you have more of a family atmosphere. You know the owners and the managers on a first-name basis. You can walk down the corridors and if you need to ask something, you just knock on the door and ask if they have a minute. If they don't, they'll tell you to come back in 30 minutes or an hour."

Another plus is the amount of opportunity available. "I was a liberal arts teacher coming from a public school, and the space industry was new to me," Hoffman comments. "I don't know if another company would have been willing to hire me, much less invest in the training on account of my age and lack of experience in this type of work." Because of that training, she was able to get a good job in Florida when her husband, an engineer, took a job with a company there. However, both of them are Texans at heart and missed life back home. Within a few years, they decided to return to Houston. Hoffman called Barrios immediately and asked if she could come back. The answer was an unqualified yes, but could she give them a month's notice? She said she would call as soon as her husband found a job in Houston. A few days later, someone from Barrios called back. Would he consider a position with Barrios? Their answer was yes.

While the pay for paraengineers at Barrios may be less than what some competitors pay, salaries for engineers and midlevel managers are competitive within the industry, once experience and job category are figured in. Senior managers, on the whole, probably make less than they could elsewhere, but some of them have stock in the company. In 1985 Barrios lost a contract for supplying flight design paraengineers to NASA to a larger company. A number of people left with the contract, a common practice in the aerospace business, and Barrios had to scale back some of its training programs. But the company still gives a number of courses, and is committed to continuing to train paraengineers as soon as they win contracts to supply them. And if you want to seek outside schooling, tuition grants of up to 80 percent of the total cost are available.

Those who chose to stay with Barrios when the contract was lost—Hoffman and Moore among them—feel not only that the atmosphere is more amiable than at a large corporation, but also that they have more mobility than they would elsewhere. Hoffman, for instance, has worked in a half dozen different areas and knows that the skills she's learned here make her highly employable elsewhere, and for more money, if that's what she decides she wants. She particularly appreciates that the company doesn't lean on her teaching experience and ask her to give training courses constantly, even though she is the natural candidate for the job. Once, when the company was in a bind and had a contract to teach simple engineering tasks to Air Force officers, Hoffman agreed to do it, but only until someone else could be found. Instead of ignoring her wish, management did find someone else, and she went back to flight design, her first love. And although they have asked her to take a management position several times, they have not applied undue pressure and continue to let her take jobs that increase her technical skills. To put it mildly, Hoffman loves her new career.

As for the number of hours one works, you can apparently work as much or as little as you want, depending on the project and your priorities. Ling N. Chang has a master's degree in computer science but doesn't want to work the 60–80 hours a week her husband works in data processing. She wants more time for her two young children. Before coming to Barrios in 1983, she had worked for another subcontractor at NASA. "It's great here," she says. "At my first company they didn't have insurance, they didn't pay for maternity leave. Here we can take a maternity leave of up to three months and come back to our job."

After her first baby was born, Chang tried day care, but since the child was sick so often, she had trouble at work. In desperation, she sent the baby back to Taiwan, where Chang and her husband are from, to live with her mother-in-law until the child was 20 months old.

When her second child was born, Chang was at Barrios and had no such problems. Now, if her children are sick, she takes off for a few hours and comes back later to do her work. "The bosses—the men as well as the women—understand the pressures of the working mother," she says. "I make up the time working through my lunch hour or working late, and there is never a problem." Other responsibilities, such as caring for aging parents, are met with the same flexibility. You won't get into trouble if you're the one who has to take your dad to the doctor frequently.

Conversely, if you *can* manage both kids and a hectic schedule, you're allowed to do that too. Vice president of finance and administration Marilyn Wiley, the mother of two, became pregnant after she had been with the company only a few months. "I told Emy right away, and she was surprised, but that was it," Wiley says. "By the time the baby was born, I had been here a year. And I was working at home within two weeks after the baby was born."

The company rolls with the punches, not letting rigid rules interfere with the kind of place Robinson wants her company to be. When Lorna Onizuka's husband, Ellison, was killed in the space shuttle accident in early 1986, she had been with the company for only about 10 days. She stayed home for five weeks and collected her pay, even though she didn't expect to. The company let her use sick time and vacation time even though she was a new employee. The checks always came with a note from Robinson. "It was a tragedy of such major proportions that it seemed like the right thing to do," Robinson said. "It was what we could do."

Later, company insurance paid for counseling with a therapist. "Emy sat down and talked with me for a long time," remembers Onizuka. "She is not what you think of as a typical boss, she reaches out to you and you are a friend, not just an employee."

Robinson works hard at making that friendly arm a part of the company's business philosophy. "The image we want to establish is that we are people-oriented," she says. "And we want to make sure that women have the opportunity to progress." The message seems to have gotten out. Barrios receives more than 300 résumés a month, more than the total number of people employed by the company. A special effort is made to recruit minorities and women with children who have been out of the work force raising them.

In such an atmosphere, sexual harassment would be met with practically a public burning, and the women hesitate to bring it up, not because they will be chastised but because the action will be swift and to the point. If it's an open-and-shut case, the guy will be fired. At least one has been. The women wish that some of the men weren't so lewd in their language and jokes—it's a case of unbridled good-ol'-boyism, with the emphasis on *boy* —but are reluctant to raise the issue with Emy because the response again will be explosive, like a Mexican firecracker. However, NASA men are, after all, Texans too, and they appreciate a good joke or a remark about a comely pair of body parts. They sometimes cross over the line. And if it's NASA employees who are the offenders, Barrios will go to bat for you also, even though NASA is the client. When a NASA employee jokingly accused a young, attractive Barrios woman of going to bed with her NASA superiors —in front of a group of people in the copying room—she took the matter up with Barrios personnel. They went back to NASA and formally complained. Result: one public apology, one private. Happily, the two were later able to work together without embarrassment.

Many of Barrios's employees report for work in the space stations in Houston and, more recently, outside of Washington in Virginia. Plans are afoot to expand to wherever space installations are located. Those who work at headquarters have a cool, dark and sophisticated place to call home, a $4.5 million building that was completed in 1983. Situated among the aerospace companies that ring the Johnson Space Center in the Clear Lake City area of Houston, there's no indication of just how warm and cozy a place Barrios is.

Until you meet Emy.

BIDERMANN INDUSTRIES

THE PEOPLE WHO BRING YOU RALPH LAUREN
WOMENSWEAR, AS WELL AS DESIGNER FASHIONS FOR MEN

▲ EMPLOYEES: Approximately 700; more than 60 percent are women.

▲ SALES: privately held; industry sources estimate $200 million, with Ralph Lauren Womenswear accounting for approximately two thirds that amount.

▲ Bidermann Industries is a young, dynamic company unconcerned about its need to recruit, hire and promote women. It doesn't have to be concerned—it's already there. Of the 700 employees, about 60 percent are women; a third of the 90 people in upper management are female.

▲ Bidermann has few written policies about anything, not even an employee handbook. No formal statement on sexual harassment exists. The rag trade is an industry in which language and behavior that might make a banker cringe are accepted as the norm for both men and women.

▲ The company has standard medical and maternity benefits and a decided acceptance of women at early stages of their careers who choose to work part-time. Deep discounts on clothes from Bidermann's designers are one of the perks of working here.

▲ Although no formal management training or career development programs exist, Bidermann regularly sends employees to seminars and brings in consultants to speak.

▲ Young, energetic and aggressive women are hired and fast-tracked from one division to another when they demonstrate talent. While starting salaries in fashion can be small, rapid promotions seem to bring ample rewards, both in salaries and in bonuses when the company is doing well. Fashion is a cyclical industry that has recently gone through hard times, so there are no guarantees of promotions or, for that matter, of jobs.

▲ Major employment centers: New York City: 200; Secaucus, N.J.: 400; the remainder at sales offices in Los Angeles, Chicago, Dallas and Miami.

BIDERMANN INDUSTRIES USA, INC.
1211 Avenue of the Americas
New York, NY 10036
(212) 730-1880

Partly because of the company's high profile, partly because of its rise and retrenchment since it began in 1973, and partly because it's known as a tough but good place to work, gaining experience at Bidermann Industries USA is somewhat akin to having P&G on your résumé if fashion, and not package goods, is your forte: if you can make it here, you can make it anywhere. In the industry, Bidermann has a reputation as a class act, something the rag trade is not known for.*

Bidermann's stature as an industry leader is obvious when employees interview for jobs outside the company. "When they see you're at Bidermann they just want to know what's going on," one woman remarked. "They want to hear all the gossip, and you come away feeling that they want to know more about Bidermann than they do about you."

The company underwent considerable restructuring in 1986–87, narrowing its focus from the stable of designers and divisions that included Karl Lagerfeld and Calvin Klein Menswear to a select three: Ralph Lauren Womenswear, Yves Saint Laurent Menswear and Bill Robinson Menswear.

As a result of retrenchment, Bidermann is no longer the brash young kid who bought the candy store and overdosed. Today the company is very much the sensible, and considerably sobered, youth who is sticking to the main chance. And Ralph Lauren is very much a main chance.

While the company is privately held by a French parent company and no sales figures are released, industry sources put Bidermann's annual sales at around $200 million, with nearly two thirds of that accounted for by Ralph Lauren Womenswear.

With the winnowing-down of divisions, the atmosphere is very much like family—tight and close-knit. But it's a family where pressure is what's for lunch. You either make the numbers or you're out—as female division presidents have learned in the past.

Although no effort has been made to seek out women and promote them, Bidermann's record speaks for itself. When it had a half dozen divisions, women were amply represented in the inner circle. As we go to press, Ralph

---

*Since we did the interviews and wrote the profile in the spring of 1986, the company's restructuring has led to many changes in personnel, including at the top, and so some of the women included here are no longer with the company. However, their comments give the flavor of the company and it remains an excellent place for women.

Lauren has a female executive vice president, and numerous directors and managers are women. At all levels except the very top, it is performance rather than sex that counts. At the very top, sex does count. As in corporate America everywhere, it's harder to be a division president if you're a woman. The Bill Robinson Menswear division did have a female president when we did the interviews in the spring of 1986, but she left when she had a child.

Nevertheless, at Bidermann women can be found in jobs one would normally expect to find men filling. Youth is not a hindrance either. This is not a place where you'll be told you can't do something because you are too young or inexperienced. This is a place where you'll be given a chance to show you've got the right stuff at a tender age. Several years ago, Bidermann had a woman—a very young woman—selling men's suits before it became an industry practice.

Twenty-eight-year-old Janet Corwin is the director of sales for Bill Robinson Menswear. In Corwin's case, it was being able to run with the ball when it was thrown her way that made the difference. In 1978, after two years at the Fashion Institute of Technology, she started out as an administrative assistant making $10,000 a year. After a few months she mentioned to the head of Calvin Klein's men's sportswear that she would like a job in his division. One of the sales representatives was leaving, he said, and would she like his job?

"Instead of starting me out as a trainee, as they do most people, they gave me a territory—the Southeast," she says. "We were all young and energetic and were thoroughly devoted to the company." After a season she was asked to head up the West Coast territory. She was 21 when she moved to Los Angeles. "I loved the job but loathed L.A.," she says, and when the chance came six months later to run the East Coast sales division, Corwin moved back to New York City and stayed at the job four years. Before being named to head sales for Bill Robinson, she was national sales manager of the Calvin Klein accessory division. Not surprisingly, Brooklyn-born Corwin would like to be president of a division someday. To do that, she knows she has to gain merchandising experience. She hopes it will be at Bidermann.

"It's not an easy company to work for," she says. "It's very demanding. But what is good about it is that I've never felt I've been held back because I'm a woman. At other manufacturers it's much more difficult to get ahead. People are surprised that I'm director of sales for a menswear company."

What they give you at Bidermann is the freedom to do the job your way. A creative person couldn't ask for anything more. "But if you screw up, they're all over you, and it's almost impossible to regain the confidence and freedom again," said a former employee who once sat on the corporate operating committee. Translation: you're given enough rope to hang yourself.

There isn't a great deal of strategic planning. There isn't a policy and procedures manual. Quick decisions are a corporate style. If somebody has a good idea, there's a tendency to try it out immediately. One of the corporate officers attended a morning seminar at which he heard that progressive companies often do not have reserved parking spaces for managers. During the lunch break that same day, he gave the order to take down the RE-SERVED SIGNS at the company's warehouse in Secaucus, New Jersey. "We want to be as innovative as possible, and so we try things, but we dump them if they don't work out immediately," remarks Simone Thornber, assistant to the president. "But this means that there's lots of opportunity for anyone because we're young enough to try something and learn by our mistakes. Nothing around here is a sacred cow. We never say, oh, we've never done it that way, we can't try it without going through five levels of memos."

Sometimes the impulsiveness can be hair raising. One woman remembers what happened to her a few years ago, when the designer sportswear market softened. Belt tightening was necessary. Company officials panicked and decided to fire people without thinking through who should go and who should stay. The woman in question is Ronnie Lederman, who was let go only to be called back within weeks, as were others, when the company realized they were needed.

Lederman was particularly unhappy when she was let go because at Bidermann she had found a company that let her work part-time, enabling her to be the wife and mother she wanted to be. "I had been looking for a long time for a job like this, where I could work part-time," she says. "People at other companies were not willing to understand that yes, I want to work, and yes, I will give you my all when I'm here, but my home and family do come first." She works 9:30 A.M. to 3 P.M. three days a week, a schedule which allows her to drop her baby at the baby-sitter and pick her up without a problem, as she has a hefty commute to Manhattan from New Jersey, where she lives.

Lederman has the option of expanding her position as much as she feels she's able to take care of. She taught herself to work a computer terminal and is now putting out a company newspaper, in addition to her regular duties for the vice president of human resources.

Motherhood is an issue that is looming on the horizon at Bidermann. A number of young women are poised for it, and maternity issues are bound to have an impact soon. How long will they let you stay out? Will they save your job or give you another one of equal responsibility when you return? Managerial women are given a standard six weeks' disability at full pay, and as for the rest of the issues, the company is dealing with them on a one-to-one basis. Lisa Casillo, a merchandising administrator for Yves Saint Laurent, found her division's president agreeable to slightly abbreviated hours. She starts her workday between 9:30 and 10 A.M., depending on traffic, works to 4:15 P.M. and takes work home with her when necessary. When the work load is more demanding, a girlfriend picks up her daughter from the baby-sitter so Casillo can work later. The key is flexibility on the part of management, which contributes to the family feeling that Bidermann exudes, a rare commodity in the garment industry. Casillo, who worked briefly for a chain of clothing stores, calls Bidermann a "picnic" by comparison. And there really is a company picnic for employees and their families. In 1986 it was held at the company president's place in Kingston, New York. People who needed transportation were bused from either Manhattan or Secaucus.

Many of Bidermann's middle-level managers came to work here fresh out of school, or a short time later, and stayed. The air of informality allows them to go in and talk to the president of their division and know that he will know who they are and what their job entails. "There's no hierarchy that says you can't go in and talk to the president because you are only a salesperson," comments Mary Lee Gallagher, director of operations for Ralph Lauren Womenswear. Likewise, there is no standing on ceremony, or strict job definitions, when it comes to getting the work done. "The type of people who work here aren't the type who say, 'I'm the president of a division, I can't punch in an order,' or, 'I work in New York, I can't go into the warehouse to pick an order, I can't help them out,'" Gallagher adds. "If something has to get done, regardless of what it is or what your title is, everybody rolls up their sleeves and pitches in." For newcomers, the catch to this *esprit de corps* is that if you don't fit in right away—if you're not a Bidermann personality, as one woman put it—you probably won't ever be truly accepted.

And what's the Bidermann personality? Someone who speaks her mind, is fast on her feet, smart, hard working and willing to take chances. And although some of the secretaries are cowed by some male bosses who ask them to run errands, take their clothes to the laundry or buy shoes for them (and return them when they aren't right), the women we met insist that turning down requests from male bosses who expected women to be their personal servants will not hurt you if you do your job well. All of them wish the secretaries had more nerve to say no to their bosses' demands that have nothing to do with the job at hand. Is it just the older men? *No.* Does the garment industry foster attitudes of secretary as hand maiden? *Maybe.*

While the requests are sometimes sexual—the garment industry is known to be loose and lusty—the women say that just as often as not a young woman wouldn't mind having an affair with her boss, particularly if the boss is the president of the division. In this industry, as in many others, power and sex are mediums of exchange. Could someone sleep her way to the top? Not really, we heard; the ones who tried didn't last. In any case, at Bidermann, sexual harassment doesn't get to the formal complaint stage. "What might be taken elsewhere as sexual harassment . . . here you'd have somebody say, 'Lord, give me a break, get your hand off my butt,'" one woman says. "It's just not taken seriously. To begin with, there's a lot of swearing and a general looseness in the way we speak. We're the kissy-kissy industry." She adds that the higher one rises, the less likely it is that any sort of flirting will take place: "I've had men ask me out for a drink and then they find out who I am," she says, speaking of the industry in general (she is a senior executive). "Then the attitude changes right away."

Whether or not women are paid equally to men is anybody's guess. Some women were sure that they were paid as well as men in similar jobs, others said they suspected the men were paid more, and some women said that they would be paid more, or have less difficulty getting the next title, if they were men. "We're very good in the middle," says one woman. "But it's not so great at the bottom or the very top. They interview women for the heads of divisions, but it's usually a man who gets the job. And sometimes secretaries are given new titles, but nothing changes—they are still getting the coffee."

All of the senior women we interviewed agree that women have to work harder to prove themselves than men do and that at these upper reaches no one tolerates women taking time off for family responsibilities. One woman admits she once raced home to the suburbs in the middle of a busy day to take her son to the first day of Little League and returned to work without anyone being the wiser. She says she would lie rather than tell the truth if she had to be home due to a child's illness or school problem. "If you're going to compete with the men then you've got to be even-steven," comments Bubbles Bott, formerly executive vice president of sales and merchandising for a division the company folded. "The guys are not running home because their daughters have colds." Bubbles (that's her real name; she says it's not unusual in India, where she was born) is married to Herman Bott, the vice president of human resources. Although she met her future boss through her husband, the fact that she was married to a senior executive meant that she initially had to work doubly hard to prove to others she had the goods when she came to Bidermann, her previous fashion experience notwithstanding.

"No matter how much we want to believe that there is no discrimination, we still have a way to go to prove ourselves in the world," she says, "and so we work harder to prove ourselves."

Regardless of the fact that the highest-ranking women at Bidermann feel they operate within a double standard, they are enthusiastic about the company, its products and its integrity. So are the junior managers. The company makes a real effort not to promise what it cannot deliver and to get the goods there on time. "There's a certain electricity there, and maybe that's because of the brand names," remarks Bott. "I felt proud when I went to the Orient and said, 'I am a part of Bidermann.'"

Denise Seegal, executive vice president of Ralph Lauren Womenswear, puts it succinctly: "I'm happy to be affiliated with Bidermann, and I'm happy to be affiliated with Ralph." She was 31 when she was promoted to her present level: the next step would be division president.

Such youth in high places makes at least one of the older women at Bidermann sorry the world wasn't a different place when she was young. George Ann Jaslow is the motherly personnel manager in Secaucus. In her fifties, she's been with the company since 1980 and seen many bright young things rise with relative ease. "This is a young company, and it provides these young women with such opportunities," she says. "There is a little seed back in me that says, boy, I wish I'd had opportunities like this when I was their age."

CBS

A DIVERSIFIED ENTERTAINMENT AND INFORMATION COMPANY PRINCIPALLY IN THE BUSINESS OF BROADCASTING

▲ EMPLOYEES: 8,375; nearly 48 percent are women.

▲ REVENUES: More than $4.7 billion. Income from continuing operations decreased slightly from $192.2 million in 1985 to $189.8 million in 1986. The broadcast group, the largest business, had sharply lower profits due to lower profits from the television network. The record division, which was sold in January 1988, accounted for 37 percent of the operating profits and 31 percent of its total revenues.

▲ Sale of the record division led to further cutbacks in corporate staff, and a restructuring of top management was under way as we went to press early in 1988. Previous cutbacks in all divisions have dampened morale, and not many jobs are available. However, CBS has been a company generally concerned with recruiting and hiring women. Personnel is headed by a woman dedicated to the concerns of women and minorities, and she is a corporate officer. CBS remains highly visible on college campuses and in women's professional organizations.

▲ Programs aimed at promoting women include job posting, a computerized search program, a career development department within personnel and 75 percent tuition reimbursement.

▲ The results are numbers that are about the best anywhere in a large American corporation. Of the 480 upper-level managers, 99—20.6 percent—are women. Fourteen percent of the vice presidents in broadcast and 6 percent of those in records are female. One of the 14 members of the board of directors is female.

▲ CBS supports a Women's Advisory Council, organized in 1973. The council meets with senior management to discuss women's issues and offers a variety of programs and events to women. The council is now less active—and less needed—than it was in earlier years.

▲ The company offers an array of benefits for parents. In addition to standard maternity disability leave, mothers can take a leave of up to 12 months with their jobs guaranteed on return. The company offers flexible work hours, paternity benefits, adoption benefits, sick leave for family illness and a cafeteria-style approach to benefits which includes subsidies for child care. Understandably, few career-minded people exercise their right to extended leave.

▲ CBS handles charges of sexual discrimination either through their open door policy of operating management, or through local and corporate personnel offices.

▲ The company has done a study on sexual harassment, and top management has periodically issued strong statements about it. Newly available is a four-hour program developed with ABC and NBC and currently being disseminated among all employees.

▲ The company is committed to rectifying inequality of pay to women. To do so, it examines what other companies are doing, reevaluates individual job descriptions, systematically reevaluates descriptions of jobs held predominantly by women and uses grade level adjustments where necessary.

▲ Major employment centers: New York State: 6,000; Los Angeles: 1,600; Chicago: 500; numerous small offices at stations in major cities throughout the country.

CBS, INC.
51 West 52nd Street
New York, NY 10019
(212) 975-4321

In 1972 Lesley Stahl was the new kid on the block at CBS national news. She has no illusions about why she was hired: affirmative action gave women their chance, she says, and she was one of them. Up until that time, the few women at the networks covered social events and first ladies and generally followed the wives of important men around. However, after affirmative action, women began to be assigned to important beats, and Stahl drew politics. Watergate blew up around this time, and Stahl wasn't left behind. But hold on—even if Stahl was doing a good job, that didn't mean men were going to give up airtime to a woman easily. Especially if they could do the talking instead.

During the Senate Watergate hearings, Stahl was to be part of a round-table discussion—together with two male correspondents—several nights a week to analyze the day's coverage. Stahl couldn't get a word in edgewise. She sat there night after night but never got to talk. "It wasn't that I wasn't asked questions, but the men—the veterans—were always arguing with each other and I could never get a word in." This did not go unnoticed back in New York. The men were asked to let Stahl speak.

It didn't work.

It was mentioned again.

No soap.

Finally a memo came down: If Stahl didn't get to talk *tonight*, the specials would be discontinued. So everybody knew that she was going to get her two cents in that night. The first question, asked by a moderator back in New York, was: What's the gossip about the FBI?

The men turned to her, but Stahl wisely decided not to touch a question about gossip. Too stereotypical. She would answer another question.

Silence.

"There was this horrible black hole on the air where nobody was talking, and so Dan Schorr jumped into the breach and said, 'Well, if it's gossip you want, that's why we have a woman here.'"

Stahl recalls blathering something and making a fool of herself. When the show was over, she ran upstairs and called home. She was ready to quit. If being on network TV was going to be so awful, she didn't want to continue. "I got my father, and he said I was great, and I said, 'Daddy, if you're not going to be honest, put Mother on the phone,' and he said, 'Mother can't talk right now. She's too upset.'"

Stahl no longer fields questions about gossip, FBI or not. Formerly the chief White House correspondent, she is now the national correspondent for and, since 1983, moderator of Sunday morning's *Face the Nation*.

As successful and visible as Stahl's career has been, she is not the only woman making it at the CBS Washington bureau. Rita Braver covers the Justice Department; Susan Spenser, medicine; Deborah Potter, Congress; and Jacqueline Adams, the White House. Five out of 15—which is the total of on-air correspondents in the Washington bureau—ain't bad, considering that the Washington bureau jobs are among the most coveted, since they are the most likely to get you on the air. "If women are good, they are rewarded," comments Stahl. "And they are good and they are doing well. This is not an opinion. It's a fact."

But it's not just on the air where women are making it at CBS. There are a number of women producers—the executive producer for *Face the Nation* is a woman, as is the executive producer for the weekend news, for instance—and they are marching up the pipeline just like the men. As we go to press, the bureau chiefs in Los Angeles, Dallas and Atlanta are women. One of the key vice presidents for news is Joan Richman. In Washington, D.C., the deputy bureau chief, Mary Martin, says this about being promoted last September to her current job: "The bureau chief, Joe Peyronnin, is 40 years old, he's worked with women as equals all his life and he chose a woman deputy, but he doesn't walk around saying, 'I can be macho-gonzo and still hire girls.' The person he happened to choose to be his deputy was a woman. No big deal. If he had come across a person with the same background as I had who was a guy, he probably would have chosen that person too."

Martin's background is extensive. She began 14 years ago as a part-time switchboard operator while still in college. A succession of jobs followed—secretary, production assistant, researcher, working on the assignment desk, associate producer, senior producer and then her current assignment. "The last sexist isn't dead yet, but in this particular company they chose this guy, and he reflects a lot of management's attitudes. And he wasn't afraid to do this. Management supported his decision, and that's why I'm here. I don't consider myself a trailblazer, and I don't think I'm seven times smarter than any guys around who've gotten this."

Martin is one of those women who seem to have it all. Although she usually doesn't get home until after eight, Martin has two boys under 10, an architect husband who has his own business—which leaves him more able to set his own hours than most—and a reliable nanny, who worked for her mother. She says she goes to school events and parent-teacher meetings. "I work very hard—this is not your nine-to-five arrangement here—but you have some flexibility. There are times when you have to be here all the time, but when there are things you have to do, there is support for you doing it. No one says, oh, yeah, she's a wimpy mother. Guys my age—I'm 36—who have families like to do this too. They don't want to act like those kids aren't there."

If life in Washington sounds positively utopian, there are a few serpents in the CBS garden. Not all women agree that their sex isn't a hindrance, and budget cutting, coupled with layoffs, has rocked the company. Though all the networks are trimming their budgets, the sharpest knife is being wielded at CBS. Between the spring of 1985 and fall of 1987, 270 full-time jobs were cut from the news organization, and the layoffs have sliced into other divisions as well. The company has lived through several presidents in the last decade. The pieties once associated with CBS News—that it was the standard by which the other networks were judged, that it had the most thorough reports—are now history. The news division is no longer seen as a place where people do good works while soaps and sitcoms pay the bill. Now the news has to carry more of its own weight, and the current president and CEO, Laurence A. Tisch, is insisting it be done on a tight budget. His quest for a healthy profit-and-loss statement can be compared with Galahad's search for the Holy Grail. The staffers who remain, at least at the New York City headquarters of the news division are demoralized, even though the layoffs appear to be over. Last fall, most salaries above $50,000 were frozen. One high-ranking woman told us last fall that she didn't see how CBS could be considered as a good company for anybody, male or female.

In reality, many other companies across the country have undergone the same kind of cutbacks and turmoil: Levi Strauss and AT&T come to mind. But networks generate a kind of loyalty, and staffers here particularly looked upon the network as a trust that belonged to them. They expected to be consulted on what happened to their family, not laid off without being consulted. "The whole relationship between you and the corporation has changed," says a survivor. "It is not the paternalistic organization it was before. You have to consider your career and your future in a different context than you may have been used to."

But while the layoffs and budget cuts are seen as heresy to CBS's commitment to quality news broadcasting, the situation is equally bad for everyone. Women and minorities are doing as well—and the women are doing pretty well, by our standards—as they were before the belt tightening. "It is difficult for everyone when a corporation contracts, and it has been as difficult as you can imagine," the woman continues, "but there's been no distinction between men and women—it's equally difficult." Joan Showalter, vice president of personnel, confirmed that the overall percentages of women and minorities did not change when the cuts were made.

Two of the women we interviewed were promoted last year, in the midst of the reorganization, proving once again that every time there is a shake-up and reorganization, new opportunities arise. Joan Richman is now a vice president for news, and Nancy Whitman is vice president of the CBS-owned radio stations, both AM and FM.

Tisch's commitment to equal employment opportunities and affirmative action appears to be no less than that of his predecessors. Number-crunching CEOs, no matter how else they impact the corporation, are often very good for women, as they typically insist that the best person for the job get it. Prejudice against women and minorities doesn't flourish in a meritocracy.

CBS's record would indicate that it has been a meritocracy for some time. Overall, more than 47 percent of all employees at CBS are female, and the percentages of women at the top are among the best we found anywhere. Of 480 people in the top bonus incentive group, 99—20.6 percent—are women. In the broadcast division, 19 out of 138 vice presidents are women; in corporate, the figure is four out of 26. As Stahl and Martin said, women are moving up the pipeline. *

Yet some would say they are not moving up fast enough and that women in middle management generally have a tougher time breaking into the top echelons. One woman, referring to a top level annual meeting, says that the number of women present, four, hasn't changed year after year. "Each year, there they are, never any more," she says. "Not four the first year and eight the next and twelve the third year, and yet there are different men in many of those positions. So there is a lot of work to be done at that level." As there is all over corporate America.

The real question, she continues, is whether women will break through to division presidents. (CBS did have a female president, Lisa Bayard, but lost that distinction when the publishing division, where she headed college publishing, was spun off in 1986.)

Marlene Sanders, one of broadcasting's pioneers and the winner of three Emmys, would put the ceiling for women lower than president. She believes women are essentially overlooked when promotions are handed out. "It's still tough for women," she says. "On the entry level it may be wide open, but it's as you rise to the top that it's still largely made up of men. The frustration of women in middle management is quite severe." Sanders,

*Late last fall, Sony agreed to buy the CBS record division for $2 billion, a move that affected some 4,300 employees in the United States. Walter R. Yetnikoff retained his post as president and the unit will remain housed at CBS's corporate headquarters for the next several years, muting the sale's effect on employees. At the time of the sale, six out of 94 vice presidents in the record division were women. CBS was the first record company to promote more than a token woman into positions where they had clout in a business that traditionally had been male dominated.

who, like Dan Rather, will be 57 this year, began in television in 1955. In 1964 she was hired by ABC as a news correspondent and later anchored a daytime newscast. In 1976 she became the first female vice president at any of the networks. Two years later, finding the atmosphere under Roone Arledge at ABC no longer receptive, she joined CBS. In 1986, during the third round of layoffs, Sanders was offered a return to radio, anchoring the hourly newscasts on weekends and at night. She declined and left.

Sanders's case brings up the thorny issue of age discrimination, usually skewed against women. While Sanders was asked to work the hours usually assigned to newcomers, it apparently isn't just women who are feeling squeezed. Nearly everyone over the age of 50 who is not clearly indispensable feels somewhat in jeopardy or perhaps should, according to an executive in the radio division. Aging employees cost more to carry than young blood: pensions and higher medical premiums can make the difference between red and black ink on the balance sheet. "They are urging early retirements and layoffs on people who are over 40," she says. "If you are 50-plus, the climate is particularly tough." Outside of Tisch, who is in his mid-sixties, and chairman William S. Paley, who will be 86 in 1987, senior management is relatively young, and that works against older employees because they are not part of the peer group in power. "If I'm dealing with a 35-year-old VP and he's been in his job for two years, I can see by his behavior that he is surprised that I know anything worthwhile or might be included because I have something to contribute," the woman adds. She is hardly washed up. She is in her fifties.

Yet the reverse of that is that while there aren't a lot of jobs for anyone, at an operation as large as CBS there are always entry-level jobs, and young people, particularly young people who look upon the broadcast business as not terribly different from any other business, could have a shot here. While idealists may not find a home at CBS, hungry young men and women might. "The company is still a meritocracy," notes a senior woman in the broadcast division, "but what constitutes the best may have a slightly different definition. One of the qualifications looked for today was not previously important—this understanding of budgets, of cost cutting, of how to make do with less rather than, in our case, focusing primarily on the quality of the product." Women wishing to rise, just as men, must be in mainstream jobs—sales, for instance. And sales is a place where women have done particularly well at CBS. No one can argue with a good bottom line.

Nancy Whitman, vice president for CBS's AM and FM stations, came up through the sales route, starting in 1972. She made $25,000 a year and was the first woman to sell radio airtime in New York City. In some jobs, she had to sit it out and wait longer than a man would have had to for the next promotion, but, now in her mid-forties, she can hardly be said to be passed over with her current responsibilities for all 18 CBS stations. "There was always a theory that I had reached the glass ceiling, but I truly think I broke through it," she says.

Like other high-level women we met elsewhere, Whitman found that once she had reached a senior level, she was accepted completely for what she could do for the company and that her sex wasn't a factor in getting the next appointment. "My being a female wasn't a plus or a minus. I was just somebody who could do the job." Incidentally, Whitman was counted as an Equal Employment Opportunity statistic when she was a station general manager; at the divisional level, EEO regulations do not apply. Whitman is no longer counted when the percentages of women and minorities in management are tabulated. As we go to press, neither ABC nor NBC has ever had a female general manager at a radio station. And while none of the 18 general managers who now report to Whitman is a woman, she says she is grooming women for the spot. Overall, 43 percent of all jobs on CBS radio stations are filled by women.

On the issue of sexual harassment, again Tisch cannot be faulted. He has continued a sexual harassment program that was already in the works. The station may have needed it. CBS has had its share of lawsuits, some of which have been settled out of court. In one case, the executive producer of *Nightwatch* resigned following an internal investigation; among other things, the seven women suing contended that others had been discharged after speaking out. The sexual harassment workshop that is now making the rounds of CBS locations is a four-hour program that includes a tape produced jointly by the three networks. An in-house trainer conducts the sessions, and they will eventually reach most employees, both men and women. Tisch isn't necessarily pursuing this program because he loves women at work. A hard-liner when it comes to numbers, he must know that quashing harassment in its tracks is a lot cheaper than being slapped with a lawsuit.

As for leeway for childbirth or child care, it's not great in any of the media. If a major story is breaking, and you're on it and your child is sick, you'd better have a way to take care of the child. But there is some leeway in New York as well as in Washington. According to Joan Richman, the lone female vice president in the news division, allowances have been made for working mothers. She recounted the case of a senior producer with the evening news who had two kids and wanted to come in two days a week starting at 11 A.M. or noon. On a normal workday, no one gets home until 8 P.M. or so. "She [the producer] is working with a small group of men who have the most pressure of anybody, and they agreed," Richman noted. "But it took them a long time to get used to that and not say, 'Well, what do you expect, she's never here.' But eventually they did." And when the former bureau chief in Paris, Jennifer Siebens, was asked to take over the Los Angeles bureau, she was pregnant. The transfer occurred during her maternity leave. Someone filled the L.A. slot until she was back.

Pay parity doesn't appear to be an issue. Women in a position to know say that the salary checks they run or have been privy to show that women are being paid equally to men. "We have some tough, aggressive women in sales, and I can't imagine them settling for less than the guys," one woman in the radio division remarked.

Women in broadcasting are by nature vocal, and CBS women are no exception. As far back as 1973, CBS had a Women's Advisory Council. It was more active in the heyday of feminism in the seventies, and it scored a number of objectives: (1) job posting for executives, (2) a maternity/paternity leave policy guaranteeing an employee his or her job or one of similar status up to a year after birth or adoption, (3) a directory of women interested in networking, and (4) a commitment to give women the skills they need to advance.

Not only were career workshops held, some women were sent, at full salary, to Simmons College in Boston for a two-year program in business management. CBS used to send one or two women a year but stopped when it was no longer difficult to find women with business skills equal to men's. Arthur Taylor, then president of the network and father to four daughters, was thought to be a friend to women, and his actions indicate he was. None of the presidents following him rolled back any of the advances women made under him, except that, in the current cost-cutting mode, the special training that was once available is no longer. The Women's Advisory Council still functions today, but in these times of relative quietude on the feminist front, most high-level women stay away.

At Black Rock, which is what CBS's sleek dark granite column in mid-Manhattan is called, employees are still reeling from the changes of the past two years. A memo from Tisch last September noted, "The retrenchment is behind us." Maybe in reorganization and dollars, but certainly not in spirit. That will take more time. Yet in spite of these difficulties, women are holding their own. And some are doing very well.

But is the network—any network—a place for women just starting out? Joan Richman says no. What she would tell someone looking to break into television isn't much different today than it was a few years ago. Start somewhere other than the network, perhaps a local station. Or look for a job in other areas of the business. "There are expanding areas of the business, but network TV is not one of them," she adds. "Cable is one. Syndication is another."

CHILDREN'S TELEVISION WORKSHOP

A NONPROFIT ORGANIZATION THAT PRODUCES *SESAME STREET* AND OTHER CHILDREN'S TELEVISION PROGRAMMING AS WELL AS RELATED BUSINESSES, INCLUDING PRODUCT LICENSING, SPIN-OFF MAGAZINES AND IN-SCHOOL INSTRUCTIONAL SERVICES

▲ EMPLOYEES: 225; two thirds are women.

▲ Children's Television Workshop doesn't have to work hard to recruit and hire women; representation at all levels is excellent. Of the 56 employees considered upper management, 28—50 percent—are women. More than one quarter of its board of directors is female as well.

▲ Pay for all staff, male and female, is lower than in commercial television, except for free-lance musicians, writers and actors, who are paid guild rates. Benefits for staff are very good; CTW takes advantage of all the savings and deferment plans available to the not-for-profit sector. Flexibility for parents is another plus.

▲ In an era of lowered monetary support for not-for-profits, CTW cannot offer job security. However, for women wishing to gain first-class TV experience in a company with a grade A reputation, where they will be promoted strictly according to talent and performance, CTW can't be beat.

▲ Major employment centers: All in New York City.

CHILDREN'S TELEVISION WORKSHOP
One Lincoln Plaza
New York, NY 10023
(212) 595-3456

Nina Elias recalls with a smile and a certain pride the day she phoned another mother in the suburbs to say that she would be able to bring her three-year-old daughter to a birthday party. Elias told the other mother that she was glad the party was on Saturday, and not during the week when she would be working and couldn't come.

"She started in—'Oh, how terrible, you have to work, the guilt must be horrible, how do you do it?' Then she asked *where* I worked. When I said on *Sesame Street*, everything changed. She said, 'Well, I guess there are some pluses to working there.' I don't think there was another place I could have said where she would have thought it was okay to work."

Elias's job takes her around the world. She's a producer in the international division of the popular children's television show. To date, most of her assignments have been in the Middle East, both Arab countries and Israel. She's quick to point out that *Sesame Street* soon becomes a favorite —if not number one—children's show in all of the countries where it's produced. Big Bird becomes a shaggy camel or a porcupine, new street scenes are created, the Muppets are dubbed, new animated spots and films reflecting the culture are produced. "You know you're dealing with a good product," Elias says, "and there's a prestige in that. What you do affects kids in a positive way. I'm very proud to be working on *Sesame Street*."

Her daughter, Lauren, apparently likes where Mom works too. When Elias took her to the studio for a day she didn't get bored the entire time and in fact "screamed when I said it was time to go home," Elias notes happily.

The educational-cum-humor show that hit the airwaves nearly 20 years ago, in 1969, is unquestionably an international hit. It's seen in nearly 100 foreign countries; home in the United States, 14 million viewers tune in at least once a week. Who doesn't know about the Cookie Monster? Or Big Bird? And who hasn't heard of Joan Ganz Cooney, cofounder of CTW? An engaging speaker and a bright, trim and yes, we'll say it, attractive woman in her late fifties, she's become one of the best-known women in America, known not for the man she's married to but for her own accomplishments in the man's world of television.

Cooney didn't set out to create a company that was good for women. When CTW was formed in 1968, the first two tiers of management and production—except for herself—were male. She couldn't find experienced women or minorities for the top jobs and knew that the show had to be good or it would fail. "At the time, the glass ceiling in television for women was associate or assistant producer," she says. "But all of the associates or assistants were women. There was a very mysterious lack of talent that none of these women had been promoted to the level of producer or executive producer." The irony noted, she continues: "And so that's how we're able to get women in and they move up because we didn't have those barriers here." Since 1980, the executive producer of *Sesame Street* has been a woman, Dulcy Singer.

A combination of reasons draws women to CTW. There's the pride of product that Nina Elias speaks of. There's the grapevine knowledge that women can make it as producers here. There's the appeal of working in children's programming, something more women than men are interested in. And for burned-out teachers or academics who want to try something different, there's the appeal of working in *educational* television. As one former teacher put it: "You don't have to stash your ideals at the door." And with today's emphasis on making money, men who might have been attracted to nonprofit organizations 10 or 15 years ago are turning instead to big business; women are filling the gap. "We're witnessing the feminization of nonprofit organizations," Cooney says. For all of these reasons, no one does any special recruiting or hiring of women; officially, no one checks to see that they are making their way upward. Why should they? Two thirds of the staff are female, and four of the eight corporate executives are women. CTW, however, continues to make known its nondiscriminatory hiring policies to recruiting agencies and in its advertisements. But given the current imbalance in this company of women over men, males right now have the edge in hiring.

Turn on the show and you'll see boys and girls, blacks, whites, Hispanics, orientals. A female mail carrier and Sally Ride, the astronaut. And you won't see minorities or women made fun of. In fact, the only target is supposedly the one who can take it the best since he's at the top of the heap: the white male. That's how Dr. Nobel Price, the mad scientist, got to be the butt of so many japes. Naturally, members of scientific professional societies have written to complain. Being funny is hard work if you stay clear of stereotypes.

Because so many former academics find their way to the Manhattan offices of CTW, it's been dubbed an educational halfway house. Emily Swenson, vice president for corporate affairs, taught school for five years before she went back to school herself, to Yale's School of Organization and Management. Swenson found the atmosphere at CTW a perfect fit for her background: "This was one of the few not strictly educational institutions where I could combine both my educational life and my financial training. I didn't have to be schizophrenic." Swenson's job is assistant to the executive vice president, David Britt, a capacity which involves her in all the diverse operations of the company. She's worked on fund-raising, the initial development of new programming, public service campaigns and making videocassettes of *Sesame Street*. She realizes that no clear career path exists for her but that her boss will let her take on anything she wants to as long as there's a logical reason to do so. "I never get the sense that because I'm a woman I can't do something."

The same is true in production, a department that continues to be male dominated at most commercial stations and the networks, where getting a chance to produce is often directly related to how close your connection is to the boss. Not so at CTW.

In 1985 Judith Webb was promoted to field producer for CTW's show on science and technology, *3-2-1 CONTACT*. The day we caught up with her she was dressed in a jumpsuit and hiking boots, for she was off to a shoot in

Vermont. A 25-ton piece of granite was to be blasted off the side of a mountain; by the end of the show, she hoped to have the granite going up the side of a skyscraper being built. It was a particularly hectic time for her, for she was still holding down the job she had been hired to fill four years ago, that of production manager, a job she would eventually leave behind. She came to CTW after six years of production work on various projects and working at a station in Pittsburgh. "I don't think I could have moved up as fast as I did if I had been at most other companies in this industry," she says. "People are extremely jealous of the producing positions. They are the hardest to get, the most competitive and are mostly male dominated. This is a liberal industry, but it's male dominated."

The person who's largely responsible for bringing along people like Webb is Al Hyslop, the vice president in charge of production at CTW. "Al is a man who is personally committed to the advancement of women and minorities, and even if you're not sure it's time to develop, if Al thinks it's time, honey, it is," Webb commented. "It's the only way you're going to learn. It's trial by fire. Overall, I'd say he pays more attention to women and minorities because they usually enter at a lower level. But he's very fair to everyone."

Webb's background is a typical route for producing, but the secretarial path is also open at CTW; one woman who began as a secretary is now a producer. While it may be somewhat more difficult to accomplish this jump as the company matures, women contend it's still possible. However, it's not easy to move from division to division in the company, since the operations are so varied—magazine publishing to product licensing. Nina Elias accomplished it by first quitting her job in financial services, where she was a cost analyst, and taking on free-lance production jobs. She was hired back as a production supervisor. She met her husband while free-lancing for CTW, since he is a free-lance producer himself, and for a while she took a number of CTW jobs before she was offered a full-time job in production. It's probably better that he isn't on staff, for the company generally tries not to hire couples even though a few do work there. In recent years, the size and staff of CTW has changed as divisions were reorganized or dropped. Two play parks were financial flops and were sold, a software experiment proved unprofitable and has been phased out, and layoffs are not unusual. One year, 80 people were let go. When one is part of a couple in a company the size of CTW, firing one partner and not the other understandably creates friction.

While company policy isn't favorable to couples, children are another matter—this is *Sesame Street*, after all. As at most creative places, the people who work there tend to be highly volatile and voluble—noisy, if you will—and yelling in the halls or cracking jokes during the workday is part of the background hum. And so even if a child banging on a terminal bothers some, chances are no one will say anything. A day at CTW might give conservative, quiet types the hives, but the women who work there call it a fun place.

Absence because of a child's illness is not an issue. "I hate making that call," Nina Elias says, "but once I deal with myself and say, 'Look, my daughter is sick and I've got to stay home,' everybody is compassionate and it's fine."

Maternity leaves are generous; unused sick days double as disability days, and three months' paid leave with your job guaranteed is the norm. The problem is that up until recently, only 20 percent of the women came back, announcing their decision on the day they were to return. This causes a crunch for everybody because your coworkers have to pick up the slack, a difficult task when only two or three people constitute a department. Only secretarial staff can be replaced with temporaries.

Although *Sesame Street* seems to go on and on—130 hour-long shows are produced a year, most of them with 15 minutes of new material blended with segments from earlier years—CTW has matured and grown since the days 15 people put the first programs together. Some shows have come and gone. *The Electric Company*, for graduates of *Sesame Street*, is no longer; *3-2-1 CONTACT* was making its final shows in 1986. Last year, a new math program for 8- to 12-year-olds, *Square One TV*, premiered. Production costs continue to rise, while the sources of revenue have remained relatively stagnant. Foundations and government agencies supplied the early funds, but today their pockets are not nearly as deep as they once were. The annual budget is around $55 million, with approximately two thirds of that coming from the licensing of toys, books, clothes and other products inspired by *Sesame Street*. The other third comes from member stations of the Public Broadcasting Service, which pay to broadcast the show.

Since licensing brings in considerable revenues, the division is far more than a stepchild. And here it's considerably less than an egalitarian paradise for women: in truth, the products group is lousy for women, even if one woman who has been with the company since 1971 is a vice president. Women say they have been routinely ignored when it comes to promotions; that men are allowed to grow into their positions without requisite experience while women are not; that they are patronized and their opinions summarily dismissed. Morale stinks in this division. "We generate the most revenue in the place, and the idea is, 'Don't mess with the formula,'" remarks one woman. "The department is actually antiwoman."

Other women from other divisions agree with these harsh perceptions, and all wish that Cooney—whom they personally admire—was more of a hands-on president who paid more attention to the day-to-day operations, rather than remaining distant and remote in her gigantic corner office over-looking Lincoln Center. They look up to her as a role model but see her infrequently.

Cooney has not been known as an active feminist, and she admits that the National Organization for Women had to prod her into having more women in nontraditional roles, or more women, period, on *Sesame Street*. As president, she surrounded herself with experienced men and didn't do a great deal for other women, per se; in recent years, however, company women say, she has been making an effort to reach out to other women in the company and assuring that some are being groomed for senior positions. Cooney wouldn't be judged under a similar microscope if she were male, but because this book is necessary, she is.

Her salary—along with those of other top executives—is considerably less than it would be in commercial television. Cooney makes a little more than half of the $265,000 or so she would outside, and while other senior management salaries are closer to their comparable worth, they are still 20–30 percent lower. Down the line, the pay is more competitive with commercial operations; every two years salaries are evaluated to see that they generally keep pace with commercial television. It's a different matter for the creative people who write the shows, and the musicians and actors; they make guild rates, and with residuals coming in for years, some of them tend to be highly paid. Because CTW is a place where women can get production experience they wouldn't elsewhere, and because in a small company like CTW the senior positions are few, turnover tends to be high as women take their skills and ambitions elsewhere.

The retirement and savings plans are unusually good, partly because CTW is nonprofit and partly because the company figured out how to make the most out of what was legally allowable. CTW contributes an amount equal to 3–5 percent of employees' salaries (based on length of employment) to a retirement plan, and members are completely vested as soon as they are eligible, three years after employment begins. A savings plan allows an employee to set aside up to 6 percent of her salary, with CTW matching the funds for three years; after three years, CTW will throw in an extra 50 percent ($1.50 for each $1 a staffer saves). None of this is taxable until the member withdraws the money. Other plans allow additional monies to be set aside and not taxed, up to the legal limit for nonprofits.

Talking to women from different divisions of CTW was somewhat like talking to women at different companies. Here it's great for women, there it's not so hot. Each division is its own entity, without a lot of communication among them; each tends to run as a separate—and sometimes warring—fiefdom. "Even if everyone shares the same philosophical goals and is expected to have a commitment to the company's ideals, there's a vacuum that exists," says one woman. "It's a political place, and it's easy to feel isolated." Management meetings are held monthly, but attendance is not a high priority. You're more likely to learn what's going on through gossip rather than a memo or an announcement. Women from different divisions make a point of having lunch with each other to keep up.

They're a fairly aggressive bunch who aren't timid about speaking out and complaining, secretaries included. Maybe Cooney's presence at the top makes them feel free to; maybe not. Maybe it's the vocal types who are drawn to television. Maybe it's the informality you get at a small shop like CTW.

The company may be small, but its reputation is not. Everybody in America who reads or watches television has heard of *Sesame Street* and how it's changed children's programming. As Emily Swenson puts it, "The place may appear to be a little pond, but once you come to work here you realize you are actually a big fish in a big pond. All you have to do is say where you work and watch the reaction. Sometimes it's embarrassing because you find people giving you credit for things you didn't do."

CITIZENS AND SOUTHERN

C&S OWNS BANKS IN GEORGIA, FLORIDA AND
SOUTH CAROLINA; OUR REPORT DEALS WITH C&S BANKS
IN GEORGIA

▲ EMPLOYEES: 8,000; nearly three quarters are women.

▲ SALES: $1.7 billion.

▲ ASSETS: $14 billion. In 1986 profits were $150 million, up nearly $25 million from 1985.

▲ Women are actively recruited, and programs to ensure opportunities for all include job posting, tuition reimbursement, succession planning and management training.

▲ To rectify pay inequity, C&S examines what other companies are doing, reevaluates job descriptions and adjusts grade levels when necessary. Sexual discrimination charges are handled through both informal and formal channels.

▲ C&S is sensitive to parenting and family needs. In addition to the standard maternity disability leave, the bank grants liberal paid and unpaid leave on a case-by-case basis. Sick leave is allowed for family illness, and flexible working hours are an option available to both men and women. A resource referral directory for child care services is provided.

▲ The company is aware of potential problems of sexual harassment, and a training program is offered to all employees to explain both what constitutes harassment and how to deal with it.

▲ Although approximately 73 percent of its employees are women, only 6 percent of the 209 people C&S considers senior management are female. However, the bank encourages women to stretch. The well-educated, highly motivated women now swelling the ranks of lower and middle management have an excellent chance of breaking through to the top.

▲ Major employment centers: C&S operates the largest network of banking offices in Atlanta—90 full service banking offices in Atlanta and environs. (In total, C&S has 188 offices in Georgia, 137 in South Carolina and 141 in Florida.)

CITIZENS AND SOUTHERN NATIONAL BANK
Box 4899
Atlanta, GA 30302
(404) 581-2121

When Isa Williams was applying for jobs at Atlanta banks in 1971, shortly after she graduated from Spelman College, one of the banks in town that wanted to hire her asked if she would mind trimming her two-inch Afro. She responded that she didn't think it was too long. Over at Citizens and Southern, "No one mentioned it," she says. "They related to me as a person, not just as a black, and whether or not I fit the job."

When Williams came to C&S, opportunities were just beginning to open up for women and minorities. "You were constantly being told, here's the opportunity, if you can do this there's something in it for you," she says. "I was given the chance to learn a lot of different things, to gain diversity without having to leave the company."

Determined to be taken seriously, Williams waited until she had been at the bank six years before she had a child. When she was ready to come back, a suitable position couldn't be found, and she stayed on leave for a full year with benefits. Leaner times now prevail, and such an extended leave wouldn't be possible.

However, women who must stay off their feet and in bed for months before the birth of a child are given the necessary leave. In return, the bank earns the women's loyalty. "I was offered a promotion when I was eight months pregnant," says Leslie Douglas Hurst, a branch manager, "and they don't discriminate against you when you come back. This has been a wonderful place for me."

As far back as the sixties, when Betty Jones came to the bank, she found that she could make of her career pretty much what she wanted. Initially, Jones, a newlywed, thought she would work for a few years before beginning a family, which is what she told the man who hired her. With a year of college, she went to work in auditing, the first woman ever to do so. After a year or two, Jones decided that if she was going to work she might as well make the best of it. "It wasn't until I decided that I wanted a career that I had one," she says. "I set a goal to become an officer when I had been with the bank for 10 years, and I let my manager know." Although the first promotion she was up for did not go through, it did the second time her boss recommended her. She became an officer in 1970, two months before her 10th anniversary with the bank. At the time you could count the women officers on the fingers of one hand; at this writing, there are 727 out of 1,695.

Jones finished college at night, graduating from Atlanta's Oglethorpe University in business and accounting; C&S picked up the tuition. Working as an auditor gave her exposure to senior officers, and she reasoned that if she did good work it would pay off. Eventually one of the general vice presidents asked if she would like to move over to the real estate division, an operation that, in the mid-seventies, was in a crunch. Her manager in auditing didn't want to let her go but was persuaded to do so in 1979, and she was able to help turn around a problem department, receiving the spotlight for doing so. It's a move she recommends to anyone wanting to get ahead. "If a situation is risky, you get a better deal. You get recognition and the promotion that comes with it. If you don't solve the problem, you also get the visibility. But if something is a safe bet, you don't get as good a deal, you don't get as much credit."

Her next major move, which amounted to a career change, was in 1978 to investments, where she is a senior vice president of operations. "I have been treated equally to any man," she says of C&S. "If you work hard, if you are productive for the bank, you are treated equally. I have never felt discrimination here."

Although confident that women will reach the top at C&S, Jones is realistic in assessing the conflict between career and family that many women face: "There is a price to pay for success. And the questions many women ask are, is it worth it? How much is too much? Would I be comfortable doing a good job in my present one, or am I willing to put forth the extra effort to take that next step? Men are usually not asking those same questions. The men at senior levels have spouses at home taking care of the family, the social obligations. They have wives." By mutual agreement, Jones and her husband have no children. They share domestic responsibilities.

Other women voice the same concern as Jones, mentioning it more often than we heard in interviews outside the South. "Your priorities shift with two children," one woman says. "You've got to step back for two or three years. I've got other things I have to do now." The problem women face is that although this is true of some women, or only for the years when the children are young, it is not true of all women.

Yet men, not only in the South, but perhaps more so there than elsewhere, tend to lump all women together, handicapping those who are willing to give their all to the company. "In recent months, I've talked to a senior manager who said that when he looks around, he sees few women he would put in senior positions because women have a more difficult time than men making the commitment because of family obligations," one woman says. Because of this, she feels it will take at least another decade of women proving they can do jobs at levels *higher* than senior vice president before women are considered for top positions in the bank.

Part of the reason is that although women have been around for 10 or 15 years, men were in place a decade or two earlier. "The guys at the top will see that the guys they supported all along will continue to be supported first, ahead of the women, the newcomers," another woman observes. "You may have a continued tiny trickle of women moving up, but it will be very tiny."

For instance, women tend to get stuck in the small branches rather than manage the big, prestigious ones. When the bank was reconstructed, somehow women were cut out of the power positions. Retail division managers will be women, but they aren't the ones making the large commercial loans. One woman, who started with the bank in 1979 and is a branch manager, says that none of the men she started with are still branch managers. They've moved up. "It is hard work and it is grueling and there is not much glory in it," she says, pinpointing what happens to most women in Southern banks. They are heavily recruited and make up nearly 40 percent of the people in the management training programs at C&S. Yet even there, trouble is apparent. One woman who graduated from college with honors had trouble convincing superiors that she be allowed to take the entrance exam for special training in credit, while a man with mediocre grades breezed in effortlessly. All he had to do was ask.

Yet generally, women have no trouble getting to entry-level management. Some divisions will have more women than men in such spots, much to the surprise of some of the young men joining the company. These women work extremely hard to prove themselves. Audits of branches women manage tend to be close to perfect, the women point out, while audits of branches men manage are more likely to be average. But perfect audits don't give the women brownie points. Regardless of their willingness to do the work, only a few truly exceptional women are able to rise above such jobs in line positions. And even when they do so, "It's easier for a woman to be selected if she is a specialist," rather than a general manager, remarks one of the most senior women. Her comments ring true for most of the eight women who had the title of senior vice president when we visited C&S in the spring of 1986; one woman says only two are managers in any real sense. And another woman is harsh in her assessment of the power these women have: "If you look at the dynamics of the organization, power has suddenly moved past the senior VP level to another level. The senior VP is not the power base it used to be when the title was important. It's no longer a senior management position. Women have the title, but they are not the movers and shakers in the bank."

A few months after our visit, one of the eight female senior VPs was made an executive vice president. She is Veronica Biggins, director of human resources for the C&S Corporation. Biggins is not only female, she is a black and the mother of two. How well she does will certainly have an impact on the opportunities for women coming up the pipeline, but the effect will be muted since she is in human resources rather than the line management of the banking business.

Biggins, who started in the retail bank in 1974, paints a somewhat rosy picture of C&S: "If you can do a job, it doesn't matter what you look like, what you wear, or anything else, the question is, can you do the job?" While she is quick to admit that women have had to put in some hard time to prove they can have a family and still stay committed to their jobs, she feels that it has been done to management's satisfaction at C&S: "This is a company where it's okay to have a discussion about your family. I know women who work in companies where they would never raise the issue of having a family, much less go to a meeting and say, 'My child has chicken pox,' but you can here and women can be as comfortable as men doing that." Overall, Biggins believes C&S is open to anyone who shows good results: "We have been very open to people achieving. You achieve, you move up. You don't achieve, you don't move."

You might also be out of a job. Times have changed from when C&S boomed right along with the expanding real estate market in Atlanta during the sixties and early seventies; when the real estate market collapsed, C&S was left holding the bag on millions of dollars of loans. Its stock, which once traded at $25 a share, went as low as $4 a share. However, a turnaround came within a few years, after the senior management was ousted in 1978 and Bennett A. Brown was named president. By 1984 *United States Banker* reported, "C&S, Once On Its Knees, Now Roars Back." In the process, the bank became lean and mean. People who did not pull their weight lost their jobs.

People who succeed work long hours. Coming in at 7 or 7:30 A.M. is not unusual, nor is staying late, night after night. One high-ranking woman says frankly that it was easier to keep up with the work after she got divorced nearly a decade ago, and that she often spends weekends working at home. "A lot of the guys say they envy me because no one is nagging me to do this or that," she says. "No one is complaining but the dog if I don't get home until seven. But I also go home to an empty house at the end of the day. Getting to the top means paying the price that not all men and women are willing to pay."

One woman who paid the price is Irene Carpenter, who in 1981 became the first female senior vice president in the bank's history. She had been with the bank for 23 years. Carpenter, a district manager of 14 branches, notes that men—not only women—often opt out of the dedication a continual career climb means, adding, "When men make those decisions they often switch companies, but that's not viewed as opting out the same way it is for women."

At C&S, and quite possibly throughout the South, women are viewed as quite different creatures from their male counterparts. While that's true in the large sense, the differences men perceive about women in business work against the women. For example, many men feel women aren't tough enough.

Mary Ann Whidby found herself caught in this last stereotype. As a group manager in systems development, she had been passed over for a promotion to development head when a man without a technical background was brought in. She made no bones about the fact that she was upset. Five months later the position came open again, but again there was a hesitancy to move her up because she was a woman. "There was a protective attitude of, what if you don't make it?" she says. "They are almost as afraid of your failure as you are, of how you will react, of what a woman's failure will mean in a job they've never had a woman in before. The boss finally said, 'I am not being as objective with you as I would be with someone else, and that's not fair. I am not allowing you to succeed or fail.' Then he stuck out his hand and said, 'It's yours, congratulations.'" That was three years ago.

Other women say that even when things get screwed up in their departments, their male bosses have a tendency to protect the women from the brunt of the situation, an attitude that keeps them from fully understanding the problem.

Another wall the women come up against is the hunting-and-fishing-male-bonding weekend, where the decisions about who fits in with the team are made. The younger women in particular feel locked out, although some of the women say they go hunting and golfing with their customers and senior bank officers. Yet it isn't likely to happen as often or as naturally as it does with their male peers and senior management. "Your customers might go if you ask them, but senior management doesn't think, 'Oh, let's get Barbara Nell and one of her customers and go hunting for the weekend,'" one woman remarks.

Irene Carpenter says that while she didn't take up hunting or fishing until recently, she did learn how to read the sports pages a long time ago to be able to converse with her peers about subjects they were interested in. And she brings up the sports analogy about why women are not often team players in business. "Little girls miss by not learning how to play football—they don't learn about team concept," she says. "Consequently women tend to appear inflexible. A woman will want what's right in the world as opposed to what's going to make something work, and if a guy is assembling a team of people, he wants to know that the team is going to play with him, and not that one of them is a maverick who's going to go her own way." In short, Carpenter thinks, women tend to create some of their own problems in getting ahead because they don't think and act more like men. It's not a problem particular to C&S.

The fact that boys will be boys poses a problem for single women at C&S, especially pretty single women. They have to put up with a barrage of innuendo, comments about their personal lives, how they look and the clothes they wear. Some managers ask personal questions about who they are dating or how it's going. And what do you do when a senior officer of the bank calls with no other purpose than to tell you how beautiful you looked at the officers' meeting that morning? But once a woman marries, the Southern gentleman style takes over, the inappropriate comments come to an end and business resumes in the formal and civil manner of the South.

The men open doors, the women smile and say "Thank you." This is an old-line Southern bank rooted in tradition that goes back to 1887. While there might be an open door policy—the employee handbook says so—the doors themselves are likely to be shut. Conversations are quiet and discreet. This is good gray banking. Given all that, it's remarkable that C&S has made the kind of progress it has in promoting women and minorities. Underscoring that commitment are the affirmative action goals that are part of each division head's annual review. An attempt is made to stick to the spirit of the law.

In summary, the women at C&S give their company mixed reviews.

Some say they have not been discriminated against, while others point to specific cases of discrimination. At least in entry-level management, sex appears to make no difference. One woman says she didn't have to work harder than a man to get a promotion, but she had to do it a lot longer. Women at the senior VP level say they have not been treated any differently than men. They have had to work hard, but so have the men. And when they give their opinions at meetings, they are listened to. It is not a perfect place, but then few are. Very few.

Leslie Douglas Hurst, a branch manager and a mother, had the final word in our discussion group: "In any corporation, there is a president at the top, and he's going to be a man. Wherever we go, we are going to face that. I'm not sure women have come any further than we have here. When I read about how women are faring in business, I have to consider C&S one of the leaders."

In the South.

COGNOS

A SOFTWARE MANUFACTURER IN THE BUSINESS APPLICATIONS MARKET, COGNOS, INC. IS A CANADIAN COMPANY WITH OFFICES WORLDWIDE; OUR PROFILE DEALS WITH THE U.S. SUBSIDIARY

▲ EMPLOYEES: 200; more than 40 percent are women.

▲ REVENUES: Compared with the previous fiscal year, which ended in February 1987, revenues grew 51 percent, to $68.4 million; net income increased more than five times, to more than $5 million.

▲ Cognos is concerned about recruiting, hiring and promoting women but has no special programs focusing on women. Four of the nine employees considered upper management are female, including the president and CEO. None of the six-member board of directors is a woman.

▲ In addition to standard maternity disability leave, additional leave (up to 26 weeks) may be granted based on length of service to the company. Cognos offers flexible work hours, especially for individual contributors, flexible workplaces and sick leave for family illness. The company has experimented with part-time work for professionals. Other benefits are excellent—medical and dental reimbursement for employees and their families is 100 percent. The company offers a liberal vacation policy.

▲ Cognos has no stated policies, practices or training programs on sexual harassment. It does not seem to be a problem.

▲ Cognos is committed to preventing inequality of pay for women and is researching various measures of comparable worth.

▲ Major employment centers: Peabody, Mass. (corporate head-quarters and Eastern Region sales office): 65; 18 small offices throughout the country.

COGNOS, INC.
2 Corporate Place, I-95
Peabody, MA 01960
(617) 535-7350

Take a young, hot company with a great product in an industry just out of short pants, and you are likely to come up with a place where women with talent and ambition can reach for the top. It's true at Lotus. It's true at Recognition Equipment. And it's nowhere more true than at Cognos U.S., a company that develops and markets application development software, where who's on top is a woman, stylish Mary Makela.

Makela, a 17-year veteran of IBM, heads up the U.S. division of Ottawa-based Cognos, a relatively young entrant in the crowded software scramble. The company began in Canada in 1969 as a consulting firm and in the 1980s started providing customized software to the Canadian market. Cognos' principal product, PowerHouse, is the world's most widely installed advanced programming language for business systems on minicomputers used at over 10,000 sites in 48 countries. What sets Cognos apart from the pack are great products—easy-to-use computer languages for business systems—that are faster than the competition's, which is why PowerHouse is taught in more than 160 colleges and universities worldwide. How much better they are is reflected in the company's financial statement. Between February 1986 and February 1987, the company's first fiscal year after going public, revenues grew at the blistering rate of 51 percent, to $68.4 million. In the six years preceding, the company had posted revenue growth of more than 40 percent annually, putting it among the top 25 software companies in the world. The forecast for the future is more of the same.

In the United States, Makela heads a staff of around 200 from head-quarters in the Boston suburb of Peabody. Although the senior sales managers Makela brought in soon after she joined the company in 1985 were all men, she claims to have no sex preference—the best person for the job gets it. Understand, females do not get promoted over more qualified men. A few sales managers may need to be nudged to see a woman's worth, but most men at Cognos are open to women who can do a job as ably as men. Makela herself doesn't give a second thought to whether it's a man or a woman up for a promotion or job. "My attitude is, give me the best person for the job," she says. "The opportunity for women is there and everybody knows it, just because I am a woman. That helps a lot."

That this was an environment where women get ahead attracted Jennifer Rogers when she was interviewing for the job of Makela's administrative assistant. Not only was the boss a woman, she noted, so were the heads of the marketing and human resources divisions. "I looked at that and thought, well, at least there's no prejudice to women moving up." Rogers had taken 10 years off to raise two children before reentering the work force in 1978. What's important to her is flexibility for parental responsibilities. "I've had to go to meetings at school, and the teachers expect to meet you between the hours of 8:30 A.M. and 2 P.M. Mary [Makela] has been very supportive—'Go,' she says."

But it isn't just parents who get that kind of understanding. It's across the board. It is also the flip side of an energetic company in the throes of a growth rush, a company that expects a lot from its employees. People who are not overachievers should apply elsewhere. "The attitude is, we want you to give a hundred percent to Cognos and do the best for it, but management feels that there is life after Cognos," remarks Lauren Levenson, U.S. marketing manager. "And the only way for you to care about Cognos and give it your best shot is if Cognos cares about you."

People do give a lot. Levenson says that after she had been with the company for several months, she realized she didn't even know what the official hours were, since there was so much going on, you just came in and kept going until you couldn't any longer. Because she writes brochures and other promotional materials, Levenson finds she's able to get her work done only when the phone isn't ringing, and that's usually at home at night or on weekends. Sometimes when she has a project she expects to delve into on a weekend, she'll get a call from her boss—a man—on Friday afternoon telling her he doesn't want her to work over the weekend. "They are sensitive to the burnout issue," Levenson notes. "They are not like some companies that burn you up and spit you out and then go on to somebody else. It's go, go, go a lot of the time, but everybody watches out to see that nobody goes over the edge."

Apparently nobody does. Lana Farmery, head of the U.S. marketing division, says that in the nine years she has been with the company, she's never not wanted to come to work. Renee Romagnole, who sells Cognos's financial software in the Northeast, says that at other companies where she had worked, she's always had one foot out the door. Not so here. "It's exciting and everybody is enthusiastic and the products are terrific," she says. "You feel like you are working for the prima donna of the industry."

Prima donnas are, of course, demanding, but Cognos has a liberal vacation policy designed specifically to combat burnout, common at the hot software companies. After a year, you get three weeks of vacation; in your fifth year, you get an extra week. Top performers in 1987, Romagnole included, were treated to a two-week trip to Hong Kong and Bangkok. It was first class all the way, even down to the gift packages that were left in their hotel rooms each evening. The hope is that everyone comes back rested and renewed—and ready to go for broke once again.

Other benefits are equally generous. Not only are employee health and dental insurance premiums completely paid for by the company, they're also paid for employees' spouses and families, a practice few companies, especially small companies, maintain. The medical insurance policy itself covers everything from prescription drugs to therapy. Tuition reimbursement is 100 percent.

But while the opportunity for advancement is there, as it is at small companies, Cognos also shares some of the minuses of small companies.

▲ There is virtually no management training at this point, nor is there clear-cut career pathing. The company is not doing a great deal to see that opportunities are made for people who are ready to move up. If you want to grow into a bigger job, you will have to go after it yourself. And in a company this small, there may not be the kind of opportunity you're after at a particular juncture in your career because somebody else has the only job that you want.

▲ Because the company is expanding in the worldwide market, a promotion may take you overseas or to Canada. Lana Farmery came to the United States from her native Canada in 1985, when Makela joined the company; whether or not she will stay for a long time is unknown. (Cognos pays all moving expenses.)

▲ Growing pains are causing some consternation among the troops. "They are expecting 40 to 50 percent increases in sales numbers, but Cognos is not giving the support to help us accomplish that," says a saleswoman. "I'm very positive about the company, but I don't think 70 percent of the people I work with feel the same way."

As in many young companies, sales is the driving force at Cognos. Makela's background at IBM was largely in sales, and it is sales the senior management of the company will come from for some time. Some of the sales staff were disgruntled that Makela initially brought in people from outside to run the sales division. In 1987 all nine regional and district sales managers were men. Yet the sales staff of 50 is 20 percent female, and an even higher percentage is found among the high performers. On that Far East trip, three of the 11 salespeople invited were women. In 1987 both the Most Valuable Player (Marsha Dowen) and Rookie of the Year (Karen Cleever) awards went to women. Top salespeople can make between $80,000 and $100,000. "We are open to women and minorities," says Makela. "We just don't concentrate on it." For women with some experience, Cognos could provide a wealth of opportunity.

The company's small size makes it necessary to have highly skilled people at all levels. While secretaries and administrative assistants are encouraged to leap the hurdle from clerical to management, and many do, figuring out how to do it is pretty much up to the individual. Secretaries, in fact, don't do much typical secretarial work, since most people do their own writing on computers. Cognos is looking for people who can take an idea and develop it on their own. Courses on the software systems that Cognos develops and markets are constantly being given for newcomers, yet college graduates looking for a professional job might do better gaining experience at a larger company before coming here. People hired right out of school usually have some special technical expertise.

Turnover seems fairly frequent here, but that's typical in this industry, and it does open a lot of spots for new people. One reason people leave is pay lower than what's otherwise available in Boston.

On the balance sheet, Cognos is a good company for ambitious women with some experience, not necessarily in software. Romagnole, for instance, has her degree in accounting. She joined the company as a financial consultant and was encouraged to go into sales. Her superiors thought she would be good at it. What seemed like a risk turned out to be a sure thing. In the process, Cognos gained Romagnole's loyalty and enthusiasm.

But where does she go from here? She's in her thirties, poised and ready for the next step. Will Cognos be able to find a place for her?

That's the main problem for women at Cognos. It's still so small that there just isn't room for all the aggressive comers in its ranks to go as far as they'd like.

CONRAN STORES

A RAPIDLY EXPANDING CHAIN OF RETAIL STORES IN THE
NORTHEAST SPECIALIZING IN CONTEMPORARY,
MEDIUM-PRICED FURNISHINGS

▲ EMPLOYEES: 875; approximately 60 percent are women.

▲ REVENUES: Not available. Conran's is part of Storehouse Group PLC, a British concern with annual sales of approximately $2.5 billion.

▲ Conran's is not concerned about hiring or promoting women. They don't have to be. There is a high percentage of women in management, in contrast to most other retail chains, where women are mainly in the sales force.

▲ Of the nine people considered senior management, four (president, a vice president, a controller and a director) are women. The president also sits on the board of directors of the parent company.

▲ Sexual harassment and discrimination are not issues. Any grievances are handled by informal discussion with company officers.

▲ This is not the place for formal training programs. Hands-on experience, long hours and a recognition of experience gained in nontraditional ways allow Conran's employees to grow.

▲ Major employment centers: Greater New York area, including New Jersey and Connecticut: 550; Washington, D.C., area: 100; Philadelphia area: 75; Boston: 50, with another 50 projected for a new store to open in spring 1988. A new store will open in Los Angeles later in the year.

CONRAN STORES, INC.
10 Astor Place
New York, NY 10003
(212) 674-4800

If anyone at Conran's wonders how top management views taking time off to have a baby, she need only to take a cue from the president: at 39, Pauline Dora had a baby and was away from the office for five weeks. That's not to say she let the Northeast retailing chain of trendy housewares and furniture run without its captain, for she was on the phone checking in the day after her son was born and remained in constant touch until she was back at her desk.

The message was clear, and it was the same one Dora gave Catherine Sadler, vice president of marketing and design, who discovered she was three months pregnant after she was hired but before she reported for work. "I don't care if you have 14 kids," Sadler remembers Dora told her, "as long as you can do your job and do it well, that's all that matters." Sadler became the head of a previously nonexistent marketing department of three. Less than four years later, she had 17 people working for her. Five of them were men. Sadler was still in her early thirties at the time. Her responsibilities include running an in-house advertising agency and design group, public relations and promotion, including Conran's quarterly catalogs, which are distributed nationally.

"There's little sense of who's male or who's female here," says Sadler. "When a position opens up, we look for the best people for the job, and more often than not the best applicants are women. Actually, I'd like to hire more men. If I could find them." That may be true, but management—with Dora at the helm—is so totally oblivious to sex that it's unlikely women of any age will have trouble getting ahead in this retail and design empire that's growing at a hare's pace.

To call Conran's simply a home furnishing and housewares outlet is to miss the point. It represents a lifestyle: good design at affordable prices for "people starting out or starting over," their publicity fairly chirps. The high-tech stores are stocked with whole rooms of furniture, down to the last teacup and bed sheet. Four richly illustrated books of Conran's design show the uninitiated how to do it.

Conran's is named after its founder, Sir Terence Conran, designer and entrepreneur, who opened his first store (called Habitat in England) in London in 1964; the American stores followed in 1977. Sir Terence is now chairman of Storehouse Group PLC, a group of 900 retail stores on three continents. For his contributions to design and retailing, Queen Elizabeth knighted the ebullient maverick in the early eighties; he then refused lunch with Prime Minister Margaret Thatcher because he disagreed with her policy on the Falkland Islands.

While in England the management tends to be largely male, here in the United States Sir Terence showed no hesitation in hiring women: Pauline (as everyone who works for her calls her) was the first person he hired to set up shop in the New World. The location was Manhattan's Citicorp Center. After a sluggish beginning, Conran's is thriving, and new stores are projected for 1988 that will bring the total to 18. The latest one will be in Los Angeles, a first on the West Coast.

All this growth makes for an informal, hectic atmosphere bordering on chaos back at headquarters, which shares airy loft space with a three-floor store in the Greenwich Village section of Manhattan. Because everything is happening so rapidly, the place nearly always seems to be under some kind of construction. As in the functional, high-tech stores, the floor is polished hardwood, adding to the noise. To be heard, you sometimes have to yell over the phones. Memos are practically unheard of. The offices are cubicles, and there are no doors. While employees admit these can sometimes be annoying, the chaos does allow people from different departments to cut through the bureaucracy.

Since the place is bustling and noisy to begin with, nobody minds that babies in strollers often end up there while Mom's working. The receptionist (who is just as likely to be a man as a woman) is often asked to watch the baby while Mother is in a meeting. By the same token, a vice president is likely to end up ticketing merchandise and putting it on the shelves when a new store is opening and the staff hasn't been fully assembled. You'll even see Pauline dusting merchandise when necessary.

The pace of expansion means that a manager's support system is likely to be herself. "You turn around to tell somebody to do something, and you discover nobody's there," says Maxine Fechter, former vice president of personnel and training. "But it also means there's a tremendous opportunity for your own growth within the company. If you're willing to roll up your sleeves and do the work, you can have a tremendous impact on the future of the company. You can be anything you want to be as long as you're willing to work hard and have some ability. And it's not a pretentious place. You don't have to come from the right company or have the right degree from the right university to get ahead. What counts is, can you do the job?"

Fechter herself is an example of that policy. She came to Conran's in 1979 after teaching school and several years of mothering and soon became one of the three women on the management committee.

Pat Grable found the same kind of opportunity open when she reentered the business world after several years of motherhood, volunteer work and acquiring a college degree during her late forties. Before she came to Conran's, she found herself in a dead-end job with a television network, where she was little more than a secretary. Trading on her volunteer work in publicity, as well as her broadcasting degree, she found a job at Conran's doing their publicity, even though she readily admitted she had no contacts in the home furnishings field and little expertise in product publicity. "They took a chance on me," she concedes, "and hired me at a low salary with the promise that if I worked out, I'd get a good hike in pay in six months." Her first task was to put together a list of 250 names for the company mailing list. Two years later, she had an assistant and was wearing the title of publicity manager. "This is a wonderful place for the older women reentering the business world—or entering it, for that matter," she says. "They give you so much encouragement and push you to do things you've never done before. You really feel that you're being pushed along to go as far as you can. And as for raises, I've never had to ask."

Opportunity to use the skills she had was what attracted Karen Coneys, who is the corporate controller, a position formerly held by a man. She is in her twenties. "I knew I could never get any farther than fixing up somebody else's mistakes at the accounting firm I was at before, and I had to get out. Conran's recognized that I was an accountant, not a glorified clerk." The accounting department is all women, not, Coneys says, because she looks for women, but because "Conran's asks you to work hard, and the men didn't seem willing to stay in the trenches and get the job done." Lunch for her, as well as for most of the other executives, is a quick take-out meal at her desk.

On the retailing side, women fare well too, for while many of the sales staff are male, most store managers are female. In contrast to most retail operations, company benefits are almost identical for both the hourly and executive staffs. These include medical, dental and doctor plans and life insurance paid for by the company, profit sharing for all employees who work at least 20 hours a week, and a 20 percent discount on all merchandise beginning on the first day of work. Three months of unpaid maternity leave are granted, but members of the executive staff almost never take that long.

Hard work, long hours, a breezy, informal atmosphere that allows people to move from department to department (any job openings are posted as well as listed in the company newsletter), and a potential for growth that the employees see as limited only by their own ambition and talent shows what it's like to work for Conran's. To keep up with the expansion, the rate of promotion is phenomenal. No one has to wait until somebody retires before he or she is promoted. And as the company expands, new positions are created and old ones assume more authority and power. As the company's continued growth fuels employee enthusiasm and opportunity is wide open, the women are highly motivated and dedicated, even though the pay scale is no better than at comparable retailers.

On the downside, Conran's isn't a place where you will find mentors to guide you through the rough times or show you how it's done. You learn by your mistakes, and you had better learn quickly. People in management either grow and are promoted or leave the company. "If your ideas don't work and you lose money, you have to leave," one woman comments. And no one is unaware that this is a high-risk retailing business and the atmosphere is highly charged and competitive. "We compete with each other," says one young woman. "There are only so many spots at the top."

Not surprisingly, Conran's has no programs aimed at hiring and promoting women, nor are there policies to deal with sexual harassment, a problem employees find amusing even to consider.

While the future looks rosy for Conran's, employees agree that any retailing chain still in its infancy could go belly-up as public tastes change, and they could all be out of a job. That seems unlikely, given today's emphasis on design in everything from teaspoons to wall clocks. It's a postmodernist world, after all.

THE DENVER POST

ONE OF DENVER'S TWO DAILIES

▲ EMPLOYEES: 1,350; approximately 30 percent are women.

▲ REVENUES: Reportedly lost $10 million in 1986. The Times Mirror Company sold it in the fall of 1987 to MediaNews Group, Inc., for $95 million. The Sunday *Post* reaches 55 percent of the Denver market but loses the daily circulation war to the rival *Rocky Mountain News*. Between August 1986 and March 1987, the *Post* increased its share of the advertising market by 5.5 percent.

▲ *The Denver Post* is concerned with hiring and promoting women. They work with women's organizations to recruit, with special focus on nontraditional jobs for women. For editorial jobs, the number of female applicants has made it unnecessary to recruit women.

▲ Efforts to promote women include a number of in-house training programs.

▲ Of the eight people considered upper management, one—a vice president—is a woman. One of the eight members of the board of directors is a woman.

▲ In addition to the standard maternity disability leave, new mothers can take leave without pay. It's not clear for how long, but the attitude seems to be one of flexibility. No other kinds of attention are paid to parenting needs at this union paper.

▲ The *Post* offers a program on sexual harassment; attendance is mandatory for all male and female managers and professionals. Charges of harassment are handled by the human resources department.

THE DENVER POST
650 15th Street
Denver, CO 80202
(303) 820-1010

The story at *The Denver Post* changed as we were going to press in the winter of 1987. But the good news here for women didn't. When ownership of the troubled paper passed from the Times Mirror Company to the MediaNews Group, the executive editor and publisher, two men who had promoted several women to senior jobs, were to be replaced by the end of 1987. A new publisher, James Barnhill, was dispatched by the new owners. On a get-acquainted visit, folksy Barnhill had alienated women by calling them "girls" and indicating that he couldn't quite get over the fact that some of his top deputies, particularly the under-30 Anne Gordon, the business editor, were women. The staff of the hard-hitting, prizewinning daily were also concerned that he would soften the paper's journalistic edge.

When one of the new owners, Dean Singleton, showed up two days later, the management committee, including attorney Carol H. Green, lobbied hard for Barnhill's ouster, citing both the women's issue and the paper's bent for hard news. To Singleton's credit, he didn't argue. He replaced Barnhill quickly.

The new editor and publisher, Maurice L. Hickey, who will be 54 next year, is a 24-year veteran of the Gannett chain (see p. 129) and has long been used to working with women as more than underlings. His tenure was scheduled to begin by the end of 1987; until then, he was aiding with the transition at his old Gannett paper, *The Detroit News.* As for working with high-powered women, Hickey says, "I don't see any difference between working with men and women," adding that as women have been making it in the newsroom, the logical consequence was that they would move into management and executive editor positions. Hickey credited Al Neuharth's policy of actively promoting women and minorities for his nonsexist attitudes.

Meanwhile, back at the *Post*, the good news that made the grapevine was that when Hickey arrived in Detroit in 1986 he refused to join the still-segregated Detroit Athletic Club (which his predecessor had belonged to) and told senior executives and editors who were members to resign. Says Kathy Joyce, manager of communications and training at the *Post*, "Women have been in power too long here, and it's too much a part of our culture to go backward."

Now, to our story. . .

The difference in how two highly capable, talented women were treated when they joined the staff of *The Denver Post*—less than a decade apart—is a microcosm of what has happened across America once the door was open to women the same way it was open to men.

Carol Green joined the paper in 1968 with excellent credentials. She had been a star on a midsized Southern daily and a city editor on a daily in Guam. She was hired at the fourth-year guild (union) level of pay; newspapers do not hire people at that level unless they have good solid experience and the clippings to prove it.

Yet Green was told that although she had interviewed for a job cityside, she would have to start in the women's department. "We run all our women through the women's department first to make sure they will make the grade before we put them on the city desk," she was told in no uncertain terms. She was tough enough to take the humiliation and boredom. As low man in the women's department, it was her job to write up meeting notices, a boring task usually filled by young, inexperienced reporters, not someone getting a veteran's salary. Need we say that men who were hired with similar backgrounds were not "run through the sports department" to see if they could make the grade? Sportswriters were sportswriters, they were not men who really wanted to be covering crime or education.

But Green proved her mettle. By doing a series exposing the false claims of health clubs on her own time, Green gained the confidence of the city editor, who said he would not only run the series, he would have her transferred to the city desk. It happened in a matter of weeks.

Eight years later, when Gay Cook joined the paper, she too had good credentials but less actual newspaper experience than Green. Yet Cook went directly to general assignment for the city desk. And in quick succession she was named assistant city editor, then one of two city editors, then editorial page writer, then went back to the city desk with more responsibility. In 1986 she was named metropolitan editor, in charge of all reporting on local, state and regional issues. Oh, yes, the national correspondent—a woman —reports to her too.

The really good news here is that Carol Green didn't get stuck in the reporting job for the rest of her career. She wasn't "too old" when the paper finally opened up for women. She is, as they say, one of the brass. Moving from editorial to the business side (via a law degree and time at an outside

firm), Green is vice president in charge of legal affairs and human resources. She is the one the craft unions—the printers, the pressmen, the
carriers—negotiate with at contract time. They do not think she is a push-
over.

Green made a major career move about the same time Cook was joining
the paper. She was selected as one of the five participants in the first group
of journalists to attend Yale Law School's program for a master's in law,
ostensibly to make her better prepared for a legal beat at the paper. Which it
did. But with the first year of law school under her belt, she decided to
finish and attended night school at the University of Denver College of Law.
By this time she had moved on to assistant editor of the editorial page, the
first woman to do so. When she passed the bar, she was offered the job of
the *Post*'s in-house counsel and labor relations manager. "The job had been
vacant for about a year and a half, and they needed me, but there was still
resistance," she says. "They weren't sure it was a good idea to have someone
who was, number one, inexperienced, and number two, a woman handling
labor relations."

Although she was eventually accepted as the paper's labor negotiator, she
wanted to fill in a hole in her background, and so she joined the largest law
firm in town, Holme Roberts & Owen. For two years, she honed her litiga-
tion skills. When top management at the *Post* changed, Green was invited
back. She wanted to come but took her time about it, negotiating for two
months to get the deal she wanted. Salary was not the only issue; she also
negotiated the level of the position and the amount of responsibility.

She came back as a vice president, and while some of the men who had
been her peers welcomed her, others openly acknowledged they were having
trouble dealing with her new status—but they promised they would do their
best to deal with their feelings. Green says they have and that all is well.

It's a bit different dealing with the diehard sexists (yes, we know we're
stereotyping) who come out of the pressroom. Mechanical and production
people—usually all men—are known to be hard on any woman they have
to deal with professionally, whether it be in the print shop or across the
bargaining table. "When we sit down, I sometimes get the sexist comment,
but it's all done in a joking manner, and I just feed it right back to them,"
she says. "I never take anything seriously unless somebody goes out of their
way to insult me... which has not happened. Somebody will say, 'I'm
going to take you out for a drink, honey, and we'll settle this,' and I say,
'The day isn't long enough where you are going to negotiate with me over a
drink.' And everybody laughs."

Green is very clear about the fact that the comments do not get in her
way. "My job is to have a dialogue about labor-management issues. And if I
detour from that and permit some basically uninformed sexist comment to

get in the way of that mission, then I'm not being an effective manager. I don't let them intimidate me. I don't turn red. And I can cuss with the best of them."

Four-letter words may not be as necessary in the newsroom, where Gay Cook supervises the day-to-day coverage of local events. Thirty-seven in 1987, she says, "I don't intend to stay metropolitan editor forever." Understand that metropolitan editor on any daily newspaper is a big job; on a paper the size of the *Post* (daily circulation in 1987 was 230,000; Sunday, 414,000), the title commands respect and wields considerable authority. All of the general assignment and most of the beat reporters (except for Washington, D.C., and international coverage) are under Cook's domain. Perhaps no other paper of this size in the country has a woman in the job. For some, the job is the capstone of their careers; for others, it has been a stepping-stone to managing editor or editor-in-chief. What's even more unusual about the situation at the *Post* is that Cook's competition for the job was another woman.

The person most directly responsible for that happy state of affairs is editor David Hall,* a Tennessean who retains his Southern drawl and style, making it all the more surprising when he says: "I am ruthlessly results oriented."

He's got the results to show it. Whenever women are judged on results alone and not on more subjective qualities, our research has shown, they can compete on an equal basis with men. By our standards, Hall's performance backs up his claim. He put a number of women in high places. One of the three people who reported directly to him is a woman; although her position, that of associate editor in charge of all the feature sections, columnists and the magazine, is not an unusual one for a woman to hold, this woman, in Hall's words, "controls half the newspaper." And that is unusual. At the next tier women show up in surprising places. There's Cook and the business editor, Anne Gordon, both filling jobs traditionally held by men. A few years ago, the photo editor was a woman, also usually a spot held by a man. The number of assistant city editors and city editors was fluid when we were writing last summer, as the *Post* had offered buy-out packages that were taken by more than 150 people. But women fill those slots just as frequently as men do. On the reporting staff, a number of key beats are filled by women, including the relatively new post of national correspon-

---

*Hall, like other sex-neutral executives we interviewed, had a mother who worked. She was widowed and left with a family to support. Hall is no longer at the *Post*; at this writing, he is working on special projects for the Times Mirror Company.

dent, which went to a woman after heavy competition. She travels the country for her stories. It is a plum reporting job.

When asked if sex ever has anything to do with assignments, Cook reflected for a moment and said that it might be brought up if the assignment was "especially gruesome and difficult," but that it most probably would be dismissed and everybody, regardless of sex, "would have a shot at it." At a police killing last year, a woman was the lead reporter on the shooting, and as she got to the scene early, she ended up dodging bullets in the middle of the night, just as the police were.

On the business side, women have done just as well, largely thanks to former publisher Richard T. Schlosberg,* who was also committed to hiring and promoting women. Not only did Schlosberg bring Green back to the paper, he has made sure that jobs were parceled out on the basis of merit, not good-ol'-boyism. And the women knew it. Former employee Peggy Onstad, who held a highly visible job in advertising, that of retail manager, said of Schlosberg: "He is very comfortable around smart women. Unlike a lot of men." Onstad supervised the sales staff who call on Denver's largest retailers.

In circulation, women still have to deal with a macho attitude, but if they work hard, they will succeed. Dee Durland, who was a single mother of four young children when she needed to find a job in 1971, took one delivering the *Post* because it paid more than other jobs. She is now circulation training coordinator. It means that she still rises some mornings at 1:30 A.M. and is on the job at 2:30 A.M. Morning papers, of which the *Post* is one, are delivered in the wee hours. "Long hours, a lot of hard work and determination are needed to overcome the traditional concept that it is a man's job," she says, understating the years of difficulty she let roll off her back as she outperformed many of her peers.

For a half dozen years, she was one of the winners of circulation contests. The prize for the men who won was a week-long trip to a nearby resort. But every year, Durland would get a check and a handshake from her boss; she wasn't even asked to the stag awards ceremony. In 1981 she complained, but to no avail. Yet the following year, they asked if she would prefer the check or the trip. She went to Vail. "The first three days were miserable," she recalls. "Pool games would stop when I walked in. They kept opening doors for me and apologizing for telling off-color jokes. But they got over it." Durland, incidentally, is in a position to complain about the treatment of women below her, and with the former management, she got results, and, as she puts it, "things started happening for me."

*Schlosberg remained with the Times Mirror Company and is now the president and CEO of the *Los Angeles Times*.

So. *The Denver Post* is an equal opportunity employer. (Minorities fare well here too.) But what's the place like? It turns out that Denver is the site of one of the last rough-and-tumble circulation fights in the country. There are no shared printing presses, no shared advertising staffs, and certainly no shared scoops. The competition, the *Rocky Mountain News*, beats the *Post* on daily circulation figures; the *Post* leads on Sunday. It is seemingly a fight to the death. It affects every department. "It causes us to work more hours than we should," says Renae Gerkin, assistant controller, who is getting a college degree as well as taking care of a young baby in addition to her full-time job. "But people who work here have a lot of loyalty. Sometimes your family gets neglected, and you forget about them until there's a problem." Gerkin started in 1972 as a billing clerk.

The intense competition with the *Rocky Mountain News* is fought on several fronts—sales, editorial, circulation—and certainly was a factor, if not the major factor, in the sale of the paper to MediaNews Group. The *Post* lost $10 million in 1986, and employees walked on eggshells wondering if Times Mirror would sell. It came as a relief when it actually happened, particularly as the new owners, Dean Singleton and Richard Scudder, are known for acquiring sick papers and nursing them back to health. Their method is radical budget cuts, but as more than 150 employees took buyouts (some walked away with as much as $250,000) that may not be necessary.

The women at the paper face these uncertainties but have lived with them for a long time and love their paper anyway. Newspapering is a business that gets into your blood, no matter what department you're in, news to human resources. Says Mary Bender, employment manager, "I worked at a bank before, but now I can't imagine not working at a newspaper. It's just so different." The *Post* apparently gets into one's blood more than most, no doubt because the circulation war breeds a we're-all-in-this-together attitude that can make going to work exciting and fun. Adrenaline flows at any paper, but maybe more so at the *Post*.

"Women have this built-in buzzer that makes them need to belong to something," remarks Anne Gordon, business editor, "and this is a great place to belong to. I can get so lost in my work when I have a troubled mind. It's great therapy. My boss always knows when I'm mad because there is more work flying out of my office than any other day." Gordon oversees the daily and Sunday business news operations and the paper's real estate and automotive news coverage. A Denver native, she was hired away from a Fort Lauderdale paper; her competition was two well-established men. She was hired for the job when she was 28.

Okay, it's a good place for women and the pace is intense. So who has time for kids? Diana Griego, for one. She just happens to be a Pulitzer

Prize—winning (with Louis Kilzer) reporter, a prize she won at 26. Incidentally, the story idea—that there aren't as many missing children as the statistics indicate—was her idea. When we interviewed her in late 1986, she was home on a four-month maternity leave. "When somebody wants to go out on maternity leave, I tell her to take all the time she thinks she needs," said Hall. "I want my people here long term, and the way I can screw that up is to pressure someone to come back before she's ready." For emergencies, management is also understanding, as long as *you understand* that people at a newspaper in the middle of a circulation war work damn hard.

You don't get paid extra for the excitement of the battle. The pay is in line with other newspapers of its size. In 1987 starting salaries for first-year reporters were $430 a week, while assistant business editors and their peers were making around $775 a week; merit pay could add up to another $50 a week on top of these union figures. In advertising, a saleswoman with four years of experience had a base pay of $562 a week and might average $500 a month in commissions. Senior managers make $60,000-plus.

The *Post* is at a center city location where it occupies a series of buildings as old as the late 1800s and as recent as the fifties. Although some of the offices are modern and the paint is mostly fresh, some of the space is old and grubby in a friendly, *Front Page* kind of way. You either like it or you don't, and it has as much to do with the hum of word processors and the ringing of phones and what's being done there as with architectural ambiance.

Note: We heard a number of quips here about how smart-talking *Denver Post* women deal with the things men say. One woman said that whenever anybody calls her "honey" who shouldn't, she lowers her voice and says deadpan: "Let's get this straight," looking him square in the eye. "I am a bitch."

Another woman, rushing into a meeting late, was met outside by a man who said anxiously: "There's no coffee." Racing past him, she said quickly, "That's all right, I don't drink it."

DIGITAL EQUIPMENT CORPORATION

THE WORLD'S LEADER IN NETWORKED COMPUTER SYSTEMS

▲ EMPLOYEES: 69,000 (in the United States); 38 percent are women.

▲ SALES: $9.4 billion.

▲ Digital Equipment Corporation lives its commitment to recruiting and hiring women and minorities. It actively advertises in minority and women's publications and engages in special efforts with professional organizations. Once hired, employees can voluntarily participate in an ongoing "Valuing Differences" program. The company has a liberal tuition reimbursement plan and provides a wealth of continuing education and personal skills workshops.

▲ Charges of sexual discrimination are handled by formal procedure; the company reevaluates individual job descriptions in response to allegations of pay inequity.

▲ DEC refused to reveal the number of upper-level female managers; from another source we learned more than 20 percent of all management are women. One of the vice presidents of marketing is female, and their treasurer—also a vice president—is a woman. One of the seven members of the board of directors is a woman. Women are aggressively recruited for the sales force; they are increasingly beginning to move up to the middle levels of management in sales as well. Data on technical managers were unavailable.

▲ Maternity leave is the standard disability (usually eight weeks), but this company provides flexible working hours, flexible workplaces, and part-time opportunities for managers and professionals. The company is grappling with child care alternatives; currently, it provides monetary support for selected community-based facilities and introduced a resource referral service in February 1988.

▲ The company has a strong policy on sexual harassment and a highly regarded training program for all professionals and managers. Complaints are handled by a formal grievance procedure.

▲ In an industry where top talent is aggressively pursued, women find unusually good opportunities at Digital. But whether they will rise to the top in engineering—an area traditionally monopolized by men—remains to be seen.

Are you tough and aggressive?
Do you like to slug it out in meetings and win?
And is high tech your field?
There may be a place for you at Digital.

Mental toughness isn't all that's needed at Digital. The ability to operate in a structure so loose you literally make up your job as you go along is a prerequisite. But if you don't need neat organizational charts and narrow parameters defining everyone's job—and if you're tough and competitive— you'll thrive here and find it an exciting place to work.

The man responsible for the corporate culture is a cowboy with a computer in his holster. His name is Ken Olsen. The company he shaped is a high-tech version of a wild Western town, a place where anything goes as long as it works. Its name is Digital Equipment Corporation. They call it DEC (pronounced deck) for short.

The company that Olsen founded in 1957 with two other engineers from MIT is today the leader in systems integration, that is, computers talking to one another. And while the sixtyish Olsen runs the company like an autocrat—no one doubts that he is the head honcho and he has named no successor—he set up his first- and second-line lieutenants as freewheeling entrepreneurs who design, build and sell their own products. Yet when all these product managers went running off in different directions without anyone keeping tabs on them, DEC ended up competing with products that were after the same customer dollar. When the company went into the personal computer business in 1983, it brought out three unrelated PCs and confused buyers; today most Digital PCs are bought to use as workstations with existing Digital networks, as they are more sophisticated and expensive than most people need in their homes.

Company organization is decentralized, and so is the physical plant. Home base is an old red-brick woolen mill on the banks of the Assabet

River in Maynard, Massachusetts, 20 miles west of Boston, but Digital has facilities all over the world. Small engineering groups in places like Tokyo, Seattle, Palo Alto and Israel work as teams with larger groups in New Hampshire, Colorado, England and the Maynard area, where there are a number of sites.

So how to rope in this unwieldy structure? How to get your VAX to talk to my PDP-11 or the DECsystem-20 across the country or around the world? In solving its own communication problems, DEC found the solution the marketplace wanted—computer networking.

It appears to have put Digital in the pink. After a slump in the early eighties, during which Digital lagged behind its competitors in new products and industry analysts were warning off investors, the company was posting healthy gains at a time when its rivals were mired in a soft marketplace. Two new VAX computers were brought to market in 1985, and in 1985 the company moved from slot 65 to 55 on the *Fortune* 500 list. Revenues reached $6.7 billion, reflecting a 20 percent gain over the previous year, at the same time inventories were reduced. By 1987, revenues were $9 billion and the *Fortune* 500 listing was 44.

To achieve this, Olsen was willing to fly in the face of the praise he has received for the loosely structured management style that made DEC one of the stars of *In Search of Excellence* and Olsen sought after as a lecturer. Olsen pulled in the reins somewhat, centralizing management and focusing on the product line. Several vice presidents and managers walked away when their jobs were reduced; those who stayed decided to base most of their computer designs on the company's line of VAX superminicomputers, a move which, while it slowed product development for a while, ultimately led to Digital's emergence as the world's largest manufacturer of networked computer systems. Partly because of this, DEC remains the major supplier of computers for scientific research, while garnering a healthy share of the market in medical research and industry.

"From the start, we chose to accomplish the harder, more technically challenging jobs, partly because of our engineering background but mainly because this was Digital's contribution to the computer industry," boasts the 1985 annual report, which is filled with page after page of pictures of DEC's applications in research and industry: monitoring earth tremors in Italy; providing access to up-to-the-minute biomedical research and patient data to staff at the Fox Chase Cancer Center in Philadelphia; collecting, transporting and analyzing data at the Lawrence Berkeley Laboratory in California; and controlling assembly and quality testing for the Ford Motor Company. When Dennis Conner got back the America's Cup from the Aussies in 1986, some of the credit was due to the Digital computer his team used to refine the design of their 12-meter yacht.

Above all else, DEC is engineering at its most advanced. And since engineering is a field that is mostly male, the culture bred at Digital is overwhelmingly macho. What counts are the goods you've got. You have to prove yourself over and over again, like the gunslinger whose reputation won't let him put away his guns. If anything goes, why not let a woman, or a member of a minority group, show her stuff? Why not indeed? Especially if you've got an industry that's growing so fast you can't find enough good bodies to keep up with the demand, period? At Digital, this willingness to hire women and minorities has been intensified as Digital grew even faster than the industry. "The intention has not necessarily been to help women, but because bodies were needed, women had the opportunity of being successful and going up the ranks," says one senior woman.

One of them is a district sales manager in Philadelphia,* a slot that makes her responsible for some $100 million in revenues annually. She is one of six female district sales managers out of 85. "I've worked hard, but I've been afforded the opportunities to move ahead," she says. Although she says she has never encountered discrimination when it came to getting promotions, she met resistance from the men who reported to her when she was first transferred to Philadelphia. "It took six months to prove to them that I really had the credentials for the job," she says. "I would have gone crazy if I had listened to everything that was being said about me." The fact that her husband is a service technician with the company and transferred from Washington, D.C., with her didn't make life any easier for either of them.

Happily, the testing period for both of them is over now, and she feels, at 39, that she has a bright future with DEC. She is also aware that how well she does will affect the chances of other women coming up. "We're still kind of new," she says. "At least you know here that you don't get a promotion because they are promoting women. We don't do that." No one would accuse her of having it easy because she's a woman. Married at the age of 16, she worked as a secretary and went to school nights while her husband went during the day. It took 13 years of night school to get both her bachelor's and master's degrees. "You've got to know what you want and go after it," she says.

And in some divisions, that means you make up your job as you go along if you're to succeed. "You have to be very self-generated here," says a group manager and one of the highest-ranking women in engineering. She oversees some 400 technical and professional staffers in the office systems group.

*Digital Equipment Corporation is the only company that did not divulge numbers of women in management, nor were we able to use the names of women interviewed and quoted. Although the company was uncooperative in this respect, we still feel that it presents unusual opportunities for bright, aggressive women who want careers in the computer field.

"There's no direct career path for anyone to follow." The advantage of this flexibility is that it allows for the individual creativity Digital is known for.

"At Digital, you can try things that other companies probably wouldn't let you try," observes another group manager in engineering. "If you succeed and accomplish a few things, you can move on to the next thing. There's not a card-stamping mentality here that says you can't do this until you do that. It's more, 'I think you can. Why don't you give it a whirl?' We're not bureaucratic."

Bureaucratic the company may not be, but make no mistake, this is one tough company—for both men and women—and you had better be able to match wits with your coworkers and be aggressive enough to move your projects forward. It's not going to happen by itself. Listen to these women talk about a company they say they like:

"DEC is a meritocracy. And consequently women can do very well because they are judged on their results. However, what's also true is that we're a very combative company. We have a strong orientation toward thinking that intense debate is necessary to determine what is the right thing to do."—A group manager.

"For a woman to survive in this environment, she has to have extreme self-confidence. Men too. The forces at play tend to whittle away one's self-confidence. It's highly competitive. And ultimately, at the top, it's a white male environment."—A senior executive.

"The kind of person DEC requires is assertive, aggressive, competitive. It's hard to maintain male-female relationships if you're that kind of woman. It's a given that there are women who are comfortable being married to men who fit this profile, but there are very few men who are comfortable being in a relationship with a woman who fits that description."—A married woman who's been at the company for a number of years.

"There are many lonely [unmarried] women in this corporation . . . there's a price to be paid at Digital if you are doing the kinds of things that the high-ranking women you're talking to are doing."—One of those women.

But while the road may be lonely, Digital has enough to offer to make very loyal employees out of the ones who do well here. Letting someone follow her own interests and create a job that suits her—whether it's in the area she's in or the one she would like to be in—is a style not many companies share. And when an employee and her manager decide that more education or professional memberships are needed to advance one's career, the company pays the bills. A sabbatical program—unlike any other we've come across—lets technical people earn advanced degrees full-time—at the company's expense—while they remain on full salary.

Women who have been at the company through the move to centralize management say yes, there is less tolerance for people doing their own thing now, and yes, this means that the product line fits together better than it did, but overall the corporate culture is one of constantly shifting sands. "Some valuable people don't like it—they have the mind set of wanting things clearly defined," remarks one woman, "and Digital tends to burn out those people."

Yet this woman, like all those we spoke to, was adamant about one thing: the freewheeling corporate culture makes it possible for women to succeed, not because they are particularly sought after, but because they haven't been locked out. Up to a point.

While the good news is that Digital has two female vice presidents, the not-so-good news is that neither is in engineering—and Digital is a company where engineering is king. Women have a harder time breaking through here than do white men. One factor, of course, is that there are so few women to choose from. Even in 1986, only 14 percent of all engineering graduates were women.

The other factor affecting women vying for the pinnacle in engineering is more amorphous: how do you fit in with the group? It is still a problem. Even though there is apparently a real commitment on the senior management level to *try* not to be prejudiced against women, comments are made and old biases emerge. One woman said that when a woman breaks through, the attitude about her boss is, "Well, he hasn't been killed by her ineptitude yet... and maybe he has gotten some attention because he was the one who promoted this woman. The problem is, some of us are going to screw up—just like the men—but the limelight on the woman who does will have a negative effect on the next one coming up. Whereas it doesn't hurt the next guy when a man screws up."

Another woman says that when she hears managers make even mildly sexist comments, she knows that ultimately it will be reflected in how she's going to be evaluated, perhaps unconsciously, and what kinds of positions she'll be considered for. "The thing to do is get away from it when it's impacting your career," she says. "But it's tough to fight because most of it is not anything you can hang your hat on. It's not direct. So you've got to leave. You either have to leave the particular area or leave the company. I've seen some women come along for two or three years, and they are just poised with the right expertise to have a significant impact on a segment of the company, but if they run into that brick wall—most women will go someplace else. That's the price the company pays."

A voluntary program called "Valuing Differences," in which groups of eight to 10 managers and professionals meet regularly to discuss a broad range of topics, should help eradicate some of the ingrained biases—one black woman said it made her rethink the stereotype she had of white males.

And women said that although the program affected hiring to some degree, overall its impact on the corporate culture was still difficult to gauge. One woman who participated said it had been extremely helpful; another said the experience had been irrelevant; most of the women we spoke to hadn't taken part; and some didn't know much about it.

However, it may be part of the reason sexual harassment, even in this macho culture, is minimal. One Texan who came in a few years ago and made lots of obnoxious comments about women eventually was asked to leave the company because he didn't fit in. Peer pressure is an effective tool here, especially at major sites. Out in the field on the sales force, it's tougher for women at some locations, as they have to be able not to let the put-downs get to them because no one is going to tell the guys to shut up.

The program may also have prevented the setting up of an old boy network, especially at lower and middle management levels. Women, and to a lesser extent minorities, fill a wide variety of slots. The vice president for strategic resources is a black man; a black woman who was the manager of a plant in Boston has since moved up to a more senior position. The plant, incidentally, was located in Boston, not the suburbs, so that it could draw from a diverse inner city population.

Yet how effective such a program is at the higher reaches is questionable. The male preserve at the top is tough to crack.

"Ninety percent of the people making the decisions about who they are going to let in are older men," comments one senior woman. "They have the philosophy that it should be equal for women and men, but they haven't internalized it. They just don't feel comfortable with you, even the ones who don't want to discriminate. It's just a fact. And so when it comes down to a selection of one of the boys for a prize job, it's unlikely that it's going to be a woman. It's going to be one of the boys."

One woman who was able to rise on the technical side says she did so by being given a project that was considered avant-garde and running with it. When it became more topical, the men wanted to get in, and they set up competing programs, a fact she accepted as a matter of course: "I don't own that space." She adds that women who are in line positions tend to be on projects that are not mainstream but on the fringe of the product line. "Women have to prove themselves in these slightly off-to-the-side projects and then move laterally into the mainstream, whereas men don't have to do that. They would go straight there."

The question in some women's minds is whether or not they want to go straight to the top, where if slugging it out is not as natural as breathing you might not survive. "Many women see the top as being a very macho environment, and not necessarily one they want to be a part of," remarks one woman. "When anyone is in a position of being a leader of a program, he is going to have to display an ability to be able to live in a very combative environment." And, she adds, the more senior one becomes, the less stable is the focus of your job. "The whole thing is moving the whole time."

Many women who are in senior management at Digital came in at fairly high levels, levels at which they could assume jobs—or create new ones— with a fair degree of autonomy. It's apparently not easy to be a woman and make points when you start at the bottom, even though the company has formal management training. "If you're good, you're good," remarks one woman. "If you're not, you're not."

Yet in making classroom instruction available to its employees, Digital is at the top of the list. More than 500 courses and seminars on subjects ranging from English as a second language to electromigration in thin film interconnects are taught at a number of locations, either on site or in nearby public schools. Instructors are from the company or universities around the country. Some of the courses can be taken for academic credit.

The company doesn't aggressively promote women, nor has it been a forerunner in looking after their special needs, that is, parenting responsibilities. But once an omission is pointed out, the company is usually more than willing to correct it—not to be overgenerous, understand, but at least to fix it. Maternity benefits were initiated in 1978 after a high-ranking woman threatened to leave the company and sue if she didn't get paid leave. A nationwide resource referral service for child care was made available early in 1988. Two surveys failed to indicate that employees wanted on-site day care facilities. The attitude is that work and family are separate. Since the company is accommodating when day care centers are closed and managers are usually understanding when a parent has to be home during an illness, most employees do not feel it's an urgent issue. Children do come to work with their parents when they must, and the parent is occasionally Dad.

One personnel manager tells of bringing her daughter to an interview for a different job at Digital one Columbus Day when her day care center was closed. She couldn't find a baby-sitter, and her husband, an engineer with the company, was away on business. She had hoped her 14-month-old would be happy with a chocolate doughnut or two and her secretary's attention. Not this day. She went through an hour-and-a-half interview with a chocolate-covered daughter on her lap and got the job. "That manager is impressive, but he's not alone," she says. Perhaps it's not surprising that he could overlook the toddler in the room—after all, in this company of rugged individualists, just about anything goes.

Just as benefits are not at the high end here, neither is the pay—for either sex. And as with benefits, when a problem is called attention to, it gets fixed. For instance, in 1985 it was discovered that one of the engineering organizations had a pay differential of 20 percent between men and women in the same kinds of jobs. The group had been pulled together by people from a number of different organizations. When the group manager learned of it, he immediately took steps. Yet such adjustments don't make up for past years—nor do they make up for the lower beginning salaries that women often accept.

What attracts women to Digital are the same things that attract men: the opportunity to harness huge resources for your own ideas. "If you need something, you just keep calling, and sooner or later somebody comes up with an answer," says a software engineering manager. "That's the Digital way. What I like about my job is always being required to think. You come up with an answer and move it forward. A lot of pressure is put on you, but you can see things happening."

Digital is not a place for every woman. Not even every woman with a technical bent. You have to be able to hold your ground in a fierce intellectual competition. You have to know how to present your ideas well and fight for them. But if you've got initiative and you need a lot of space to move around in, it will be your kind of place. You'll probably love it. And the fact that your suit has a skirt may not make much difference.

DRAKE BUSINESS SCHOOLS

A FOR-PROFIT SECONDARY SCHOOL SYSTEM WITH A SOCIAL MISSION

▲ EMPLOYEES: 80; 75 percent are female.

▲ REVENUES: Numbers are unavailable for this privately held company.

▲ Drake is a company dedicated to recruiting and hiring women; they use advertising, word of mouth and agency referrals to do so. Programs aimed at promoting women include in-service training, management development through industry seminars, on-the-job training and a policy of promotions from within.

▲ All five upper managers of this privately held company are women; all four members of the board of directors are women.

▲ Drake offers the standard maternity disability leave and a re-source referral directory for child care facilities. Part-time work for managers and professionals is available.

▲ Not surprisingly, Drake needs no special policies, practices or training on sexual discrimination, sexual harassment or pay inequity. It strives to keep compensation equitable with that within its industry.

▲ Major employment centers: Drake is a company based in New York City. Schools are located in Manhattan, the Bronx, Queens and Staten Island.

DRAKE BUSINESS SCHOOLS, INC.
10 East 38th Street
New York, NY 10016
(212) 725-5757

Drake Business Schools is the smallest company in this book—with fewer than 100 employees—but we are including it to show what can happen when a small group of women with a social mission are in business for themselves. Not all businesses run by women will operate the way this one does, and certainly not all businesses run by women have altruistic aims, but we feel Drake is special enough to include as an example of how business as usual can be business by consensus. And be successful.

Drake is not only run by women, it operates a business largely for women: training high school dropouts to gain the confidence and skills they need to enter the business world as clerical and secretarial workers. The typical Drake student is black or Hispanic; she's 24, single and has two children under 10. In many cases, she needs to get her high school equivalency diploma, polish her language skills, and learn how to dress and act in a business office. She needs, in other words, more than a few courses in typing, word processing and accounting. Drake supplies it all at one of four locations throughout New York City's boroughs. When the year or two-year program is completed, a placement service helps graduates (men and women) find jobs as medical and legal secretaries, administrative assistants, clerk-typists and all types of office workers.

Working with students who badly need assistance to better themselves and their lives is part, if not most, of the attraction for many of the women who work at and run Drake. Bea Ross, whose responsibilities, until she retired last year, included counseling students throughout their years at Drake, can't imagine a more rewarding life than the one she's chosen. She started with Drake in the Bronx in 1964 as a typing teacher. "I found the job so fulfilling," she says. "We really change lives. That's why I loved working with the students." Her sentiments were echoed by many.

The women at the top have the same sense of social commitment. Fay Joyce, one of the owners who is now a consultant to the school, kept the school going financially during the dog days of the early seventies, when enrollment was under a hundred and it appeared that the school would go under. At one point she sold a home in Washington and risked the proceeds by investing in the school to save it. "I felt I didn't have a choice—you talk about doing something for minorities, about how to treat employees—all these things were just words and I saw that I had a chance to put my money where my mouth was."

The woman running the school at the time was Mary Ann Lawlor, the CEO, whose determination to save Drake was inspired by Joyce's commitment. The women insist that they worked as a team and that the rescue mission couldn't have occurred if each hadn't done her part. Lawlor frankly admits that her role models were the Catholic nuns who taught her in high school in Brooklyn. "We are doing important work that is needed by New York City," Lawlor states. "The students need what we are doing." Yet she is not so idealistic that she neglects profit and loss. "Of course, we need to make money, but this has been a wonderful way to support myself and feel good about myself at the same time. Doing business for profit injects reality into what we do here, but we feel that if we are doing the right things, we will figure out a way to pay for them."

Lawlor, like Joyce and president Diane Scappaticci, all participate in ownership of the company. When they have to, they forgo paychecks; and when business is booming, usually when the economy is in a downturn, they share the profits. The largest percentage of workers are, quite naturally, teachers; pay is competitive with the public schools, although the school year does not break for a three-month vacation in the summer. It is year round. While recruiting teachers is difficult for Drake—as it is in the public school system—the advantages of teaching at Drake include working in a smaller, cozier environment with less bureaucracy than the public schools and, for some, working close in the borough where they live, say, Staten Island or the Bronx. "We are essentially a democracy," says Lawlor. "The whole staff is a work team—it's not us against them."

Teachers also get incentive pay when their students do well on progress tests; bonuses are handed out several times a year. When the school makes a profit, everybody participates in the profit-sharing plan, which essentially is a pension plan.

The kind of person that is likely to be hired at Drake is one who makes clear her commitment to the kind of work being done there. "I look for people who want to care about students," says Diane Scappaticci. "You have to look for the academic credentials, but I'd rather take a C student who's a mother earth type in the classroom than an A student who is going to look down on our students." Understanding and patience might not be qualities encouraged in most businesses, but here they are paramount. "We view our students as the customers, and the customers come first."

While most teachers need to be just that, teachers, for a woman with an interest in administration, Drake offers unusual opportunities to advance, partly because everybody's worth is seen clearly in an organization this small. Anita Brownstein started in 1979 as a teacher but had some ideas how things could be changed. Her innovations at her school were noticed by Scappaticci, who implemented them in the other schools. She eventually became the dean of the Queens school and today is director of academic affairs for all four of the Drake schools. "The timing was right, and I was right and Drake was open," she says. "It still is. They don't look at you and say, this is a woman or this is a man, they look at you and say, you've got an idea, let's make it work." And if it doesn't? "Then we try a different approach. You don't have to agree with your boss either. There's a lot of healthy criticism around here, and as a result animosities don't build up."

So it's not only in student-faculty relations that the golden rule is followed. The women belie the old stereotypes about how women can't get along and, most especially, can't agree on anything long enough to get the job done. Hidden agendas apparently don't exist. These women agree to disagree and get on with business. Employees say that while management training is on the job, the senior people are always willing to let you do whatever you can and help you at every turn. The women unanimously stated that the school had helped them develop and grow because they were given freedom and responsibility.

They also say they learn from one another, since their backgrounds are diverse. Some come from other trade schools, others were in various fields where progress for women was blocked. Sexual discrimination is something these women have to deal with only in the outside world. They joke that the place is akin to a nunnery. And the ones who stay love it.

There are a few men at the school, so it is not a totally female environment. It's just that here, women are running the show. The five people in upper management are all women.

Flexibility depends largely on one's position. Teachers have to be there five days a week, as they do at any school. More leeway is allowed on the administrative staff. Some women come in at 7:30 A.M. and leave by 4 P.M. If Scappaticci wants to see someone that day, she'll ask them when they are leaving and schedule a meeting around that. But everybody works a heavy load, putting in long hours and weekends when needed.

While all the good works have been under way, business has not been neglected. The women sometimes sense an attitude in outsiders that they are women simply running a school and don't have to worry about business. In a school that operates for profit, that's like suggesting that IBM makes computers because the world needs them. In the last 20 years, the student body has grown from around 50 students to more than 1,500. Business, in a sense, is booming. In the future there are plans to open schools at other sites in the New York metropolitan area and work toward accreditation, which would allow the school to grant associate degrees. An indicator of how well regarded Drake is by others is Lawlor's standing in the industry. This fall, she will take over as chairman of the national Association of Independent Colleges and Schools.

Scappaticci sees the business of running a proprietary school as one in which women can succeed. "It is a very entrepreneurial industry, one where you can go off and get ownership in a company or start your own business. *If* you thrive on keeping a lot of balls bouncing in the air. . . ."

FEDERAL EXPRESS

THE NATION'S FIRST AND LARGEST PROVIDER
OF OVERNIGHT DOOR-TO-DOOR DELIVERY OF
PACKAGES AND LETTERS

▲ EMPLOYEES: 45,000; more than a third are women, many in nontraditional jobs.

▲ REVENUES: Approximately $3.2 billion in 1986. An average of 850,000 letters and packages a night is handled by Federal Express.

▲ Federal Express's commitment to equal opportunity is stressed in all its advertisements and recruitment. A strong affirmative action program ensures that female and minority applicants are considered for all jobs. Promotion from within is the norm, and many college students hired to do package sorting aspire to join management, a practice that is encouraged. The company posts weekly lists of job vacancies with relevant information.

▲ Maternity leave is handled as short term disability, at 70 percent of base pay; additional leaves without pay, position assured, are available with approval. The company's excellent benefits package includes medical, dental and vision insurance, current and deferred profit sharing, an employee stock purchase plan, a liberal suggestion award program, and discount airline travel.

▲ Sexual harassment and discrimination, along with all other employee grievances, are handled through the Guaranteed Fair Treatment (GFT) program, cited as one of the top three grievance procedures in the country by the Education Fund of Individual Rights, a private foundation that researches employee rights. GFT provides a due process procedure that may ultimately be heard by the CEO, chief operating officer and the chief personnel officer. This, and an extensive and anonymous program of feedback from employee to management, lowers the probability of sexism hampering anyone's ability to be treated fairly and get ahead.

▲ Employees are encouraged to utilize company-sponsored training and the Education Assistance Program, which includes tuition refunds and programs such as Smoke Enders.

▲ Jobs are evaluated every 12–18 months to ensure pay equity within the company, and employees have the opportunity to express their feelings about the fairness of pay in an annual attitude survey. Groups expressing dissatisfaction are evaluated by the compensation department.

▲ Slightly more than a third of employees are women, and 24–12 percent—of senior management are female. Two are senior vice presidents. However, this proportion should improve as the 745 female managers gain experience. Of the managers trained in 1984 and 1985 in Federal's Leadership Institute, approximately one third were women.

▲ In 1984 the Federal Reserve Bank of Atlanta cited the company as a flexible, innovative model of success.

▲ Major employment centers: greater Memphis area: 14,000; Calif. (several locations): 825; Somerset and Baltimore, Md.: 450; Newark, N.J.: 400; Chicago: 250; other employment centers are in Atlanta, Boston, Cincinnati, Dallas, Fort Lauderdale, Kansas City and Phoenix.

FEDERAL EXPRESS CORPORATION
Box 727
Memphis, TN 38194
(901) 369-3600

Talk to a Federal Express employee long enough, and eventually you might come up with some area where the company falls short. But first you'll hear repeatedly what a great place it is to work, whether you're male or female, black, white or yellow. As long as you're willing to work hard.

That, in a nutshell, is what employees at the nation's first and largest "absolutely, positively overnight" package courier say about their employer, a super fast track, high-energy company where the level of dedication and loyalty sounds like what we hear about Japanese workers. This positive attitude is underscored by a turnover rate that is almost unheard of in this country—less than 1 percent.

Down in Memphis, Federal's reputation as a "people first" place is so well known that once you get into the company, you can expect to be bombarded with requests from acquaintances who want to know if you can help get them a job there too. "After I got my job in personnel, I told my mother not to tell anybody I was working at Federal," says Nina Thornton. "Understand, we get a few thousand résumés a day in the mail." Yes, it does help to have a friend at Federal.

Barbara Ashcroft, who joined the company in 1984 after running a student placement office at a local college, said that when Federal Express asked her to send over 25 students, she took the names at the top of a list of 200 who wanted to work there. "Then I'd make them promise that they would show up for classes and not drop out of school. I've heard of cases where kids register for three hours of class just so they can get on the list."

What is it these college kids are dying to do? Work hard and fast in the middle of the night sorting letters and packages at the Hub, a huge cargo-sorting facility at the Memphis airport. They are expected to make 55 sorts a minute; they have to memorize over 550 three-letter identification codes and when they're tested must be 99 percent accurate; they have to be able to lift 70 pounds. The noise level is high and so is the tension. If that doesn't sound like anybody's dream job, consider that the starting pay is $7.33 an hour, nearly twice what most of these young people could be making elsewhere. Add on regular raises, terrific benefits—medical, dental and vision insurance, tuition rebates of up to $750 a year for part-time employees (double for full-time), a no-layoff policy, profit sharing, a stock option purchase plan at a 15 percent discount, an extensive awards program, an open door policy that allows access to all managers and supervisors all the way to the top, and one of the most popular benefits, a chance to fly free in the cockpit jumpseat anywhere Federal's 64 jets are going, and greatly reduced fares for oneself and family on commercial airlines.

Sharon Hall, who was 23 and a recent college graduate when we were there in late 1985, said that she's flown jumpseat to New York City to do her Christmas shopping and to Florida on vacations. Since she was a sophomore, she's worked from 11 P.M. to 3 or 4 A.M. at the Hub, taking afternoon classes when she could. "Sure, it's hard work out there, but I know the real meaning of slavery—it's working at Kmart. When I got my first paycheck, I realized I would've had to work exactly twice as long to bring home as much money. And I saw the unbelievable opportunity in the company. Half a dozen managers are under 25." Now that she's got her business degree, Hall, who owns 45 shares of Federal bought under the stock option plan, is considering which of the hundreds of available jobs in the company she will go after.

New openings are posted every Friday on numerous bulletin boards throughout the Hub and the complex of office buildings that house the bulk of the 4,000 Memphis employees. The notices are as likely as not to have somebody in front of them taking notes, looking for a better job somewhere in the company. Hall and the others know they will be considered before somebody from the outside is brought in.

Does she feel being a woman might hurt her chances? Not in the least. "We've got Carole Presley [a senior vice president] and two other female vice presidents," she point out. "I figure I give myself five years to make VP, and then Fred Smith better look out."

Fred Smith is the Vietnam veteran in his early forties who started the door-to-door overnight delivery industry in 1973 with a dream, extensive market research and several million dollars of loans and venture capital funds. A lot of people thought he would fail, from the man on the street in Memphis to banking officers. Start-up costs were enormous. Sixteen packages of mail showed up the first night of operation.

Cindy Landers-Henson, who started full-time with the company on her 18th birthday that year, recalls that acquaintances scoffed when she went to work for such an untried operation. She started in billing; she's now managing director of revenue accounting operations. Her husband, whom she met at work, is a supervisor in another department. Such in-house marriages bother no one, the only proviso being that the two people do not report to each other.

Since the early shaky days of Federal (Smith was once tried but acquitted for trying to defraud a bank by using false documents in an effort to save the company), the company has become a $2.6 billion corporation. An average of 850,000 letters and packages a night travels through the system, or more than half of all the overnight express shipments in the country. Most of them still pass through Memphis, but regional sorting and trucking, as well as a new sorting facility in New Jersey at the Newark airport, handle shipments for the East and West coasts, the Midwest and Florida as the company continues to decentralize. In 1985 an overseas operation was opened.

Federal's meteoric rise—over the past decade revenues have doubled every two years—stalled somewhat a few years back due to substantial losses with the failure of ZapMail, a network of computers designed to facilitate delivery of an exact duplicate of a document in hours, but the company is now back on track.

Headquarters in Memphis is a complex of buildings that resembles a modern college campus. The hallways are lined with paintings chosen by an employee committee. The carpeted customer service area is surprisingly quiet, considering that the several hundred workers present are taking hundreds of incoming calls. Agents are clustered at circular "pods," and in December the place was festooned with Christmas decorations. The cafeteria is bright and airy; so are the "quiet" rooms, separate ones for smokers and nonsmokers, where workers take their breaks.

A visit to headquarters gives the impression that no job is closed to women. The tour guide mentions that her husband tried to get a job in sales at Federal, but that a woman got the position instead. A large percentage of the package sorters are female; one woman, formerly a mechanic herself, now supervises 49 male mechanics. More than 3,200 women (out of a total of 12,000) are couriers connected to the more than 300 cities where Federal has offices. Over 400 women hold management positions in field operations, and 40 female pilots—out of 600—makes Federal the airline with the highest number of female pilots in the country.

Janie Akin, a captain who's married to another Federal pilot, says that how you are regarded by your colleagues depends entirely on ability. "Pilots are usually a very macho group," she says, "but the men we fly with are a progressive bunch and they don't resent us at all. Do your job well and you'll be respected. If you can't, you'll be blackballed, male or female." Akin points out that when pilots are interviewed, one of the questions asked is how they would feel about flying with a woman as captain.

Minnie Sims, a ground fuels coordinator, works in the "oil business," as she puts it, a field not usually mastered by women. At Federal, however, her department consists of four men and four women. Sims, a black, started at the company as a secretary in 1981 but transferred to a different division doing a whole new kind of job, buying fuel and getting it to the more than 12,300 ground vehicles Federal owns. When a problem crops up somewhere, she's off and flying to straighten it out.

"If a woman has the edge, she'll get the job," Sims insists. "But only if she has the edge. Federal is a young corporation, and top management is young and have young minds. They don't have the old heads that I found at General Motors [where Sims worked in Michigan before coming to Memphis]. At GM, I sensed there wasn't much opportunity. You're either a secretary or a benefits representative. Here you can be anything. Federal has been good to me in that now I have a career. Right now I'm up for a position as an analyst. Things have just been wide open for me."

In return for all this opportunity, Federal asks a lot of its employees. If the job needs to be done, you stay and do it, no matter that your shift ended an hour ago. If you're flying on company business, it's preferred that you travel at least one way on Federal flights since the cost to the company is nil. If you need to survey the pilots, you show up uncomplainingly in the middle of the night at the Hub while they are there waiting through the package sort. The stay-till-the-job-is-done philosophy stems partly from the kind of business the company is in—overnight delivery—and a determination to remain number one. Besides, everybody else is on the same wavelength. Or they don't last at Federal.

When a surprise snowstorm hit Memphis a few years ago, making it nearly impossible for sorters to get out to the Hub, a lot of them walked the five or six miles from town. Office workers and professional people who could get there showed up and said, "What can I do?"

"I work very hard in my job," says Julie Wilson, a communications representative, "because I feel I would be letting somebody down if I didn't. The company has taken good care of me."

Naturally, some people find the tension tuned too high and leave—even people in senior management, where the pace is more demanding than at other supposedly fast track companies, according to Mary Alice Taylor, vice president of logistics. "People who come from Procter & Gamble, which is supposed to be a model for management, say they can't get over the pace here."

Taylor is one of three female vice presidents. She took over her job in 1985—after competing with 18 men for the spot—when she was 35. Some 700 people report to her. She has two daughters in elementary school, an understanding husband and an almost-never-sick housekeeper. Taylor usually leaves the office between 6 and 7 P.M., later when necessary. "I have been called a workaholic," she admits.

While child care has not been a problem for Taylor, other employees say that how understanding a supervisor is about days absent due to a child's illness depends, to a large degree, on the supervisor. Some are understanding, some are not. In the customer service department, where people must be present to answer the phones, workers have four paid holidays a year they can use for emergencies. If someone must leave after having worked a half day, it does not hurt his or her attendance record. The hours are also flexible, and if someone arrives a half hour late, she need only stay a half hour longer to make it up. Even the professional staff is allowed flexitime. Some come in at 7 A.M. and leave at 3 P.M.; others might work four 10-hour days.

Federal employs a phalanx of communicators and human resources specialists who ensure that management gets its message across to every level of worker and vice versa. Videos from Fred Smith and others in senior management are common, and there is an endless stream of memos and booklets informing everyone what's going on. Supervisors and managers evaluate those immediately under them; these employees, in turn, evaluate their managers and supervisors. The ratings are filtered through personnel to assure that an employee who gives his boss low marks won't be punished. Managers do not learn who said what. And when someone gets a low rating, a personnel representative comes back to help figure out how to fix the problem, be it racism, sexism or trouble communicating what needs to be done.

In addition to an official open door policy at every level, the company has an equal employment opportunity department and a grievance procedure that allows any employee to take a complaint all the way to Smith. Every Tuesday morning, beginning at 8 A.M., Smith, the senior vice president of personnel, James Perkins (who is, incidentally, one of the highest-ranking blacks in American business), and the chief operating officer, James Barksdale, hear grievances until lunchtime. It's the last stop in a five-step process that begins with an informal talk with your immediate supervisor. Often the grievances that concern top management have to do with an employee firing; workers in Memphis know that if being fired by Federal shows up on their employment record, they are likely to have trouble getting another job since the Guaranteed Fair Treatment (GFT) procedure is so well known in Memphis. It is, in fact, considered to be one of the best grievance procedures in the country.

The grievances that reach top management may concern trouble anywhere in the country, such as deciding the fate of a courier in Spokane who failed to report an accident—should he be fired or merely receive a warning letter?—or what to do about the three men running a small Texas office who made the place unpleasant for women with their constant sexual innuendos and dirty movies playing on the company VCR. (They were demoted, and the atmosphere was laundered.)

However, the system has been known to break down. In 1980, before GFT was instituted, a secretary lost her job over a lengthy affair with her boss, a vice president, when another woman with whom he was allegedly also having an affair was to be transferred to his department. In court testimony, according to the *Commercial Appeal*, the woman "literally begged" for her job but couldn't convince Smith and Perkins that the vice president was lying. He denied being sexually involved with the woman. Eventually she took her complaint to the courts and won a $157,000 settlement in 1984, in what the judge called "a classic case" of sexual discrimination. The vice president, not too many years from retirement, was transferred to Federal's overseas division in a position nowhere near the top. Not quite Siberia, but close.

Since then, it appears that Federal has taken a harder line against sexual harassment, and in early 1986, 11 cases had reached the last step in the GFT process. The firings of four men by lower management were upheld. Sexual discrimination cases are also heard in the equal employment opportunity office, but if an employee doesn't get satisfaction, or the one charged feels the punishment is too harsh, she or he turns to the GFT process. One or two men have been known to complain of sexual discrimination, but the complaints were straightened out early on. One story making the rounds when we were there concerned a man who accused his female supervisor of favoritism to a man he thought she was having an affair with. Apparently the woman was not, the matter was settled, and the woman admitted to being flattered by the accusation.

Although the strong and clear message from top management is that sexual harassment or discrimination is not to be tolerated, and most women we spoke to agree that is the case, some say that naturally old-fashioned male attitudes still crop up, particularly at lower and middle management levels. One woman we spoke to is not satisfied that her job has significantly expanded while her grade level has not, and she is seeking redress. Another woman says that some years ago she learned she was being paid a thousand dollars a month less than a man who had come in from another company to do exactly the same job she was, and her complaints to her immediate supervisor led to her being made to understand that she should not complain, that it would do her more harm than good.

But by and large, women who have been with the company since the early days say that the tokenism—and much of the chauvinism—they saw in the 1970s has pretty much disappeared. Back then, most women were in clerical jobs, and they would not be listened to about how to fix a problem, a situation that apparently no longer exists as the secretarial jobs themselves have become more skilled. Two of the three top winners in Federal's extensive awards program—winning a $25,000 bonus each—were women. One of them, Susan Stanton, is an Orlando courier who developed a storage rack for Federal's familiar white, purple and orange vans. Vice president Taylor, with the company for five years, says that in general she doesn't "feel that there is as much chauvinism or reluctance to see women succeed" as there was in the past, and that's true at Federal as well. Many women said they have never been discriminated against at Federal due to their sex and insist the pay rate for males and females is equal because it's based on grade levels.

How well a company treats all its people is best measured by how hourly employees fare. The enthusiasm of the Hub worker who's sure her future is at Federal is shared by Susan Jones, a customer service representative with two young children. She's one of the approximately 300 people who answer the phone when you call Federal's 800 number. "Federal is totally different than any other company," she says, "the way it's structured and the way it's not structured. Sure, working the terminal is repetitious, but when you're not talking to a customer, you can read magazines or newspapers, communicate to the other people in your work area, knit. I bring in my bills and do them. And if you get stressed out, you can go to a quiet room on the floor and relax. If you need to go to the ladies' room between breaks and lunchtime, you can." Jones took off 11 weeks when her last child was born and was paid 70 percent of her base salary; the typical maternity leave is six weeks.

Jones is waiting to hear about two other jobs in the company she has applied for. "Federal is just so good to its employees. Everything is just handled so much better than at other places, beginning with the interaction with the employees. Everybody is just so caring."

Jones's laudatory comments appear to be earned by the senior vice president who runs her department, Carole Presley. "Tell me," she asks, "what have you learned from my people in customer service? I come from pounding a typewriter eight hours a day, and I know what it's like to be pretty bright and know you can do more. I want to give them a chance to do something above and beyond answering a telephone. They're happier when they're off the phone for a while rather than just taking inbound calls. So I'm going to spend time trying to figure out how to carve up their day to do important things for the company and not keep them in that react, react, mode they must be in when they answer the phone."

FIDELITY BANK

THE PREMIER COMMERCIAL BANK SERVING SOUTHEASTERN PENNSYLVANIA AND THE DELAWARE VALLEY

▲ EMPLOYEES: 3,500; 75 percent are women.

▲ REVENUES: $10 billion in assets; $6.9 billion in deposits. This spring, Fidelity Bank, with its parent company, Fidelcor, merged with the First Fidelity Bancorporation, becoming one of the country's superregional banks.

▲ Fidelity Bank is concerned with recruiting and hiring women. Although they use agencies and networks that can refer qualified women, the female Fidelity executives actively and visibly refer and support other women.

▲ Programs aimed at promoting women include job posting, 100 percent tuition reimbursement and a host of training programs. In 1987, 55 percent of the 20 employees attending the Professional Banking Training Program were women; in the Accelerated Management Training program 68 percent of the 22 enrolled were female.

▲ At the very top level of 28 managers, one—the president—is a woman; 19 percent of the next level of 112 are women, including three senior vice presidents. One of the 21 members on the board of directors is a woman.

▲ In addition to the standard maternity disability leave, any employee may take three months of unpaid leave, position guaranteed. The bank offers part-time work for managers and professionals, flexible workplaces and adoption benefits, as well as a referral resource service for child care facilities.

▲ Complaints of sexual discrimination are handled by internal problem resolution, as are charges of sexual harassment. The bank has issued strong statements on harassment and offers a training program on the subject for male and female managers and professionals.

▲ The company is committed to rectifying inequality of pay. It went through rigorous reevaluations as a result of a 1975 consent decree.

▲ Major employment centers: Corporate offices are located in downtown Philadelphia; there are 125 branch offices in southeastern Pennsylvania and the Delaware Valley.

FIDELITY BANK
Broad and Walnut Streets
Philadelphia, PA 19109
(215) 985-6000

Imagine you are in a marble-and-crystal house of money with pillars reaching heavenward four or five stories, with brass fittings and railings gleaming like fool's gold, with giant chandeliers sparkling like Christmas lights, with elevators whose wood-paneled doors have the dull patina of years of polish, the whole place reeking of tradition and establishment banking, so much so that just walking into the place makes you feel r-i-c-h, like the money in your purse just had to be inherited. The place is a Hollywood set designer's dream. In fact, it *was* the set for the old-line financial institution Eddie Murphy took over, in a manner of speaking, in *Trading Places*.

This is banking, Philadelphia style. This is Fidelity Bank.

It is not run by Eddie Murphy. It is run by a woman.

She is the first and only female member of the prestigious Reserve City Bankers Association, whose membership is drawn from the senior management of the top 150 banks in the country.

Her name is Rosemarie B. Greco, and she was unanimously elected president of the $9 billion bank in 1987, 19 years after she was hired as a branch secretary. Talk about rags to riches! When she was hired, fresh out of the convent, the 22-year-old lacked business clothes and the money to buy them. Half of her sister's wardrobe was altered to fit her. At the time, she thought the bank would be a good place to work while she finished her degree in education. She had no plans to be a banker.

But, as the story goes, education's loss was the bank's gain.

To backtrack a bit. When Greco left the convent in 1968, it was before the mass exodus of nuns from the religious life, and she had a hard time convincing potential employers that she wouldn't be passing out holy cards on her lunch hour or be offended by strong language. By the time Fidelity hired her after a month of job hunting, Greco was short on confidence and terrified that she would fail. Her job was to open new accounts in one of the branches. To make sure she succeeded, Greco took notes on how to do it and wrote them out every night, stapling properly filled-out forms to the instructions. In a few months, others in the bank got wind of what she was doing, and her notes became the bank's first training manual.

Soon she was teaching Vietnam veterans how to be branch managers, assignments they usually got three to six months after joining the bank. Greco's title remained the same: secretary. "At the end of a year, I said, 'Enough of this' and decided to start teaching in the Catholic schools while I finished working on my degree," she recalls. "But the day I was going to resign, a regional vice president needed a secretary and he asked me to be it." The job paid $15 a week more than the teaching job, so she decided to stay with the bank for another year, save her money and then quit the following year, go to school full-time and be done with it.

Better jobs kept coming along, and after she graduated magna cum laude from St. Joseph's University in Philadelphia, she was training director for operations. Being a banker no longer seemed like a bad idea.

But not all women were doing well. In general, they were the tellers, secretaries and bookkeepers, with little chance of getting ahead. Another woman who has been with the bank since the sixties, Denise Shields, recalls that when a male boss tried to get her a title that mattered in the early 1970s, "the company would have none of it." What got senior management's attention was a sexual discrimination suit a computer programmer filed after she discovered she was making less than the male programmer who sat next to her doing exactly the same job. A consent decree followed in 1975.

Greco was on the task force whose job it was to straighten out the mess. More than 700 job descriptions and manuals for every operating unit were written. To get the work out, Greco sometimes ran the presses in the photocopying unit herself. Eventually, she got her first big break and was named deputy head of personnel; her job was to do the nuts-and-bolts work of the department. Two years later, she got the top job. By Greco's admission, the consent decree was an easy one—it didn't require that women be put in certain jobs, only that they were in the pool from which candidates would be chosen. It was Greco's responsibility to make sure there were qualified women in that pool. "If you keep putting qualified women in front of men making the decisions about a job, after a while their consciousness is raised and they become sensitive to talent," she says.

Unlike elsewhere, the consent decree generated a minimal amount of backlash among the men, partly because the message was: don't put a woman in a job because she's a woman, but don't prevent her from getting one either because she's a woman.

But problems of sexual discrimination weren't the only ones the bank had. Huge losses from unpaid loans caused a crunch; so did sloppy management practices. In one year alone, the bank lost $13 million. The bank was in such desperate straits the Federal Reserve Board intervened in the late seventies, requiring the bank to deal with its problem loans. Raymond Dempsey, a banker from New York City whose name garners respect here, came in to save the bank. He immediately put everyone on notice that the times had changed: unless you were prepared to work long and hard, you should apply for a job elsewhere. And if you were simply doing a marginal job, you were probably going to be out of it. Many of those fired turned out to be white men who weren't performing up to snuff. Simply by concentrating on results, Dempsey gave women and minorities the shot in the arm they needed. "He didn't care if you were a monkey," remembers one woman, "if you could do the job better than somebody who was there, he was going to fire that person and bring you in. And he brought in women."

Dempsey vested considerable weight in the personnel post, and Greco thus became one of his inner circle. That she happened to be a woman reinforced the attitude of gender equality. She became head of community banking in 1981 and an executive vice president in 1983.*

While the bank was undergoing changes, the world outside was resisting them. The grand midtown main banking office sits directly across the street from The Union League, an exclusive men's club dating back to 1862. In 1980 The Union League took its first vote on whether women should be admitted. It was defeated. Greco went in and spoke to Dempsey, saying that if the bank was going to make a statement about women's equality, this was the day to do it. Within 20 minutes after the vote was counted, Dempsey had hand-delivered his resignation. Officers' memberships, which had been paid by the bank were canceled; no bank functions—not one single lunch —were held there. Other Philadelphia businesses followed suit. Greco herself attended no functions of any sort held there.

"It took six years for the economics of their decision to catch up with them, but it did," she says. When they took a second vote in 1986, women were admitted. And last year, when Greco was honored by the Sons of Italy as their first "Woman of the Year" (instead of man), it was at a black tie dinner at the Union League. At the dinner she told them how it felt to be a poor kid in Philadelphia and go to her prom in a dress her mother had rented for $10. She accepted the award in a Mary McFadden original. There were a lot of damp eyes in the audience.

When she was elected president, there were tears of joy at the bank. Greco herself burst into tears. Over the next few weeks she received over 100 floral arrangements and 500 notes and letters, including this one from a second-grader, printed on lined paper: "I am so glad you are the first [female] president of a bank. I bet you are very proud. I am very proud. I hope you keep your job." The letter hangs in Greco's office at home.

But Greco is not the only success story at the bank. Not one single woman we met—black or white—felt that her rise or lack of it had anything to do with sex. It was merit alone. "I can never say I was discriminated against because I was a woman," remarks Elizabeth Styer, senior vice president, whose job it is to collect problem loans. "Nor can I say the doors were ever open because I was a woman. It's been a lot of hard work, a little bit of luck and being in a high-visibility area." Styer, incidentally, chose Fidelity as a place to work because it had tuition benefits and she, like Greco, had a few years to finish when she took a job as a teller in 1973. This is clearly a bank that prizes homegrown talent as well as that from the outside.

---

*In the early eighties, Greco was not the only high-ranking woman at Fidelity. Claire Gargalli was the executive vice president overseeing international banking and commercial banking in the mid-range and national markets, responsible for $1.2 billion in deposits. She is now president of Equibank in Pittsburgh.

Deborah Levin, a vice president who was in an accelerated management training program, says that being black doesn't cause her any problems in the bank; if she runs into prejudice, it is with customers at the branch she manages.

But if some customers are slow to change their minds about racial prejudice, everyone—including the Federal Reserve Board—has changed their minds about the financial health of Fidelity. In 1986, following a series of mergers with smaller banks in the area, an article about the parent company, Fidelcor, in *American Banker*, was headlined: "The Cream of a Vibrant Philly Market." Analysts give the stock a top rating and praise Fidelity for its emerging preeminence in consumer banking and its low operating costs. This spring Fidelcor merged with First Fidelity Bancorporation, becoming a superregional bank.

Dempsey, who moved on to another bank (European-American Bank on Long Island) after turning around the numbers at Fidelity, left behind more than a healthy financial institution. The seeds of a meritocracy were firmly established during the years of crisis and consent decree; when the new management team came in 1984 things took off again for women, this time without a consent decree but with Harold Pote, chairman and CEO, letting it be known that in determining promotions, the reckoning would go like this: talent, 10; sex, 0; race, 0. Pote, who will be 42 in 1988, represents a new breed that is likely to change the way corporations think about women and minorities more than any government-mandated order can.

As at most companies that have been through tough times, people work hard and put in long hours. One woman in her twenties says that although she made assistant vice president in two years, she had to give up going to the gym altogether and didn't know if she could keep up the pace. Jokes vice president Diana Gilson, "When they stopped looking at men and women in terms of jobs, they wanted us to give up sex." Gilson is married to another Fidelity employee, someone she met when he was a trainee in a sales department she was running. Gilson is now special assistant to Greco, and Gilson's husband manages the main banking office. Lest you think that only a man would be given such a prestigious job—it has over $300 million in deposits—let it be noted that one of his predecessors was a woman, Sara Schmid, now a regional vice president.

When the bank went to lean and mean, generous early retirement benefits were offered, and although Schmid could have taken one, she didn't. She now manages a small group of branches in a growing upscale area and is confident that something even better is waiting for her. "If there's talent and professionalism, it doesn't matter how old you are or what color you are," she says. Schmid, who married in her late forties at the height of the bank's troubles, put a worktable in her bedroom so that she could get up at 4

A.M. and catch up on paperwork while still being near her husband. Even if he was fast asleep.

But if everybody's working this hard, what happens when there's a family emergency, when the sitter doesn't come, when you can't find good day care until your new baby is four months old? No problem. That's what happened to Constance Bach-Nobel, a computer programmer. She had three children at home and had already been appraised of the bank's flexibility when she wrote a proposal on how to handle the leave she needed after the birth of another child. Her plan was to take home a terminal that would be hooked up to a computer in the bank through a modem. Some coworkers were skeptical, but Bach-Nobel persisted anyway. Management went for her plan. A phone line was put into her home in New Jersey so that she could be transferring data while she was on her private line with the bank discussing what was coming in. Her husband, a postal clerk, had Mondays off, which enabled her to spend one day a week in the office attending meetings, picking up and dropping off paperwork and so on. On the few occasions she had to get paperwork to the office sooner, she met another women who works at the bank at a train station. "Sometimes it was hard, I admit," she says, "but I knew I had to keep up at least the same pace I had in the office or they would never want to do it for anyone else. Sure, I was appreciative, but my loyalty to the bank was already there. It didn't make me think, now I'll stay with them because they did this. I already felt that way."

For women who want maternity leave, the bank allows three months with no loss of benefits. Not only are you guaranteed a job back, you are guaranteed the same job, desk, papers, and portfolio if you are a loan officer. "We have to reassign the accounts, naturally, if the woman is out," says Kathryn Endlein, manager of human relations, "but we're very protective that the woman get her same portfolio base back instead of giving it to one of the younger guys nipping at her heels."

Endlein was instrumental in figuring out what to do about the number of women, particularly in the lower ranks, the bank was losing to motherhood. A day care center was rejected as too unwieldy, but a resource referral service was made available and noon seminars are regularly held on topics like "latchkey children." Counselors with training in stress management were put on call. Managers were urged to be even more flexible than they had been. The plan seems to have worked. Endlein reports that far fewer women are quitting when they have children.

In this kind of atmosphere, sexual harassment is a nonissue; so is being asked to get the coffee at meetings or trouble being heard. Besides, you're likely to be at meetings with a number of other women. Anybody can get the coffee, even somebody's male secretary. The bank is an equal opportunity employer at all levels.

In fact, the women gave their bank high marks on everything. But you will work hard here, very hard, if you expect to rise.

Does Greco have any advice for women who would be president? Don't focus on the fact that you are a woman. "You shouldn't think of yourself in the one very narrow definition as female," she says. "Once you think, 'I am the only woman in this job, I am the only woman at this meeting,' you send out certain signals and you will be recognized first and foremost as a woman, and not simply as someone doing a job. Focus on why you are there, not on the difference between you and the men."

FIRST ATLANTA

ONE OF GEORGIA'S LARGEST BANKS AND PART OF A
MAJOR REGIONAL HOLDING COMPANY,
FIRST WACHOVIA CORPORATION

▲ EMPLOYEES: Approximately 4,500; three quarters of them are women.

▲ ASSETS: First Wachovia's assets are $18.7 billion. While the corporation does not break out First Atlanta and report its finances separately, assets were approximately $8 billion before the merger of the two banks in 1986. In 1986 *Forbes* magazine ranked First Atlanta as the top bank in the Southeast over the 1979–84 period, with the highest five-year annual return in equity (18.8 percent) and with the top five-year average increase in earning per share (24 percent).

▲ Since commercial banking attracts large numbers of women, First Atlanta feels no special efforts are necessary to recruit them. Approximately 50 percent of its management trainees are female. It actively supports the National Association of Bank Women—a recent national chairman, as well as regional and local officers, are First Atlanta women.

▲ First Atlanta is committed to rectifying inequality of pay to women, reevaluating individual job descriptions and adjusting grade levels where necessary. The company does not hire couples but does not insist that one spouse leave if employees marry.

▲ Sensitive to parenting needs, First Atlanta allows leave without pay with your job held for up to three months following standard maternity disability leave. The bank provided start-up money for on-site day care as well as financial support for community-based facilities. A resource referral directory is also available. Flexitime and part-time work for some managers and professionals are additional options.

▲ Although comfort level options are high for working mothers, the flip side is that the highest-ranking female is only a vice president. The controller is a woman. The 17-member board of directors is all male.

▲ The bank has no training program on sexual harassment. Complaints are handled either by informal hearing or formal grievance procedure.

▲ You can be a comfortably cared for middle manager at First Atlanta. Can you rise higher? Not yet.

▲ Major employment centers: 127 offices in 45 communities in Georgia.

FIRST ATLANTA CORPORATION
Two Peachtree Street
Atlanta, GA 30383
(404) 332-5000

In the summer of 1985, three times a week, a dozen or so tots walked out of their day care center, across the street and through a parking lot into the Information Resources Division of the First Atlanta Corporation's operations center. There, under the guidance of First Atlanta staff, they learned how to use a computer. They were such apt pupils that by the second day, most didn't want help in setting up their machine. They already knew how. Over eight weeks, the 3- to 5-year olds, from their perches on phone books placed on adult chairs, learned about numbers, letters and spelling. Now the center has its own IBM PC, and one of the day care instructors teaches tots as young as 2½ years old, who learn how to pick out the letters in their name.

That kind of program is one of the reasons First Atlanta parents are so enthusiastic about the day care center the company opened in 1983 after an employee survey—at the instigation of First Atlanta's chairman, Thomas R. Williams—indicated a need for one. First Atlanta became the first bank in the nation to sponsor a day care center. The company gave a $130,000 grant to purchase a building across the street from the operations center, where more than a third of the company's employees work, and renovate it. The company continues to subsidize the center by an undisclosed amount in the hope that it will eventually reach a break-even point and no longer need aid. Fees are unusually low, even for the South, and particularly for the kind of programs the day care center offers. Toddlers take field trips to places like the airport and learn about helicopters and how the police use them by having one parked in the lot one afternoon and letting them climb all over it. The cost is less than $50 a week for one child, with a 20 percent discount for additional children. The center has 42 spaces for tots from 15 months to 6 years of age. For parents who work at the company's downtown and largest bank, the First National Bank of Atlanta, 20 spaces are allotted in a day care center organized by a consortium of downtown businesses, First Atlanta included.

The day care centers are understandably a big attraction for working parents, but they are by no means the only way First Atlanta draws workers with special requirements. "The opportunity to be professional *and* be part-time certainly makes this an enticing environment for me," says Lois Rickard, an assistant vice president in human resources and mother of two tots. She's been with First Atlanta six years, three of them part-time, during which she continued to receive proportional benefits. Christine Reynolds, a systems officer in information resources and the mother of two small children, also spent six months part-time and went back to full-time. "I've been on two maternity leaves," Reynolds comments, "and while those leaves slowed down my progress in the company somewhat, it hasn't been dramatic. Not as much, say, as it might have a few years ago." Andrea Settles, an operations manager, says her maternity leave didn't slow her down in the least: "I got a promotion right after I came back." Since her child was born prematurely, Settles came back to work before her baby came home from the hospital, and when she finally did, Settles worked for a few months on a reduced-time schedule. Men going to school can also work part-time on a professional level.

For people who want to switch careers and go into banking, First Atlanta makes it possible. Judy Smith was a teacher when she went back to school for her MBA. "Because I had 10 years in a very traditional field, that stuck out much more than the MBA," she says of the interviews she went on before she took a position at First Atlanta in 1983. "The MBA didn't seem to matter to anyone but me. Many of the other places said, 'We've been seeing a lot of you, we've been thinking of doing something.' But First Atlanta already had something in the works." Smith was one of an initial group of six individuals hired with several years of work experience in different fields. They were rotated through different divisions in the bank for two years, and when their time was up, bank officials went back to them and asked them what had worked and what didn't. The program was then revised. Smith was managing a small banking center when we interviewed her in Atlanta in April 1986.

If you don't have the education the bank officials think you need to advance, they will suggest that you get it—at their expense—and give you the time off you need. Sherry Gordon, who's been with the bank since 1969, rose to vice president without a college degree. At First Atlanta's behest, she completed a banking program offered by Louisiana State University. "They gave me the four weeks off a year I needed and paid for the tuition and books as well as the night school," she says. "It was an opportunity that I wouldn't have pursued elsewhere."

Gordon has held a number of positions throughout the bank, moves that were not difficult to maneuver. "I started opening new accounts in the branch banking centers and knew right away I did not want to be a lending officer, that I had more of a flair for marketing." When last heard from, Gordon was a product manager in the marketing department; when we had met a few months earlier, she had been in corporate communications.

Gordon also applauds the bank for not asking for her or her spouse's resignation when they wed in 1972. At the time, all the other major banks in Atlanta made one spouse quit when they got married, a policy that has since been relaxed.

Marriage and maternity were much on the minds of the women we met. It is not unusual at First Atlanta for women to quit when they either marry or have children, factors the women who stay feel work against them: if Anna quits when she gets married to a boy in Winston-Salem, how does management know Rachel's not going to do the same, and if that's the case, should women be promoted into positions of authority? Managers who are affected by this phenomenon complain to anyone who will listen, naturally making the women who don't leave—or who come back after having a child—rightfully edgy about their status and chances for promotion.

One MBA, who joined the management training program in 1984, noted that less than two years later, eight of the 29 women who joined the program with her left when they married. Their husbands had jobs in other cities or were transferred soon after. The woman who ups and leaves is typically in an entry-level job, her spouse older and further along in his career, and thus his work takes precedence. "Every time this happens, it puts us two steps back for every step forward we take," she says.

While it is true that a great number of young men leave entry-level banking jobs—apparently it's done as often as women leave entry-level jobs—their defection to Daddy's business or a better job does not hurt men down the line. The message is: it's okay to leave for a better job, but not to follow your man and have babies. "It is simply more frustrating to management when women leave to get married than when men leave," another woman says. "They come here to get their training instead of going for an MBA, but that's seen as all right." This is the South, remember it well, and the good ol' boys who run the shop are not comfortable with women's reasons. Besides, they provide such a handy excuse for not promoting women up the pipeline and into senior management.

And it is here where First Atlanta falls short of the mark. Yes, it has day care centers and flexibility for the people who need it and programs for individuals who want to switch careers in midlife. It is a great place to begin a banking career. You will get great training. If your aim is a job in middle management, First Atlanta has plenty of them, and the bank will take great care of you. Why not? Women at such levels are known to be harder workers because they feel they have so much to prove. But women get stalled here at the vice president level. As we go to press, no women were any higher.

The women gave two reasons for this: women haven't been at the bank in great enough numbers through the years to provide candidates who were up to it; and we're in the South and a woman's position is more tenuous than north of the Mason-Dixon Line. "The male echelon at the top does the recruiting," says one woman. "The head of personnel, of operations, or corporate communications—they were all recruited on the outside and I ain't seen a skirt coming in at the division manager level yet."

First Atlanta does have a phalanx of female vice presidents. Fifty-seven were listed on our survey. But in banking that's a title given to senior *middle* management. Individuals who really wield power are senior or executive vice presidents. "You have free entry into the bank," says one woman. "There is no discrimination at the lower levels. There is no discrimination at the VP level. But then you have to start looking at what areas they put women in. Are they positioning them to get ahead? For instance, we've never sent a woman to the Harvard Business Management School—only group vice presidents or above get sent, and if there are no group vice presidents who are women . . ." And so what we have at First Atlanta is a classic catch-22 situation.

"Women aren't being given the right background to be ready to move ahead to senior jobs," she continues, "and then when the jobs are open, management says, the women haven't gone to Harvard or they don't have the right experience." The woman, who clearly has her mind on a senior-level position somewhere, doesn't expect to break ground at First Atlanta. She expects to leave. Others before have done the same. Waiting and hoping and praying will simply take too long. First Atlanta—and Atlanta itself—isn't going to change all that much during her lifetime.

"When it comes to promotions, the female has to go in and say, 'I did this, I did this, I can do this.' But the man doesn't have to do anything but show up at his desk and answer the phone and leave early for the golf game," comments another woman.

One vice president, Vicky Miller, who spoke positively about her chances to advance and was optimistic that her sex wouldn't hold her back, has since left First Atlanta for the Florida National Bank. She is the treasurer.

The younger women who have "vice president" on their business cards concede they had much less difficulty getting it than the women who are 10, 20, or 30 years their senior. Those women had to be patient and persistent and work six times harder than the man at the next desk. "You've got to keep knocking on the door telling them what you've done until they can't ignore you anymore, and they say, 'I have to put this woman in the job because she's obviously the best person,'" comments one woman. It's no secret that an earlier chairman of the board once said that First Atlanta would not have a woman vice president except over his dead body.

Those days are gone, but getting into the coterie that runs the club isn't simply a matter of doing your job well and waiting to be noticed. You've got to make yourself stand out, you've got to be there having drinks after work at the Kimball House, you've got to belong to the right clubs, have the right connections, wear the right kind of suit (conservative and well made), get involved in the right community affairs (cultural and philanthropic) and have a mentor who will really support you. Without a mentor, you might as well forget it. And it would help if you were married to someone suitable, someone who will fit in at private parties at bank officers' homes. If you get invited. The men have to do these things too. Women have to do them better. And they can't be too obvious about it. You can't really run twice as hard down in the South because that tempo isn't accepted. Running twice as hard will only mark you as someone who doesn't know the rules, and that will slow you down. First Atlanta is most definitely in the South.

First Atlanta traces its roots back to the days immediately following the Civil War. And any company that's been around that long, particularly any Southern company, is going to be traditional and paternalistic toward women. Given that, it's not surprising that First Atlanta doesn't have women in more senior positions. Although women at some of the smaller Atlanta banks have "senior" and "executive" in front of their "VPs," they are still not handling the most important line jobs at those banks. And when women are given powerful positions, some of the men become decidedly nervous, a condition that was exacerbated before First Atlanta's merger with the Wachovia Bank and Trust Company in 1985, when First Atlanta was grappling with what kind of institution it would be. Anyone's job could be eliminated. The general consensus is voiced by one woman: "The men have to change. And I'm not so certain that we as human beings can change that easily. So maybe what I'm saying is that we have to have different types of men with different attitudes at the top before we see women rise to the senior positions."

As for sexual harassment, women say it was the same decades ago as it is today. You have to learn how to handle it yourself. "If you think you're going to be nice about it and let it take care of itself, it rarely does," one woman says. "I don't mean you have to be ugly about it, but you have to let them know it is not appropriate." How to do that presents a big problem for younger women who must take the heat from senior bosses whose language in meetings gets down to the gutter. What do you do when you're the only woman in the room and everyone is laughing at the foul allusions? Since it's a group vice president making the jokes, there's no one to tell him he shouldn't. You are being tested. The problem is, no one knows what constitutes a passing grade.

A more difficult problem is the unwanted advance from a prospective bank customer, a customer who says flat out, if you want the business, you have to be nice to me. The women we met agree that most of the women who call on customers face at least one such incident somewhere along the way. And then there's the older gentlemen who insist on kissing you before they do the deal or before you walk out the door. Thank heaven for younger men with working wives, the women agreed.

Yet however slowly, women are getting ahead at First Atlanta. They are bringing in business without sleeping with the customers. They are filling middle management ranks in quantity and proving they can do the job. Eventually they will get the right jobs, and the glass ceiling will shatter.

Fleda Hensley, retired vice president and manager of administrative services, is quite sure no one will ever have to repeat her career path. She joined the bank in 1944, right out of high school. "No woman is ever going to have to wait 21 years, six months and 21 days to be one of the first officers," she says. "No woman is ever going to have to do that again."

GANNETT

THE NATION'S LARGEST NEWSPAPER GROUP, WITH MAJOR HOLDINGS IN BROADCASTING

▲ EMPLOYEES: 36,000; approximately 38 percent are women.

▲ SALES: $2.8 billion.

▲ Gannett has long been a leader in recruiting and hiring women and has the numbers to prove it. Not only are 40 percent of its managers female, so are 27 percent of the top 150 people in the company, including a regional president and a division president. Three women, one executive vice president and two senior vice presidents, are on the management committee. Four of the 18 members of the board of directors are female. At entry level, a third of the employees in the management training program is female, and the newspapers and radio stations around the country are encouraged to hire and promote women. Bonuses for management are based, in part, on how well they meet specified goals regarding the hiring of women and minorities.

▲ Here is a company that candidly agrees women have been historically shortchanged in pay when compared to men. Gannett uses a variety of methods to rectify the inequality, including grade level adjustments and paybacks for past offenses. However, Gannett is known for paying low salaries up to senior management.

▲ At present, there is no set policy on maternity leave, but each case is worked out with management, allowing at least the standard disability leave in that state. At some newspapers, part-time work for reporters, managers and other professionals is an option. Paternity leaves of absence are permitted. Adoption benefits are $1,500 per child. The Gannett Foundation gives financial aid to selected community-based child care facilities.

▲ Reporters at the local newspapers can sometimes transfer to Washington, D.C., to work on *USA Today* for a few months, thus gaining exposure to national stories. The local paper pays the employee's salary, and *USA Today* provides a furnished apartment plus a cost-of-living stipend.

▲ Although training programs on sexual harassment are given, it appears to be a nonissue among the women interviewed. In the atmosphere Gannett's management has fostered for decades, someone seriously trying to get away with it at any management level would likely be laughed at.

▲ Age, family background and schooling don't matter here: talent and performance are what counts. Being a woman or a minority group member may actually give a slight edge, except at the very top.

▲ Major employment centers: Washington area: 1,300; New York City: 275; plus 90 daily and 39 nondaily newspapers across the country and eight television and 16 radio stations.

GANNETT COMPANY, INC.
1000 Wilson Boulevard
Arlington, VA 22209
(703) 276-5900

When Carol Richards went up the hill in Albany in 1967, the first woman to be assigned on a regular basis to Gannett's bureau at the state capital, one of her first assignments was to go out and buy a tie for the bureau chief. He needed a Christmas gift for the elevator operator.

This was not exactly what Richards had in mind, but she complied rather than complained. The guy handed her $20. She found a tie for $19 and change, which she knew was more than twice as much as the guy expected to pay. When he asked for the change, she said there wasn't any. Richards was never asked to run errands again. She is now an editor for the Gannett News Service.

Today, although there are still fewer women than men on the bureaus in Albany, no one expects them to bring the coffee in the morning. And when newspaper women in their twenties and thirties hear such stories, they listen politely but with some amazement. It wouldn't happen now. And it particularly wouldn't happen on a Gannett paper or bureau.

Even in 1967—although the news hadn't reached every bureau chief or city editor—Gannett was a pioneer in the hiring and promoting of women. The company's good record goes back to 1963, when Al Neuharth became the general manager of Gannett's then flagship papers in Rochester, New York. While most other middle-sized dailies rarely had women in the city room and only seasoned veterans when they did, both dailies had one woman apiece, fresh out of college, on general assignment within two years. By the mid-sixties, Neuharth was making speeches about the sex gap in the newsroom; in 1969, in a speech at a journalism workshop at the University of Missouri, he was challenging women to take the initiative: "If you will, you can shake the stereotyped role some men have cast you in the past. You can close the sex gap in communications. And if you do that, not only will you benefit, but so will our profession and our society."

Even with Neuharth's strong commitment to women, it didn't happen overnight at Gannett. Editors and reporters who thought women could only write soft stories weren't eager to make way for the young Turks in skirts, and they made life difficult for them. Women were usually assigned the crap. But Neuharth persisted, as did the women, and after he married an outspoken feminist in 1973 he put real muscle behind his words. The following year, publishers' bonuses became tied, in part, to how well they met specified goals regarding the hiring and promotion of women and minorities.

"I don't care about sex or age or family name," Neuharth says. "We think companies that do that penalize themselves. Let's face it. Middle-aged men like myself are in the minority. And women represent the majority—fifty-two percent of the people in this country. Why should a minority of us white males make the decisions in a media company that tries to reach the vast audience out there? It's good business to hire women and minorities. It's philosophically and ethically right. And I'm for it."

Neuharth grew up an outsider himself. And while he doesn't talk about it, his poor beginnings in a small town near Sioux Falls, South Dakota, may have as much to do with his insistence that women and minorities be allowed a chance to get ahead as his belief that it makes good business sense. Take Nancy Woodhull, one of the top people on the news side. She grew up in a factory town in New Jersey and went to a teacher's college for a year and a half. Ask about her background, and she tells of small steps made when an opportunity presented itself, of "taking on jobs nobody wanted." In 1975, with a decade of newspaper experience behind her, she was offered a job with Gannett as a night city editor in Rochester; five years later, she was managing editor. She was 34 at the time. Few newspapers in the country had women in jobs like that, and they still don't.

When Gannett decided to start up USA Today, Woodhull came to Washington with her husband and child, as part of the task force, and was its first managing editor for news. Today she is president of a division, Gannett's R and D arm, New Media Services, which makes news available via computer to businesspeople. She runs the Gannett wire service as well. "Sure, I have a sense of gratitude for being given a chance to work hard and get ahead," she says, adding, "I'm very aggressive and very opinionated," implying that that's the style that works best for anyone at Gannett."

Aggressive is certainly a word that fits the company. Under Neuharth's stewardship, the company went from a small chain of papers centered around upstate New York to the largest chain of papers in the country. Most of them are in places like Chillicothe, Ohio, Fremont, Nebraska, and Elmira, New York, but recent acquisitions include *The Des Moines Register*, the *Detroit News* and *The Courier-Journal* and *Louisville Times* in Kentucky. With 90 daily newspapers, Gannett owns more daily papers, representing more circulation, than any other chain. It also owns 39 nondailies. Gannett also owns the largest outdoor advertising company in North America; *USA Weekend*, a Sunday supplement formerly known as *Family Weekly*, and eight television stations, as well as 16 radio stations.

In 1986 the company reported operating revenues of $2.8 billion, with earnings of $276 million. After suffering more than $450 million in operating losses, Gannett reported last May that *USA Today* turned a $1 million profit.

Neuharth is in the process of phasing himself out and has named John J. Curley both president of the Gannett Company and CEO. But it's unlikely his stamp will soon fade away when he retires as chairman at 65 in 1989, as he has announced he will. A hard-working entrepreneur from the wrong part of town, he favors people of the same ilk. "The overall rule of the company is that individuals succeed because they are results oriented," comments Woodhull. "If you can show your results and be aggressive, there's a good chance you'll be successful whether you're male or female, black or white. This is an action-oriented company, an entrepreneurial company. That's good for women. If you have a good idea and can make something happen fast, all the politics don't count as much. What counts is—what did you do for me today?"

Woodhull herself likes the kind of place where what she wears to work, or how she talks, or what alliances she has formed don't count as much as what she does. A frequent public speaker, a skill she was pushed to learn by a male boss at Gannett, she advises women to seek out companies where they don't have to fit a mold—usually set by a white male—if they want to get ahead. "I could come to work wearing a bathing suit and if I was doing my job, no one would care," she says rapid-fire. "Now, of course, if we had to go up and meet the president and I was in my bathing suit, they would say, 'Hey, I don't think that flies.'" While no one actually wears inappropriate garb, fashion plates, particularly at the smaller papers, are rare.

They are not making enough to support a clotheshorse. Although corporate and sales salaries are competitive with the marketplace, reporters' salaries are another matter. You go into this field knowing it is not high paying. Susan Church, the health and medical writer on *The Press and Sun-Bulletin* in Binghamton, New York, said that her income was almost halved when she took a job as a reporter after five years in a university public relations department. Her weekly pay is $357. She is working for rewards other than monetary.

"I love my job and wouldn't go back to PR unless I was starving," she says. "I like the stress, I like deadline pressure, I like the subject matter, I like writing moving stories. I feel I have an important role in this town—to let people know what's happening in their hospitals and what things affect their health." When asked what the main difference between public relations and working for a newspaper was, she replied without hesitation: "Power. I have access to anybody I want. You don't when you are on the other side."

What Church and other women who like writing and are good at it face is pressure to move up in the ranks, to give up reporting and writing and move into management. For men, except for the very best writers or political pundits who ran bureaus or had columns, it has always been a natural progression. Young women at Gannett who want to keep writing and do not take an assistant city editor's job before they are 30 often wind up leaving the company to try their skills at larger papers, which for many is where success lies—not in becoming publisher of a small town paper.

"If you are a reporter like I am and like I want to be, it can almost be frustrating at Gannett," says one woman in her late twenties. "You have to ignore the pressure. I've been approached a few times by a woman who is an editor, and she tells me I ought to think about being an editor myself, that there are lots of opportunities in the company for women. It's all real subtle, but it adds up. And when I started talking to other women about it, I always heard the same thing. You know those bonuses they give for promoting women? We call them bounties."

Whatever they're called, they work. As we go to press (and this number has moved noticeably upward since we began our research), 21 of the 91 publishers of the Gannett dailies and *USA Weekend* are women, a hefty 23 percent; three women are on the 17-member management committee, and one of the three regional presidents is a woman. Another woman is president of a division, and seven other women are at a VP or comparable level at headquarters. Overall, well over 100 women are in senior editorial, production and advertising jobs throughout the chain, in an industry that continues to be male dominated. One of those women is Cathleen Black, publisher of the national daily *USA Today* and the only woman among the 54 board members of the Newspaper Advertising Bureau. Before coming to Gannett, Black was publisher of *New York* magazine. She, along with three other women, is a member of Gannett's board of directors. Black, like everybody you talk to, stresses the long hours the company demands. "This is not a nine-to-five job, this is a mission, and we are not there yet," she says, speaking of *USA Today*. "I say this to people when I hire them, but I know they are not going to hear me, because selling at most places is nine to five and they can make just as much money as here. But here I'm going to ask them to give, and give some more, and then tell them it's not enough."

People here might have accumulated enough seniority for a three-week vacation, but it's rarely taken, and almost certainly not in one chunk. It's the kind of place where you don't announce that you're going to Portofino. Instead, you'll mention that you've been asked to go along when the company jet flies to the Super Bowl or a World Series game. Major advertisers are usually along, but company executives and sometimes even reporters from *USA Today* join the champagne-and-lobster crowd. Women are not cut out of this select circle, and if there's space, they can bring their spouses or friends along. Neuharth is fond of holding annual meetings for executives and editors at his Cocoa Beach home in Florida. "If you have a meeting beginning on Sunday, Al will say, 'Come down a day early,'" says Black. "So you have a minibreak."

The operative word here is "mini." To some of the meetings, not only can you bring a spouse or friend (this is not the kind of place where you will be criticized for having a live-in lover), but kids occasionally come along too. Karen Howse, a single mother with two adopted children, took them to a meeting in Florida. It's not that Gannett is all work and no play, but it's playing with other people from the company that gets the nod of approval.

That kind of intensive involvement with your job at Gannett is a given if you are to rise. It's not just that the hours are long, it's something akin to religious fervor that's expected. And nowhere is this more true than among the corporate staff and the people who put out *USA Today,* Neuharth's brainchild of how communications might be changed in the television age. Most stories are eight inches long; a big color weather map is a regular feature; graphics are eye catching; a state roundup is likely to inform you that a teachers' strike in Livonia, Michigan, is the most crucial bit of news coming out of your home state. Serious journalists scoffed when the paper hit the street in 1982, but its circulation (1.5 million) has passed that of several major dailies, including *The New York Times,* the *Los Angeles Times* and the New York *Daily News.* Now it is second only to the *Wall Street Journal.* Putting the paper in the black was not just an end, it was a "mission." Howse describes it this way: "There's a whole different feeling here than I've ever encountered anywhere. I wouldn't call it camaraderie but a sense of commitment to the place." Howse is managing editor of the international edition of *USA Today.*

Gannett is famous for its penny pinching, but there appears to be no shortage of money at *USA Today* or corporate headquarters in Arlington, across the Potomac from Washington. The public areas are appointed in the sexy black leather, high-tech style Neuharth favors. Editors are likely to receive company credit cards the first day on the job.

Back in the trenches, it's a different story. Belt tightening is endemic.

Editors are reluctant to send reporters even an hour's drive out of town because of the mileage cost. It's 18 cents a mile. Most newspapers are down staffers because they don't have the budget to hire additional people—or keep as many as the paper had before Gannett took over. When Gannett bought *The Des Moines Register,* a paper with a good reputation and winner of numerous Pulitzer Prizes, its staffers were reported not to be wildly enthusiastic. They would have favored a company known for journalistic excellence rather than a winning bottom line.

The women there may change their tune, however. Only two had been promoted to department editors when Gannett took over; it's likely that the balance of power will change in the future. And thus encouraged, the women might also be inspired to form their own women's caucus, as those at some of Gannett's other dailies already have. The first was in Rochester, New York, and Neuharth's then wife, Lori Wilson, was in charge. Neuharth credits her for awakening him to the insidiousness of male chauvinism on most papers. The fact that she was Neuharth's wife incensed some women, but others say she was the best thing that could have happened to them. "The men didn't want Lori to be in charge of the women at the company," comments a woman who was in Rochester at the time. "She could snitch right to the top about who was being passed over."

At Binghamton, the purpose of an antisexism committee (dubbed the Gender Gestapo) was to make editors and writers aware of the inadvertent sexism that crept into their pages. "We asked questions like, do all the pictures to promote TV shows have to be so sexy?" recalls Diane Bacha, the 28-year-old city editor of the *Press and Sun-Bulletin.* "We talked about how the beauty pageants were covered. The changes were slow, but they seemed to have a ripple effect through the paper."

And indeed, throughout the company, up to and including upper middle management, women have made their mark. A few have gone beyond. Carolyn Vesper, vice president for national circulation sales of *USA Today,* tells how a man she recruited from her old employer, Xerox, called her one day and asked how he could break into the inner circle of women who were running the marketing side of the business. "He didn't know how to get to know his managers—the women were going out to Elizabeth Arden on their lunch hour," Vesper says. "What we have here is an old girl network." Ask Vesper if Gannett is a good place for women to work, and she shoots back: "We have no complaints. But you should ask our spouses."

Newspapers are notoriously hard on marriages. The hours are crazy—when you come in you almost never know when you'll be going home—and commitment is expected, regardless of the puny monetary rewards. Reporters' spouses have long complained—and then left. "So many nights do I call Joe and tell him to fix something for himself and our daughter for supper, that I'm working on a story and I'll be late again," says Susan Church about her job in Binghamton. "Then when I get home I have a couple of Oreos and a glass of milk." Church, whose daughter is 6, says she would like to have another child, but "you can't have a kid who's 6 months old and be a reporter."

Diane Bacha, one of her editors, wonders if it's even possible to have a relationship. "What kind of man is going to be sympathetic to the kind of hours I put in?" she asks. "I come in at ten and go home anywhere between seven and ten-thirty at night. Not many outside the news business can sympathize with the hours." Women going into the business should realize it's a calling, not just a career.

And the higher you follow your star, the rougher the going gets. Even at Gannett. The three women on the management committee are Cathleen Black, Madeline Jennings, senior vice president for personnel and administration, and Mimi Feller, vice president for public affairs and government relations. All came in at the top, and none is on the editorial side, the route, quite possible the only route, to the cadre that really runs the Gannett machine. Way up there, it's a bunch of guys playing hardball. The game can get vicious. Women have been purposely sidetracked when they got too close. The emphasis is on solo playing, but even there, alliances are made that keep women out. "If there are six people of equal rank, and one is a female there's a feeling that if the woman does better or is equal to what a guy could do, Neuharth will promote the woman," says one woman close enough to know. "He'll promote the woman because he is so fair to everyone and he loves the PR he gets from promoting women. So what happens is that these five guys group up because the one thing they have in common is their sex. The attitude is, if we let her do too well, or if we let her show her stuff, she's going to get the goddam job and we'll wind up working for her. They would rather cut the female out and elect their own leader."

At the outset Gannett looks fabulous. Women have been given a push for a quarter of a century. They have had a chance to stretch, to grow into jobs and become editors and publishers and directors of this and that, even presidents of whole divisions. They can screw up without wrecking it for the next woman down the line.

But it ain't easy at the very top. If aggressive solo playing has been rewarded all along, you can damn well be sure that those who rise are very good at it. And very tough. And if you want to be a winner, you've got to play the game their way.

But at least here, ladies get invited to the game.

GENERAL MILLS

A DIVERSIFIED FOOD GIANT

▲ EMPLOYEES: 57,000; 52 percent are women.

▲ SALES: $5.2 billion.

▲ General Mills states that none of its hiring or promoting policies are directed toward women or any other group. Programs that facilitate promotion include job posting for nonexempt and certain exempt positions, a performance appraisal program, tuition reimbursement and succession planning.

▲ In addition to the standard maternity disability leave, General Mills provides leaves of absence without pay, job held, on a case-by-case negotiation with managers. The company also has flexible work hours, again on a case-by-case basis. Other parenting benefits include a referral directory of child care services; employees may set aside up to $5,000 a year in pretax income for dependent care.

▲ To ensure pay equity, General Mills regularly monitors compensation.

▲ General Mills's top group of officials and managers consists of 5,507 employees, 28.6 percent of whom are women. The upper management group of 617 is 19 percent women. These include two presidents, five vice presidents and an assistant treasurer. Twenty women hold director-level positions. Of the 16-member board of directors, two are women.

▲ General Mills has written policies on sexual harassment. Approximately 7,000 people attended a training program on sexual harassment. Grievances are handled through informal or formal procedures, as are charges of sex discrimination.

▲ Major employment centers: Minneapolis area: 2,600; Chicago: 300; Orlando (base of the restaurant group): 200; in addition, large food plants are scattered from coast to coast, and restaurants and retail stores may be found in every state.

GENERAL MILLS, INC.
9200 Wayzata Boulevard
Minneapolis, MN 55440
(612) 540-2545

It's cold in Minneapolis in the winter, so cold that your breath makes ice crystals in the air, and the town fathers realized that to get people out to shop in the wintertime they had to do something, so they installed a skyway that snakes through 30 blocks of downtown shops and offices, linking store after store so that you can buy flowers and shoes and tobacco in stores that are some distance apart and never have to step outside. But if it's cold outside, there's a company in town to warm the heart of many a woman. True, it's a big conglomerate with its fingers, so to speak, in a lot of pies, from breakfast cereals (Cheerios, Wheaties, Total and more) to sit-down dining (Red Lobster, the Olive Garden) to clothing (Talbots, Eddie Bauer) and—what started it all—Gold Medal flour. But while it's big, General Mills is anything but a cold, impersonal place.

Rather than cold conglomerate, think down home, the kind of place where the lunchroom talk is more likely to be about vacations and kids or what's playing at the Guthrie Theater than it is about profits and losses; where it's not unusual to pull out pictures of your youngest taking her first steps; where people work hard, make no mistake, but they don't kill themselves while doing it. Not only do they have time for their families, they are encouraged to volunteer for community activities and keep them up after they retire. They are expected to be good solid citizens and family men and women.

It's difficult to talk about General Mills without talking about family. That goes not only for the way the company is structured—lots of small companies that are part of the General Mills family—but also for the way it treats its employees. Kind of like family. "Even though we've been through a major restructuring in the last couple of years, most things happened gracefully," remarks Chris Steiner, vice president and director of new business.

"There's a warm, taking-care atmosphere here. I remember when I went to tell my boss I was pregnant, I went in with a little trepidation. I know they have to give me my job [when I come back], but I wasn't expecting him to say, 'Oh, that's great!' But he did."

Having babies usually makes even the most confident of fast-trackers a little nervous, and the same is true to a degree at General Mills, but the women here are more relaxed than most about it. And we are talking not only about secretaries and middle management women. We are talking about women who are entitled to lunch in the executive dining room, a group that totals less than a hundred. We are talking about women who are making a hundred grand a year or more.

Not that all new mothers take off several months to get acquainted with their newborns. Most don't. "People here have gotten used to the fact that life goes on when you have a baby," says Martha Robertson, director of Betty Crocker Enterprises, who was on the phone with her office within a week following the birth of her daughter in 1984. "I was able to get my mail every day since my husband works at the company. People came to my house to present key issues, and we didn't skip a beat." Not everyone feels the need to stay so involved, but few high-ranking women feel they can afford to take off anything past the standard six- or eight-week medical leave, a feeling shared by many—if not most—career-minded women in America.

Longer leaves are possible, but there are no guarantees about what kind of job you'll be given when you return. Good jobs at a company that is learning how to be lean and mean don't wait while mommy spends six months bonding with baby. "Sure, I could have said, I'll take a leave and take a job of like status when I come back," remarks attorney Ivy Bernhardson, senior associate counsel. "But you could be sitting on your thumbs for who knows how long before you find that challenging job again." Bernhardson has two preschoolers.

Yet there are always exceptions to the rule. Some women work it out with their bosses to come back on a part-time basis for a few months; others arrange to work at home. Leslie Frecon, director of acquisitions, took a three-month unpaid leave when she had her firstborn and was planning on doing the same when she had her second in 1987. Frecon, who has been with General Mills since 1981, comments that she has seen an attitudinal change on the part of senior management: "Five years ago there wasn't the comfort level with working mothers that we have today. There are more of us who had babies and came back, and we are still going strong." Frecon makes it clear, however, that her work is covered while she is gone. She gets her mail once a week and keeps in touch with the office, dictating memos and coming in for important meetings.

She's undoubtedly wise. Frecon has been in the middle of the back-to-basics restructuring that the company went through in 1985–86, shedding 26 businesses with sales totaling about $1.7 billion. Along with other big companies, General Mills had gobbled up lots of companies in the 1960s and 1970s and diversified into such businesses as stamps and coins, costume jewelry and Play-Doh. The acquisitive binge came to an end in the 1980s when those same companies found they were in businesses they knew little about how to manage. At General Mills the fat became painfully evident when business units began reporting profits on a stand-alone basis, and earnings could be compared not only with each other, but with those of competitors. That got senior management's attention, and they began to question what to keep and what to sell. Toys and apparel manufacturing went. Returning to its roots as a food company, with a few exceptions, did not seem like such a bad idea.

Restructuring affected everything, from attitude to investment strategy. Some management positions were done away with, and 17 percent of the headquarters staff was let go; deeper cuts were made in some of the operating divisions. The company had prided itself on how well it was managed; now doubts appeared. In research and development, energy went into a handful of the most promising ideas, rather than dozen of maybes. Eddie Bauer was overhauled to appeal to more than gentleman farmers and mountain men. Talbots was updated from boring and dowdy to fresh and classic. The company's flagship restaurant line, Red Lobster, which has worldwide sales of more than $1 billion, is capitalizing on the eat-fish-it's-healthy trend and beating out the competition with friendlier service, updated decor and broiled instead of fried entrees. Between 1981 and 1986, sales grew approximately 50 percent faster than those of the restaurant industry as a whole, and the future looked healthy.

Both Talbots and Red Lobster are on growth curves. Red Lobster USA plans to add an average of 25 units per year through 1989, so that total units will top 450; in Canada it is buying up the competition and converting restaurants to their own. Talbots is positioning itself to catch the windfall in apparel appealing to the working woman. Once a small collection of stores catering to New Englanders, Talbots is scheduled to have more than a hundred stores open by the end of 1988 (up from 21 seven years ago) and another 50 by the end of 1989. And with an aggressive marketing strategy, the mail order business is thriving. Presiding over it all is a president and CEO stolen from Ann Taylor, Sally Frame. Talbots's sales in 1986 grew 55 percent, to $224 million; earnings grew by an even greater percentage.

The company's $3.4-billion-a-year food operation is also healthy. Betty Crocker layer cake mixes have recaptured the lead they lost to Procter & Gamble's Duncan Hines in 1958; its share of the cereal market is a record 24 percent; consumers are eagerly gobbling up Pop Secret microwave popcorn and its dried fruit snacks. Not every business that General Mills owns is a smashing success, but the few slow performers are still turning a profit. Overall, the company's earnings from continuing operations rose 24 percent in the first quarter of 1987, and early in 1987 the return on equity was topping an enviable 30 percent. It's hard to see how management could be worrying about whether they could be better. By any standards, General Mills's performance is stellar.

The company has managed to rack up these impressive numbers by attracting and keeping good people, people who have a mutual respect for one another because they recognize they are among the best in their fields. The energy and dynamism at corporate headquarters is palpable. "It's a fun place to work," comments Steiner, who joined the company immediately after graduation from the Amos Tuck School of Business at Dartmouth. "People are very congenial, very goal directed. There's a lot of teamwork, a lot of open doors, one-on-one discussions that take place in hallways. It's competitive too, but there's not a lot of back stabbing. I know that I am competing with my peers for the same jobs, but we help each other all the time."

Managers are frequently organized into work teams that cut across rank and discipline, and titles and levels are forgotten in the process of trying to accomplish something, reflecting the overall informality. Memos are likely to be one-page handwritten notes. Dress is more casual and low key than at most companies on either coast. Hundred-thousand-dollar-a-year women here can get away with dressing like secretaries would in the East; however, women who advance are expected to dress with sophistication and leave the safe blue suit and red bow tie behind. And if high fashion beckons, no one will be bothered because you look like you order from the Neiman-Marcus catalog rather than Talbots's. "One of the best things about working here is that I have freedom to be my own person," says Leslie Frecon, who dresses more fashionably than is typical here. "You don't have to adhere to a certain type."

It is expected, however, that everyone will maintain high ethical standards, which are integral to this part of the country. Minnesota is a place where people pride themselves on being the backbone of America, where they vote liberal but live conservatively. Minneapolis is a city of strong, staunch Protestants and Catholics, and while the churches may not be full, moral values are in the warp and woof of the culture. This is one of the few places in the country whose city council adopted an antipornography code, later vetoed by the mayor on constitutional grounds. Fittingly, integrity is a corporate virtue that gets more than lip service. Doing the right thing is taken seriously here, whether or not some government agency is breathing down the company's neck.

In 1978, when General Mills was the world's largest toy manufacturer, it took a product off the market after two children died from inhaling small parts, even though the Consumer Product Safety Commission said the labeling and precautions were satisfactory. Regardless, the toy was pulled. It happened around Thanksgiving and cost the company an estimated $8–$10 million in Christmas sales. More recently, when an industywide alarm went up because flour products had been found to be tainted with a harmful insecticide, General Mills acted with candor and speed to calm unnecessary fears. Several "800" numbers were set up and refunds given with dispatch. "The company has done a number of things that I can point to with pride and say, that was my company," says Marcia Copeland, director of Betty Crocker Food and Publications Center. "I don't want to have to apologize for what the company does."

Nor does anyone need to apologize for the company's record of corporate giving. General Mills and its foundation donated nearly $8 million to various philanthropies and schools in 1986. Volunteering for everything from the Big Brother program to serving on various community and arts boards is looked upon favorably, and the many women and men who are so involved give the company a reputation for being a good neighbor.

The women also expect that the company will do the right thing by them, and to date they haven't been disappointed. They can point to Jane Evans, who was an executive vice president for four years before Monet Jewelers was spun off and went along as president. (She is now a partner with Montgomery Securities in San Francisco.) Although Sally Frame isn't an old-timer, *she* is the one the company brought in to run the revitalized Talbots. Ivy Bernhardson has one of the highest ranking legal jobs, just below general counsel. Women have come up through product management to the level of marketing director, with profit-and-loss responsibility for as many as a dozen products, and have moved on to new assignments to broaden their experience. They are being groomed the same way the men are, and the women don't expect their sex to hold them back. "It's true we don't have any female general managers yet, but the environment is right," remarks Bernhardson. "All we need is one breakthrough. The women are convinced that there are enough strong young women in the pipeline that it will happen. This is the best atmosphere that I can imagine, and if it's going to happen anywhere, it's going to happen here."

Although everybody hired for jobs in product management needs to have an MBA, it is possible for people in other areas to come in as secretaries, get an undergraduate degree or MBA with company money and then move into management. It won't be held against you, and it's not out of the question that your boss might bring it up before you do. Starting salaries for fresh MBAs are between $37,000 and $45,000, depending on work experience and schooling. The differential for a top school is only a thousand or two, and the difference will probably be made up within two years. A generous bonus plan for managers, tied to individual performance and divisional and companywide profits, can add as much as 50 percent to one's pay. Salaries throughout the company are competitive, perhaps a tad on the generous side, and the same is true of the benefits, which are better than average but not great.

At Red Lobster, it's possible to reach for upper management even if you start with the company as a server, the company's neutral term for waitress or waiter. That's the way the vice president of employee relations, Linda

Sampieri, did it. Her move into management came within months of joining the company in 1974. A single mother with three young children, she left operations and her home in South Bend, Indiana, to take a staff job at company headquarters in Orlando two years later. Not yet 40, she is working on her MBA (having fulfilled the undergraduate requirements by examination) and is thinking about going back into operations. What she has in mind is a divisional vice presidency, and she doesn't think it's out of line for her to be talking about it.

Although there were no women to mentor her, she has found champions in male superiors, one of whom told her a few years ago to stop being so helpful at meetings. "He said, 'Linda, if you want to get ahead, I don't want you volunteering to take notes or getting the coffee. And if I think you are talking too much—even though you don't but most men think women do—I'm going to kick you under the table.'" Good advice for any woman.

We don't know if they are kicking women under the table in Minneapolis, but what they are not doing is pinching anyone's bottom or making rude remarks. Strong peer pressure to be gentlemen and ladies appears to keep anyone with lust in his heart in line; the few who cross over it are quickly booted out of the company, years of experience and rank notwithstanding. One senior manager was summarily fired for sexual harassment, and the news quickly made the grapevine. "When something like that gets around the company—and everybody knew about this one case—that's a real strong deterrent," remarks Joan Engstrom, Equal Employment Opportunity director. Salesmen naturally will be salesmen (and we know we're generalizing, but we heard this over and over), and sometimes the remarks can get raunchy, particularly after the end of the business day. Women who rise learn when it's appropriate to get their hackles up and when it's not. What doesn't go, however, is to ignore that some of the people present at meetings are women; referring only to "he" and "his" or calling female subordinates "my girls" is likely to result in a rebuke afterward. From another man. A nice touch.

All the nice touches, and a physical plant to match. Because corporate headquarters are in the suburbs, the company made space in the building for a variation on the company store. There's a haircutting salon and a small variety store with everything from over-the-counter medicines to toys. You can bring in your dry cleaning and dirty shirts, undeveloped film and shoes that need repair, and they will come back in a few days with the work done. The grounds are large and rolling (148 acres) and contain a duck pond, modern sculpture by the likes of Richard Serra and lots of places for open air lunches when the weather's right. When the weather's not, a mechanic from a nearby garage patrols the parking lot to jump start your car if necessary.

Walk through the halls and visit the offices, and you are struck by the extensive art collection which has a full-time curator and an assistant. No one can hoard a Jim Dine or a Jasper Johns print forever in her office. It rotates (ask and you will receive, eventually) among offices, halls and reception areas.

Because of its reputation and opportunities, General Mills doesn't have a hard time recruiting people from all over the country to come to cold Minnesota. There's a fair amount of culture—the Guthrie Theater is considered one of the best regional theaters in the country—and touring ballets and symphonies frequently stop here. Some people are attracted by the family orientation of the city, the clean streets and the fact that most people live within a 20-minute radius of the company.

"It's a place where I can feel secure in who I would get to raise my baby," says Steiner, who moved here with her husband after they finished school in the East. "We live in a nice neighborhood around a lake where I can walk my baby and take my dog without a leash. The company is fast paced, the jobs are challenging. But you can walk out the door, and it's a lot easier to live here than it is in a lot of other places where you can find this kind of job."

GREY ADVERTISING

THE NINTH LARGEST ADVERTISING AGENCY IN THE WORLD

▲ EMPLOYEES: 2,200; slightly more than half are women.

▲ SALES: $2 billion worldwide; the New York office accounts for $1.1 billion of that amount.

▲ Grey Advertising actively recruits women. Management training programs are approximately a third women. A career development program for entry-level employees (mainly women who start as secretaries) includes liberal tuition reimbursement and the setting up of interviews with managers throughout the company who have executive openings on their staffs. Thirty percent of senior management (vice president or above) are women. Four are presidents of subsidiaries; three are executive vice presidents, and nine are senior vice presidents.

▲ Since advertising is a client-oriented industry, flexibility in parenting is limited; however, practices at Grey vary widely, and women say the agency is unusually accommodating for one in the advertising business. Parents can set aside up to $5,000 of their salaries for child care, not taxed as income; others can set aside nontaxable funds for individual medical needs, such as eye care or physicals.

▲ Sexual harassment is not an issue.

▲ Major employment centers: New York City: 1,900; Los Angeles: 100; San Francisco: 60; Fountain Valley, Calif.: 40; Chicago: 100.

GREY ADVERTISING
777 Third Avenue
New York, NY 10017
(212) 546-2000

Whether or not Grey Advertising is a good place for women to work depends to a large degree on whom you ask. The younger women say emphatically *yes*. The older women say, well, yes, maybe and then maybe not...

The real problem may not be Grey Advertising. It's Grey's clients. Not all of them, of course, but some simply don't like dealing with women on an equal level. One client, a manufacturer of a popular brand of panty hose, insisted that no women work on the account. Women at Grey say that other clients have a hard time looking a female art director in the eye. And still other clients—like the panty hose manufacturer—let it be known that they prefer to work with men.

The problem goes beyond office hours. It is customary to socialize with clients, and difficulties arise, for example, when a married client and his wife aren't comfortable with a single woman taking them out. What we are talking about here is a night on the town—dinner at some trendy, *expensive* restaurant and theater tickets to the hot new show, all paid for by the advertising agency as part of the cost of doing business. "Socializing with clients —with the guys—is part of my job that I've learned how to do," said one vice president in account management, an area that was one of the last to open up to women at Grey. "I don't think I go out for drinks with clients as often as my male colleagues do, and I think it's definitely hurt me at Grey. What happens is that this becomes part of the social life of the client. It's the theater tickets to the play you want to see, it's dinner at the restaurant you want to go to. My not being married and having a partner to bring has definitely affected me."

The speaker, an articulate and self-assured woman in her forties, said that as she rose in the ranks, many of her male colleagues had trouble dealing with her as an equal. "I believe firmly that Grey has never had a policy against women," she says. "I don't think Grey treats women any differently than men." Because her chances for promotion were so much greater at Grey than at J. Walter Thompson, where she had been working for a number of years, she came back to Grey, where she had first started out in advertising.

Yet when she was promoted to account management, at a level where all her peers were men, she found that she was initially ignored by many of the men she had worked with in a subordinate position, men whom she had thought of as friends. "One man in particular asked me to come to work for him on Monday, and when I was promoted on Friday—to his level—he didn't speak to me for an entire year." But it wasn't just him. "I had nobody to go to lunch with for a year." It happened, she believes, because "as women come into positions historically held by men alone, we diminish their sense of importance."

According to another high-ranking woman at the company, Grey is not alone in harboring chauvinists: "It's the industry. Yes, we have many women who have good jobs. I have one of them, and maybe a half dozen other people do. But I don't think that's the real question. I look at the accounts department, and there is not one woman executive vice president. Why? I can't tell you why, because I see the ability, I see the brights and all the rest of it, but I don't see the women in the positions." The same, she adds, holds true for the creative department, where two men run the department and there is only one woman creative director. "The truth of the matter is that women have an incredibly long way to go in the advertising business. The power in the agency is male."

Her comments also ring true for the media department, which determines to a large degree where advertising dollars are best spent and arranges to buy time or space in the media. The top four media directors in late 1985 were all men, backed almost exclusively by female staffs. "You go to a meeting, and you get this funny picture because there is one man and behind him are seven women running around with all the numbers and all the backup," said Nancy Utley, a vice president in the department. "You feel like you're playing the wife role—that of being the perpetual backup."

One area where that is not true at Grey is market research, a field long dominated by women. Barbara Feigin, who heads the department, is an executive vice president and the only woman on the seven-member policy council at headquarters in Manhattan. She has been at Grey for nearly two decades, since the days it was a feisty little agency. Unlike some of the other women in traditionally male departments, she feels that across the board the agency is open to creativity, male or female. "The currency at the agency is creativity and ideas, and if you work hard to bring those ideas to fruition and make things happen, your contribution will be well received," she says. "I personally have been able to do what I want and feel I can rise as far as I want. And as the agency continues to expand, there is tremendous potential for continued personal growth. I don't feel hemmed in or restricted in the least because I'm a woman—I don't even think about the male-female issue. Maybe because of my particular area of expertise, I haven't had to fight these big battles. People have always wanted whatever I've been able to bring to the party."

This is at least partly because at Grey marketing reigned supreme for so many years. In fact, the disparaging term "marketing sweatshop" characterized the agency. This is undoubtedly due to the man in the president's seat, Edward H. Meyer, who began his career at Bloomingdale's learning firsthand what the consumer wanted, and, as he saw it, what she wanted was straightforward product information, not splashy commercials that leave one wondering what the product was. Powerful, charming and autocratic, Meyer assumed the presidency in 1968 and emphasized market research and strategic planning, speaking the same language as the marketing types in the package goods companies that make up the bulk of Grey's business. The market research department is known as the best in town, a plus when servicing such industry giants as General Mills, General Foods, B. F. Goodrich, 3M, RCA, Procter & Gamble, ABC, Revlon and several divisions of Bristol-Myers, an obviously satisfied client that has given Grey a big slice of its advertising pie for nearly a quarter of a century.

In recent years, however, as funny, futuristic and fantastic commercials —from other, zippier houses—captured the public's attention, Meyer began spurring on his people to come up with the kind of creative flash that wins awards. In 1986 Grey's worldwide operation picked up 192 awards; the following year the number dropped off by more than half.

Financially, the company is doing extremely well. In 1986 Grey pulled in more than $292 million in new billings and showed a rise in growth from current clients of $85.3 million.

However, how preeminent the creative department will be at Grey overall remains to be seen, since not a single woman in two focus groups spoke of this shift and instead generally agreed that marketing and account management had the upper hand at the agency. Executives at Mitsubishi Motors frankly admit they were attracted by Grey's ability to handle the strategic planning they were looking for. The marketing formula has worked smoothly and profitably for so many years. It may be difficult to dethrone such a viable profit center. Effective but bland ads for products like Downy fabric softener, Stove Top Stuffing and Minute Rice are probably likely to continue to roll out of the agency and onto our screens for the foreseeable future.

But if marketing is where Grey shines, it is also an area wide open to women, since men, in general, are used to listening to women tell them what kind of soap, softener and cereal they want. Feigin's predecessor as head of the research department is also a woman, Shirley Young, who now heads one of the company's subsidiaries, Grey Strategic Marketing, which provides in-depth marketing planning. Feigin and Young have no trouble getting the president's ear and are considered two of the most powerful people in the New York office.

While Grey *may* be the place for a hot young writer or art director looking to dazzle the advertising world, it is without question a haven for those business school graduates and marketing majors who are attracted to advertising as a business. And increasingly, the people being attracted these days are women: more than half of Grey's 2,200 employees are women, approximately a third of the more than 300 vice presidents are women, and, perhaps the most telling, 10 of the 13 people in the management training program at the end of 1985 were women. Men with the same backgrounds are not going into advertising as they once did but are turning instead to fields where they can make big bucks really fast, such as investment banking and industry. The women are filling the gap in advertising, coming equipped with credentials every bit as good as the men's were five or 10 years ago.

It helps to have a business degree from one of the best business schools (you'll start off approximately $5,000 higher than your colleague who doesn't) or to be one of the stars of your university's liberal arts department (French, English, history, etc.), to get your foot in the door. The company looks for people who are well rounded and have some knowledge of business, but it's still possible to get into the executive suite the old-fashioned way: start as a secretary. You are asked to make a 13-month commitment to staying a secretary; after that, while there are no guarantees that you'll be promoted, the personnel department does keep track of your interests and desires, alerts you to openings, even helps you rehearse for the interview you'll face with the person who could be your new superior. The company pushes its young people along so that the secretarial staff doesn't get stale but remains eager and committed. This entry route somewhat discriminates against young men, since older men, particularly, feel uncomfortable with a male secretary.

After you're in, what counts is what you produce. "A slave is a slave is a slave," joked one account executive. "Either you produce or you don't. Nobody cares if you're a woman or not. That's why it's a good place for women. You're judged on absolutes, not the more subjective things you might find at other companies, and in that context women will do as well as men."

Vice president Jan Dobris, summing up the general feeling of younger women at the agency, also insists that Grey is not broken down by sex lines. "We're concerned with just one thing—can you make money? If you're good at what you do, management couldn't care less what sex you are or what your background is. If you can get the job done and make money, you'll be recognized. There are examples of women in unbelievably high positions at Grey, and it's not because they were put there because of affirmative action, although we do that, it's because they were running a profit center and were just as capable as their male colleagues."

People at Grey tend to be aggressive, outspoken types who aren't afraid of disagreeing with each other—or the client. The women who participated in the focus groups were outspoken and critical of their company, and these were the people that management had elected to send. And as Shirley Young was quoted in *Savvy*: "You don't stimulate creativity by telling people what to do. They should be saying what they think is best for the client." The directness can be refreshing, allowing you to "get a lot done without a lot of bullshitting," as one woman put it, adding that it sometimes comes across as brash, even rude. "Social graces are not a prerequisite to getting ahead at Grey."

Because the emphasis is the bottom line, not sex or how you look or speak, the people who come to call Grey family tend to be highly individualistic and less what the world thinks of as the woman in the gray flannel suit. "We're interested in content rather than form," comments Harvi Robinson, a vice president and group management supervisor. "Our people tend not to be as mainstream as what you find at other agencies."

She has noted a slight shift, however, in that the younger people the agency is hiring generally have the same style as the individuals found at the large corporate clients they would be servicing.

But it isn't all disharmony in the ranks. Once you decide to settle in at Grey, camaraderie runs high. Management breakfasts at a hotel four times a year keep everybody informed of how the company is doing and gives Meyer a chance to publicly pat the creative or account stars of the last quarter on the back. When new major clients sign on, some kind of celebration usually takes place. The day after Red Lobster came on board, two people in lobster costumes met employees in the lobby and invited them all to a continental breakfast in the company cafeteria. Every fall, a choral group rehearses at lunch hour for a program of Christmas music in the building's lobby. And Grey women, in constant contact with dozens of major industries, meeting people at their levels, are acutely aware that it's easier to go farther in advertising—at least at Grey—than it is in any number of the industries they service. "You go to these companies and you wonder, where are the women?" commented one Grey account manager.

That may be one reason the rehiring rate at Grey is so high. Although advertising is a business where switching companies is as common as changing your brand of toothpaste, coming back to Grey seems to be unusually frequent. "It's gotten so that now when someone leaves I feel there's a fifty-fifty chance they'll be back," says Nancy Utley, a media vice president who's been with the agency since 1978. "I feel like it's silly to say good-bye."

While no one would return to Grey for its terrific benefits package, it does allow a working mother (or father) to defer part of her (or his) income (up to $5,000, the legal limit) toward child care subsidies, and this will then not be taxed as income. This cafeteria-style approach to benefits can be used for special medical needs as well, such as eyeglasses or a complete physical.

What is special about Grey is the profit-sharing and stock ownership plans. Although the exact amounts vary from year to year, the result of a decision by the seven-member executive committee, they are high by most other companies' standards. In 1984, for instance, someone who was making $35,000 annually would have had nearly $4,000 set aside for profit sharing and another $5,000 in stock. While someone leaving the company couldn't take all of this with her in a year or three, after eight years the entire amount—in stock or dollars—is hers to take. Compound these figures over several years, and you come out well rewarded for your time and effort. It's worth noting that eight years is a short time to be completely vested.

Pay equity with the men at the agency is a matter of constant speculation without any definite answers. Several women said they thought they ought to be more aggressive in asking for raises and that speaking up would *probably* yield results.

Sexual harassment is virtually nonexistent. The few cases that have cropped up have been dealt with informally by the personnel department. In recent years only two complaints were registered, and both women have since left Grey in due time for other reasons. "Our policy is, we don't like it and don't do it," says one woman. To that end, in 1985 Meyer sent out a memo dealing with both discrimination and harassment, quite simply saying: Grey tolerates neither.

Working mothers—hard-working mothers, that is—are accommodated easily at Grey, which gave maternity leaves a long time before many other companies did. In 1969, a week after she began working at Grey, Feigin learned she was pregnant. She immediately 'fessed up, and the response was "fabulous," she says, in contrast to that of a previous employer when she had her first child. She worked up until the time she delivered—going to the hospital from the office—and had to take a longer leave than expected because the birth of her twins was complicated.

Since advertising is a business where it's not all quiet in the halls and offices, children are tolerated easily and seem to bother no one. Mothers often bring their youngsters in on school holidays or Friday mornings in the summer, when the agency closes at noon and a quick getaway to the Hamptons is planned. "Sometimes I feel like I should borrow a kid on Friday to fit in," jokes one woman. The art department is likely to yield up a big pad of paper and colored markers to be spread out on the floor of Mom's office.

One woman in the personnel department found not only that her job was waiting for her after a four-month leave to have her child, but also that she could work part-time for the next year and a half; in the meantime, her secretary had been promoted to her old job. Early in January 1986, Jane Van Saun returned to work full-time. "They couldn't have been more understanding," she says. "My working three days a week didn't prejudice them against me. But understand, they didn't do it for a favor—we were swamped. We are always looking for people." Van Saun hires the nonexempt, or secretarial, staff. Her former secretary and she are now at the same level.

And what happens when Johnny's running a 104° temperature, the nanny won't do, and Mom—or Dad—*must* be there? Vice president Patti Dyson, a supervisor in account management, and her husband solve that problem by deciding whose workload is most crucial that day. The other parent stays home with their 3-year-old. "There are days when they know my child is sick and I've come anyway," Dyson says. "And they say, 'What are you doing here? Get your priorities straight.'" When her first child was born, Dyson was on leave from May to September; she came back to new assignments (planned before she left), a promotion and a newer, bigger office. Dyson, however, made it clear that the company's understanding was a two-way street. "I don't freak out if I'm not home by seven," she says. Dyson was five months pregnant when interviewed, and she planned to be gone for the less hectic summer months.

Maternity leave is handled as a regular medical leave, and the number of weeks you are on full salary depends on the length of time you have been at Grey. A 10-year veteran, for instance, would have 11 weeks of leave with pay, to add to accrued vacation time if she so desired.

Much of the credit for the quality of life at Grey goes to Robert Berenson, executive vice president for administration, who frankly admits that to continue to attract the kind of top people they are known for, the agency has to offer "a good measure of love" along with dollars. "If we're going to continue to be represented by the smartest, brightest, toughest people, we knew we couldn't compete on the basis of money alone, since other businesses offer more," he says. "To keep our competitive edge, we began to develop programs that would attract and keep good people."

Berenson went on to say that women may actually make better account executives—whose job is, in essence, to mediate between the client and the creative people—than men. He apologizes for seeming to sound sexist and observes that "women are potentially more able to convince people to work together by virtue of their personality and intelligence, since they have spent years learning how to handle difficult situations and keeping peace." Berenson adds that they are now finding "30 capable women for every man" when they interview.

Grey's offices are spread out on 25 floors of a mid-Manhattan skyscraper, and except for a few recently remodeled areas with high-tech charcoal-gray walls and turquoise accents, black chairs and the requisite black vases of white tulips, they could be the offices of any accounting or consulting firm. For the most part, jazzy they are not.

What happens next at Grey is the question on many women's minds. While they are making their way in the lower and middle management ranks, will they rise to the few spots at the top?

"We've got a lot of women in their middle thirties who are ready to roll, and the real drama is going to come in the next ten years," says Dobris. "Are women actually going to be promoted to the highest levels?"

Barbara Kurka, director of personnel planning, feels quite certain they will. "Ten years from now advertising will be run by women. Women are becoming mainstream at the agency now. If we don't have more women at the top now, it's just a matter of time."

GTE

GTE DEVELOPS, MANUFACTURES AND MARKETS TELECOMMUNICATIONS EQUIPMENT AND SERVICES, LIGHTING PRODUCTS AND PRECISION MATERIALS; OUR REPORT PRIMARILY DEALS WITH *GTE DIRECTORIES,* A SUBSIDIARY THAT SELLS YELLOW PAGES ADVERTISING AND PUBLISHES MORE THAN 900 TELEPHONE DIRECTORIES IN THE UNITED STATES AND ABROAD

▲ EMPLOYEES: GTE Corporation: 123,200; 43 percent are women.
GTE Directories: 4,975; 68 percent are women, including 50 percent of the sales force, 54 percent of professionals and 47 percent of officials and managers.

▲ SALES: $15.1 billion in 1986 for the corporation as a whole, down a bit from 1985.

▲ GTE as a corporation does well at recruiting and hiring women at the entry level for professional and managerial positions. GTE Directories, among all the business groups, excels at rewarding them for performance with money and promotions.

▲ Of the 496 employees throughout GTE who are considered upper management, only 12—2 percent—are women. The corporate secretary and four vice presidents are women, as are 45 directors. One of the seven regional vice presidents of GTE Directories is a woman.

▲ The company offers a good package of benefits, including medical, dental and life insurance and pension.

▲ A particularly nice extra is the beautiful training center owned and operated by GTE. Situated on the extensive grounds of a former monastery in Norwich, Conn., it is an elegant atmosphere for off-site meetings and training.

▲ Flexibility for parenting varies according to the business group; GTE Directories does not tolerate long maternity leaves or parenting emergencies well. At corporate headquarters, manners are genteel and policies are paternalistic. GTE Directories is a place where success-oriented women with some sales experience, with or without college degrees, can and do excel.

▲ Major employment centers: GTE operates in 48 states and Puerto Rico; major concentrations of employees include: California: 33,500; Florida: 13,000; Texas: 13,000; Illinois: 9,000; Massachusetts: 8,900; corporate headquarters in Stamford: 900; GTE Directories: Dallas: 900; Los Alamitos, Calif.: 1,000; Mount Prospect, Ill.: 400; St. Petersburg, Fla.: 300.

GTE CORPORATION
One Stamford Forum
Stamford, CT 06904
(203) 965-2000

GTE DIRECTORIES HEADQUARTERS
Box 619810
West Airfield Drive
Dallas, TX 75261
(214) 453-7000

While we started out looking at the entire GTE Corporation, after interviewing a number of women and looking at the numbers—12 of 496 employees considered upper management are women, or 2.4 percent—we decided that the company as a whole isn't a place we can recommend.

Management *says* it wants to move women up, and a few have: twelve women were part of senior management when we went to press; seven women were in senior management in 1986 when we did our interviewing.

Nearly all of the seven belonged to a small group of women who had started with the company between 1977–78. Most of them said that they feel that they have topped out and are discouraged that they don't see women swelling the pipeline behind them. The company has formulated no clear directives and set no numerical goals to bring women up past middle management. Sexism appears to be rampant, particularly in the manufacturing units. The only response when we went to press was to admit there was a problem.

Downsizing has made matters worse for everybody, women as well as men, as GTE, along with other major telecommunications companies, struggles to restructure in today's fiercely competitive environment. There aren't a lot of jobs for anyone moving up the pyramid. Furthermore, the laissez-faire attitude of the Reagan administration toward affirmative action seems to have been adopted by GTE as its own. Given the situation, many women are unwilling to stick around to see what will happen. Discouraged and frustrated, they realize they have topped out well before they should. And some walk. One of the women the company arranged for us to talk to said that she had recently advised a young woman who was considering a job with GTE to seek employment elsewhere. Not a very bright picture for today's graduates.

Yet in contrast to that bleak picture, GTE does a fine job of recruiting and hiring women at the entry level for managers and professionals, particularly in mathematics and engineering. In 1986, 50 percent of the new engineering employees hired were female, an amazing feat given that only 14 percent of 1986 engineering graduates were women.

Another bright spot is GTE's legal department, which has a fair number of women (33 out of 122) and is headed up by corporate secretary Marianne Drost. She worked for the company for seven years before leaving for a nearby corporation but was recruited back for her current position. Drost herself feels that being a woman has never held her back, encouraging words for anyone looking for a legal job in Stamford, Connecticut, where GTE is headquartered. Should we say that Drost serves as a reminder of the corporation's good intentions? We don't know.

We do know that GTE has a Dallas subsidiary—GTE Directories—that is doing just fine as far as women are concerned. Like so many good companies for women, GTE Directories is oriented to the bottom line. Here women have every chance of succeeding. Here they get a chance to show that even in a highly competitive, intense environment, they can perform. The job is selling.

They are selling ads in the telephone directory, and they are doing one hell of a job. It's almost expected that the new crop of high performers will have more women than men in the group, because, as the highest-ranking woman at GTE Directories says, "They're willing to work harder."

Their unquestionable ability was proven in a few short years. Up until 1982–83, women handled nearly all the "inside" sales, meaning that they would contact customers over the telephone. They handled approximately 70 percent of the accounts numerically, but brought in only 30 percent of total revenues. The big money in sales was with the male "outside" sales staff, who brought in 70 percent of the revenues and naturally earned the highest commissions. Women weren't given the jobs calling on advertisers in person. The idea was, they couldn't hack it. Too tough, too competitive, too much travel.

But when women were given a chance—surprise! Not only did they do well, they generally did better than the men. Now the company finds no lack of women willing to compete in the driving atmosphere of a sales force that prides itself on being macho. It's a Lone Ranger mentality—where there's a job to do, we'll be there to do it.

Understandably, the atmosphere is not genteel and the language is rough. "I get awfully tired hearing about basketball games and women's tits," says one woman. You're likely to be on the road between 30 and 100 percent of the time, covering a territory that can take in several states and often traveling with male coworkers. None of this stops the women. And no one can argue with high numbers.

"Everything is very quantified, and your successes and failures are very glaring," says Marilyn B. Carlson, vice president for the central region. "That has really helped women, because you don't have to go through the same political games that you do elsewhere." Carlson is one of seven regional VPs; the six others in the spring of 1987 were men. By the time you are reading this, the numbers will probably have changed.

Carlson started out as a clerk with the company in Florida in 1968, fresh out of high school, and after following her husband during his hitch in the service came back and was offered a job in sales because she was "outspoken," as she recalls. Success was rapid, although she had to take a number of transfers on the way. She and her husband made five moves in 11 years, no questions asked. Her husband, also a sales rep, was able to move as she was transferred and opened up new territories all over the country. Carlson is back in Texas for the second time.

The transfer situation hasn't changed and can be brutal. You're likely to get a phone call informing you of your new territory or promotion, and you are not expected to say no. This makes it somewhat difficult on women who are not mobile. Similarly, pregnancy and flexible workdays aren't well tolerated. The directories have deadlines. A sale missed because you're out on leave is a sale missed for good.

Of course, some women thrive on the pace, especially when the rewards are so tangible. In 1986 the minimum salary for a salesperson was $43,000; the average is $47,000. High performers can break $100,000. Not bad for someone without a college degree, although if you do have one, you won't be told you're overqualified. What is necessary is a few years of sales experience, preferably in nontangible goods such as stocks or insurance. At those salaries, the company finds it can pick the cream of the crop among experienced saleswomen, and that the men applying for the same spots aren't usually so sparkly. The best way in is to know somebody on the inside. The sales force numbers around 900.

Those applying would do best to have a thick skin and not be offended every time they hear a comment about some woman's anatomy. Carlson's advice: "You have to make the men feel comfortable being around you, and by that I mean, you don't set out to change the culture. You realize there are certain things you cannot do."

But there's no longer any question about what women can do. "I hear a lot of opinions about why women do so well, but the bottom line is, they just work harder," says Carlson. "They need the success more, or they need the money more, but whatever the reason, our women work harder than the men."

HALLMARK

THE NATION'S NUMBER ONE GREETING CARD COMPANY

▲ EMPLOYEES: 12,000 full-time and 4,800 part-time; 64 percent of the full-time employees are women.

▲ REVENUES: Approximately $2 billion. Hallmark controls more than half of the $3.5 billion greeting card market in the United States. (If public, Hallmark would rank near the middle of *Fortune* 500 companies in sales.)

▲ Hallmark is concerned about recruiting, hiring and promoting women. They recruit from women's colleges and have used female recruiting firms. Programs aimed at promotion include job posting and career development classes; today, two thirds of college recruits entering the program are women. The company subsidizes women's memberships in Central Exchange, a Kansas City club that nurtures women's leadership development. Tuition reimbursement is routine for undergraduate courses, MBA, art and other graduate courses. Hallmark employs a dual-track career advancement system for artists, writers and photographers.

▲ Of the 124 people considered upper management, 14—or 12 percent—are women. These include 10 senior management people and eight department directors. Of the nine members of the board of directors, one is a woman.

▲ Hallmark states that it achieves pay equity by participating in numerous national pay scale summaries, as well as updating and reevaluating job descriptions.

▲ Hallmark is concerned with the needs of new parents. In addition to standard maternity disability leave, new mothers *or* fathers as well as adoptive parents can take up to three months' unpaid leave, with their own or a comparable job guaranteed upon return. A resource referral service is available for child care or eldercare, and the company supports community-based facilities. The company adopted a flexible benefits program in July 1987. Although part-time work is not available for managers, many artists and writers work part-time through free-lance contracts.

▲ Other benefits include 50 percent discounts at on-site stores. Through profit sharing, one third of this family-owned company is owned by employees.

▲ A strong statement against sexual harassment has been issued by the company. Complaints are handled by department personnel or, if necessary, by formal review. A program on sexual harassment, "New Roles, New Relationships: Men and Women Working Together," is part of management training and has also been used extensively throughout the company. Individual remedial counseling is sometimes done for longer-service supervisors.

▲ Major employment centers: Kansas City, Mo.: 7,000; Enfield, Conn.: 750; nearly 2,000 at production and distribution facilities throughout Kansas.

HALLMARK CARDS, INC.
2501 McGee Street
Kansas City, MO 64108
(816) 274-5111

You can often guess—with some certainty—when someone's from the Midwest because of her friendly, open manner and unassuming smile. By that measure, Hallmark Cards couldn't possibly be any place but the Midwest. And Kansas City is about as Midwest as you can get.

And at Hallmark the people are as friendly as they get anywhere. Walk through the building, and lots of people will smile at you as if you've been passing them in the hall for years. When you do meet someone, there's more than a simple assumption that everyone will get along; immediate intimacy is assumed. Reserve here is a word seen only on wine labels. To someone not used to it, the style falls somewhere between ingenuous and gullible. It's not for everyone. But for a lot of people, it's why they love working at America's largest greeting card company. It's like one big family.

That familial feeling is most definitely what attracted Anne Sebesta, a vivacious 1982 graduate of Duke University and native of Florida. Set on a career in politics, Sebesta spent a summer working as an intern in the White House, enough time to convince her that she was "too ambitious and too impatient," as she puts it, to wait the length of time it takes to get ahead in Washington. She was also bothered by the knowledge that factors other than what she could control would affect her career. So she decided to channel her energies into business.

To practice her interviewing skills, she signed up for an interview with the first company that came along. It turned out to be with Hallmark, and that was fine, since she knew that she didn't want to work in Kansas City, and so what would be the harm if she flubbed it? She was so ill-prepared for the interview that halfway through, when asked why she wanted a job in sales, she blurted out: "Is this for sales?"

The interviewer suggested that she might do better by talking to the people who came around to Duke's business school and applying for a job in marketing. Something about their talk convinced Sebesta to follow up when the recruiter for the business school came back. "I really enjoyed talking to him," she recalls. In the meantime, she interviewed with a number of other companies. "At a lot of big companies in New York and Washington you aren't getting away from politics, and that's what I wanted to get away from," she says. "I wanted to work someplace where I felt my career was in my own hands. And Hallmark seemed like a company where everybody was straightforward."

She admits that when she flew to Kansas City, she didn't know what to expect—would the people be wearing suits, would they have hayseed in their hair? In fact, they weren't wearing suits the day she came. There had been a fire the day before, and many of the offices were flooded. Most people were in jeans helping with the mop-up. "People had been working all through the night," she remembers, "and I just thought, there's a lot of loyalty here. That's important to me. I wanted to have a reason to be loyal, and I could sense that people felt that Hallmark was like their family. I thought, If I'm going to take a job in a faraway place, I would at least like it to be someplace where I'm comfortable with the working environment."

Sebesta hasn't regretted her move. When we interviewed her, she was an assistant product manager for greeting cards, trying to find a way to avoid being a sales representative working out of her home for the next few years. As we went to press, Sebesta was at Harvard working on a master's degree in public policy. Although technically she had to quit, she had every intention of returning to Hallmark, convinced that most firms wouldn't allow her to have as much control over her career. Or her life.

No one claims that Hallmark isn't political, but the politics have more to do with taking the initiative and getting to know who's important than who your daddy was and where you went to school. Being political here means scheduling lunches with senior managers, a move that takes some guts but is encouraged. And senior managers are expected to meet with the new people and become their mentors.

One of the mentors is a single parent. Sally Groves, creative director for writing and editorial, has a son who was in the second grade in 1987. Groves manages with a housekeeper who works from 3 P.M. to 7 P.M. weekdays. Because she can't get to work much earlier most days than 8:30 A.M., she says she doesn't do breakfast meetings. Unless it's very important. Then she has someone else take her son to school. "Sometimes I say, 'Start without me, I'll be there at eight-thirty.' You make these compromises." They certainly haven't hurt her career path or stymied her ambitions. Groves and the other woman at the director level, Phyllis Nolan, both have their eye on becoming corporate officers. It's one step higher.

If either makes it, she won't be the first woman. Jeanette Lee, who started with the company in 1946, was vice president of design from 1971 to 1983. Now her daughter, also Jeanette, works in product development. "Jeanette set a marvelous precedent for many years, so the people who own and run this company don't feel women are innately inferior," says Groves. "And we have to keep in mind that the consumer is 90 percent female. Anyone who works here—male or female—has to keep in mind the consumer and understand how she operates. And I can do that."

While nearly all the women were gushingly enthusiastic about their employer, a few doubts that senior management is all that concerned about pulling women up to the very top level surfaced. Was the path easier for Jeanette Lee than it is for women today because she started with the company when it was much smaller? Did she really open things up to women, or is she seen as the exception? "I wish there was a stronger commitment from the company to put women in senior management," one woman says. "I'm not sure they have given it much thought." She adds that she didn't see women advancing as quickly as men.

Yet Hallmark has moved with the times. Women who began working in the sixties and didn't think about career planning were invited to attend management development seminars and to set their sights up several notches. Deanna Hormel, who started as a dietitian in 1967, now oversees a cafeteria and in-house catering service that serves some 4,800 meals a day. The Crown Room, as the company-subsidized cafeteria is called, is open for breakfast, lunch and dinner and sells take-out cakes and pies as well. Hormel also sits on an employee relations staff that's part of the personnel department and manages two on-site Hallmark shops for employees. "I have not reached a plateau," she says. "There's always opportunity when people retire or pieces of the company move in a restructuring. But if I had not gone through the management development program I would still be in my white uniform and white shoes and not know how to handle the opportunity when it came along a year later." She is referring to the fact that shortly after the seminar, she was given the chance to run the food service. Other women tell similar stories of Hallmark encouragement to push them along.

So while the questions remain about what's happening for women at the very top, women appreciate the nurturing kind of environment it is. Perhaps it's only fitting that a company that boxes sentiment and goodwill for the rest of America—and prides itself on being the *very best*—should be the kind of place it is. On your birthday, you're likely to be inundated with cards, even if you're a relative newcomer. How do they do it? Personnel sends out birthday lists. Parties with home-baked brownies and cherry winks seem to be going on in one department or another all the time. You have a party for a fifth anniversary with the company, and of course the tenth, and so on. One department was having birthday and anniversary parties so often that everybody was gaining weight. By mutual consensus, they decided to schedule them only twice a month. People don't swear much here. When men were excusing themselves at other companies for saying the F word at meetings, men here were asking the woman present if she minded if they removed their jackets, since it was hot in the room.

That kind of formality is gone now, and as times relaxed, so did the dress code. Artists and writers, for instance, usually don't wear suits and ties; they're likely to be attired in more flamboyant garb that would fit right in at art departments in Chicago or New York City.

Hallmark employs a vast creative staff—with some 700 people it's the largest in the world—that turns out more than 14,000 greeting card designs annually for both the Hallmark and Ambassador lines. (Ambassador cards are sold in mass market outlets; Hallmark cards are sold in card shops and department stores.) With 600 artists and another 100 writers all working in creative synergy, romance is sure to bloom. Marriages among the artists are common. "Artists marry artists," remarks one woman succinctly. Marriages elsewhere throughout the company are not infrequent either. A 1984 count found 718 couples who were both "Hallmarkers." Whether you marry a coworker or not, you'll get a silver-plated tray when you wed; an engraved silver cup follows with each child. In other words, Kansas City might be a good place to find a job—and a husband.

It also is a terrific place for a new B.F.A. to continue on a learning curve. Technique can be taught, and sometimes by the best. "If you are very good at airbrush but want to learn more about wash, all you have to do is go up to Gary Head, who won the Society of Illustrators Gold Medal last year, and say, 'Could you help me out?'" says Jani Mohr, a recruiter for the creative staff. "Everybody's very open about it."

A creative workshop brings together a small group of rotating artists and writers with production people who work out new concepts and try new methods of making cards. The "blue sky" thrust of the workshop rejuvenates stale artists and writers, as do trend-spotting trips to Europe. Groups of 15 to 20 are sent for two weeks to major cities to absorb the culture and come home with fresh ideas. In a Victorian mansion in Colorado Springs, eight artists are charged with the mission to be as zany and creative as possible and bounce their ideas off each other. It's also possible to be sent back to school, in this case the prestigious School of Visual Arts in New York City, for a semester. Or be sent to the Aspen Design Conference in June. Or closer to home, enroll in classes at the Kansas City Art Institute, one of the top small private art schools in the country. At the University of Kansas, 45 minutes away in Lawrence, you can take art courses, attend the Hallmark-sponsored lectures by major artists and designers from around the country or hone up on marketing if that's your interest. Hallmark will pay the tab, up to $1,500 a year. All in all, the company works hard at overcoming its location far from the creative centers of New York and Los Angeles, but a certain insularity is inevitable. However, the artists themselves are an interesting bunch, and some of their energies are directed to interests other than greeting cards and paper plates. Writer Terry Matz sold a story to *The Twilight Zone* and artist Teresa Roberts performs weekends as a stand-up comic in a local club.

Whether you stay for a long haul or not, a few years at Hallmark will certainly stand you in good stead should you decide to move on. A Hallmark background can open a lot of doors at advertising agencies elsewhere. But many who come to Kansas City with that idea end up staying, says Mohr, who found the company a refreshing change of pace from the academic world. Mohr taught graphic design for 18 years at Western Michigan University. Visiting Hallmark to learn why she should encourage her students to try for a job here, Mohr herself was recruited in 1984. "I was one of those people who thought I would come down here for a year or two," she says, grinning, "but Kansas City is very captivating. I tell the New York people that we've got the Saks and Ralph Laurens. We've got lots of jazz and a wonderful museum that brings in contemporary masters."

What Kansas City also has are great apartments with character that aren't hard to come by and don't cost most of a month's salary. One-bedrooms in the Plaza section (the best part of town) can be had for around $500. And when you come in from out of town, you won't be apartment hunting on your own. A part-time Hallmark employee will try to match your needs and desires to what's available. She picks you up at your hotel and drives you to see places she's preselected by going over the classifieds herself. Incidentally, all moving expenses for fresh college graduates are paid by the company. It is like a family.

The familial feeling starts at the top. The chairman of the board, Donald J. Hall, is the son of the founder, J. C. Hall, who is the only other board chairman in the 78-year history of the company. Day-to-day operations are run by an outsider, Irvine O. Hockaday, Jr., president, and although the flattening of the market in the last several years has increased pressures to cut costs, it has been done without laying people off while profits remain healthy. The company's long-standing reputation for benevolence is deserved.

Hockaday has managed to cut costs without cutting people in a number of ways. The creative staff, for instance, has begun pumping out 15 percent more designs than it did a few years ago. When management workers leave, some jobs are not filled immediately, some not at all. To keep factory workers busy, production schedules are juggled among the company's several plants. At slack times, manufacturing workers may take a turn in the kitchen (at manufacturing wages) or be retrained to do the kinds of jobs that are needed now. In such a fashion, it's even possible to make the move from manufacturing to clerical.

Hallmark takes care of its people in other ways too. If you run into a catastrophic emergency and need ready cash, the company will lend you some or pick up your bills while you're incapacitated; if your children are college bound, the company will give you a low-interest loan with no payback until graduation; adoption assistance of $1,000 is available. The medical and dental benefits are excellent, as is the profit-sharing plan. Each year the company takes a percentage of profits, puts it into an employee fund and invests the money in Hallmark stock. In 1987 the company's contribution was $48.2 million. Through the fund, employees own approximately a third of the company. The Hall family owns the rest. With investments and profit sharing, each employee's annual share has averaged 15 percent of salary over the years; in 1987 the amount topped 20 percent. What this means is that longtime employees are taken care of very comfortably upon retirement. Very comfortably.

Family emergencies are met with understanding, but attendance records are carefully kept of nonmanagement employees, and too many absences can result in termination. People here are expected to work hard; Hallmark is nurturing, but a welfare state it is not. Although there is no official policy on flexible hours, deals can sometimes be arranged with accommodating bosses. Job sharing, even in management, is sometimes possible, and a number of writers and artists work on a contract basis at home. The pay is reasonably good; in national surveys, Hallmark ranks in the top quartile. If pay inequity exists, according to a woman manager who would know, she has found it goes back to the salaries women accepted when they were hired. Some Hallmark managers make an effort to correct salary discrepancies, but new people should be forewarned.

There is a physical fitness building at corporate headquarters (a place to work off all those extra calories from those parties), and the offices are among the most comfortable we've seen anywhere. The cluster of buildings near downtown Kansas City is low key, pleasing to the eye and mind. White noise emits from the heating system; well-tended plants are everywhere, as is some of the art collection the Hall family has collected over the years. The furniture is top-of-the-line Herman Miller, and there is hand lotion on the marble counters in some of the ladies' rooms. Like the cards it makes, Hallmark is a class act.

Taste and quality mean a lot here, and although the language on many of Hallmark's hipper card lines is a lot racier than in the old days (some four-letter words do get into print), it's still possible for a factory worker to stop production if she thinks something is in poor taste or shoddy. It happens. "When you care enough to send the very best" is America's most recognized tag line, and it is taken seriously here.

What aren't taken seriously (except for their nuisance quotient) are claims that some Hallmark cards, particularly the contemporary funny ones, are ripoffs of cards made by competitors. Except for one, a handful of suits against the company a few years ago were either dropped or settled out of court. To avoid such plagiarism problems, the creative staff is charged to be original. One firm, however, Blue Mountain Arts, is claiming that an entire style of cards—soft sky, sentimental prose, deckle edge—is their domain and Hallmark is unfairly infringing upon their copyright. Hallmark counters that they first introduced a similar style in 1971 but the line was dropped due to poor sales. It was revived in the eighties, when marketing trends were more favorable.

None of this affects the pleasant atmosphere of Hallmark as a place to work. Artists' portfolios continue to arrive, and each is given careful consideration, age and previous experience notwithstanding. Someone who displays talent and flexibility will be asked to Kansas City for an interview. Writers can ask for the writing test, a 25-page document you fill in at your leisure. It probably helps if you are a touchy-feely kind of person, even though some irony and cynicism are evident in the Shoebox line of cards.

You don't find a lot of cynics, however, working at Hallmark or, for that matter, in Kansas City. "The best part about Kansas City and the fabulous part of Hallmark is the people," allows Jani Mohr, whose job is selling the company on college campuses. "The people are so warm. There's little or no aloofness in this town. And I have never seen the kind of interaction among workers I have here. People ask, how's your family, how's your dog, and it's not artificial. People want to know and want to help if there's a problem."

And if there's a problem, you'll probably get help. And a Hallmark card. One of the on-site stores, at which employees can buy merchandise at a 50 percent discount, is the largest-volume Hallmark store in the world.

HEARST TRADE BOOKS

A DIVISION OF THE HEARST CORPORATION WHICH OWNS TWO SEPARATE PUBLISHING HOUSES; MORROW PUBLISHES HARDCOVER ORIGINALS, WHILE AVON BOOKS IS A PAPERBACK REPRINTER

▲ EMPLOYEES: Approximately 300; nearly two thirds are women.

▲ Although the magazines and newspapers the company owns form the bulk of the company's business, we have focused on the book publishing division, where women have fared the best.

▲ Morrow and Avon Books share a justifiable lack of concern for recruiting, hiring and promoting women. Here are the numbers:

	Morrow	Avon Books
Employees:	150	149
Women:	100 (67%)	89 (60%)
Upper Management:	24	13
Women:	12 (50%)	7 (54%)

▲ Book publishing, in general, employs a great many women, and at Hearst Trade Books Division, female talent rises to the very top. Publishing, at least on the editorial side, is often described as more of a calling than a career. Highly educated graduates of fine schools compete fiercely for jobs as editorial assistants, and the entry-level pay is terrible. However, top editors and publishers make incomes in six figures. Besides jobs as editors who acquire books, jobs are available in sales, publicity, marketing, design and graphics, and copy editing.

▲ Benefits at Hearst are not very good. And if you want to combine your career with parenting, no one at Hearst will stop you, but certainly no one will help you.

▲ Yet for women who really want to be in book publishing, both Morrow and Avon seem like a good bet. The companies are described as fair, professional, casual and, most important, gender blind. Because of the sheer numbers of women, sexual harassment is not an issue.

WILLIAM MORROW & CO.
105 Madison Avenue
New York, NY 10016
(212) 889-3050

AVON BOOKS
1790 Broadway
New York, NY 10019
(212) 399-4500

WILLIAM MORROW   Bridging the gap between assistant and editor in publishing is not automatic by any means. It can take years and often does. It usually requires moving from publisher to publisher. Maria Guarnaschelli made the leap nine months after she joined William Morrow & Company.

It had been a long haul. After a few years of teaching Russian at the university level, she joined Harper & Row as a secretary and later became an editorial assistant. She stayed for four years. For a brief time, she was an associate editor at a small art publisher. While she had an expense account, she didn't actually sign up any books, the feat that normally transforms an assistant to editor. When she joined Morrow, she went back to being an assistant and took a pay cut of $5,000. Her salary was $9,000. The year was 1978.

Today Guarnaschelli is respected in the trade for the literary and serious nonfiction books she buys, a niche she's carved out for herself at Morrow, a publisher better known for its commercial books than its literary ones. She is an editor of the *Paris Review*. Commenting on the low entry-level salaries offered editorial assistants, she says that people have to look upon their first years as apprenticeships and realize that the price tag on the training is a salary that many would consider unlivable in New York City, the seat of the publishing world. But even with starting salaries as low as $11,500, the competition is keen. Degrees from good schools are run of the mill.

"Many people who are attracted to publishing come from families where Mommy and Daddy can give them money," she says. "It's always been that way. The desire to be an editor rather than a lawyer or a doctor requires a certain enlightenment on the part of the parents. Among the first generation in a family to go to college, you aren't going to find a lot of editors."

Salaries leap upward as soon as one is promoted to editor with an expense account, money to take agents and authors to lunch and woo their books. Mary Ellen Curley is one who managed to sign up a book from England from the assistant's slot. "You have to seize an opportunity or try to make one," says Curley. "You have to be a real hustler in this business to make it to editor, and when you do that, you still have to hustle—you're always trying for the best-seller so you can hustle the greater and greater agents. There's always something that you're trying to reach for."

One of her peers, Dawn Drzal, adds: "You're either an acquiring editor or you're not, and there's no formal channel for promotions. And so when the ball drops in your court—and it's often some kind of fluke—you had better be able to handle it or forget it." Both men and women compete for those entry-level jobs, and the editorial assistants who answer the phones these days are just as likely to be male as female.

With the low salaries and the difficulty in making the jump to editor, the dropout rate is high. The people who stay are committed and clear about their reasons: "The thing I love most about publishing is the people you interact with," says Curley. "Everyone from the top down to assistant is an interesting person to meet."

Drzal compares publishing to acting. "It gets into your blood. I can't imagine doing anything else."

Although the salaries escalate once you become a full-fledged editor, publishing is known as a business where nobody makes a huge pile except those at the very top. It's fair to say that salaries in the six-figure range at Hearst companies (or any publisher) come only after a steady flow of best-sellers or one gigantic book that stays on the list for months and months, and even then it's not automatic. You often have to wait until another publisher tries to steal you away at a big salary; either you go, or you report back and ask your company to match it. However, if you don't make the numbers, you can be cut off quickly at Morrow. "Sometimes editors can come and go so fast I don't even get a chance to know them," comments one woman.

But the women who pull their weight at Morrow say there is plenty to like about the place. The atmosphere is casual, loose and congenial. No one feels the need to be into power dressing. Even the lobby has a down-home quality about it, with something that looks suspiciously like a plate from a supermarket set of dishes serving as an ashtray. Offices for most editors are small, crowded quarters. Doors are seldom closed. Each editor is allowed to operate somewhat autonomously, bringing in the kinds of books she likes.

That's why a literary editor like Guarnaschelli can operate happily side by side with Pat Golbitz, whose instincts have led to more best-sellers than most editors will have in three lifetimes, as Guarneschelli puts it. Golbitz is probably known best at this stage for signing up *One Minute Manager*. A vice president and senior editor, she has had a checkered career in publishing that began when she wrote fashion copy for Sears & Roebuck. Ten years ago she landed at Morrow by bringing her résumé in personally rather than sending it in as she had been asked to do. At Morrow she was given a chance to move from paperback publishing to hardcover, a transition some houses are unwilling to let you try.

"This is a great place," she says. "Before this I didn't stay any place longer than two years before I got bored. I've been here ten and have no plans to move." What she particularly appreciates about the company is that "it's easy to be straightforward here—if I have a problem, I can simply go to the person I'm having the problem with or who I think can solve it and lay it out straight," she says. "There's not the kind of politics around here where you have to watch over one shoulder for this and the other shoulder for that." Golbitz was a widow and the mother of an adolescent son (as well as a grown son) when she joined Morrow. On the infrequent occasions when she had to be absent due to his illness or an emergency, she never had a problem. "So much of the work can be taken with you wherever you are," she notes. "You have an assistant who can answer the phone and take care of everything. And you're at home and you've got a phone and are available, and you've got your work with you."

Nonetheless, frequent absences are frowned upon, as they are in all publishing houses, since an editor must be present to shepherd her books through the maze that begins when a proposal is first submitted through contract signing, working with the author, writing catalog and jacket copy, getting a good jacket, championing it to the publicity people, presenting it to the sales staff and seeing that it gets shipped on time.

Golbitz says it may even be easier for a woman than it is for a man at Morrow: "This has been an open company for women—you don't have to be a man to get ahead. Sherry is the perfect example of that."

She is speaking of Sherry Arden, former president and publisher of Morrow. Arden started with the company in 1968, when she was hired to set up a publicity department. The man who hired her was Larry Hughes, who was then running Morrow and is now chairman of the Hearst Trade Book Group. Arden says that she and Hughes connected right from the start, adding that he was the one who allowed her to learn and grow into her present job.

Arden moved from publicity to subsidiary rights and had that job a decade ago when paperback advances were setting new records and the money seemed to be limitless. A famous story about Arden's ability to make a deal is what happened at her first lunch as sub-rights director. She had Gael Greene's first, very sexy novel, *Blue Skies, No Candy*, up for grabs and mentioned it to her lunch partner, an editor at Warner Books. Arden suggested that a really creative thing to do would be to make a floor bid on the novel without seeing a word of it—that way he could undercut the competition on the spot. He thought for a minute. What did she want, he asked. Six figures, she said. Which ones, he asked. A hundred thousand, she said. Okay, he said.

"I got in the cab and thought, what have I done?" Arden remembers. "I've either done a wonderful thing or a terrible thing—maybe I should have said two hundred thousand. By the time I got back to the office I was hysterical. I thought it was terrific, but I ran into Larry's office and said, 'You may fire me for this,' and told him what I'd done. Larry said, 'That's fabulous.'"

Arden believes her ability to make on-the-spot decisions is one reason she has been so successful. "The decisions won't always be right but you've got to make a decision and get on with it because there are hundreds of decisions to make during the day. All the members of the staff are coming and asking what to do, and you can't be tortured about making a decision. If you can't do that, you can't be an executive."

A handful of major players in publishing have been playing musical chairs in the last year, moving from company to company, and Morrow was affected. Arden now heads her own imprint, Silver Arrow Books, at Morrow.

AVON   At Avon there is Rena Wolner, a *force majeure* in paperback publishing. Tiny (5'2"), fiery and feminine she made her name at Berkley Books, where she took an also-ran house in 1978 and turned it into a formidable paperback publisher with sales of more than $70 million before she left in 1984. At Avon she was called in to revitalize a company that had been floundering with a revolving door staff and an unclear focus as to what it wanted to be. It was also losing money to boot. When we met Wolner, she had been at Avon little more than a year and the red ink was just about to turn into black, by her own admission. That would be in the $45 million range, as Avon has a 5 or 6 percent share of the $876 million paperback market.

Although initially there had been some industry curiosity over how Arden and Wolner would get along, both said they had no trouble working together, as they do when Morrow and Avon put together a hard-soft deal, in which the hardcover and paperback rights are part of the same package. To date the most famous deal involving Morrow and Avon is the $5 million purchase of James Clavell's *Whirlwind*. "I happen to love working with Sherry, but I don't think about her being a woman," Wolner says.

Wolner is in her early forties and old enough to remember when she had to prove to men that she could perform as well as they could and that the stereotypical ideas they had about female executives weren't necessarily true. "I didn't have to be bitchy or whatever to make progress," she says. "I'm sensitive to making men feel they don't have to act any differently toward me because I'm a woman executive."

Wolner says she was attracted to Hearst primarily because of Larry Hughes and his long-standing mentor relationship with Sherry Arden, whom she's known for years. "What I knew about Hearst is that—male or female—they place a very specific value on talent. If there wasn't a willingness to do this throughout the entire organization, I don't think I would be here, but that's the case. The job is difficult and demanding, but it's giving me what I need in terms of rewards and fulfillment. I don't think about the fact that I'm a woman. I just know this is the right place for me right now."

Wolner thinks that publishing itself—not just at Hearst—is a terrific industry for women. Many of the most talented line editors have been women, and today there are many important female editors who dispense huge advances and command respect. In the last few years, women have made great strides on the publishing side and have assumed positions of corporate power. One possible reason for their rise is that the business is basically entrepreneurial: you sign up the best-sellers, or edit them, or sell the subsidiary rights (paperback sales or magazine excerptions), and you get the credit. The only review that counts is the bottom line.

"Women have shown that they can do it," says Wolner. "There are lots of success stories out there. I'm just one of them." Wolner adds that women don't make it to the top in publishing and then disappear, as they sometimes do in other industries where they may be promoted without solid grounding or a long list of successes behind them. "You're as good as your entire body of work," she says. "Once you've been put in a high place, it takes a lot to knock you out. And unlike in the film industry, there isn't a lot of female burnout in this job. It's constantly challenging."

As president and publisher, she's put together a staff that places no emphasis on sex; seven of the top 13 people in the company are women. The editor in chief is a woman, Susanne Jaffe, and so is the vice president in charge of sales, Amy Rhodes, a job usually held by a man. "Working for a woman is not significantly different than working for a man," says Rhodes, "except that I might tend to indulge in more emotional behavior. And there are times I'm not sure that's a particularly good habit to get into."

The atmosphere at Avon is not dissimilar to the casual, informal style of Morrow. "We look like we're having fun," comments Rhodes. "We are not stiff here at all. It really is a loose environment but with a lot of people who care."

When the group from Avon goes calling on clients such as Walden and Dalton, major bookstore chains, it's a quartet of Avon ladies who show up to make the biannual presentation: Wolner, Jaffe, Linda Quinton, the sales manager for the chains, and Rhodes. "We make jokes, and we aren't pompous and heavy," Rhodes remarks. "We take a low-key approach and wow them with our intelligence and our logic. The accounts respond very well. But we have to be the only publisher who shows up all female."

HERMAN MILLER

MAKER OF THE CLASSIEST OFFICE FURNITURE IN AMERICA

▲ EMPLOYEES: 3,342; more than a third are women.

▲ SALES: $574 million in 1986—87; net income was $33.3 million, down from $37.8 million in 1985—86.

▲ Herman Miller, innovative in design, is also a groundbreaker in management style. Since the 1950s, a participative management program in which workers and managers set goals together and then share in the gains has set the tone here. Annual bonuses are based on how performance exceeds goals and have averaged more than 10 percent for the last several years. Stock is given to all workers after a year's employment.

▲ Benefits, including medical and dental insurance and a pension plan, are generous. Maternity leave is the standard six weeks, but flexibility in parenting is excellent. A countrywide child care information and referral service, to which the company contracts, provides help for working parents.

▲ Although the company has a program on sexual harassment for managers and professionals, the issue is not particularly pressing here due to the religiously conservative area in which Herman Miller is located. When complaints arise—most likely in the plants—they are dealt with swiftly and severely.

▲ Herman Miller promotes from within whenever possible. Whereas in 1980 only one of the upper-level managers was a woman, six years later, five women (7 percent) were in this top crew. One is a vice president; the other four are directors. One member of the board of directors is a woman.

▲ To encourage promotion, jobs are posted and generous tuition reimbursement is available. Managers and professionals are permitted to work part-time, which is unusual in a manufacturing company.

▲ As good design is part of the company's credo, it is not surprising that the workplaces—including the plants—are clean and pleasant. On ambiance, Herman Miller rates a 10.

▲ Major employment centers: western Michigan: 2,700; Roswell, Ga.: 250; Irving, Tex.: 200; Irvine, Calif.: 125; Dayton, N.J.: 100; in addition, there are sales offices in 15 major cities throughout the United States. A major manufacturing site is scheduled to open near Sacramento, Calif., in early 1989. Subsidiaries are located throughout the world.

HERMAN MILLER, INC.
Zeeland, MI 49464
(616) 772-3300

They say you can tell a lot about a company by looking over its annual report. If the chairman is posed formally on the cover, he probably runs the place like an autocrat; if you don't see at least a few women, there probably aren't any who count. Herman Miller's 1985 annual report opens with 22 pages of inch-and-a-half-high full-body shots of employees: here's one standing on his hands, here's another with her dog, here are three ladies in an impromptu chorus line, everywhere there are smiling folks with their arms around each other, holding hands or otherwise clowning around. And here's the same kind of tiny etched photo of Max DePree, then president, CEO, chairman of the board, alongside two of Herman Miller's retiring directors. So what's going on here?

Simple. Everybody owns a piece of the action. "When you call us, you're always talking to an owner," notes Max—as he is called by everyone—in his letter to shareholders. Since the 1950s, this maker of office furniture has been organized along the principles of participative management, which in part means sharing in the company's profits through monthly bonuses based on performance against goals. Over the years, the bonuses have amounted to somewhere around 10 percent. Another aspect of the plan encourages suggestions on how to increase profits or improve the workplace. In 1983 more than a thousand changes were suggested. Those accepted and implemented saved the company over $7 million. Additionally, stock accrues to all employees who have worked for a year, and purchases are encouraged through options and a 15 percent discount off the going price. More than half of the employees buy stock through payroll deductions.

"People who make it here care about what they're doing and care about the company," comments Nancy Green, a senior communications manager. "Having employees own stock is one way of making sure that happens." Green is typical. After six years of employment, she holds 140 shares and, like most employees, has a well-honed sense of involvement in and loyalty to the company. "The attitude is, if you've got to work for a corporation, this is a good one to work for."

Herman Miller is not simply a maker of office chairs and sofas. Since the thirties, this company in western Michigan has attracted some of the best and brightest people in American design and played an important role in taking furniture design away from the traditional to the functional and modern. In 1946 George Nelson, who designed the company's stylized "M" logo, joined the firm and brought in Charles Eames and Isamu Noguchi. Eames's molded fiberglass shell chairs and molded plywood "potato chip" chairs became well known worldwide and today are hot collector's items, as is the Noguchi free-form birch-and-glass coffee table and all of Nelson's pieces. In 1956 Herman Miller began manufacturing the famous leather-and-plywood Eames chairs and ottomans, as well as a slinky chaise longue. Both are on permanent exhibit in the Museum of Modern Art's design collection, along with several pieces by Nelson. In total, Herman Miller has 35 pieces in the museum and has received numerous design accolades and awards.

In the past 20 years, the company has influenced the shape of business interiors with its open plan office with movable partitions that support work surfaces, storage units and furniture. The partitions work as part of an integrated system and can be moved and redesigned as needs change. The newest designs include partitions that are more like walls to give workers more privacy and a chair that is so user friendly that orthopedic specialists prescribe it to their patients with back problems. Herman Miller is a company that likes to think of itself as being on the cutting edge, and toward that goal spends 3.5 percent of its total income on design and research, an unheard-of amount in the industry. Miller designs are frequently knocked off by firms right in its own backyard, as most of the manufacturers of office furniture are clustered in and around Grand Rapids.

While Herman Miller is the undisputed design innovator, it ranks behind the industry giant, Steelcase, in sales and profits. But the focus here is not the bottom line alone. An environment where individuals are pushed to reach their potential, and the old-fashioned virtues of hard work and fairness—along with quality design and technical proficiency—color the corporate style as much as the desire for profits.

That approach is what attracted Vicki TenHaken, who was ready to leave business for academia to find the kinds of social values she believed in. "Being a child of the sixties, I didn't even know if I should be in business, and frankly, after five years at GE, I was a little bit disillusioned," she says. Because her husband had strong family and business ties to the area, picking up and moving elsewhere wasn't a real possibility. TenHaken was looking for both a corporate headquarters in the vicinity (to avoid having to turn down transfers to the home office) and a company she could respect. She remembered meeting people from Herman Miller in her senior year at nearby Hope College in a seminar and was impressed with what they had to say about their employer. "I thought I would give business one last chance —if I could work for a company that seemed to be progressive and oriented toward the social causes and approach to management I could identify with." That was in 1978.

She began in human resources, where she had experience, but was determined to "get my hands at more of the core of business," as she puts it, a move that proved not too difficult, since one of the company tenets is that the more you know about various areas of the business, the better manager you'll be. Consequently, moving from one division to another is encouraged. When she was nearly finished with her MBA, TenHaken saw a job posting for a corporate planning analyst. She was five months pregnant. The notice said that because of the highly competitive area in which the company was located and the sensitive nature of this job, personal and job stability were of the utmost importance. She had doubts that she would be a serious contender, but went after it anyway. Her pregnancy didn't seem to matter at all, and much to her surprise and delight she got the transfer and promotion. "It turned out to be one of the best things that ever happened to me, because our baby died at birth," she says evenly, "and had I not gotten that job . . . at least I knew that I was still in the job that I would have been in had I not gotten pregnant. That's one reason why Herman Miller—and that manager in particular—will always be special to me. Because in this case there was just no discrimination at all."*

She was in her early thirties when she was promoted to the director level, one of four women directors at the company. Although she is not, at this point, driven to make vice president by the time she is 40, she has no doubt "that would be a possibility if I decide that's something I want." TenHaken, petite, soft spoken and feminine, shatters the stereotype of the kind of

*After we interviewed TenHaken, she had a healthy baby girl.

woman who gets ahead in business. At Herman Miller, you clearly don't have to step over dead bodies or jockey your way through the bureaucracy to move up. Hard work and competence are rewarded. Some men and women in management do not have college degrees; a number have two-year associate degrees. Some who started out as administrative assistants (secretary is a word that is rarely used here) or in the plant are now directors. In general, TenHaken says, "You don't have to be so far superior to men in every aspect in order to make it at Herman Miller."

Although women are beginning to succeed in all operations of the company, not everyone believes sex bias does not exist. True, a regional sales manager whose territory takes in four states is a woman, as are a half dozen production supervisors, who oversee the men and women who work in manufacturing. Yet some women said unhesitatingly that it was easier for men to get ahead.

One woman who had previously worked in a large urban area on the East Coast and came to Michigan for personal reasons says that women definitely have to work harder than men to be promoted. "Sometimes men are given the vice presidency title, and everyone wonders why," she says. "There are never any questions when a woman gets a director or VP title." Working elsewhere had raised her expectations. "You get this mind set that anything is possible, and when I moved back here, I had this rude awakening. There weren't as many women moving into management. Everyone in New York thought it was tough, they just didn't know the way things were in other areas."

The region is undeniably ultraconservative, with a strict Dutch Reform Protestant populace. Traditional values are upheld to such a degree in Zeeland, a small town of under 5,000 where the corporate headquarters are located, and Holland, a somewhat bigger town where other facilities are located, that not too many years ago a group of churchmen from the Netherlands came to see how their American cousins were managing to keep to the straight and narrow in these rambunctious times.

For one thing, not a lot of mothers work. For another, single women without ties to the area (or even with them) fare better living in and around Grand Rapids, a half-hour drive away. Most of the women we met preferred to live some distance from the insulated Dutch colony, while couples attracted to the simple life may find it a pleasant place to raise a family. One divorced woman who doesn't go to church moved to Zeeland when she first joined the company but felt out of place, even though she had only moved from a working class town in central Michigan. "It was a terrible cultural shock," she says. She now resides in a resort town on Lake Michigan. "Now I have a good home life, and I take the Herman Millerisms in stride."

What might they be? For starters, no alcohol is served at company functions, including the annual picnic. And if you're a saleswoman in the field entertaining clients in, say, New York or Los Angeles, don't expect Herman Miller to pay for the client's drinks, let alone yours. Food, yes, booze, no. It wouldn't be a good idea to duck out of the Bible reading before the Thanksgiving holiday begins, and if, God forbid, you should set up housekeeping with your boyfriend without marriage, don't let it be known at the office—especially if he's a coworker. Someone is likely to speak to you about it.

Yet the emphasis on clean living is taken in stride by some relatively sophisticated women, both single and married, a number of whom lived and worked elsewhere before returning to home base or to their husband's home town. Quite possibly they don't object to Herman Miller's idiosyncrasies because they feel they're getting back a fair share for honest labor. It isn't the pay they rave about—since there is a suspicion they might be making more down the road at Steelcase—it's the ambiance, the civility, the feeling that their contribution counts. Everyone speaks fondly of Max, the 63-year-old chairman, and more than one woman said that he makes them feel almost like daughters. Incidentally, his office is not much larger than anyone else's—approximately the size of an average to small bedroom.

The workplaces are among the most inviting anywhere: not only all that great furniture, but plenty of natural light and lots of greenery. Along with hair spray and hand lotion, there's ivy in the loo and pots of violets on cafeteria tables. The food is of exceptionally high quality. It is subsidized by the company, which lured the chef of the best private club in the area to head the food service.

The ambiance extends to the factories. A few years ago, the journal of the American Institute of Architects featured a story about the seating plant in Holland, citing it as "A Splendid Workplace." An acrylic clerestory bathes the factory in daylight. Walking through another plant when she was applying for a job, Michelle Hunt knew right away something was different about Herman Miller.

"You could eat off the floor," she says. "There were flowers in the break area, the shipping department was full of light. When I was there, somebody was telling somebody else that they couldn't ship out a box because the label was on crooked. Oh, I said to myself—they had to set this up for me. Later, when I peeked into an auditorium, I found a woman in there lining up the chairs. She was making sure they were in *perfect* alignment—I asked myself, what kind of environment is this that can engender this kind of commitment?"

The answer stems largely from the participative management style that Herman Miller adopted in 1950, when the idea of cooperation between labor and management was considered a novelty at most corporations. The man responsible is D. J. DePree, father of the current chairman. D. J. had taken over the Michigan Star Furniture Company, after beginning there as an office worker 10 years earlier, and, with some hefty financial backing from his father-in-law, was able to buy the company in 1923. He promptly changed the name of the company to his father-in-law's. Although D. J. was a deeply religious man, he ran the company more or less traditionally.

Until the day the millwright died.

He was the man who ran the steam engine and boiler and kept the whole process flowing. When visiting the family after the funeral, D. J. learned that the man had been an accomplished poet. The fact that D. J. had thought of him only as a man who could fix things affected him profoundly, and he determined that he wanted to run a company that nourished the whole person.

Some changes were made and ethical values were espoused, but the major shift in how the company was run would not come until two decades later, when D. J. adopted a management program called the Scanlon Plan, named for the Michigan labor leader who originated it. Although it has been revised several times, the basic tenets remain: workers are given voice in management decisions, and performance is rewarded when it exceeds goals. Weekly or monthly meetings of work teams provide a forum for all employees to sound off about their complaints and make suggestions for increased productivity or improving the workplace, as well as learning what is going on throughout the company. "What this means is that anybody can offer suggestions to anyone about anything," notes Nancy Green. "If I want to influence something, the opportunity is there. Conversely, anyone can comment on my work. If you don't feel confident, you may have an ego problem with this." Additionally, peer group meetings, without the boss, let workers discuss problems—possibly with the boss—freely.

Participative management, however, is not democracy, a fact that employees tend to forget when a company decision is announced. Recently, when the company's Millcare division was made into a wholly owned subsidiary to handle the health- and science-related products Herman Miller makes, unhappy workers made a bit of a brouhaha. *They* didn't all agree— *they* wanted to work for Herman Miller, not Millcare, and why was this being shoved down their throats without their say-so? Many said that Herman Miller's greatest failing may be that it doesn't live up to all that it promises, but when questioned, all said that their expectations were high, perhaps unreasonably so. "You expect 10 times more than you get elsewhere," says Deb Keen, "and if you get eight times more, you're still better off, but that two times that's missing becomes disappointing."

"We tend to forget how good we have it here," adds Linda Powell, a senior manager in communications and graphics. "It would be hard for me to find another place to do the design work that I can get away with here—

the standards are high, and so is the level of creativity. You can try just about anything. You get the room to grow."

The opportunity to do things your way can be both scary and exciting, according to Marg Mojzak, a marketing manager responsible for training the salespeople. "My manager doesn't say, 'We need to do 25 things to be successful and they need to be done in this way and you do them,'" she says, "but rather, 'This is what we need to get done, how would you suggest we do it? You write an annual plan, you set objectives,' and then you're held responsible for meeting them."

This accountability for taking charge of your job filters down to the people who answer the phones, says Keen, a graphics production manager, who began with the company seven years ago. "It's not just, do your job and take orders," she says. "You're expected to think about what's important."

Not everyone fits into the Herman Miller style. Reorganization is practically a constant in the company, and if you're not flexible, you will have trouble. People are transferred and new bosses put in place just as soon as you're getting used to the old ones. Because of this, no defined career paths exist; you have to make your own. Mentors can be helpful, maybe—up to a point, as the constant reorganization dulls their influence. Self-motivation and self-direction are a must; so is a positive attitude. "You are not looked upon favorably if you complain a lot since we have such a good system to take care of problems," says Pat Walker, a financial planner. And if you can't make the system work for you, you probably won't be happy at Herman Miller.

In the late seventies the company went through a period of intense growth, with sales more than tripling in three years. Management types were recruited from other parts of the country, but the number crunchers who prefer the big city and the emphasis on the bottom line alone tended to part ways after a year or two. "If you are autocratic or don't believe in the full potential of human beings, you shouldn't work here, because in the long run you're going to be rubbing against the grain," Michelle Hunt observes. Her title is quite possibly the only such title in the world: vice president for people. Her job incorporates human resources, EEO, the participative management program and a holistic health wellness program, open to all employees. Spouses are welcome to come to the smoking cessation clinics and such, but they must pay a fee. Aerobics classes are held three times weekly, following both shifts at several plants. How many places in the country are you likely to find factory workers beginning their jumping jacks at 11:30 at night?

"Sure we work for profit," comments Hunt, "but how we get there is as important as the profit." What Hunt finds difficult is switching off corporate concerns when she leaves the office to pick up her youngsters at a day care center. "What concerns me is how consuming it is," she says. "Because you believe in something so strongly you don't tend to compartmentalize your life. So Herman Miller becomes a whole lot of you."

Other women spoke of the same dedication the company requires, particularly at high levels; some frankly said they had other interests in their lives, were comfortable in the jobs they had currently and didn't want a promotion, thank you, and they praised the company for finding a niche for them without penalizing them.

Whenever possible, part-time workers are accommodated. In accounting, for instance, job sharing is not unusual because it's easy to divvy up the work. There's been a part-time product manager, whose responsibility included only one product, a practice unheard of at most corporations. Penelope Pestle, a senior manager, was able to maintain her career climb while reducing the number of hours she worked to spend more time with her young children. Following the birth of her first child, she came back full-time for more than a year, but switched to part-time for the next six and a half years. "The responsiveness of a number of managers to my particular needs has been remarkable," she says. "They look at whether the business lends itself to that particular request, but there is really some openness in meeting your requirements." Pestle admits that while working part-time, she felt she had to prove herself and did more because she was a woman—and a mother.

Because at Herman Miller working mothers were scarce in 1978, when her first child was born, the general attitude she faced was that she wouldn't come back or, if she did, she wouldn't give all to her job. For Pestle, who had worked in the Detroit area before coming to western Michigan with her husband, that attitude only fueled her desire to prove everyone wrong. Now that working mothers are more common, how coworkers treat you depends largely on your own commitment and ambition.

What every new parent will get is a choice of a Herman Miller rocker—with a plaque inscribed with the baby's name—or a $100 savings bond. The typical problem-free leave is six paid weeks; workers can usually tack on their vacation time after that or request additional leave without pay. Whether or not their old job will be waiting is at the discretion of their manager, who usually tries to be accommodating.

Professional women who need time off to care for children or other emergencies usually face no difficulty, as most managers assume you're not trying to cheat the company. Some women say they often take work home on those days. "The attitude is not, 'What can I get away with?' but 'How can I stay with my sick kid and still do my job?'" comments Pat Walker. "If you think that way, it's not too hard."

All the ambiance and civility and down-home niceness—along with high standards—has not been at the expense of good business. However, after 13 consecutive years of earnings increases, profits have dropped its last two fiscal years. Yet in returns to shareholders in the last decade, Herman Miller ranked fourth among *Fortune* 500 companies, which is particularly unusual for a family-run business. Max's older brother, Hugh, ran the place before him, but earlier this year the CEO slot was given to someone from outside the family, Richard H. Ruch, a 32-year veteran of the company who is not expected to change policy much. Max expects to be an active chairman.

Women not born and bred in the area might feel out of sync with the conservative attitudes of western Michigan, parochial attitudes that naturally find their way into the corporate offices of Herman Miller. After all, the firm incorporates the values of the Dutch Reform populace.

But it's not at the expense of a progressive management style. Or an insistence on being at the forefront of design and technique. And anyway, the religious conservatism is tempered with a touch of whimsy.

Life-size papier-mâché workmen are sprinkled throughout the offices and factory areas of the company's facilities. They stand on girders with tools, appear to be painting walls, watering plants and sweeping rubble from under machinery. They were commissioned several years ago when Herman Miller was undergoing construction and the work never seemed to be done; now they serve as humorous reminders that work and enjoyment need not be mutually exclusive.

Which, in short, is the Herman Miller credo.

HEWITT ASSOCIATES

ONE OF THE LEADING CONSULTING FIRMS IN THE
EMPLOYEE BENEFIT AND COMPENSATION FIELD

▲ EMPLOYEES: 2,000; 60 percent are women.

▲ SALES: $152 million in fiscal 1987; $175+ million projected for 1988. Growth rate for the last 10 years has averaged 23 percent, with no year lower than 17 percent.

▲ Hewitt Associates makes no special effort to recruit and hire women—it doesn't need to. Approximately 50 percent of those interviewed and hired are female. Promotion is also without regard to sex. Programs for associates include tuition reimbursement, succession planning and management development.

▲ The company is committed to equality of pay for women. To correct possible past inequities, they examine what other companies are doing.

▲ In addition to standard maternity disability leave, Hewitt Associates allows limited leave without pay, negotiated in advance. This company pioneered the concept of flexible cafeteria-style benefits with their clients and implemented their own program in 1980. They also did research on adoption benefits and began their own program in 1982. Sensitivity to the needs of parents is abundantly evident. Hewitt Associates reimburses associates for baby-sitters while they are on overnight business trips, provides sick care in an area hospital when ordinary arrangements fall through because a child is sick, and have recently hired a "parents' helper," whose full-time job is to serve as problem solver for working parents.

▲ Of the 61 employees labeled upper management, 10 percent are women. In this privately held company, conventional titles do not apply, but upper management consists of regional managers, regional office managers and group managers. Hewitt Associates has 148 partners; 15 percent (22) are women. Of 12 partners named in 1987, four were women.

▲ Sexual harassment and sexual discrimination seem to be nonissues for this company. Should grievances occur, they are handled by informal procedure.

▲ Major employment centers: Lincolnshire, Ill.: 1,100; Rowayton, Conn.: 200; Santa Ana, Calif.: 150; Atlanta: 75; The Woodlands, Tex.: 70. The remainder of employees are scattered throughout the country in 18 offices.

HEWITT ASSOCIATES
100 Half Day Road
Lincolnshire, IL 60015
(312) 295-5000

Our initial survey came back from Hewitt Associates with a lot of spaces left blank, such as the number of women who held certain titles. "Titles do not apply" had been written in by Christine Seltz, one of Hewitt's partners and the person in charge of public relations. Had a study ever been done about sexual harassment? we asked. No. Did she favor issuing statements forbidding it? "?—Policy in place," Seltz wrote. "No reason to hype it." Does your company have an active recruitment program aimed at attracting women? "Gender isn't an issue—in the last three years, 50 percent of the candidates for professional positions have been women" and "Promotions not focused on women. Instead we look for candidates with greatest potential and fit with long-term goals."

In a letter, Seltz wrote that one of the company's goals is to provide a satisfying work experience, and that it takes great pains to develop people through rigorous testing, training, feedback, screening and evaluation. When a consideration for a promotion or change in responsibility arises, they have so much information about their associates that "gender" is "immaterial and irrelevant." We cheered and read on.

Seltz noted that Hewitt has recently hired someone to work as a "parents' helper," whose sole job is to assist parents—men, women, singles—to find the kind of child care resources they needed, whether that be a place to take a sick child for a few days, day care or an emergency overnight baby-sitter when someone is out of town on an unexpected business trip. The company also reimburses baby-sitting fees for all such overnight trips.

Hewitt Associates' home office, in the Chicago suburb of Lincolnshire, is situated in a woodsy, 43-acre setting on a road that curves around a man-made pond that was put in strictly for ambiance. It handily achieves its goal. The building is a cedar-sided three-story modern structure that slips quietly into the environment. With its floor-to-ceiling windows, sunlight fills the lobby on bright days. Walk through the halls and you'll notice trays of chocolate-covered doughnuts and other noshes next to the coffeepot. In the afternoon, cookies and soda usually replace the breakfast rolls; whatever, it's all free, as is the food in the cafeteria.

What strikes one immediately is how high everybody is on their company. They can't imagine a better place to work; they say in a matter-of-fact way that there is no sexual discrimination; sexual harassment is something they only know from previous employers or magazine articles. They speak well of each other. And everyone is polite and considerate. Roberta Fox, a consultant in the compensation group, says that what makes Hewitt special is its respect for its employees: "That permeates the whole atmosphere. Where I worked before, you were a number. Everyone was dispensable. Here you don't get that feeling. You are valuable and every person has a place and you all work together for the good of the company."

In fact, no one had anything bad to say about Hewitt. Zip. When pressed, someone in the discussion group made a joke about the parking—since some construction was under way when we were there, you had to park out in the far reaches of the lot as the construction workers got there early and took a number of places close to the building. But if you are working late, not atypical in a consulting firm, a night watchman escorts you to your car. Then somebody else jokingly grumbled that since they use clients' products whenever possible, the club soda in the lunchroom was not Perrier. Then somebody remarked about the free Tampax in the ladies' room—had we noticed? Hewitt is too good to be true, we said. We hoped that would get a rise out of someone. The women chuckled and said they thought we might get that idea. They had talked about it beforehand and tried to come up with some warts, but couldn't. It really *was* that good.

A former employee, whom we met while investigating another company, was equally enthusiastic about her former employer. "It's a real democratic place to work," she said. "It's great for men or women. Even though I was only a secretary, they make you feel valuable, like what you did mattered." She herself was no longer at the company because her husband had transferred to an area where Hewitt didn't have an office.

Partner Judy Whinfrey's enthusiasm is typical. Hired right after graduation from the University of Illinois in 1971 with a mathematics background, she said that during the interview she was so impressed with the company that she kept hearing herself say "Wow!" much to her chagrin. Although she's fuzzy about what was specifically said, she recalls that the interview was unlike those with other firms. "You can tell when people are enthusiastic, and I was being interviewed not by professional interviewers, but people who actually did the work." The main question associates consider when interviewing, she said, was whether or not the interviewer would want to be working with that person at 9:00 at night.

The acronym for the kind of people Hewitt hires is SWANs, which stands for Smart, hard-Working, Ambitious and Nice. Superstar types who work best alone and don't mind stepping over others need not apply. MBAs from fancy schools usually aren't the right fit, possibly because they have been trained to be more aggressive than is the Hewitt style or they expect to make more money more quickly than one will at Hewitt.

Although partners here make what partners make at Big Eight accounting firms, between $150,000 and $200,000, and probably near the high end of that, salary is not usually a reason an individual joins Hewitt, nor is it why he or she stays. Salary grades are extremely broad; people are paid their worth in the marketplace. People who progress rapidly will find their salary keeps pace. Starting salaries for people with a mathematics background coming right from college will range from $28,000 to $35,000, depending on how many of the 10 required actuarial exams they have passed.

Many apply but few are chosen. For each 150 jobs, it's likely that a few thousand will be interviewed, and approximately half those positions will be for new college hires. Hewitt recruits at 90 schools throughout the country, with a heavy emphasis on the Midwest. The largest block of new hires is programmers and actuaries, but people with skills in writing, research, accounting, law and investment services could also find a home here. The remaining positions are filled by people with a few years' experience, and almost no one is hired at a very high level. Hewitt likes to grow its own; they've found it works best. People who are used to a political atmosphere where you send lots of memos and carbon-copy 20 people to let them know what you're doing do not fit in. Coworkers question why they send so many memos: Whom are they trying to impress? Whom do they need to impress? New hires at whatever level represent mostly growth, as the annual turnover is an incredibly low 7 percent, half the national average.

But Hewitt has a reputation as more than a wonderful place to work. The clients include over 70 percent of the *Fortune* 500 companies plus many banks, insurance companies, retailers, hospitals, utilities, transportation companies and industrial firms of all sizes, including a goodly number of the companies profiled here. The client list was hovering around the 2,000 mark when we visited in the spring of 1987, and growth for the year was projected at 19 percent. According to *Business Insurance*, Hewitt Associates achieved the greatest percentage of revenue growth among benefit consulting firms in 1986 without any acquisitions. Regardless of how rapid its growth, Hewitt doesn't take any clients it doesn't like or doesn't think are ethical and, since the majority of its work is for corporations, does not take unions as clients. If nice is the kind of person they hire, it follows that ethical is the kind of company that results.

And loyal is what workers become. It's not hard to understand, given what Hewitt gives back to its people—besides the freebies at home base, there's flexibility when you want to move around the country. In Whinfrey's case, when she wanted to move to California, she was able to transfer to the Los Angeles office; when she was ready to come back to the Midwest, she moved into the downtown Chicago office. Moves like hers are not exceptional. Because associates (no one ever says the word "employee" here) get extensive training, the company wants to hang on to them if at all possible —and it often can because its regional offices are located in 23 cities. If a spouse is being transferred to a city where there isn't one, it could be that it's a spot where Hewitt was looking to open a new branch anyway. If that's not the case, the company goes so far as to try to find a new job for the spouse who is being transferred, a job in a location where the Hewitt associate can stay within the firm. Clients will be asked if they have any openings, or the spouse might be hired into Hewitt itself, if he or she passes the fine filter of the interview process.

And the interviewing is rigorous. Cynthia Straub, who joined Hewitt early in 1987, had two years of experience at a public relations firm following graduation from Northwestern University. Her interviews lasted three days. Not only did she meet with five people, she spent a half day being evaluated by a psychologist, whose evaluation is taken into account but is not the final word. "They want to make sure that the people you are going to work with like you and you're going to like them," she says, echoing Whinfrey's words.

The kind of kinship this breeds lends itself to stories like the ones Susan Koralik tells. Koralik is a single woman who adopted a son in 1987. Not only did she have the full support of everyone; the baby shower given for her at the home office was well attended by the men. "I don't know who bought them—the men or their wives—but the guys were there with their little outfits for the baby." She also received a $2,500 adoption benefit and took a month off to settle in with baby Adam.

Then there was the time she was hospitalized for surgery. A birthday party was arranged in the hospital. "They wheeled me into the doctor's lounge, and there were 40 people standing around at a party for me. And when I needed blood, Pete [Friedes, the chief executive] went down to the lunchroom and said, 'Who has A positive blood?' and they sent a whole van of people." Since Koralik radiated a pleasant disposition, it seemed natural that her fellow workers would be caring. But then, her geniality did not stand alone here.

Koralik's friendliness does not detract from her strong will. She vividly recalls the ruckus she created when she was made account manager, the first woman to be so promoted. Before that, she had been an analyst in the New York office, writing reports and discussion guides, and before that, she had been the research department in the Illinois office, joining the company shortly after graduating from Miami University in Oxford, Ohio. At the time, the company had something like 175 employees; growth since then has been tenfold.

It was at a meeting in 1975 in Illinois that Koralik decided it was time for her to become an account manager, regardless of the fact that no women were. At the meeting, it was announced that Judy Whinfrey would be going to California and "doing what *Susie* is doing in New York." It was also announced that several young men were going to regional offices as account managers, young men with less experience and fewer years than either Judy or Susie. During a break, Koralik approached the man who was running the meeting and asked him what he meant by singling her and Judy out from the men. "It sounds like we're not going to be doing the same things that the men are doing," she told him.

"But you aren't going to be doing the same things," he answered. "They are going to be account managers and you and Judy aren't."

"Wrong," Ms. Koralik recalls saying, now amused by her boldness. "I am going to be an account manager," she told him.

She remembers his exact words: "But *Susie*, girls can't be account managers."

She didn't press further that day, but when she got back to New York, she and her boss, Tom Paine, always a strong supporter of women, discussed the matter, and he told her to "go and arm wrestle with the guy."

When he came to New York, Koralik was ready. "I kept insisting," she says with a wry smile, "and giving logical reasons why I could do the job, and he finally agreed that Judy and I could try. I'll mention his name—Tom Wood—because he became one of my strongest supporters. At the end, he said, 'Susan, you've got to understand that I've had the feelings I've got for years, and it's going to take time for me to change.'"

Change he did. When Koralik was proposed as manager of the New York City office, whose billings of more than $20 million make it the largest regional office, she says Tom Wood backed her all the way. She spends about a quarter of her time managing people and the rest of the time servicing clients. No one, not even Pete Friedes, does not have some direct client contact. The New York office has two men on the nine-member support staff, five female consultants (including herself) and nine male consultants. "Sex has nothing to do with it," she says. "People get promoted on pure qualification." Even for partner? "Even for partner." As we go to press, Hewitt Associates has 148 partners, and 22 are women. Between the time we did our interviews and we went to press, the percentage of women increased, and it is a sure bet that it will grow as women move up the pipeline. While Koralik and others combine partnership and motherhood, not all mothers want to put in the effort and time required to make partner. The women stress that this is their choice, not the company's, as having children does not ipso facto put you out of the running.

Moving up does mean working long hours. Yet the women insist that the work isn't drudgery and that they enjoy it. But unlike many firms, it isn't the kind of place where you have to show your face on weekends even if you don't have any work to do. Some women said if weekend work is required, they came in really early—5:30 A.M. or so—on Saturday and are gone by 10 A.M. to have the rest of the weekend free. They might not even run into anyone who would be impressed with their dedication.

What impressed us was the team spirit. No one is too busy to help someone else. New associates learning the rules find this particularly gratifying, and seasoned partners realize what a time-saver this is. As Susan Koralik says, "If you are asked to do a report on, say, the fate of the Laplanders, you can send out an all-points bulletin and ask if anybody's done it before. And you'll get it."

All of this bonhomie is why Judy Whinfrey retains her "Wow!" attitude about her company. "I love my firm," she says. "The work is constantly challenging." She explains that each assignment calls for separate work groups, so that she might be working with six or so people on one project and then with an entirely different set of people on another. "The clients add another set of dynamics," she adds. "They can range from extroverts like myself to shy types. You get all types, and you have to remember that they have somebody breathing down their necks."

Presumably those heavy breathers are executives who are looking to cut costs, as benefits represent a large portion of the compensation costs of any company. In the sixties, benefits expanded with the economy. Foreign competition and new tax laws have necessitated changes, sometimes constriction. Another factor is that a majority of employees are no longer the sole breadwinners, each with 2.2 children. To suit the diversity of employees, benefits packages across the land are being redesigned. Consequently, benefits consulting is a hot area and anything but stodgy. Flexible benefits, which Hewitt pioneered back in the sixties, allow an individual to choose various options from a comprehensive package, and we've noted which companies among those included here have them. A typical package might be designed so that one person could have an annual checkup, another a child care option. Surprisingly, although life at Hewitt seems positively sybaritic, Hewitt's benefits package, workers say, is not all that spectacular compared to some of the companies they work for. But certainly the benefits are good enough to squelch complaints before they are uttered.

What else isn't heard are sexist comments. As might be expected, women have no trouble being taken seriously at meetings, and should someone forget that and refer only to "he" or "him" when discussing associates or partners, there will be a lot of throat clearing until the message hits home. "It's like you're talking to your brother—sometimes he slips up, but you can kid him about it," says Whinfrey.

While good feelings and team spirit abound, there is no doubt in anyone's mind that their leader, Pete Friedes, is indeed their leader and, you could say, pledge chairman of this fraternity. He manages by consensus and is an integral part of the day-to-day operation, not someone rarely seen. New associates meet him at informal orientation sessions. Young and personable, Friedes has few of the power trappings that people in charge often favor. His office is no larger than anyone else's, the size of a maid's room in an old New York apartment (tiny) and furnished with decidedly plain (Spartan) tables and chairs. The areas clients see—the grounds, the conference rooms, the lobby—are something else again. They are handsomely decorated to the point of luxury.

This is, after all, a company whose product is service to the client.

Should a client call during someone's half-hour lunch break (yes, we said half hour), the call will be forwarded to the cafeteria. Clients can be in different time zones, it was explained matter-of-factly, and Hewitt people need to be available when the client summons. By the same token, dress is determined by how the client expects their benefits consultants to dress, and that means natty business attire. Flamboyant outfits should be saved for parties. Flashy dressers won't be taken to client meetings until they tone down, and should you need coaching, someone is likely to help you understand what goes and what doesn't. Even pale pink shirts on the men were suspect until clients began showing up in them. While dress is fashionable, at the cutting edge of fashion it's not. With all the concern for the client, it's no wonder that Hewitt Associates has the reputation for service that it does and such a healthy chunk of the *Fortune* 500 companies as clients, even though Hewitt ranks fifth in size in its field.

So, what's Pete Friedes like? How did he get to be such an egalitarian fellow? Does all the emphasis on niceness make for a certain lack of aggressiveness among employees? Could this sometimes hurt?

In answer to the last question, Friedes said that the problem he has noticed is that people are reluctant to speak their minds at a meeting—lest they hurt somebody's feelings—when they don't agree with a proposal. Consequently, meetings often don't result in conclusive decisions. Politeness doesn't breed action when it comes to decisions.

As for how he came to run such a gender-blind company, Friedes said he had more or less inherited it, since the man who started the company in 1940, the late Ted Hewitt, didn't feel that women couldn't do the work. In fact, Rosemary Tagge, who joined the company in 1952 as a mailroom clerk, eventually progressed to become Hewitt's secretary, and, with one thing leading to another, in time she was running all of the company's support services. Lest you think she never got her due, Tagge became the first female partner in 1970.

When Friedes took over that same year as managing partner at the tender age of 30, he saw no reason to change the policy. And as more women began working, more of them began finding jobs at Hewitt.

Friedes says he became sensitive to the needs of working women, and single mothers in particular, because his mother was widowed when he was 11 and worked as a secretary to make ends meet. When he was growing up, he adds, his best friends were women, and he was always comfortable around women. "I find women more interesting than most men," he says, a comment not frequently heard from the heads of successful companies. "At a cocktail party, they are more interesting to discuss things with because they will talk about their feelings and you can get a little deeper than you can with most men. Most men are always trying to preen themselves and trying to show off. They are always on stage, always competitive. I personally have found it easier to get along with women."

As we said, he's our kind of guy. And Hewitt is certainly our kind of place.

HEWLETT-PACKARD

AN ELECTRONICS COMPANY KNOWN FOR ITS HIGH-QUALITY PRODUCTS, MAINLY ELECTRONIC TEST EQUIPMENT AND COMPUTERS

▲ EMPLOYEES: 53,000 (in the United States); more than 40 percent are women.

▲ SALES: $7.1 billion; net earnings are $516 million.

▲ Hewlett-Packard actively recruits women, particularly those with engineering backgrounds.

▲ Although they've issued firm statements on sexual discrimination and sexual harassment, such complaints are handled via an "open door policy," which women report is less than effective. Women who do well here take care of problems themselves; other women have been known to leave rather than attempt to complain. A short program on sexual harassment is part of the orientation process for all employees.

▲ The percentages of women in middle management seem to be increasing particularly well in marketing and are even advancing in R&D and manufacturing. Of 35 general managers, three are women; at other companies, their title might be division president, putting the percentage of women in the very highest ranks of management (51 individuals) at an impressive 6 percent. Of 27 corporate officers, one is a woman. One member of the board of directors is a woman. Since training is done within the individual HP entities, which number around 100, figures for women in management training programs were not available.

▲ Hewlett-Packard offers flexible working hours and permits sick leave for family illness. Some divisions offer a resource referral directory for child care services, while others do not. The company reports that it is considering a number of child care alternatives. On a case-by-case basis, managers and professionals can arrange part-time work.

▲ Overall, this company wins kudos in the press for its egalitarian treatment of all employees. With three appointments of women to general manager positions in the last few years, it appears that well-educated, talented women are able to break through the ranks into senior management.

▲ Major employment centers: northern California: 22,000; Colorado Springs, Fort Collins and Loveland, Colo.: 7,000; manufacturing plants in Idaho, Massachusetts, Oregon, Pennsylvania, Washington.

HEWLETT- PACKARD
3000 Hanover Street
Palo Alto, CA 94303
(415) 857-1501

When Sara Dickinson was getting her engineering degree from the University of Illinois in 1976, she had no trouble setting up interviews. A number of companies were eager to talk to her. The problem was the interviews themselves. Except for one, the recruiters didn't ask about Dickinson's ability. "Hewlett-Packard was the only company that gave me a technical interview," she says. "Every other recruiter from Bell Labs to Texas Instruments told me about the weather and the apartment prices and how soon I could get a credit line to buy a car. They must have wanted me for some quota, because they certainly didn't know how good I was or wasn't technically. HP dragged me across the coals for ten hours straight." Dickinson was given a transistor circuit and asked to analyze it.

It was the toughness of the interview that made her decide on Hewlett-Packard: "I knew they were looking for an engineer and not just a token, and they offered me a real job. I was afraid the other companies would just give me a desk to shuffle papers on. And how are you going to prove yourself if you don't have a meaningful challenge? If you don't have a circuit to design, how can you prove you are a good circuit designer?"

Yet after Dickinson joined the company, she saw the recruiter's summary: "Pretty good for a girl," it read.

Damn straight.

In the decade she's been at HP, Dickinson, currently an R and D laboratory manager, has been promoted an average of every two years. To prove that she had the right stuff—even though she was a girl—Dickinson recalls that it was not uncommon to work two all-nighters a week for the first couple of years. "I had to prove that I could handle my share of the load," she says. "I was the only female engineer at my level—what's that saying? 'A woman has to work twice as hard to be considered half as good?' I felt I was in that role." Dickinson now works an average of 50 hours a week, down from her original 80.

Because of Dickinson and others like her, women are making progress at HP. In the lab where Dickinson was once the only woman, women now make up 20 percent of the engineering staff. Some 50 women are currently ranked as functional managers or above. True, approximately half of them are in the personnel department, long a women's ghetto, but the remainder are making inroads in nontraditional areas, such as operations, R and D, manufacturing and general field management. In marketing, 21 percent of all managers are women. Since 1986, three women have been appointed to general manager of major divisions. One of them, Nancy Anderson, was promoted while she was on maternity leave. She now heads the division that is responsible for the company's best-known computer system, the HP 3000; the two other women head divisions in key areas of the computer industry—networking and remarketing.

But.

Hewlett-Packard is a vast, decentralized company with divisions throughout the United States and the world. And while the company is constantly being stroked as a great place to work, a place that pioneered in amenities such as flexitime and no layoffs, a woman's experience here apparently hinges on what division she works for and who heads it up. This is a company with a reputation for some of the best engineering in the world, remember, a company that stresses that its electronic testing instruments and computers are made by engineers for engineers. Add it up, and you're going to get a macho mind-set that's dubious about the skills and abilities of any engineer wearing a skirt, no matter what the official policy is.

Due to the disparate experiences of the women at HP, we found divided opinions over HP as an employer. Some women feel that HP is one hell of a place to work. Women in their twenties and thirties who haven't topped out yet and women with close connections to corporate were especially keen on their company.

Mei-Lin Cheng, a manager in corporate administrative systems, says, "They are very fair. If you can do a good job, you will get it. I can't think of any incident that made me suspect that I didn't get something because I'm female, or that there were any second thoughts about me because of my sex." In fact, it was Cheng who anticipated problems that never materialized. When she was offered the job of information systems manager for intercontinental operations a few years back, she was wary of how the Latin American managers, all men, would take to reporting to her, not only a woman, but a *foreign* woman, as she points out. Cheng is Malaysian. "I asked my boss to call the managers in the Latin American countries to find out if they were going to be supportive of me." One doesn't know how the issue was presented to them, but the promotion went through without a hitch—or a problem thereafter.

And unlike women at other companies who feel it's necessary to practically have their babies in the parking lot to stay on the fast track, Cheng stayed home for up to three months when her three children were born, combining disability leave (six weeks) and vacation time carried over from a previous year. She feels that having babies didn't slow her down in the least.

Barbara Kommer, a public affairs manager in Seattle, is equally enthusiastic: "I've never run into sex stereotyping here. I've never run into anybody saying, 'Well, you can't do that,' or 'That's not an area you should be involved in.' If you've got an interest and it makes sense for the organization, it's likely you are going to have a go at it if you've got the energy." In her mid-thirties, Kommer transferred from headquarters in Palo Alto, where she handled investor communications. Her new job gives her exposure to operations, background she feels she needs to advance at HP. Her spouse, who she says is not as career oriented as she, is the one who packs up and follows when she takes a new job or accepts a transfer.

Kommer gives the company high marks for creating an atmosphere free of snide put-downs, the kind she faced at previous employers. "What you don't hear around here are comments like, 'It's so simple even Barbara can do it, ha, ha, ha'... I have not personally encountered any sex discrimination here—I can say that flat out because I had a lot of it at other places."

And Ann Baskins, an attorney who's been with HP since 1982, says that any kidding directed at her is a sign that she's accepted as part of the team, and she kids the guys right back, even when a light goes on in her head and she questions whether she should be offended. Baskins is apparently right in her assumptions, since the guys she works with make sure she isn't cut out of important conversations.

During long negotiations with another corporation over a joint venture, Baskins and three men from HP met for up to 14 hours a day. "We'd have breaks where you go to the bathroom, and finally one of the guys said, 'You've got to come in here, we're getting things done and we're not being fully represented by counsel,'" Baskins recalls. "They decided that the conversation about the deal stopped when we walked out of the room."

All well and good. But when we spoke to women not so close to corporate, or women somewhat older who felt they were bumping up against a glass ceiling—beyond which women wouldn't make it—we got a different story. A senior manager blew a chill wind into the good news we were hearing. "You ask yourself what is the next step, and the answer often is, the next step is to look elsewhere," she says, adding that women who have left the company have gotten the kinds of jobs they were denied at HP elsewhere in Silicon Valley.

If they stay, women often transfer to staff positions or to outlying areas and divisions. "You see all these women starting up now, but gee, it's not like we had no one in the past," she says. "We had women in these positions before."

Another woman said that she's seen jobs reclassified and downgraded when a woman got them, even in the personnel department, where women have made the greatest push at HP. What it all boils down to is, how progressive is the person who runs your division? "One bad manager can ruin a whole lot of people's lives," says one woman. And some of those people are going to be women.

Yet because Hewlett-Packard has always fostered a spirit of we're-in-this-together, there isn't a great division between "them" and "us." Management talks to workers, and listens. HP's San Diego division formed a task force on women's concerns, surveying all the women in the division. The findings were presented to both division leaders and corporate management, and although corporate didn't officially respond, shortly thereafter corporate issued a statement on child care, a concern that only some divisions had dealt with. Some divisions, for instance, had resource and referral services; others had no child care assistance at all. The corporate statement mandated that all divisions appoint someone to look into the matter and begin to deal with it as a people problem, both to make life easier for HP's employees and to be able to attract the most qualified workers. A review of what all facilities are doing is called for in a year. But the general feeling is summed up by one woman: "HP doesn't do anything for the working mother. You figure it out yourself."

And while company women say that overall they don't believe salary differentials exist, one female manager says that although she compared them in her division and found no male/female discrepancy, she also discovered she had been hired at $75 a month lower than her male peers hired at the same level and with the same background. However, all salaries are subject to market whims. What's hot today may not be tomorrow. Right now the right ticket is software; yesterday it was hardware.

As with nearly everything else, we heard opinions on both sides of the fence regarding sexual harassment. Some say flat out that the corporate culture squashes it; not so, say other women, adding that no effective way to deal with it exists. Ostensibly, each employee has a liaison person to whom she can take a grievance, including sexual harassment, and that person can take it up with the employee's boss. In reality, however, the liaison usually doesn't have adequate status to speak up to the boss; besides, it might be his or her boss that's the offender. The boss ends up hearing a watered-down version of the complaint. When there are sexual harassment grievances, one woman remarks, "It ends up one guy talking to another guy, and if he denies it, that's that." She knew of one case where a woman left rather than take it higher. And one of the senior women we spoke to agreed that's how she would handle it herself: she would leave. "Top management conduct themselves very well, not only in what they say but how they act," she says. "But that doesn't filter down to the bottom level." Once again, it's the division manager who calls the shots.

Hewlett-Packard has always been a loosely knit federation of highly autonomous production divisions, almost since the beginning, when it was started by William Hewlett and David Packard in Packard's garage in 1939. An entrepreneurial spirit and "management by walking around" has been credited for much of the company's success—and its reputation as a great place to work. HP started out making electronic testing instruments and became known as a quality operation selling terrific customer service along with its products.

Computers and software accounted for a large share of HP's $7.1 billion revenues in 1986, and a slump in that business in the early eighties didn't spare HP. Instead of layoffs, workers took 10 percent pay cuts, supposedly taking a day off every other week. The policy went all the way up the line to company president John Young. Most executives came in on their days off anyway. Manufacturing workers were offered early retirement. The company reorganized somewhat, bringing more unity to both the structure and the product line. HP's ace in the hole is a new technology that speeds up computer function, but without much additional cost. The pay cuts are over, and the future looks healthy.

Overall, there's not a lot of business done over drinks or during after-hours socializing. Maybe it's because more people are jogging five kilometers after work than are belting back Johnny Walker Black. But HP is in Silicon Valley, and the place does have the Foothills Tennis and Swimming Club and the University Club up the road. The story that gladdens the hearts of HP women is the one about a group of employees, including a woman, who stopped at the University Club after work one day. They went up to the bar. The men were served, but when the woman gave her order, she was told that she couldn't drink at the bar. William Hewlett, who's now vice chairman of the board, heard the story and fired off a letter protesting the policy. The policy changed. Now women need not be escorted by men if they want to go to the club. Power and money carry a big stick.

The women who appear to be the most comfortable at Hewlett-Packard have found hard work and humor their best offense in the company of engineers. Saying, "It's a man's prerogative to change his mind" or "Just like a man to get emotional" apparently goes a long way in squelching the obverse. One woman said that when she was discussing wage cuts with a manager, a woman's name came up. "Oh, we don't want to cut her," she recalls the man said, "She's so cute and has great legs." The woman said nothing. Later, when a certain man's name came up, the woman said, "Oh, we don't want to cut him. He's so well hung." The man didn't comment either. Next case.

It's not that Hewlett-Packard is a bad place for women to work. By and large, it's a good place for people. But here, perhaps because its reputation as a good employer is untarnished, expectations run high. "Time is running out on the argument that women with the right credits haven't been around long enough to qualify for the major slots." The quote comes from a 1985 issue of HP's employee magazine. It's an encouraging sign. And so are the three female general managers.

Pretty good for an engineering company.

HOME BOX OFFICE

THE LARGEST PAY-TV SERVICE IN THE UNITED STATES

▲ EMPLOYEES: 1,517; 56 percent are women.

▲ SALES: $886 million. In 1986 HBO was the primary business of Time Inc.'s programming operations, which reported income from operating of $111 million, a drop of 8 percent from 1985.

▲ HBO is actively concerned about recruiting and hiring women. The entertainment industry has historically attracted women, and HBO is no exception.

▲ HBO's record of promoting women is excellent: 24 of its 89 upper management employees are women, including two senior vice presidents, 22 vice presidents and 38 directors. The five-member executive committee is all men, and the CEO's direct report is a woman. One of the 18 members of the board of directors at Time Inc.—HBO's parent company—is a woman.

▲ A study was done on sexual harassment, and strong written statements have been issued.

▲ HBO interprets its parent company's liberal benefits in its own style. The company is particularly sensitive to parenting needs. In addition to standard paid disability, parents can take up to six months' unpaid leave with position guaranteed on return. (It used to be a year—that changed when HBO experienced its own personal baby boom.) Flexibility is the rule rather than the exception—working hours, part-time work, sick leave for family illness. The company has a dependent care tax advantage program consisting of pretax dollar deductions. Medical benefits are excellent, and the company has an active health center and an Employee Assistance Program.

▲ Major employment centers: New York City: 1,200; Hauppauge, N.Y.: 100; Los Angeles: 100. Regional sales offices are in Philadelphia, Atlanta, Chicago, Dallas, Denver, San Francisco and Kansas City.

HOME BOX OFFICE, INC.
1100 Avenue of the Americas
New York, NY 10036
(212) 512-1000

You'd think that at a company still in its teens and with the average age of its employees in their thirties, and a CEO in his early forties, an old boy network at the top would be as unlikely as Tina Turner being cast as Mother Teresa.

You would be wrong.

The old boy network at Home Box Office didn't happen by design, but it's there. As far as the women can see, they are not dealing with a bunch of die-hard chauvinists; for the most part, quite the opposite. But just as fraternities and sororities perpetuate a certain sameness, so usually does the clique of people running a corporation. If white males are running the place, the odds are that they will surround themselves with other white males, unless they make an effort not to. Thus, while no one was watching, did an old boy network quietly slide into place at Home Box Office.

While the women at HBO overall were positive and enthusiastic about their company (more about that later), they have no illusions: at the top, it's a boys' club. The five-member executive committee is all men, and all of those who report directly to the CEO, save one, are men. Bridget Potter, senior vice president of original programming, is the exception. The other female senior vice president, Shelly Fischel, is head of human resources. HBO women wonder if they are really being groomed for the top jobs. On paper, HBO looks pretty good. Of 89 people considered senior management, 23 are women. In addition to the two senior VPs, 21 other women are vice presidents. But they question if they are given the same kinds of responsibilities as the men. They don't think so. If one of the top guys left, would a woman get the job? Or would somebody from the outside—most likely a man—be brought in? Would the thinking be, we don't have any women ready yet? In sales, for instance, the lower ranks are largely women, but promotions don't seem to be passed out purely on the basis of performance, and women sometimes have trouble justifying them. "There are many of us trapped at the manager-director level," says one woman, "and we're really frustrated. They pass over women when a job's open, and then later they say, 'We've got to promote a woman.' It sounds as if they are being nice, but thanks for nothing. It's quite demeaning. Why can't they just put the best person in the job?"

Yet some areas of the company get very high marks. Marketing had a turnaround in 1986, and several promotions went to women. In the legal department, assignments are passed out purely on capability, and bright young women who defected from prestigious old-line—and chauvinistic—law firms are given a chance to shine here. That's what happened to Shelly Fischel, who made Law Review at Columbia University, but correctly read the no-win situation for females at Sullivan & Cromwell, one of the nation's leading law firms. She got out in 1979. Within six months at HBO, she was assigned to an antitrust case that, if the company lost, could have severely hampered the pay-cable business. The movie studios were banding together to deny movies to pay-TV networks like HBO. "Within seven months I had credibility, and within a year we had won the case and won it very big," she says, "and so I kept getting good stuff to work on." Her pregnancy didn't impede her or put off her boss, not even the edema that plagued her. "I conducted a lot of meetings lying down," she says. "We'd have conference calls with me lying on my boss's couch or with my feet up. As long as it didn't bother me, it didn't bother him."

Although Fischel wasn't sure that she wanted to leave the legal department and take the human resources job in 1984, she did because she knew it was important to be considered a team player, and fortunately she had a boss who told her so. Now she loves the job.

Part of the reason she likes it is that it puts her in a place where she can deflect some of the silent sexism that rears its head when boys will be boys. In 1986–87 she and a few other high-ranking women began holding forums of women throughout the company to find out what they thought was going wrong. That old glass ceiling is what the women talked about. "There is a real question in many women's minds whether they are being given the same decision-making authority as a man with a similar job and title," remarks vice president Linda Frakenbach, one of the women who put the forums together. "Many women feel they have less input when it comes to making line decisions."

That the forum came about as a grass roots movement from the women themselves is indicative of the company. Everybody seems young—34 appears to be the median age—and the women were educated in an era when they believed that they would get ahead in lockstep with the men. When they found it wasn't happening, they had no qualms about getting together to complain. And management listened. When salary inequities were noticed by a female vice president who was handling the purse strings, she had to argue a bit to make her point understood, but eventually she did, and a number of women's salaries were adjusted upward. One of the women responsible is Pat Fili, vice president of business affairs and production. "I wasn't afraid that I would be cast in a bad light or that they would say, 'Oh, she's a rabble-rouser,'" Fili says. "What makes this place work for me is its openness."

HBO's women's movement, as they say, is in its second stage. A decade ago, when just about everybody was in their twenties, the place resembled not so much a business as a cross between summer camp and a frat house. The language was straight out of *Animal House*. It wasn't unusual for a woman to be at a meeting, be taken seriously, but then be called out of the meeting by a boss who would say to her: "Get your tits in here." The jokes were raunchy and sexist, and everybody was supposed to think it was a gas. When women accused the men of being sexist, they said, "How can we be sexist? We grew up in the sixties!" Things came to a head at an off-site meeting where a prom night, complete with dance card, was scheduled. A woman who was leaving the company and two others who weren't cornered one of the worst offenders in his room and "yelled at him halfway through the night," according to a woman who was at the meeting, "after which he believed there might be a problem." To his credit, the man immediately set about rectifying the atmosphere. He took small groups of women to dinner to hear what they had to say. Afterward, the company hired a female consultant who came in and ran male-female sensitivity sessions. Higher-ups at the parent company, Time Inc., had heard about the trouble and gave the plan their blessing. In no uncertain terms.

"Things changed dramatically overnight," says one of the women who witnessed the change. "The same person who had made it rotten at its head turned completely around." The man is no longer at HBO; he went to Time Inc. "It's true there are pockets of sexism," remarks Fischel, "but I've never known any place that was as good a place for women to work." The women may have something to gripe about, but it is at a whole different level than at most corporations in America, something like the difference between complaining that you can't find your favorite kind of hair mousse at the corner drugstore and being in a Third World country where they have never heard of mousse.

About that old boy network. Women say there are ways to crack it, at least at its lower rungs, but crack it you must if you expect to rise. Pretend that it doesn't exist, and you might as well check out now. In a young, energetic company like this, sports is the easiest way to become friendly with the boys on top. There's bowling, volleyball, tennis and a coed softball league that people get crazed about. A few years ago, the softball teams had much the same problem as the company: an assumption of male superiority. Sales manager Brent McKinley recalls that while women would be in position, men would run in front of them to catch the balls because they assumed that the women would miss them. "Being a good softball player, I was absolutely incensed that men would run in front of me," she says. "Finally, I said, 'Why am I here? Just make it a men's league.'" McKinley and a number of other women were ready to resign, whereupon "the male population on the softball circuit just went crazy," she says. At their insistence, changes she suggested were implemented. The best was yet to come: her team won the championship that year because two women made crucial plays. "We were down by two runs in the bottom of the seventh [the final inning in softball]. We had two outs and runners on second and third. I hit a double, which tied the score. When I came up to bat, you could hear the other team say, 'Oh, oh, a woman at the plate,' and they pulled in their infield and I said, "Suckers," and hit it right over their heads." McKinley's was the winning run across the plate.

If only everything was that easy to fix in business.

If you don't play the game, you can still come along to cheer and go out for drinks and cash in on the camaraderie afterward; if that's not your style, take up tennis or learn to talk boxing or take a share in the Hamptons and socialize with your coworkers, including CEO Michael Fuchs, in the summer. But do *something*, don't just go home at six every night.

When the company started in 1972, it was very much like a fraternity of young people. People worked hard, stayed late and went out for dinner afterward; there was plenty of intramural sex, all of it voluntary; marriages with people who didn't work for HBO were on the critical list, and many of them didn't make it. This was in the heyday of pay-cable, when new subscribers were sprouting faster than sushi bars. It didn't last. By 1985, as movies became available on videocassette months earlier than on pay networks, subscribers began dropping out by the thousands. Trouble had already hit HBO. An inflated staff working with inflated titles had lost credibility at Time Inc., on Wall Street and in the industry. The flattening in revenues only made things worse. HBO cut its staff (Fischel's first job was to oversee the downsizing) and got its house in order. Today it remains the largest of the pay-cable services, with more than 19 million subscribers to its HBO and Cinemax (for a younger, hipper crowd) networks, but it still had trouble in 1986. Operating profit at Time's programming operations—primarily HBO—fell more than 8 percent, to $111 million, as sales rose 13 percent, to $886 million.

While the company is going through the adolescent blues, the employees are in the midst of a baby boom of their own. It appears to be quite painless. You can take a six-month leave and be guaranteed the *same* job upon return. This is after the paid disability leave, which can be up to 12 weeks for a cesarean delivery without complications. How you are treated afterward depends to a great degree on you and your boss. If you're lucky, he or she will ask if you still want to travel as much as you did in the past or take on the extra assignments that mean you're still on the ladder moving up; if you're unlucky, the assumption will be made that you are no longer as interested in working hard as you once were. It will be up to you to prove differently, or your career, as one woman says, "will be dead in the water." HBO is a very demanding company; run on slow for a while and it will probably be hard to recover.

It may be easier if your boss is a woman. Pat Fili, who had six women go out on maternity leave in a short time, sent one of them to Wimbledon with her infant for seven weeks. Because other people were out, the new mother was needed there. Because the baby was only a few months old, Fili agreed that Mom could take her and the company would pay for a full-time nurse overseas.

But men too get high marks for their handling of the situation. "My boss is a man, and he is unusually accommodating," says Chris Ehrenbard, director of network operations. "He might say, 'Can you go on this trip?' and I'll say yes. But I target the travel more. There really has to be a reason that I'm the one who goes and not someone else. I know he thinks of me now as a mother also, and that's good." Ehrenbard is convinced her motherhood will affect her career only as much as she wants it to. Ehrenbard, incidentally, has an engineering background.

As far as accommodating special needs (read part-time) is concerned, whatever flies with your boss is fine. All kinds of part-time arrangements are made.

With so many people having babies, the atmosphere today runs to family sitcom. Lunch conversations are just as likely to be about Apricas as Adidas. Single mothers are made to feel comfortable, and fathers as well as moms bring in the kids on Friday afternoons in the summer before the early getaway to the Hamptons. A high premium is still placed on humor, as long as it's nonsexist when women are within earshot. Get a group of HBOers together, and somebody will grab a mike and try to make everybody laugh. This is show biz, remember? Wardrobes are hip, the midtown Manhattan offices are stylishly deco (and often used for fashion shoots) and the peach-colored lunchroom has a great view of the park behind Manhattan's main library. The cafeteria also has tables with tops of Carrara marble and food catered by Marriott. In the minigym on the premises, TV monitors in front of the stationary bicycles make the workout a lot less boring. This enticing list only skims the wide array of benefits and perks packaged by Time Inc. as interpreted by HBO. As secretary Joanne Taylor says, "I've worked a lot of places, including some advertising agencies, but this is by far the best."

As far as the entertainment industry goes, she could very well be right. Her boss, Bridget Potter, who oversees all original programming for HBO, finds what she likes best about the place has nothing to do with male-female issues. She likes the energy, the fast-paced business style, the aggressiveness in seeking out new business. "We've had some ups and downs, but we're never afraid to reevaluate, never afraid to turn on a dime, never afraid to change our minds about an issue," she says. "We're constantly looking to the future."

For the present, men dominate the entertainment industry. They are the ones who do the deals. What the future holds for women at HBO appears to depend to a great degree on the women themselves. What a refreshing idea. If women can make it here, and they are more likely to at this young, hip company than elsewhere, maybe it will start a trend.

And that would be the best news of all.

HONEYWELL

AN INTERNATIONAL ELECTRONICS COMPANY
THAT SUPPLIES AUTOMATION AND CONTROLS SYSTEMS
FOR HOMES, INDUSTRY,
AEROSPACE AND DEFENSE

▲ EMPLOYEES: 59,000 in the U.S., 79,000 worldwide; 24 percent are women.

▲ SALES: $5.4 billion in 1986. After five bad years, the company went through a major restructuring and took a net loss of $398 million. The company had sales of $6.7 billion for 1987 and earnings of $5.75 per share—of $254 million—in 1987.

▲ Honeywell is concerned about recruiting, hiring and promoting women. Evidence of success is the fact that of the 8,850 engineers at Honeywell, 925 are women. This does not include software engineers, a classification in which women tend to concentrate.

▲ Programs aimed at promotion include liberal tuition reimbursement, job posting, specific training and workshops, tracking, succession planning and management development procedures. The Honeywell Women's Council develops goals, programs and activities to address perceived needs. Of the 630 employees considered upper management, 24 — 3 percent—are women, including three vice presidents.

▲ Honeywell is concerned with needs of parents. In addition to the standard maternity disability leave, flexibility is the rule. You work it out with your manager. The company provides flexible working hours, flexible workplaces and part-time work for managers and professionals. The company provides a resource referral directory for child care facilities and a cafeteria-style approach to benefits.

▲ Charges of sexual discrimination may be handled by informal or formal procedure. To rectify inequality of pay, Honeywell examines what other companies are doing; they've also conducted internal conferences with expert speakers on the subject. In short, they agree that inequities have existed.

▲ Honeywell is one of the few companies that has conducted a study of sexual harassment, and it has issued strong statements on the subject. A training program on harassment is mandatory for all employees. Grievances are handled by informal hearing or formal procedure. The environment is such that women are not afraid to go to the human resources department with a complaint. They've seen punishment meted out to offenders.

▲ Major employment centers: Minneapolis: 19,500; Phoenix: 10,200; Boston: 1,290; Los Angeles: 2,300; Tampa: 5,440; Seattle: 1,120; Colorado Springs, Colo.: 1,370; Denver: 1,170; Chicago: 1,350; Philadelphia: 1,180; Washington, D.C.: 1,190; Freeport, Ill.: 2,980; Albuquerque, N.M.: 5,800.

HONEYWELL, INC.
Box 524
Minneapolis, MN 55940
(612) 870-5200

Ask women at this industrial giant why more women don't come here looking for jobs, and they wonder themselves. They assume it's because it's such a traditionally male-dominated industry—making everything from thermostats to lightweight torpedoes—but, they counter, aren't many of the biggest companies in America in the same boat? All things considered, younger women, who started working in the seventies, think Honeywell is a pretty great place for women. They feel quite certain that their sex neither helps nor hinders them.

Thirty-six-year-old Adelaide O'Brien, a business development manager, says, "The best person qualified for the job is the one who will get it, and that's the best news we have. If you were to take a cross-section of people—maybe not from the highest level, because you wouldn't see enough women who have been around—you'd find that it isn't a big deal to have women throughout. Five to 10 years from now, women will be in those higher positions too, no question about it."

Other women in the same age group, engineers among them, also present this rosy picture. Sure, sexist comments are heard now and then, but not so often, and they don't get in anyone's way. Not quite what we expected to find at this electronic giant.

But not everyone sees such fair-mindedness in their employer. Ask a high-ranking vice president if she thinks there is a glass ceiling for women, and she will assure you she has no doubts there is. "All of the general managers are male," says Irma Wyman, vice president of corporate information management. "I have been hearing them say, 'We just can't find a woman to be a general manager, we've been trying for 10 years, but we just can't find one.'" Wyman is too much a lady to use an expletive in conversation, but you're sure she's thinking it. "The way you make a female general manager at Honeywell is the same way you make a male general manager. You promote someone." Wyman says that she takes every opportunity to point out the women she believes are ready for the job, women she says are sitting there and waiting or having their careers redirected.

Wyman herself has no illusions about how she became the head of an organization of 540 people with a multimillion-dollar budget. She nurtured her job and watched it grow right under their noses. "I am still convinced that if they had realized this was going to be an operating job and not a staff job, they would have thought differently about offfering it to me," she says. "It started as a staff job with 16 to 20 people." Wyman is one of two vice presidents with an operating function. She does not believe it is because no other women at Honeywell are qualified.

Wyman herself has seen a great deal of progress from when she signed up for engineering at the University of Michigan in the 1940s and encountered professors who told her that no matter how well she did in their courses, they were going to flunk her because they didn't believe that women should be engineers. Her solution? Sign up for another section.

At Honeywell in the sixties, it wasn't much different. A vice president told her, "Too bad you're not a man, you would have a great future if you were a man." By the seventies, she decided that more than patience was needed. "I said to myself, hey, wait a minute, I'm not getting any part of the action here," Wyman recalls. When she saw an opening she wanted, she requested it, the first time she did anything other than go along with what was being offered. What had been offered was to move her around every time the next obvious step would be to management. Although it kept her treading water for more than a decade, it also gave her varied experience that turned out to be useful when she finally got feisty.

Wyman believes that the company will change only when the attitudes of the people at the top change, when men who are comfortable working alongside women are the ones in charge. Given the realities of Honeywell's senior management—Midwestern, older, conservative—Wyman thinks its openness to women and minorities has been remarkable, if not quite enough. No matter how it happened, she did become a vice president of a high enough grade to park in the heated garage beneath headquarters in chilly Minneapolis, a move that raised more eyebrows than when she became a vice president. There are approximately 125 vice presidents. There are 62 spaces in the garage.

She's not the only woman eligible. Dana Badgerow, recruited from the outside in 1985 for the job of vice president of contract management in the aerospace and defense business, will park there as soon as her name reaches the top of the waiting list and a space opens up. Badgerow knows that some of the people were surprised when *she* turned out to be the candidate of choice for her job, but says that she doesn't think the mental adjustment took them very long. "I have been accepted wholeheartedly right from the beginning. And this is a company and an industry where they are not used to people coming in from the outside. So I had two strikes against me—I was an outsider and a woman. But the acceptance has been phenomenal."

What's also phenomenal is the corporate tolerance of parenting needs. Admittedly, we were surprised, considering the industry, but then, why not? Women here work out all kinds of deals with their managers, and nobody is surprised. Flexibility is expected. Adelaide O'Brien took a three-month leave—and was offered a new job—the day before she was due to deliver. The job would remain vacant until she came back. But of course there were things to be done in those months. A week after her daughter was born, she interviewed someone for her department over lunch; when crucial meetings came up, she was there. She and her new boss kept track of those hours on a slip of paper—they totaled 13 days over three months. When she needed a morning off to go to the doctor's or to stay home with her sick child, she dug into that bank of days, crossing them off as she used them up. When the days were used up, the slip of paper was thrown out.

The official maternity leave is a medical disability period of four to eight weeks, but scores of women seem to work part-time. Nobody knows how many. Managers have a more difficult time arranging part-time work than do engineers or clerical staff, but it's still done in the first few months after childbirth. Because the company is highly decentralized, some divisions grant more leeway than others; aerospace and defense, where almost everything is done under government contract, is somewhat less flexible than divisions that make products for residential or commercial building customers. "We have an extremely powerful women's network, and we would look with hard eyes on any supervisor who wasn't accommodating," says Marjorie Brimi. She is manager of the chemical and metallurgical laboratory in the division that makes environmental controls for homes and small buildings.

Employees requesting up to 90 days' leave are guaranteed the same job upon return, as long as the position hasn't been eliminated in the interim. With Honeywell's cost-cutting mode (which includes getting rid of bodies), it may be somewhat more difficult to preserve your job than in the fat old days of American industrial supremacy.

Honeywell went through some rough years, resulting in a net loss of $398 million in 1986. Many of the industries Honeywell serviced were in a slump, and foreign competition also hurt deeply. In several markets, the company had only a small piece of the pie. In the computer business, for instance, the question was whether Honeywell could compete with Digital Equipment, lately dazzling the market with state-of-the-art products, and the much larger IBM. In 1986 the company spun off its information systems division to a newly formed joint venture owned by Groupe Bull, a French computer company, the NEC Corporation and Honeywell. The alliance creates one of the world's biggest players in the computer business, starting with $2 billion in revenues.

Another of its major businesses, aerospace and defense, was diversified when Honeywell bought the Sperry Aerospace Group for just over $1 billion. With Sperry a leader in flight controls and displays and Honeywell solidly established in the guidance and navigation market, together they are looking to reap profits in the commercial aviation market, a market that is expected to grow at least 8 percent annually, while defense spending is flattening.

In 1986 employment was cut by 3,200 in Honeywell's continuing businesses, and everybody was on notice that belt tightening was in order. Salary increases were limited to 1 percent of payroll. Employees were asked to share the cost of medical insurance and now pay 20 percent, up to $1,000. First-class tickets are a thing of the past.

In spite of the troubles, the women remain positive about working for Honeywell. And if something is bothering them, a grass roots movement eventually gets management's attention. When the medical insurance fee structure was announced, workers saw that it was, in effect, a flat tax, and lower level workers would almost pay just as much as senior executives. Petitions taped to the coffee machine asking that this be rectified eventually got action. Difficulties in dealing with work and family issues resulted in a task force that conducted a detailed survey of employee needs. Last year, corporate issued a list of recommendations to its various divisions. The main message was that flexibility, which previously had been up to each individual manager, was now a corporate policy. Managers were urged to learn more about work and family problems, from the difficulty of finding a baby-sitter when the day care center is closed and the company's not, to the demands of caring for elderly parents. Supervisors were urged to be as lenient as possible while meeting business needs.

An active women's council, partially funded by Honeywell itself, was to some degree responsible for the work-family task force. The steering committee comprises 30 representatives from all divisions and all levels, vice presidents to clerical workers. The women's council got rid of the Japanese division's girlie calendar but weren't making much noise about company women's movement upward as of early last year. Should they be? Depends on whom you ask.

With locations and plants all over the country, the flavor of Honeywell depends somewhat on where you are located. Boston will be one way, Los Angeles another. In Minneapolis, where the largest concentration of employees is, Honeywell is decidedly Midwestern: open, straight shooting, democratic, polite. So polite, in fact, that you can be done in without becoming aware of it until it's too late. Decisions are made by consensus. If there's a problem, a task force is appointed to look into the matter. One popular subject has been the slow progress of women and minorities into the upper reaches. Goals will be set, the following year they will be unmet, and another task force will be appointed. The heads may be in the right places, but the hearts aren't always following.

There's little unofficial socializing where decisions get made, but business does get done on off-site weekends for executives. "Be at fishing dock at three P.M., bring fishing gear," is how one senior woman characterized the weekends.

A certain paternalism is evident at most companies this large, and Honeywell is no exception. You are pretty much hired for life unless there is a downturn in business; seniority is as good a reason as capability to promote someone. Being seen as putting in long hours may be as important as the output. Nothing happens quickly. As one woman says, it's like a battleship turning around. It takes a long time, but once you get going in that direction, then you're definitely going in that direction. The military allusions fit and are heard a fair amount: many people from the military, women as well as men, find homes here and in the divisions with defense contracts. It's a plus. It doesn't mean that a less qualified person with a military background will necessarily have a leg up. Badgerow, with a legal rather than a military background, knew that she was competing with a retired admiral for her job; she's the one who was wooed to Minneapolis from her previous job in Washington, D.C.

It's estimated that fully half of all of Honeywell's 52,000-plus employees in the United States are engineers, a great percentage of whom are working on the business side. Of the 8,850 employees classified as engineers, 925— about 10.5 percent—are women. This does not include software engineering, where women tend to concentrate. The human resources, public relations and accounting departments are well-peopled with women.

Although the near freeze on raises may bring down Honeywell's salaries, company women say they are better paid than most of their neighbors. Whether or not they are being paid equitably with the men is not certain. Some women who have managed to see salary schedules say they are paid equally with their male peers; other women find they are consistently being paid in the low range for their jobs. Until they complain. Some typical salaries: brand-new vice president, $128,000 plus stock options; human resources director for a medium-sized division, $88,000; entry-level job in human resources, $24,000; entry-level engineer, $28,000.

What's a nice girl like you doing in a place like this? isn't a question asked around Minneapolis. The women there know exactly what they are doing: carving out careers. They come from Midwestern engineering schools, they come from the military, they come from neighbors like Control Data. They are becoming fully integrated into the pipeline, and if they are not holding their breath waiting for the first female general manager, they are waiting.

INTERNATIONAL BUSINESS MACHINES

BIG BLUE IS THE LARGEST COMPUTER AND OFFICE
EQUIPMENT COMPANY IN THE WORLD

▲ EMPLOYEES: 237,274 (in the United States); nearly 30 percent
   are female.

▲ SALES: $51.25 billion in 1986. Worldwide net earnings were
   $4.8 billion, down 26.9 percent from 1985.

▲ IBM is concerned about recruiting and hiring women and minorities. The company employs extensive outreach and affirmative
   action programs to assist women, minorities, handicapped and
   Vietnam-disabled veterans to compete on an equal basis. The
   company has a well-known program of promoting from within. In
   addition to training and workshops, tuition reimbursement, tracking and succession planning, the company has a women's high-
   potential program and a mentor program.

▲ Of the top 250 executives of IBM, 11—4.4 percent—are
   women. Of their top 6,000 managers, 10 percent are women.
   Two of the 20-member board of directors are women, as are two
   out of 59 officers listed in the 1986 annual report.

▲ Much more encouraging, especially in light of IBM's policy of
   promotion from within, is the fact that 48 percent of the 3,500
   new employees hired in 1986 were women. Of the 1,000 new
   college hires, 37 percent were women. However, it takes many
   years to grow a top executive.

▲ IBM offers maternity disability leave, as well as up to 12 months'
   leave without pay for either parent. The company offers flexible
   work hours as well as personal time off for family illness. Adoptive
   parents are given $1,750, and either parent may take extended
   leave without pay to care for the new child. IBM's comprehensive
   nationwide resource referral directory for child care facilities is a
   model for other companies in this country that are contemplating
   similar services. In 1987 the company added Eldercare Service,
   available to employees, retirees and their spouses.

▲ The company has studied sexual harassment and issues frequent messages about the unacceptability of such behavior. Attendance is mandatory for all at the company's program on the subject.

▲ Charges of sexual discrimination are handled by line management review and action or open door investigations. The women we interviewed maintained that discrimination is not an issue.

▲ Major employment centers: New York State: 69,000; Maryland: 9,500; Georgia: 6,700; Illinois: 4,400. IBM has offices and manufacturing facilities in all 50 states.

INTERNATIONAL BUSINESS MACHINES CORPORATION
Corporate Headquarters
Armonk, NY 10504
(914) 765-1900 or (800) 426-3333

Number 117F
February 13, 1985

IBM's policy of equal opportunity is founded on sound business judgment and our basic belief in respect for the individual.

I expect IBM managers to hire and promote based on job-related requirements and an individual's qualifications. All personnel-related programs are administered without regard to race, color, religion, sex, national origin, handicap, or age. These programs include training, compensation, benefits, and IBM-sponsored social or recreational activities, as well as transfers and terminations. This policy of non-discrimination is reflected throughout all areas of the business.

Implicit in our equal opportunity policy is a working environment free of harassment based on sex, race or ethnic origin, religion, age, handicap, or veteran status.

In order to ensure equal opportunity, IBM carries out affirmative action in such areas as recruiting, training programs, and accommodation of the handicapped. In the U.S., for example, IBM has programs on behalf of employees and applicants who are minorities, women, handicapped, and Vietnam-era or disabled veterans.

Senior management at each location or operating unit takes the necessary action to fully comply with our equal opportunity policy. However, I expect each manager, at every level, to ensure this commitment is honored in all of our business activities.

> *John F. Akers*
> CEO

We're running the company's official statement here for several reasons: first, IBM was among the very first companies to issue such a statement. Back in 1953, then president Thomas J. Watson, Jr., laid down a company policy making it clear that racial and religious discrimination would not be tolerated; later it was expanded to include sexual and national origin as well. A woman who owned an employment agency in the fifties, Ann Anderson, recalls the company as one of the few places she could send female college graduates where they wouldn't be given a typing test. Instead, they would be tested for their math aptitude. Just as male college graduates were.

Two decades earlier, Thomas J. Watson, Sr., was quoted in the *New York Sun* as saying that a crop of 25 women professionals who had been hired to form the systems service department to help customers install and use IBM products would "have neither handicap nor an advantage over the young men." He further added that men and women who did equal work would get equal pay.

The year was 1935.

The second reason for running the statement has to do with the corporate culture. IBM's revolves around rules and official statements like the one above and not releasing much, if anything, else. All information not official is akin to a leak, even if the information presents the company in a positive light.

The third reason is that the interviews with IBM women were as cut and dried as the official statement. IBM would not allow us to run a focus group at headquarters; instead, they offered us interviews with women around the country. Except for an anonymous interview done without IBM's knowledge and interviews with previous employees, the interviews were done on the telephone, and IBM insisted that someone from the public relations department be listening in. The connection on the three-way call was less than clear—metaphorically indicative of the filter IBM places on information gathering. Consequently, the arranged interviews were bland and somewhat formal. No amusing anecdotes spilled from anyone's lips, no hint of humor, no wild card of insight. That is not the IBM way.

Yet while what the woman had to say might not have been colorful, it was more than encouraging; indeed, it was downright remarkable, considering that IBM is among the nation's largest employers.

They categorically stated that IBM is an untarnished meritocracy, that they had been promoted fairly. These were satisfied women in high-ranking jobs. Typical was Barbara Grant, product manager for high-end systems printers, who said, "I have always felt very positive support from my managers—both in the research division as well as in the information products. There have been many times when IBM asked me to do something I wasn't sure I could do. They stretched me further than I might have thought I could be stretched. My own career has certainly not been one of beating my head against something that was in the way of what I wanted to do." It has, in fact, been quite the opposite.

Grant, who joined the company soon after receiving her Ph.D. in chemistry from Stanford University, rose through several managerial positions in research before making the switch to marketing in 1986. It happened seemingly without a hitch, thanks to IBM's extensive management development program, a program revered in the corporate world. Its basic tenets are amazingly simple: courses and seminars in tandem with varied job experience. People flip back and forth between line and staff positions; for fast-trackers it can happen every 18 to 24 months.

Training has always been a cornerstone of IBM success. It has a reputation for cultivating its people and planning their careers. Critical to its early dominance in the computer industry was its funding of university programs (most notably at MIT) back in the fifties to train systems engineers and programmers. At the time, the computer business was growing more rapidly than IBM could find skilled managers and computer scientists. Today, IBM spends approximately $750 million a year on employee education and training.

Grant, like all of the women we interviewed (past employees included) categorically stated that capable women didn't top out at IBM. There is no glass ceiling at IBM, they said.

Do we believe them? Not quite. Of the top 250 positions at IBM, only 11—under 5 percent—are filled by women. Two out of the 59 officers listed in the annual report are women. This is despite the fact that the company had female professionals and managers well ahead of most other companies; nevertheless, it may be a tad ahead of other giants in the same industry.

As proof of their convictions that women do not bump up against a glass ceiling, women can point to Ellen M. Hancock, who heads the communications systems unit responsible for several billions in budget annually.

Hancock will be 45 this year, putting her in synch with male fast-trackers. She started at the company as a programmer in 1966 with an M.A. from Fordham University; *Business Week* estimated her salary last year at $275,000.

Hancock's rise wasn't without sacrifices. IBM is legendary for asking its employees to pick up and go wherever they are needed, and Hancock has not been immune to those moves. Three times she had to relocate elsewhere and have a commuter marriage to her fellow IBMer, W. Jason Hancock, currently on a year's leave to Western Connecticut State University. The moves were undoubtedly critical to her promotion. "Those Friday night and Sunday night planes get to you," she told *Business Week*, "but I got a good promotion out of it."

A few years ago IBM tried to cut back on asking employees to relocate, but the company's no-layoff tradition and the practice of making sure employees get varied work experience make it impossible to cut back much beyond moving between 3 and 5 percent of their employees annually. That means that approximately 9,500 workers a year are combing the want ads for a new place to live. It's almost a sure bet that if you join IBM, you will be asked to relocate at some point in your career, probably more than once, if you intend to rise. The women we spoke to either had portable husbands and children or commuter marriages or were not married.

Judy Johnson, site director for business application systems in Bethesda, Maryland, manages a work force of 950 people. She started with IBM in Houston in 1967 as a programmer and moved into marketing before her current job in operations. "When I made the decision to leave Houston, I'd had every marketing job that I could have had," she says. "Either I could stay and be a marketing manager in Houston until I decided to go to another company, or I had to move. It was as simple as that."

Johnson, a black, says that neither sex nor race has impeded her career. "The tone is, no matter what sex you are, we are all professionals and we have a job to do," she remarks. "If I have to work a little harder on the front end to make sure that people realize the reason I got the opportunity is because I am competent, that's okay. I see men having to do the same thing."

While Johnson's record is too clear an upward path to call it into question, one woman, interviewed anonymously, said that women and minorities are sometimes slotted into positions for which they are unsuited and unqualified. Troublesome as they may be for the people who work for them, they do maintain IBM's image as an equal employment opportunity company. When IBM is audited for equal opportunity, they have never been out of compliance.

According to *Think*, IBM's employee magazine, the company has come out clean in more than 620 government audits. This doesn't mean, naturally, that IBM harbors no male chauvinists; of course it does. What it means is that they can't get in one's way for long, because somebody is watching him watching you. Do a good job, and you will be moved up, regardless of the sexist attitudes of a particular boss.

And to move up, you will move around. The company makes it as painless as possible. Not only is there a paid house-hunting trip, the spouse is also entitled to one job-hunting expedition to the new site, as well as paid résumé assistance and career counseling. If he or she is an IBMer also—and there are hundreds—the spouse will be given job priority at the new location. It could be anywhere, as IBM has installations in 50 states and 131 countries.

That kind of assistance gives the flavor of what it's like to work for IBM: your every need is taken care of, including strokes—it's management by merit badge, and the employees bask in it. Their appreciation is akin to religious fervor. In fact, joining the company is more like joining a religious sect than simply taking a job. The overriding zeitgeist is a proprietary concern about employee attitudes, behavior and appearance. The reins have loosened somewhat from the old days when the Watsons, father and then son, ran the company. When Watson senior was in charge, one could be dismissed for being seen during working hours in a saloon or being obviously inebriated. Even today IBM keeps a tighter hold on employees than other corporate giants.

It does this seemingly effortlessly by wrapping the job in a virtual cocoon of security, much like life in a monastery. Worry and tension are miraculously absent. To begin with, IBM pays extremely well. Other companies located in the same towns where IBM has a plant or corporate office find that it can be difficult to compete for workers.

IBM's benefits package—pension, health and dental insurance for employees and families, aerobics classes, adoption assistance, antismoking programs, pension plan, stress management seminars, voluntary free health screening, you name it—is one of the very best in the nation. At a few locations—Poughkeepsie, Sands Point and Endicott, New York—IBM has country clubs with nominal dues. For a family of three, the charge is $10.

For all this, you need not work too hard unless you are very ambitious. Late nights are for the few. If you merely want a good job with average effort, IBM is an extremely comfortable place to nest. Unless you are grossly incompetent or dishonest, you will not get fired. And even with the current downtrend in their business, people are not laid off. They are given incentive packages to take early retirement; 13,000 workers took IBM up on that offer in 1987. Others are retrained and redeployed to different areas of the country, wherever they are needed. And short of being fired, workers who are promoted over their heads are moved down and then around from job to job, lateral move after lateral move, until a place is found where they can quietly be forgotten.

There is a laundry list of programs to take care of employee needs away from work; there are rules to govern the most minute details on the job. Is an account in trouble? *File a yellow form.* With all the attention, one doesn't need to do a great deal of creative thinking about how to run one's life. IBM will do it for you. Have a drink at lunch? *Take the afternoon off.* What to wear? *The most conservative business outfit I can find.* Tomorrow? *The same thing, maybe substituting a blue shirt for a white, as long as it's not too blue.* What should I do about my ex-wife who won't let me see my kids? *Dial up a counselor.*

The company is known for one of the best employee assistance programs in the country. For anything from drugs to divorce to job-related problems, your computer will blip up the number of the nearest outside counseling service. The first eight visits are automatically covered by IBM; after that, health insurance picks up the rest. Total confidentiality is guaranteed, since the therapists bill only for total services; no names are ever given to the company. Like many of IBM's programs, it's one of the best in the country, and, like IBM's PCs, it has been copied by many companies.

IBM has also been a trendsetter in the child care arena and back in 1984 started one of the first resource referral services, well before other companies were alert to the difficulties of two-career couples with children. IBM workers are given a 40-page booklet on what to look for when considering child care options and a 14-page booklet (booklets abound at IBM; the one on business conduct and ethics is 30 pages long) explaining how the child care referral service works. Since its inception, some 21,000 employees with more than 24,000 children have been helped, whether the need was for a recommendation for a good school or a live-in nanny. Last year, Catalyst, an organization that collects data about women in corporations to promote their advancement, singled out IBM's program for its highest accolades. With IBM's encouragement and some aid, more than 5,500 new day care centers have opened in communities across the country, and nearly 1,500 in-home providers have been trained. An employee survey (IBM does surveys about everything, from the food in the cafeteria to the performance of senior managers) found that 92 percent of the employees would use the service again. Last year, an eldercare program offering both referral services and counseling was instituted for both current and retired employees.

As to flexibility on the job, there are official policies, if not an entire booklet, to cover that too. At most locations, the normal starting time is 8:30 A.M.; workers may come in 30 minutes earlier or later and leave appropriately. There are four personal choice holidays, such as Martin Luther

King's Birthday and Columbus Day, and flexible vacation scheduling. Whatever you work out with your manager is fine. One option is to take half days in the summertime when the children are out of school, or Fridays off in July and August to head early for the Jersey shore.

But—and it's a big but—fast-trackers are not expected to have their attention diverted from the main chance. They are expected to have child care under control. Our anonymous source says, "You can get flexibility for a child's emergencies, but once you do that you are very aware that you are treated as a woman and you will not forget it." Interpretation: Forget about rising too far. This company means business, and so should you if you want to rise.

If that's your goal, it's almost always necessary to start fresh out of school or soon thereafter. Rare is the individual who makes a move to IBM even at a middle management level. Promotion from within is the rule. If anything is clear, it is that IBM knows how to pick the people it needs, groom them and motivate them. And what kind of people does IBM select? The same kind MBA schools look for: people with a good academic record, evidence of leadership, a positive attitude, self-confidence and good common sense. An advanced degree is a plus. In the past, most people in senior management were Christian, but that seems to be changing, if only slightly.

Before being hired, you will be filtered through a screening process that includes rigorous job-related tests and numerous interviews. It's likely that the people you are working with will have similar backgrounds and education. The homogeneity practically assures that IBMers will want to socialize with other IBMers. They play golf, tennis, softball, basketball, have drinks after work, get together with their families for backyard barbecues, and take vacations together. It's not surprising, since they have so much in common, not least of which is working for IBM. "Pressure Breeds Camaraderie" a headline read in a 1982 *Wall Street Journal* profile of the company.

IBM's policies of taking care of its employees, if not from cradle to grave, then from date of employment till death do them part, apparently appeals to the kind of people IBM selects—or changes them into once they are there. Employees may have to rein in some of their rough ego and energy, work patiently as team players and wait for their rightful turn for the next promotion, which will come in an orderly fashion. In return, IBM extends a paternal embrace with its cocoon of creature comforts, forever keeping one from want and fear about the future. The system works. IBM has very, very loyal employees; according to industry sources, fewer than 1 percent a year leave by choice. Why should they? It's cold out there. IBM can be so soft, so easy, so lulling. One woman who left after nearly two decades to head up a small software company said it was "like leaving the womb."

Describing what is widely accepted to be IBM, Alan Harrington wrote,

"We are not worried about our jobs, about the future, about... much of anything. This is a curious sensation, not to have any real worries. Try to imagine it. How are you going to get ahead? The company will decide. *Quo vadis?* The company will take care of that too. Furthermore, your affairs will be ordered fairly and squarely with maximum sympathy for your well-being." Where does all this benevolence leave employees? "Alive but not kicking: that is the trouble." Harrington's book, from which the above is taken, *Life in the Crystal Palace*, was published in 1959, but nothing we learned indicates that it isn't as true today.

Viewed from the outside, IBM's corporate headquarters appear to be an impenetrable fortress. It sits on a hill in the suburbs of New York City, a location that intensifies the company's insularity. During most lunch hours, there's no contact with the outside world, since it's much easier and cheaper to eat at the company cafeteria. Even after working hours, the paternalism swoops down into one's life.

One woman who had risen from secretary to marketing manager was demoted back to a nonmanagement post at the same salary. To an IBM lifer steeped in the get-ahead culture, it was analogous to being released. Her infringement? She was dating a former IBMer who now worked for a competitor. He might snoop into her briefcase. Virginia Rulon-Miller quit rather than take the demotion and sued. A San Francisco jury awarded her $300,000 in compensatory and punitive damages, according to the *Wall Street Journal*, which reported the case in a 1982 profile of the company.

As an isolated incident, Rulon-Miller's story seems unbearably oppressive. Yet it perfectly suits the company that gives a great deal; it expects payment in kind. Accept IBM's paternalism, and you have to accept a certain amount of control. One of the basics of control is the control of information; give that up, and power is lost. The natural end product of this is secrecy and the kind of paranoia we encountered. One woman we interviewed didn't want to say how many people reported to her. We didn't ask why. Why was not the point.

Whether or not this is the kind of company that Huxley had in mind when he wrote *Brave New World* is probably immaterial. There will always be lots of people who want to work for IBM. As author Harrington noted, "There are two ways of looking at it: (1) If you are not going to set the world on fire anyway, it is better to spend your life in nice surroundings; (2) looking back, you *might* have had a more adventuresome time and struggled harder to make your mark in the world if the big company hadn't made things soft for you."

As a business entity, IBM is hard to beat. For several years IBM was the most admired corporation in America, according to *Fortune* magazine's annual list. It slipped southward to seventh place in 1987, but that's still pretty good. Poor performance was the main reason. Revenues totaled $50 billion, and profits were probably close to $5 billion, more than any other company in the world. But because growth for so many years has been in the double digits, anything else looks like a poor showing. It is thought to be an enclave of managerial and technological strength. Most Americans consider it one of our national assets.

What is happening now is that IBM is failing to keep pace in an industry that has slowed down, and it is being beaten out by competitors, especially its archrival, Digital Equipment Corporation, where rugged individualism is prized. Could Digital's tougher style be the reason for the edge? The company that once seemed invincible when the world was less knowledgeable about computers is no longer the expert. Perhaps the competition will scare up some excitement at Big Blue. Earnings in 1986 were down nearly 27 percent, to $4.8 million; earnings in 1987 didn't scare up any great enthusiasm. Yet the dire predictions from analysts that made news earlier last year didn't quite materialize. IBM is scrambling, and Chairman Akers is proving a nimble manager. The lore says that while IBM is often a late starter, it is prodigiously adept at reacting. As Morgan Stanley analyst Carol Muratore noted last year in *Fortune*, "The single most important thing about this company is that it prevails."

LEVI STRAUSS

THE LARGEST MANUFACTURER OF BLUE JEANS
IN THE WORLD

▲ EMPLOYEES: 24,000 (in the United States); 79 percent are women.

▲ SALES: In excess of $2.6 billion. In 1986 *Forbes* magazine ranked Levi Strauss the 20th largest private company in America.

▲ Levi Strauss, which reduced its work force a few years ago, continues an active interest in recruiting women; it frequently sends job postings to community-based organizations, including programs for women reentering the work force. Recruiters talk at women's resource centers in California.

▲ Of 123 upper management employees, 28—23 percent—are women, including one senior vice president, three vice presidents, and 15 department directors. Thirty-three percent of officials and managers and 51 percent of professionals are women. Tuition reimbursement is available; jobs are posted, and careful attention is paid to succession planning. Since Levi Strauss is a privately owned company, the board is comprised of family.

▲ Levi Strauss is a company sensitive to the needs of parents. In addition to standard maternity disability leave, informal arrangement of flexible workplaces, paternity benefits, up to five months of unpaid leave and sick leave for family illness, the company offers the possibility of part-time work with proportional benefits. Although an experiment with on-site child care didn't work, Levi Strauss offers pretax child care subsidies, monetary support of community-based facilities, and a cafeteria approach to employee benefits.

▲ Charges of sex discrimination may be handled by formal procedure or by open door policy. To ensure equality of pay, the Hay
system of compensation allows objective examination of job content; necessary salary adjustments have been made.

▲ The company's program on sexual harassment must be attended
by all managers and professionals. The program includes education, EEO guidelines, reporting procedures and self-help strategies.

▲ Major employment centers: San Francisco: 1,300; Knoxville,
Tenn.: 2,200; El Paso, Tex.: 4,200; and San Antonio, Tex.: 1,100.

LEVI STRAUSS & COMPANY
P.O. Box 7215
San Francisco, CA 94120
(415) 544-6000

A few years ago, Levi Strauss put its top executives—beginning with the
president—through an intense exercise designed to make them examine
their attitudes toward women and minorities on the job. In groups of 15–20
made up of half senior management and half their immediate subordinates
who were either members of minority groups or women, they spent three
days talking about issues at the secluded Meadowood Resort in the Napa
Valley, 60 miles away from company headquarters in San Francisco. In all,
four different groups went on the retreat.

At each opening session, the minorities and women were broken off into
one group, the white males in another. The first topic of discussion—Does
Levi Strauss have a problem? You can bet the two groups came back with
different responses.

"The white males said, 'I don't think so,' but the minorities and women
blasted them off their chairs," says one woman who was present. The
women accused the men of having a white male fraternity women and
blacks couldn't be a part of. The men responded that the women and blacks
wanted everything handed to them on a silver platter and didn't make their
career goals known. Hard issues were raised. Do sexual and racial differences unconsciously color performance evaluations? Do the white males
prefer to work with other white males and thus promote the guys they are

most comfortable with, sometimes bypassing people who might be better for the job? Could the men please clean up their comments? Would the women speak up and tell them when they were out of line? Feelings ran high. Some of the men were amazed at the level of frustration and futility the women and minorities voiced, while some of the women wondered what all the noise was about. They personally were doing fine. One man on the first day of the first session said pointedly that women who wanted careers shouldn't have families. *Who's going to have the children?* the women demanded.

In all, some 75 people took part. The object was not to come back with a new set of candidates for promotions but to change attitudes in an attempt to stop derailing affirmative action goals. Levi Strauss has plenty of women in the pipeline (a third of the managers and half of the professional staff are women) but has had some notable failures at senior levels. Two high-ranking women left the company—one because she couldn't cut it, one to go into business for herself. And the company didn't want it to happen again. Thus the retreat. In the following months, women were offered classes designed to teach them how to handle themselves better in business situations, such as speaking up at meetings or presenting ideas more forcefully.

Since then, similar conferences have been held at the home office, as well as in El Paso, San Antonio and Knoxville. Follow-up sessions are part of the plan. In San Francisco, graduates of the retreat at Meadowood have a quarterly lunch.

But there's more. All eight members of the executive management committee—including president Robert D. Haas—meet monthly with 10 employees, men and women of various ethnic backgrounds and in jobs that cut across grade levels from secretary to the top. Enthusiasm for the EEO Forums, as they are called, runs high, since employees know the issues they raise are being taken seriously by the most senior group of executives in the company. Innovative programs like this put Levi Strauss near the top of our list as a good place to work.

Paradoxically, the company doesn't think it's doing so well. When *Savvy* magazine wanted to put one of its women on the cover, Levi Strauss came back with a polite refusal; when a school for the handicapped wanted to give the company an award, that also was refused. When we asked to include Levi Strauss in our research, we were told the company probably shouldn't be included.

Yet once we got there, in the midst of downsizing and layoffs, the women we met had plenty of good things to say about their employer. They didn't whitewash the fact that the white males at the top have not opened the door all the way to women and minorities, they didn't pretend that to get ahead it wouldn't be best to be a handsome white male, aged 40–42, who can jog a 6.5-minute mile while talking business, or that risks are taken with men that wouldn't be with women, or even that some white males have been protected from layoffs because they were members of the right club, figuratively speaking.

But given all that, the consensus is that Levi Strauss is still a good—if not great—place to work.

Consider Lory Cogan, who came on board as a secretary in 1975. She'd been a French teacher before, with zero business skills. Her first boss was someone who didn't mind answering his phone while she was off taking advantage of the numerous management courses the company offers. It took Cogan a year and a half to become assistant to the national production manager, and from that point forward it was not difficult to make the right moves. She gained experience in finance and then moved into a line position, eventually becoming a merchandise manager in the Jeans Company, the main division of Levi Strauss.

"I don't feel that I've ever been held back from progressing, but I've worked for men who are not the ordinary kind and were totally supportive of me," Cogan says. "I came in as a secretary, and now I'm a merchandise manager who is part of the bonus plan. I have no personal complaints, but I have not tried to be a general manager . . . yet."

Other women have started as clerks or secretaries and 10 or 12 years later have important jobs; however, they say that because of the trouble in the garment industry, and Levi's troubles in particular, it probably wouldn't be so easy to make the leap today.

Levi Strauss went through a period of dizzying growth in the seventies and found itself bloated with businesses that seemed far from the jeans, shirts and slacks the brand name represented. But the fashion and designer lines and the accessories such as hats, purses and belts didn't bring in the profits management had hoped for. At the same time, what had always been a family-run company with a conscience felt itself becoming just another big business out to make a fast buck. And so, in 1985, family members, who had taken the company public in 1971, said *Whoa!* and bought the company back.

This meant assuming a huge debt—$1.6 billion—with initial interest payments of $200 million a year. Contraction was the order of the day. Forty factories were closed. Whole divisions were shut down or sold. The worldwide work force went from 48,000 to 32,500 in 1987. People who survived at corporate headquarters were moved back to jobs where they had proven themselves. More shuttered plants and layoffs were likely. All this goes counter to the family reputation for benevolent paternalism, but the new, narrower focus seems to be working. The long-term debt is being paid back ahead of time, and in late 1986 the company was enjoying a run of steady and increased earnings. The overall problem the garment industry finds itself confronting—cheap foreign labor—remains, but Levi jeans, plain, standard button-fly 501's, have been regaining favor with a public tired of paying high prices for designer names on jeans that were always an imitation of the real thing. Levi's are on exhibit in the Smithsonian. Levi's are what you pack to give to new friends when you visit Soviet bloc countries.

People who are laid off aren't simply left in the lurch. The company has an extensive policy to help retrain them and assist them to find new jobs. It's the best layoff policy we've come across. Employees are told of layoffs three months ahead of time, well ahead of what most industries do. Extensive placement services are available. Local vocational schools, community colleges and private companies are contracted to assist in retraining. Female plant workers are encouraged to try a series of modules in which they do some of the work associated with male-dominated fields to see if they are interested in further training. Full medical benefits are extended for three months to a year, depending on length of service.

But if the policies sound excellent, the execution is sometimes clumsy. In an effort to be up front with everybody as soon as a decision is reached, information sometimes leaks out in spurts, giving rise to even more gossip and turmoil than is already there. "The image of caring about people is still there and strong, but management gets off the track because they don't understand the reality of what their actions mean," says one woman.

But if Levi Strauss is having its problems—and what company in the garment industry isn't—there's still plenty that's right at this place. The perks are numerous. For instance, people in fairly high positions (such as marketing director) are allowed to work part-time, as are people in lesser positions; job sharing, especially at the secretarial level, is common; some people work part of the time at home on computers; after the birth of a child your job will be held for 60 days; both men and women can take child care leaves for up to five months following birth or adoption, and a comparable job will be found upon return—most often, one's old job. And when you have to stay home for a family emergency or a child's illness, you don't have to lie.

"Being pregnant here is great," says Linda Walker-Smith, a senior product manager. "I don't feel people have a different perception of me because I'm a mother. The company is flexible enough to allow you to be a mother and a businesswoman at the same time without making you feel terribly pressured. You don't have to make a choice. My friends in other companies know they will have a hard time, and so they are waiting longer and longer to have children." Walker-Smith was 27 when her son was born in 1985.

Although the company does not have on-site day care (it was tried at one location, but not enough children enrolled), it does have just about every other imaginable benefit for parents, including resource and referral services, parenting classes, pretax deductions for child care, a choice of benefits that can be tailored to individual needs and monetary support for community child care facilities.

In some companies, women don't feel free to form their own old girl network, to talk among themselves about their concerns about their jobs, to offer advice and support. Here they do. By the same token, the women feel little or no hesitation in letting a guy know that a joke or a comment was in poor taste and would he not do it again? That usually takes care of it. Real harassment appears to be nonexistent. Of course, like most sales forces, Levi Strauss's has its own standards about language, which are somewhat looser than the rest of the company's.

Here you don't need to go drinking after work to make the contacts that move the business along; you can make them at lunch or in the gym. Jogging, however, isn't a bad idea. Neither is being able to talk knowledgeably about vintages, growths and grapes. When you entertain buyers, the company won't pick up your chits if they're from a club that discriminates against women, blacks or Jews. Management means to be fair.

To ensure that pay is equitable, the company carried out a thorough job evaluation in the mid-eighties. Job and skills in different functions were compared without considering who was actually filling them. The process took well over a year, and when it was over, pay and grade level adjustments were forthcoming. No other company we know has gone to such great lengths to ensure that pay and job status are fair. It's no wonder that Levi Strauss is the employer of choice in San Francisco. A spirit of fairness and accommodation invests everything the company does.

Then there's the lay of the land. Some think that Levi Strauss has one of the most spectacular corporate homes in America, sitting as it does at the base of Telegraph Hill near San Francisco Bay. Headquarters consists of four low-slung red brick buildings, looking, from a distance, like steps leading down from the hill. They are surrounded by greenery and wildflowers, a huge open plaza and a fountain with a waterfall. Pass the second floor, and your office might have a view of the bay.

The buildings themselves are designed as if the workers themselves had voted on how to do it right. There are open balconies and skylights. Each floor has two or three break rooms with couches and chairs, and kitchenettes with free coffee and microwave ovens. In the quiet rooms you can practice yoga or read Proust. Before or after work, you can check into the spacious (7,000 square feet), handsomely outfitted gym and lift weights or take classes in yoga and aerobics. No building is taller than seven stories.

You don't get the feeling that top management is off in the clouds somewhere.

They tried it once, and it didn't work. In the early seventies, when the company was spread out among several downtown buildings, it decided to consolidate and move into a new skyscraper in the Embarcadero Center. But the place didn't feel like home. Too many tall elevators, too much cold steel and glass, too much like any old big business. And so, even though there was a long lease to run, Levi Strauss decided to build its own corporate headquarters and chose the site by the bay. They turned their corporate campus into a showplace.

Levi Strauss has plenty of women in good jobs, women who have been with the company about a dozen years, maybe a few less. But jobs at levels much higher than they are today are hard to come by because of a group of men who got there ahead of them and didn't start as secretaries, who came with degrees not in French and psychology but in business and accounting. They have worked together through thick and thin. They know and trust each other. These guys are only in their forties, and they are not planning on early retirement. Even president and CEO Robert Haas, the founder's great-great-grandnephew, is in his mid-forties. Job openings at the top of the pyramid are scarce indeed. And not everyone subscribes to the Levi standards of fairness wholeheartedly. One woman spoke for many when she said: "The hearts of the people who own the company are in the right place. They have a social conscience and a responsibility to the community. There is, however, quite a distance from the executive offices to the rest of the organization. If you expect everyone in management to be an open conduit to this wonderful Haas family philosophy, you would be wrong."

And then she went on to say that she personally had never been discriminated against at the company. Maybe she's more typical than she thinks.

LOTUS

ONE OF THE WORLD'S LARGEST INDEPENDENT SOFTWARE COMPANIES

▲ EMPLOYEES: Over 2,000; half are women.

▲ REVENUES: $283 million in 1986; in the first quarter of 1987, revenues were $280 million.

▲ Lotus relies heavily on its own employees to recruit new employees. The company employs job posting, tuition reimbursement, a management development program (50 percent of attendees are women) and careful attention to succession planning.

▲ Of the 60 employees considered upper management, eight—13 percent—are women. Although Lotus has had female vice presidents, it has none as we go to press. All five members of the board of directors are men.

▲ The company openly addresses charges of sex discrimination. Its commitment to rectifying inequality of pay includes examining what other companies are doing, research to establish measures of comparable worth, reevaluation of individual job descriptions, grade level adjustments and paybacks for past inequities.

▲ Lotus provides standard maternity disability leave and up to eight weeks of additional leave without pay, position assured. The company provides paternity benefits, adoption benefits and a resource referral directory for child care facilities.

▲ In addition to its comprehensive medical benefits, Lotus has liberal vision, hearing and dental benefits, prescription drug benefits and three weeks of vacation after one year.

▲ Major employment centers: Cambridge, Mass.: 1,340; San Mateo, Calif.: 50; sales offices are located in Atlanta, Chicago, Cleveland, Dallas, Detroit, Houston, Los Angeles, New York, Newport Beach, Calif., Philadelphia, Pittsburgh, San Francisco, Seattle, St. Louis, Toronto and Washington, D.C.

LOTUS DEVELOPMENT CORPORATION
161 First Street
Cambridge, MA 02142
(617) 577-8500

"The toughest bargainers in the universe" is how the head of information systems for a major drug company describes Lotus's sales staff. "There's going to be some real mean bastard who drives a hard bargain, and it's as likely to be a woman as a man. They're arrogant and tough because they know they've got good stuff—the best. And when you go in, you never can tell who's going to make the presentation—it could be a man, it could just as well be a woman."

The outsider's view of Lotus basically tells the story of this Boston-based software house: they're good, they're hot and they're egalitarian. Sexism is not just dead here. It's never been alive. If some outbreak of it appears—in the form of a new man on board—you can bet your first edition of *The Feminine Mystique* that it will be routed ere long. The guy will shape up or be sent packing.

"There's an implied message from the top that you will not be sexist, that's not how we behave," says the former vice president of human resources, Janet Axelrod, shortly before she left the company. She was the company's first employee, hired after Mitch Kapor decided to go into business for himself in 1981 to develop an idea that he couldn't sell to a previous employer. "I didn't have to fight any battles at the top about equality," says Axelrod. "I didn't have to prove that women were equal. Mitch was at Yale in the late sixties and early seventies, and he was one of the men challenged by the women's movement. And he comes out of that New York Jewish intellectual progressive milieu."

But Mitch Kapor, who evoked a kind of gurulike reverence in his employees, is gone too. He resigned as chairman in 1986, shortly after Axelrod left. Gone also is Jonathan Sachs, who with Kapor designed the software package called 1–2–3, whose phenomenal success made the company the world's largest independent software house. With a lot of the talent at the top gone, some of the glamour has evaporated. The running of the business has been left to Jim P. Manzi, who is cooler, quieter and much more of a numbers cruncher than Kapor. No one knows how much the corporate culture will change under Manzi. What is undeniable is that it will become increasingly corporate, the direction in which it was already moving as Lotus grew from a few flower children with big ideas to a public corporation with more than two thousand employees and revenues climbing toward $500 million.

Like the IBM personal computer, Lotus 1–2–3 has become an industry standard. It turns a PC into an electronic spreadsheet for financial analysis and lets users make graphs and file data without stopping to summon up separate programs. First-year sales projections were underestimated by 1,700 percent, and Lotus was able to emerge quickly as the leader of the personal computer software industry, a position it still holds. The growth of the company hinges on 1–2–3, rather than any blockbuster success since then. Symphony and Jazz, two later packages, did not perform as well as hoped. Lately, Lotus has focused on the business and scientific markets, since its products are generally more expansive and sophisticated than what individual users need in their homes. In 1986 Lotus brought out Manuscript, a word processing program designed to work with 1–2–3's spreadsheet, and Measure, a data acquisition software package designed for the growing desktop engineering market.

Because of its past success and easy dominance in a few short years, Lotus gives off an aura of youthful arrogance and invincibility. "We're hot and we know it" might as well be printed on their business cards. The price employees pay for this is a kind of consuming passion about their work. Very few people walk out the door at 5:30 P.M. You stay late not only to work, but to schmooze with people in your department, to find out what's going on and exchange information. "We are a company of overachievers across the board," says Ann Arbuthnot, manager of international marketing. "We are type A's, whether male or female. The peer pressure here is so intense the only thing I can compare it to was when I was in college and they had to close the library on Saturday night to keep the students out. It's like that at Lotus; they have to lock the doors to keep people out." In fact, the company sometimes does lock the doors. The day after one of its new products was shipped, everybody had the day off. When people tried to come in anyway, they found that the elevators wouldn't stop at Lotus's floors.

But the golden years of 1982–83, when product moved as fast as it could be shipped, appear to have come to an end. People hung around then at all hours to inhale the success; now they do it partly because that's the Lotus way and, more important, to come up with new products that will keep them in the number one slot. They say they enjoy the grueling hours, that they would rather be there on weekends than doing a lot of other things, that they stay after work even if they don't have to. But they also admit there's pressure to do so. "There's a subtle but pervasive tone coming from the top that says, we want you to stay up all hours and do whatever you have to for that next success," one woman says.

But as the culture changes and the people get a little bit older, they are beginning to find that they want to focus on other aspects of their lives. A baby boom is sweeping the company. In some departments, it's okay to go home at 5 P.M. In some departments, you won't be penalized. However, to keep up you'll probably be dragging lots of work home. And it still may be impossible to dispel the notion that the person at the next desk who stays until seven, goes out and grabs a quick bite and returns to work until ten isn't the one who should be promoted ahead of you. "The company may support the concept of leaving at five and devoting time to your family, but the reality is that people who can work longer hours produce more results and they are going to move ahead faster than the people who can't," she adds.

But if Lotus is a company of workaholics, it gives back in kind for that commitment. The benefits are among the most innovative we've come across (more about them later), and the atmosphere—even as it becomes increasingly corporate—remains exciting and electric. Creative emotional types with six ideas to try at once will enjoy the freewheeling atmosphere. When you flub up, no one will hold it against you for very long, even if you cry in front of your boss. It's okay to bring your kid in when you need to. It's even okay to walk around in stocking feet. At headquarters, there's no rigid dress code: you can wear leather minis and neon pink tights if you want. Techies here are barely distinguishable from the preppies that people Cambridge, where Lotus is located. Once a year the technical staff gets dressed up in proper business suits for an annual meeting, and everyone thinks it's a gas. Out in the field, it's a different story. Women who want to get ahead dress for success.

Whether they are in suits or Hawaiian shirts, the issue for Lotus employees is not boredom. It's burnout. How long can anyone put in 12- or 16-hour days, week after week? How long does anyone want to? And underneath the free-spirited culture is always 1–2–3. "We all run at such a high rate, you reach burnout at that pace," observes one woman, summing up the comments of many.

But if you want to shoot for the top, sex won't get in your way. "If we choose to make the sacrifices, there is nothing to stop us," says Katherine Paine, director of corporate communications. "It is our choice to make." Now this doesn't mean that women are represented equally at the top. However, Sandra Gunn, former vice president of engineering and scientific products, was definitely senior management, and the word is out that Lotus is always looking for talented women and minorities. (Gunn, incidentally, wore suits.) Lotus has attracted women with double-digit experience from engineering giants such as IBM and Hewlett-Packard. These women said they had topped out at their previous employers and were willing to risk security for opportunity.

In this tight little club at the top, the culture has all the grace of boys' night out. They sit together at meetings and talk through presentations. They smoke cigarettes and make cool comments. "They have a high sense of macho," observes one woman. "There's a certain bravado about them. We have a reputation for being arrogant, and it comes from the top." And if you want to operate at that level, you have to play into their way of doing things.

Yet the macho overlay doesn't mean this is a no-frills company. Quite the opposite is true. This is exactly the kind of place you would imagine kids from the sixties would dream up. Monthly meetings are held at a downtown hotel, and everyone is invited. Rumors are quashed, and the news—good and bad—is announced. New employees are introduced. If a complaint registered anonymously in the Grapevine—bright purple boxes in various places around the building—is worthy of comment, it will be talked about. A council of employees, balanced as to sex and race, discusses the corporate culture and how it could be made better. Leadership courses are likely to be given by a woman to a roomful of men. Vice presidents have offices within their groups that are not much larger than anybody else's—they are not off on a floor by themselves. Nearly everybody eats in the eighth-floor company cafeteria overlooking the Charles River, and it's not difficult to approach anybody. In warm weather, there are tables and chairs outside on the terrace. If you don't need a parking space because you ride the subway to work, you'll be given a pass for the MBTA. And a shuttle will pick you up and take you to your building from one of several stops, starting at 7:30 A.M. After a year, you get three weeks of vacation plus your birthday off. If you need time off for a family illness or your own, or special working conditions for a while, the company will support you wholeheartedly. One woman who was hospitalized for a time held staff meetings at her bedside. Not surprisingly, unusually large stock option and stock purchase plans are available, along with comprehensive benefits; a prescription will cost you a dollar. There are nutrition workshops as well as exercise classes and showers at headquarters for noontime joggers. And so on.

What Lotus doesn't have at the moment is succession planning; the company is too new and too unstructured overall for such a corporate subset. This means you're on your own, but the opportunities are wide open. Making the jump from the secretarial pool to the professional staff isn't impossible and is encouraged. At all levels, you get a lot of leeway to grow into your job. "You can bring in your ideas and explore them and see how they help the company," says Christine Bresnahan, a recruiter whose idea it was to start all secretaries off in a pool for a month to see how they fit in the company. "If an idea fails, it fails, and you can start on something new."

To maintain pay equity, Lotus sometimes finds itself giving women huge raises over their old pay scale when they join the company. Translation: you might end up getting much more than you ask for. "Men get more money because they yell about it longer," observes Katharyn Faulkner, human resources director. "And so the inequities in the world often get fixed when people come here."

Because the company is so hot and the perks so great, this is not an easy company to join. Lotus is flooded with dozens of unsolicited résumés each month. The best way in is to know somebody. And if she gets you a job and you work out, she'll get a $500 bonus.

In its heyday, Lotus was seen as such a sexy place to work that employees often didn't say they worked there when they went to parties, comments one former employee, a self-admitted victim of burnout. They said they were teachers or something else to avoid being deluged with questions about what it was like or how to get in. Whether Lotus can maintain that kind of profile is doubtful. Most glamorous companies can't. They follow a predictable scenario: a hot product, employees having a ball, investors scrambling to get in. The danger is elitism bordering on hubris. Nobody believes the company can fail or that the competition can catch up. Stay tuned.

MANUFACTURERS HANOVER TRUST

THE NATION'S SIXTH LARGEST BANK

▲ EMPLOYEES: 24,700 (in the United States); approximately 59 percent are women.

▲ ASSETS: Approximately $75.3 billion.

▲ Manufacturers Hanover does an excellent job of recruiting and hiring women. They advertise in women's publications, carefully balance for sex in recruiting brochures and send women in line positions to on-campus recruiting sessions.

▲ Efforts to promote women include job posting, corporate training programs, careful monitoring of career progress and tuition refunds. Approximately 40 percent of management trainees are women.

▲ The bank handles charges of sexual discrimination through informal hearings at first and formal procedures if necessary.

▲ Manufacturers Hanover states categorically that there is no pay inequity.

▲ Of the 194 employees identified as senior management, 13—7 percent—are women. All of these women are senior vice presidents. Manufacturers Hanover may have the highest number of female SVPs in the country. Of the 17 members of the board of directors, one is a woman.

▲ In addition to standard maternity disability leave, the bank seems flexible to the needs of parents. Flexible work hours, flexible workplaces and part-time work for managers and professionals are all possibilities. The bank allows leave for family illness and offers a resource referral directory for child care services and a cafeteria-style approach to employee benefits.

▲ Manufacturers has as part of its personnel policies and procedures manual an explicit written statement prohibiting sexual harassment. Training, including education, EEO guidelines and reporting procedures is part of presupervisory and supervisory training for men and women. Complaints are handled by informal hearing, by formal grievance procedure or, in extreme cases, by lawsuit.

▲ Major employment centers: New York and New Jersey: 19,500; California: 700; Pennsylvania: 475; North Carolina: 315; Illinois: 245. The bank has 1,000 offices in 43 states and 100 facilities in 41 foreign countries.

MANUFACTURERS HANOVER TRUST COMPANY
320 Park Avenue
New York, NY 10017
(212) 286-6000

When Nancy Mistretta was going on maternity leave in 1982, the then president of Manufacturers Hanover, John Torell, called her on her last day to wish her well. "And when I came back, a couple of the head guys called me up to their offices to welcome me," she says. "They seemed to think my having a kid was the greatest thing since canned beer. They were so supportive and made me feel there was a genuine interest in me. Somebody may have tipped Torell off that it was my last day, but he made the call, and that locks you in. I was a company man after that."

For Mistretta, a lending officer whose corporate customers are in the New York area, that means entertaining clients once or twice a week, nights when she gets home anywhere between 11 P.M. and 1 A.M. Mistretta takes it in stride, for she strongly feels that the juggling act required to be a vice president of the bank, wife and mother is her responsibility. According to her, it's a policy the bank subscribes to. However, Manny Hanny obviously believes in helping out where it can.

While line jobs like Mistretta's do not allow for anything other than the standard workday hours (and long ones at that), staff employees can make all kinds of special arrangements to meet their needs. Part-time professionals can work out the hours they will be in the office with their managers; mothers who want to ease back into their jobs after giving birth can begin on a part-time basis or work four long days and have the fifth off; one woman who quit when her husband was transferred to Tokyo was called once she was there and asked if she wanted to do research on Eastern markets; and nobody looks askance when attorney and vice president Joan Levy, who comes in early every day, walks out the door at 5:20 to catch a train. "The general counsel knows I'm going to put in my time and I'm going to take work home," says Levy. "And nobody says anything the day I call up and cancel meetings with everybody because somebody at home has tonsillitis. Understand, nobody will cover for you either. You have to keep up and not skip a step."

What we found remarkable about a bank this understanding is that this is also a place where being female is considered strictly a nonissue, at least in most divisions. (Retail banking is a somewhat different story, which we'll get to later.)

As Magna Dodge, a senior vice president, tells it, sure, she's had to work hard to get ahead, but no harder than a man would have: "Male or female, you don't sit back and coast and expect to get ahead. A woman can do anything anyone else can do, she just has to be prepared to work hard, be smart and diligent. Nobody is going to create opportunities, but nobody is going to go out of the way to hold you back."

Is there a point beyond which women can't advance? Dodge says that while there may be such a ceiling at Manny Hanny, its height hasn't been tested yet. "I have always been rewarded in a timely fashion for what I've demonstrated I could do. Of course, there have been times when I've been frustrated, but I've always had the sense that it's a temporary situation and that something more will be coming. People are watching out for me and taking good care of me."

Dodge runs the bank's media group, which handles the publishing, broadcasting and entertainment accounts. She says that she probably has more women working for her than men. "I've always been aggressive in getting the best people to work for me, and they have tended to migrate toward the women," she says. Is she guilty of reverse sexism? Not at all. Investment banking is attracting a goodly number of men interested in amassing small fortunes before they are 35, and they have left open a wide number of slots at commercial banks.

Unlike many other companies, Manufacturers Hanover didn't discover a pool of able women knocking at the door yesterday. In the early seventies, well before other companies were hiring women in substantial numbers, the bank had them on board. Not only were they there, the bank was accepting what that means—i.e., that some women will have babies. Wendy Richman became an officer when she was seven months pregnant in 1974; today she admits that she was even unsure if she would come back after her daughter was born. Four months after the birth, her manager started calling and asking what her intentions were. When she voiced a desire to work part-time at first, he arranged for her to come back three days a week for the first six months. Now it's a common practice. "It was absolutely what the doctor ordered," she says. "I had to make a decision after six months, and I came back full-time. My boss took a risk and it paid off, but without that kind of leeway, I don't think I would have been able to come back." Richman, who began as a program analyst, made senior vice president in 1986.

Obviously, having kids won't be held against you here. And you'll be given the option to move at whatever pace you want. Stay on the fast track or slow down, it's your choice. One senior manager told of a discussion she'd had with another—a man—about whether a new mother should be asked if she wanted to attend a seminar in London. The man was hesitant of asking her because he felt it might place undue pressure on her with an infant at home. The female manager suggested that the new mother be given the option of going but that it be made clear that she didn't have to go. She went.

Richman and Dodge are among the 13 women who are senior vice presidents. One woman is a senior managing director. By the time you read this, the numbers are likely to have increased. Manny Hanny is near—if not at—the top of the list of banks with the highest number of women up there. And the women we spoke to said that their male peers seemed genuinely pleased when women were promoted up, joking only that now there were too many to keep track of at monthly senior management meetings. "There's damn good opportunity at the bank, and women joining now won't be disappointed," adds Richman. "If they do their job, they can move up very quickly. There's a couple of people who started out seven years ago as management trainees, and they are now vice presidents."

The good news about Manny Hanny gets even better. Banks are not known to be warm and cuddly places, but to hear the women talk, this place is a storehouse of good feelings. People are nice to one another. The killer instinct (encouraged at Citibank) apparently doesn't exist here. "I don't mean to sound goopy," one woman says, "but in general the people around here are nice." It's a theme we heard over and over. Though the bank is chock-full of convivial Irishmen, no one is blocked from getting ahead. Jews, WASPs and minorities seem to have an equal chance here. Individuality in style—both dress and office decor—is more evident here than at other banks. No one's running around in really short minis, but not everyone's in a tailored suit. Lots of silk dresses, lots of bright colors. These ladies are chic.

The single glitch we heard about is in the retail banking center. One woman says, "These men have not come to grips with the concept of a woman who is not a teller." However, retail banking does have a female senior vice president, Joyce Healy. She's been there since 1981 but obviously hasn't been able to bring the misogynists into line.

Judy Norton, senior vice president for human resources, is aware that problems remain. "We get troubled if women are not advancing as they should be," she says. "We'll talk to the managers and say, 'Look, Mary is qualified, why wasn't she promoted?' If nothing happens in a year or so, we'll go back and ask again or, if she qualifies, offer her the opportunity to be promoted elsewhere. We take affirmative action very seriously."

To that end, the bank has a number of systems in place. Job posting has been around since 1969, earlier than at most companies, and a data bank makes it possible to track women's and minorities' progress. Tuition reimbursement is available for job-related courses and degrees; for high performers who want an MBA from a big name school, time off at full salary (plus the full cost of the program and incidentals) can be arranged. At present the bank has women at the Wharton School and Columbia University. "And if they think investment banking is the sexy place to be, we'll say, 'Go for it,'" comments Norton. "But you have to plan for it, you have to figure out the kind of experience you need. But even there, you'll see women at the top." Although Manny Hanny is the kind of bank where team playing is much encouraged, that's less true in the investment banking division, where risk taking and entrepreneurship are needed commodities. "We're serious about not wanting good people to leave us," adds Norton. "We'll do what we can to make sure they want to stay."

What the bank does not do is systematic succession planning; it's thought to be too static. Instead, particularly talented people (as many women as men, Norton insists) are identified, and they are considered when opportunities arise.

Like sex and motherhood, sexual harassment is not an issue, but since this is a big place and naturally someone is going to overstep the line now and then, a formal grievance procedure handles the complaint. Once in a while the complaints come from men about their bosses. Their female bosses. And should some hapless man have the audacity to utter a sexist put-down, the women—and men—jump all over him. It sounds like one-trial learning. At a place this good, it was disappointing to learn that male officers sometimes entertain clients at clubs that discriminate against women, such as the nearby Racquet and Tennis Club or the New York Athletic Club. While the women quickly added that lunches they would be attending were never scheduled at such places, they did bring it up, noting that the bank also paid for the memberships to these clubs. Women use private clubs for entertaining too. "The Yacht Club isn't too shabby," one vice president remarked ironically. "And it's totally integrated."

To get hired by the bank, the right degree from the right school will give you an edge, but only temporarily. After you sign on, you're in competition with everybody else. The bank recruits not only at big name schools but also regional and city schools (if you grew up a New Yorker, you'll probably stay a New Yorker, the thinking goes); to seek out women, Manufacturers Hanover recruits at women's colleges, advertises in women's magazines and depicts them in the recruiting brochures and the annual report. Women in line positions accompany recruiters to campuses.

Benefits are good but not spectacular. Profit sharing is available to all workers after a year's employment, and one becomes fully vested after six years. Pay inequity is not an issue, and we were assured that men and women are equally compensated for like positions.

But can Manny Hanny's good-guy image and gentility make it in the cutthroat eighties? Although its growth in the seventies was spectacular—it went from a single bank in 1969 to become one of the nation's largest financial services companies within a decade—it slipped in the early eighties and has been having a tough time pulling itself up again. It has been slow to put together its plans for middle market investment banking, and continuing trouble with its loans to Third World countries has been draining resources. Stories of internal wrangling have made it into the financial media. The bank's image of intense loyalty to the customer, perhaps to the detriment of profitability, has not helped either, despite the fact that the bank has reorganized and announced new marketing strategies. One was to back away from several hundred unprofitable corporate customers and double fees on some services. The balance sheet is somewhat brighter than it was a few years back, but outsiders still view Manny Hanny with skepticism. *Business Week* reported that investors were so uninterested last year, despite a rich dividend yield, that some analysts have stopped following the stock.

John McGillicuddy, the chairman of the board, has been with the bank nearly three decades. Although he has done some tough talking—including asking those who can't adapt to the new thrust to leave—some wonder if he and the management who let the bank slip can oversee a turnaround.

Some of the work still gets done on the golf course. And the group that is making the decisions that shape the bank is still all men. Women aren't being kept out because of their golf scores. There aren't any slots at the top, nor are there likely to be soon. Nearly all sector heads—less than a dozen people—are men in their forties. They will probably be in their jobs for more than a decade.

As for a woman ever becoming president of the bank, senior vice president Magna Dodge is realistic in her assessment: "The rest of the world isn't moving as fast as the banking community is in promoting women. Maybe that's an excuse, but until the rest of the world changes, we're not going to see a woman as president of our country or the CEO of a major bank."

MERCK

▲ EMPLOYEES: 15,000 (in the United States); more than a third are women.

▲ SALES: More than $4.1 billion in 1986. More than 12 percent was targeted for research, unusual for an established firm.

▲ Merck & Company is known throughout the corporate community for its benefits, which include flexitime, unusually generous maternity and paternity benefits, adoption allowances and near-site child care at some locations. Flexible workplaces and part-time work for managers and professionals are being tried on a limited basis.

▲ The company does an excellent job of recruiting and hiring women in all areas—including financial, research and sales—and managers are monitored on their ability to meet hiring goals. To ensure promotions, Merck uses job posting, career development workshops, assertiveness programs and succession planning, which requires that a certain number of women and minorities be designated as high potential. Detailed development plans are constructed for them.

▲ Of the 680 people identified as upper management, 9 percent are women. Of the 15 members of the board of directors, one is a woman. A woman was appointed vice president and treasurer in the fall of 1987.

▲ Merck developed an innovative program that deals with sexual and racial discrimination and harassment. The program is now being used by over 50 major U.S. corporations. It was first implemented with 500 senior managers, who then became the trainers for all Merck employees. The women we interviewed agreed that sexual harassment is no longer an issue. Should it occur, it is handled by an informal hearing, followed by a formal grievance procedure.

▲ Major employment centers: Rahway, N.J.: 4,200; West Point, Pa.: 3,700; Pittsburgh: 500; San Diego: 500; 26 plants throughout the United States; 12 experimental farms and research laboratories; and 51 plants overseas.

MERCK & COMPANY, INC.
P.O. Box 2000
Rahway, NJ 07065
(201) 574-4000

In 1978 a scientist who was expecting mentioned to her boss that she was going to have problems finding good child care after her baby was born. Not wanting to lose her, he voiced his concern to a company personnel director and asked what could be done.

That inquiry pinpointed a growing awareness in the company that they were having trouble keeping many good employees who happened to be mothers. What happened next is typical of the way this pharmaceutical giant does business. Its reputation for taking good care of its employees did not materialize out of nothing. A round of discussions with mothers and mothers-to-be who worked for Merck revealed the not so surprising need for readily available day care. A feasibility study followed, and the next year Merck donated what it calls a sizable sum, as well as professional advice and guidance, to a group of its employees to set up their own day care center a mile from the company's headquarters in Rahway, New Jersey. The center opened its doors in 1980 to 15 tots and is a huge success. Merck provides ancillary services such as telephones and brochure printing, but aside from that it is totally self-supporting and run by a board of directors made up of parents of children at the center and the professional staff. Merck has stayed out of the child care business, but without its generous aid the center probably wouldn't exist.

The cost is around $400 a month for infants and toddlers up to the age of 5. Parents may drop off their tots beginning at 7:30 A.M., an hour before the main work force arrives, and the lights go out at 6 P.M., an hour after the usual close of business. There is a waiting list of approximately a hundred families for its 65 places, and women who are planning to get pregnant often sign up before they do to ensure their child a spot.

At another Merck location, West Point, Pennsylvania, a number of child care facilities were already operating, but Merck employees had trouble finding one that wasn't completely filled. Merck officials looked the centers over, picked what they considered to be the best, and gave it a grant in return for preferential admission for children of Merck employees. With the grant, the facility was able to expand, increasing both the available spaces and the amenities. About half of the 92 spaces are filled by children of Merck employees.

Helping out financially with the knotty problem of child care isn't the only way in which the company has made a substantial effort to accommodate the needs of working mothers. Workers may come in as early as 7 or as late as 9:30 and leave accordingly. The policy is in widespread use in all divisions of the company. Newer programs in the trial phase include part-time work and the use of in-home computer terminals for mothers who want to work but don't want to leave their infants quite yet. The company newsletter encourages them to make wider use of these options.

Merck is also unusually generous in how long it allows an employee to stay home with Baby. While paid leave is usually only six weeks, Mom *or* Dad can stay home for up to six months and be guaranteed her or his old job—or one of like responsibility. If a parent wants a longer leave (up to 18 months), that's permitted, but there are no guarantees that a job with the same status as the former one will be waiting. However, during this time, Merck's excellent medical and dental coverage, paid for entirely by the company, stays in effect.

Yet all is not paradise for mothers at Merck. It's not keeping the job that's difficult, it's convincing your peers and boss that your career is important. In other words, how hard are you willing to work now that you have a child? The general perception here is that children lessen one's willingness to give all to the company, and the company responds in kind. One mother of three states, "Single women are promoted and pushed ahead more than women who have obligations outside the company." Another woman says that if she was vying for a particular promotion and another woman were the competition, her chances would be greatly enhanced if the other woman were to become pregnant. Working mothers who want to stay on an upward career path have to prove that they aren't overly distracted by the demands of motherhood.

The generous maternity benefits of the last decade didn't come out of a hat. Historically, Merck has always been in the forefront of benefits and has had maternity leaves on the books for more than 30 years, something of a record for American companies. And it isn't in child care alone that Merck's benefits shine. Its entire package, including pay, is among the best in the nation. The pension plan is also entirely paid for by the company, and long-term disability and life insurance plans are available. A savings plan adds $1 to every $2 you save, up to $750 a year, to be invested as you see fit—stocks, bonds, mutual funds or savings certificates. The overall attitude can be summed up by the following lines taken from a company position paper prepared for the United Nations: "It is Merck's strong belief that family support policies and practices can help significantly to reduce the stress the employee feels from the increased demands of a fuller life style. The reduction of stress has an obvious benefit to the employee; it also can positively affect the employee's productivity on the job."

While it sounds almost too good to be true, Merck is repeatedly cited as one of the nation's leaders in trying to help employees balance the conflicts between work and family life. Merck gets good grades from more than employee relations experts: the financial folks also give the company the nod, and *Fortune* ranked it first among the 10 most admired companies in America last year. In its industry, Johnson & Johnson pulled ahead only for its community and environmental responsibility. Merck was rated first for all other attributes: quality of management, wise use of corporate assets, quality of products, long-term investment value, financial soundness, and the ability to attract, develop and keep talented people.

But as often happens in companies where the benefits and pay are fabulous, its ability to attract and keep people turns into a mixed blessing. "Merck pays you well, and so you don't want to leave, even when the job has become routine and there are no challenges left," says one woman. "You aren't forced to use the kind of energy that you might be somewhere else. You get complacent, and ultimately you get cheated out of being the best you could be."

Another woman in the discussion adds, "People tend to stay here too long. You're making a lot of money and you think, 'Why should I change jobs?'" There are only so many places at the top, and so people tend to get stuck doing the same job for 30 years. You forget that you want to get ahead, not just take home a fat paycheck." And if the people above you don't move up, you often can't either.

If rampant complacency were a disease that could be cured with a drug, Merck's chemists would be on the case. Merck's research effort is considered quite possibly the best in the country, as considerable funds (approximately 12 percent of sales) are plowed back into research. R and D is the lifeblood of Merck, something that is not expected to change under the leadership of the man who took over the reins in 1985, P. Roy Vagelos. A physician and biochemist, he is the first scientist to be at the helm of America's leader in the prescription drug business. Merck consistently ranks in the top 10 of American companies rated as to how many research dollars stand behind each employee, unusual for established firms. Competition from generic drugs cutting into the sales of established drugs makes the expense necessary.

Merck has a formidable track record to show for the money and effort. Merck chemists discovered vitamin B_{12} and streptomycin and were the first to synthesize cortisone, way back in 1944, opening the door for a new class of drugs for the treatment of arthritis and other inflammatory conditions, including allergies. Clinoril, an antiarthritic medication, has long been one of its profit leaders, although sales in the United States have leveled off.

Recent discoveries include Vasotec for treating high blood pressure and Primaxin, an injectable antibiotic for severe infections. Merck is also a major manufacturer of vaccines; one against hepatitis B has been marketed in more than 50 countries since its introduction in 1982, and another, a combination vaccine against measles, mumps and rubella, saved the United States $1.4 billion in 1983 alone, according to a study by the Centers for Disease Control.

Add it all up, and Merck emerges as the employer of choice for research biochemists not attracted to academia. Indeed a company where science is happily married to commerce, Merck has no trouble attracting topflight researchers. Having a Ph.D. isn't a prerequisite to getting a job in the laboratory, but it will probably smooth the way for ambitious people. Of some 2,000 men and women who work in Merck's labs in the United States, 830 have degrees at the Ph.D., M.D. or D.V.M. level. That's doctor of veterinary medicine, for a goodly share of Merck's business is in animal health and agriculture. Fifteen percent of the people who hold advanced degrees at Merck are women. One woman who doesn't have the letters after her name says that if she could start all over again, she would go to Harvard and get a Ph.D.

Scientists tend to marry scientists, and Merck has a number of in-house marriages, as well as a program to help the spouse of someone who's transferred to a new location or joining the company. Couples are hired as long as one partner won't be reporting to the other. But marriage doesn't always mean that the two people will be working at the same place. Engineers, for instance, can be sent to sites around the world. One such couple, assigned to sites in different states, own a house in New Jersey and get together on weekends. "We'll probably never end up working in the same spot, since we're at the same level, but we knew that when we got married," she says. Merck's attitude is that the company benefits from such marriages.

Another engineer says that when she was first hired in 1978, being an outsider and being a woman made her life difficult because she felt she had to prove herself on each new job. "When they finally decided that I wasn't going to break down and cry if they yelled at me, and they could see that I could handle the job, they accepted me. It took about a year or so." Now that her days of trial by fire are over, or nearly over, she's not so sure it was discrimination based on sex, but rather her youth. The problem was especially acute when she was sent overseas to be the process engineer on a $30 million job. She had five men reporting to her who were at least 10 years older than she. She was in her mid-twenties at the time. "They are not used to women engineers in England," she says ruefully.

The problems women were experiencing because they were women — this is an old, established male hierarchy, after all — were not lost on the company, and typically Merck set out in 1979 to right the problem with a massive educational program designed to make employees rethink their attitudes about women and minorities on the job. Some 2,000 managers attended seminars that focused on affirmative action roles and responsibilities; the next step was a training session for production supervisors, shop stewards and union officials. In the last phase of the program, all of Merck's 15,000 employees in the United States spent a day with a dozen or so other employees watching a 30-minute film and videotaped vignettes depicting real-life situations that often lead to misunderstanding, listening to presentations and going over case studies. The leaders were other Merck employees. The idea was to spur lively discussions on the hiring and promotion of women and minorities. Sexual harassment was not skirted.

How open were the discussions? Well, in one, a man who worked for a female boss spent most of the morning complaining about her, and how she had been unduly promoted over him. The discussion leader took him aside and said, "Don't you understand what this woman is going through?" That had never occurred to him. The woman who told this story was the boss in question, and she said that he phoned her during the lunch break to say how sorry he was for all the grief he had given her. He later admitted that he had tried to make her life so unpleasant she would quit. The woman has since been transferred to a different department, and her former nemesis has her old job, that of a sales manager. "Now we're best of friends," she says. "The best compliment I've ever had was when he told me that I was the best boss he'd ever had."

The educational program has won numerous awards, and today more than 50 major corporations use it. A follow-up program specifically dealing with sexual harassment was developed but left to the managers' discretion whether or not to implement it. But by the mid-eighties harassment was not a significant problem, and few managers did. Company women say that while there were incidents in the past, they have by and large stopped.

While the official programs attack the problem head-on, Merck's strong response to affirmative action has sometimes spotlighted women in ways that are not necessarily welcome. "You're very aware of being a woman here, and you are often made aware that you got a particular job because you are a woman," is how one woman puts it. Naturally, this causes resentment in the ranks of white males, who feel they are entitled to compete with their peers on an equal basis, and the women say the resentment isn't only from the older men: "I would love to say that the younger men are better and they aren't discriminating, but that's a bunch of baloney. It makes it all the worse because you feel they should know better. I would say that only very successful younger men don't mind the competition."

Another woman told of someone getting a promotion and being told point-blank that she was getting it because she was a woman. When she said she didn't want the job, she was told she would be *without* a job. She took the promotion. And once a woman is promoted into a visible spot, other women below her know that their chances are limited. *The company has its woman.* "There's another woman five years ahead of me in my department, and I know that unless something happens—like she has children—I won't get promoted," says one woman. "You are always very conscious here of being different, of being a woman."

Yet some women—particularly older women who have watched the company change as the times did—feel that young women joining Merck now face few or no barriers due to their sex. "Merck is a first-class company where the opportunities to learn and grow are mind-boggling," says Dorothy Bowers, a senior director of environmental control for the chemical division. She has been with Merck since 1974. "Sex is a nonissue. If you're a woman here and you're not qualified, you're in a lot of trouble. Just as much trouble as any man would be."

And if you're a woman, it apparently helps to be attractive. "It's the feminine, attractive woman who gets ahead at Merck," remarks one woman. "The tough, aggressive type doesn't make it here." Yet beauty has it downside. Senior men—and even male peers—are reluctant to spend too much time with you or have lunch lest it be misinterpreted.

While the right degree from a good school does make a difference at Merck, some women have been able to make the transition from secretary to executive. But the going is rough. Growing up in a family where girls didn't go to college, a woman we'll call Madeline started as a secretary right out of high school more than 20 years ago. After nearly a decade of typing letters, she rebelled. "If I had to make one more cup of coffee, I knew I would dump it on his head," she says, referring to her boss. Instead of quitting, she enrolled at nearby Rutgers University and eventually received an MBA. Merck paid for the entire cost of tuition. She is now a manager with a budget of $15 million. Once she had the credentials, she concedes, she moved up faster than she would have if she had been male. While the jobs were challenging, most troublesome was the animosity of her co-workers, men as well as women. "The men in the department who felt they deserved my job made it extremely difficult," she says, "and when I first started I said that I would buy myself a new car if I could last a year." She bought it six months later, aware that she would not buckle under pressure. However, a woman was the hardest to be won over. She was 20 years older than Madeline, and used to reporting to male superiors. She was ready to resign rather than adjust. Madeline talked the problem out over drinks after work. Today they are friendly.

Although Merck appears to be committed to pushing women ahead and the statistics the company provided show that 9 percent of senior management are women (at the director or district manager level), the women interviewed agreed that only six or so women—out of 350 people—had any real power in the company. Partly, this is the result of limited numbers of women vying for the top spots over the decades that it takes to climb at a large, traditional, by-the-book firm like Merck. New policies, like new drugs, don't happen overnight. But that's not the whole reason. The power base is male, and it appears likely to stay that way for the next generation.

Women have been known to take over specific duties of their male superiors when they are promoted or a division is reorganized, but they will not be given the title—or the salary. Jobs have been downgraded and called something else, worth fewer pay points. It is not clear how often this has happened.

One good route for women to go is to find an area that is new and emerging, and where a complement of men isn't already in place. In other words, come in through the side door. That probably won't lead you to the very top rungs at Merck, but it will make for a comfortable niche. And in that case, being a woman can help, since it gives you visibility and you are less likely to be thought of as part of a certain team when management changes. Being special—a woman—keeps you out of the line of fire when a division is reorganized.

In summary, Merck emerges as a company for women that looks good on paper but in actuality is akin to a paternalistic father who secretly harbors the notion that boys ought to get ahead more than girls. He knows he shouldn't feel this way, and he tries to rectify the imbalance by doing *something*. But there it is. Women say that the new CEO is making headway in the right direction, but he hasn't been in power long enough for this to be clearly evident. Women who apply to Merck can look forward to good pay and great benefits. And a damn tough fight to get on track to the top of the pyramid.

MOUNTAIN BELL

THE LARGEST OF U.S. WEST'S SUBSIDIARIES

▲ EMPLOYEES: 29,520; approximately 52 percent are women.

▲ SALES: $3.7 billion in 1986.

▲ Mountain Bell tries to recruit and hire women, particularly on campus, where women and minorities are encouraged to apply for the management development program. The company is particularly interested in attracting women to technical jobs.

▲ Tuition reimbursement, up to 100 percent of costs or $3,000 a year, has helped many female employees to obtain both undergraduate and graduate degrees. An MBA seems to be an entry ticket to promotion. Mountain Bell's management development program is the other piece of the ticket, and in the last three years, 50 percent or more of those enrolled have been women.

▲ Mountain Bell handles sexual discrimination charges by informal hearings, including an open door policy, or by formal procedure, including union grievances. It was subject to the AT&T consent decree, which was in effect from 1973 through 1978.

▲ The company is concerned about rectifying inequality of pay to women. Methods used include examining what other companies are doing, reevaluation of individual job descriptions and whole classes of jobs held by women, and grade level adjustments.

▲ Of the 479 employees labeled upper management (third level and above in AT&T nomenclature), 18 percent are women. These include one CEO, 18 department directors and 62 district managers. One of the 14-member board of directors is a woman.

▲ The company has a policy on sexual harassment and a training program that is presented to all employees. The program includes education, EEO guidelines, self-help and coping strategies and reporting procedures. Charges of sexual harassment may be handled by informal hearing, by formal grievance procedure or, as a last resort, by lawsuit.

▲ The company is sensitive to parenting needs. In addition to standard maternity disability leave, mothers may take up to six months' unpaid leave with position assured. Other child care benefits include flexible work hours, the possibility of part-time work for managers and professionals, paternity and adoption benefits and a resource referral directory for child care facilities.

▲ Major employment centers: Colorado: 12,772; Arizona: 7,150; Utah: 3,206; New Mexico: 2,447; Montana: 1,323; Idaho: 1,198; Wyoming: 962.

MANAGEMENT EMPLOYMENT
Mountain Bell
1125 17th Street
DN 1690
P.O. Box 1300
Denver, CO 80201
(303) 896-2355

MANAGEMENT EMPLOYMENT	MANAGEMENT EMPLOYMENT
Mountain Bell	Mountain Bell
4041 North Central Avenue	250 Bell Plaza
Building C, Suite 200	Room 138
Phoenix, AZ 85012	Salt Lake City, UT 84111
(602) 235-8888	(801) 237-7810

There's no way around it: Mountain Bell caused some soul searching when we were compiling our list of good companies for women. It's not that there isn't a healthy percentage of women in senior management. There is. Women hold 18 percent of all senior management jobs—87 out of 479. One woman is a vice president and the chief executive officer of one of the state divisions. Other women are poised for promotion into the very top executive rank.

The benefits are excellent too. You can take off six months to care for a newborn and come back to a job of like pay and status; the medical, dental and vision plans, like those of all U.S. West companies, are excellent. Vacation days and personal days are also generous. If you want to get your MBA, the company will foot the entire cost, as well as giving you time off with pay to attend classes.

So what's wrong?

Mountain Bell is in cowboy country. The male backlash here is greater than any we've encountered elsewhere. When we visited the home office in Denver late in 1986, nearly nothing was being done about it. The seminars and workshops that had been held were ineffectual, all the women seemed to know it, but nobody in the corporate suite was paying attention. Most men were angry about women getting ahead and didn't feel the need to hide it.

The resentment appears to stem from how Mountain Bell came up with reasonably good numbers in the first place. A brief history is in order. Until women sued for discrimination in the late sixties, their treatment at the phone company was grossly unjust. Women with college degrees started as operators or service representatives; the best they could hope for was to become a supervisor. Men headed for management training programs and were assured promotions. The courts agreed women were getting the shaft. Although AT&T would not be liable for back pay, a court order mandated that AT&T redress the grievances by promoting women and minorities to jobs that had previously been out of reach. AT&T signed a consent decree, which included quotas, in January 1973. It expired six years later.

"Between 1970 and 1975 we had a phenomenal growth period, and with the consent decree in place, it was a great time to be a woman here," says

Sherry Sherrill, a district staff manager, whose first two promotions came quickly during those years. After that, however, advancement for women came to a screeching halt. Why? "The profiles of women and minorities looked reasonably decent, the government was off our back and the economy was terrible," she explains. The few available promotions went largely to white males. Just like before.

Women organized again, not to sue this time but to form a support group to lobby for fair treatment. The male hierarchy had only grudgingly gone along with the consent decree, and when they didn't have to do more, they didn't. In the spring of 1982, statistics in hand, U.S. West Women held a well-attended dinner meeting. Officers of the company (at the time, all men) also came. The highlight of the event was a speech documenting how the company had slipped. "Women and minorities were going down the tubes," says George Ann Harding, the gutsy woman who read off the numbers. Harding's speech created an uproar, and hasty promotions followed.

Then Jack MacAllister, who had been head of Northwestern Bell in Omaha, was named CEO of U.S. West, the parent company. MacAllister is deeply committed to pluralism in the workplace, and his move to the corporate offices in Denver put him in touch with what was going on at Mountain Bell, whose headquarters are located there also. He quickly appointed a task force to look into the problem. Today it is a permanent advisory body. When AT&T split up in 1984, MacAllister was at the helm of U.S. West, and a voluntary affirmative action plan that all the spinoff Bell companies had agreed to was in effect. The affirmative action plan—and MacAllister's enthusiasm—once more moved the company forward. The numbers began to look good again. Women were back on track and moving up. Today, a number of women say a vice presidency is within their grasp, something you don't often find at giants the size of Mountain Bell. MacAllister or one of his top officers now lunches quarterly with officers of U.S. West Women and the other support groups, one for black managers and another for Hispanics, and all are given ample opportunity to air their grievances. "MacAllister has been very effective in this area," comments Harding. "His message is coming on loud and clear."

But forcing egalitarianism on macho cowboy types doesn't mean they are going to turn in their spurs. "The company instituted this program of pluralism with the idea that you could train everybody to get along and value diversity," says Regina Jackson, a staff manager in strategic planning. "But a lot of people resent having it shoved down their throats, and this has created a backlash among the white males."

Enough to create an atmosphere where's it's not easy to be a woman. Men get away with crude wisecracks about women we won't repeat here.

When an attractive woman gets promoted, men openly ask whom she's sleeping with and question her credentials, even if they are impeccable. Racist comments are less frequent but still acceptable patter in some quarters. Put-downs in meetings are common. A man in the middle of one woman's presentation at a meeting—she was not telling them what they wanted to hear—remarked that she must have forgotten to take her Midol that day. All the men laughed. When she complained in writing to a vice president who had been present and who had joined in the merriment, he wrote back that she had taken the comment out of context. Soon after, she left the company for another U.S. West subsidiary.

Much of the blame must rest with the former administration, since their efforts to redress the situation did not amount to much, according to the women we interviewed. Workshops on racial and sexual prejudice have not been intense enough to make much of a dent. Gary Ames became president in 1987. The women have more faith in him.

But how quickly and how deeply Ames and MacAllister can change attitudes remains to be seen. The men want back what they've lost: absolute dominance on the job. In the meantime, it's a hostile world for most women at Mountain Bell, and the lower you are down the totem pole, the tougher it is. While some areas, such as human resources and information systems, are amiable, most women who want to work at Mountain Bell had better be thick-skinned and tough, especially if they are not white.

Women are particularly vulnerable to hostility if they apply for a craft—or nonmanagement—technical job, such as that of an installer. Male-oriented rules about how things must be done, such as how a ladder is carried (on the shoulder, not the hip), make it difficult for most women to meet the requirements of the job. The heckling and harassment don't help either. Equipment has been "acidentally" dropped on women and manhole covers put on while a woman was down in the hole because somebody "forgot" she was there. The result is that today fewer than 1 percent of all outside technical people, who are paid more than inside clerical workers, are women. Those advertisements we saw in the seventies showing woman installers were largely that—advertisements.

A thorny issue for nonmanagement women is the area of comparable worth. Some craft or nonmanagement jobs, such as that of dispatcher, have been downgraded as women moved into them. The company argues that computerization, not sex, made the difference. What is crystal clear is that life is much harder for women in nonmanagement jobs. The men feel no need to put a lid on their hostility.

What about the women who do make it at Mountain Bell? There are enough success stories, as we said before, to keep Mountain Bell on our list, and in spite of problems, the future for women looks good. Take George

Ann Harding, the woman who stood up and told everyone how the company had backslid. Being the bearer of bad news hasn't hurt her, as it might have elsewhere. An attorney in the legal department then, she is now Mountain Bell's highest-ranking woman and only female officer. In 1986 she was appointed vice president and chief executive officer for Wyoming. This meant that she and her husband, a bank president in Denver, would have a commuter marriage. She doesn't expect it to be that way forever. Her ultimate goal is to head up a major function at U.S. West's corporate office in Denver, a step she believes is probable.

She says she doesn't soft-pedal her feminist message—not even at officers' meetings, where she is the only woman present—but does make an effort not to alienate anyone. She has a sprightly, straightforward manner and can talk a good game of football as well as play a mean game of gin rummy late into the night.

Another woman whose career climb has been swift and sure is Jennifer Jones, whose area of expertise, data processing, is what the company is looking for now. A Phi Beta Kappa math major in college, she joined the company as a programmer in 1973, during the good years for women, and six years later she was overseeing the company's pension fund. Her next assignments were teleprocessing and systems development, and at 34 she became one of the company's youngest directors. A son was born in 1986. Jones stayed home for seven months. Before her leave, she was taken off her regular assignment and given a special project, and upon return her job was another special project, one she knows will end. "I made the choice to have a baby, and I'm not averse to slowing down for a little while right after having Christopher," Jones says. But she isn't at all concerned that the company will forget about her when she is ready to jump back onto the fast track. "My progression has been good, and I haven't had to worry about career planning. Whenever I've been in a position where it's been time to think about something else, something else has come up almost immediately."

Jones and her husband both work at Mountain Bell. Since he left law and embarked on a new career in data processing, the same field as hers, she is three levels above him. They share emergency baby duty, and both work longer hours and days off to make up for any time lost, keeping their bosses happy and understanding. "I changed bosses when I came back, but that has worked out well," she says. "Both have been extremely accommodating to my needs."

Then there's Bonnie Osborn, one step away from a vice presidency. She's been with the company for 28 years, and while now she wears business suits, she once donned a hard hat and supervised a group of eight installer-technicians, all men. On the first day she reported for the job, seven of them had their requests for promotions or transfers on her desk. The eighth couldn't because he hadn't been on the job long enough. However, Osborn was able to convince them to give her a try, and after she volunteered for some of the messier jobs herself, not only did they accept her, her crew often had the best results in their group. They celebrated regularly with pizza and beer after work. "Some of them always were kind of obnoxious, but some of them were super," Osborn says. "Ultimately, we respected one another and had a good working relationship."

While a fair number of women have done well at Mountain Bell, the black and Hispanic women say they have a harder time than white women. "If the backlash has been hard on white women, it's particularly bad for the minority women," says Regina Jackson. Promotions are never dropped into their laps; they must be even more qualified than white women to advance. However, an informal complaint could bring the coveted promotion.

For a woman to rise in management, an MBA is not simply a nice plus, it's a necessity. Jackson is working on hers. Osborn got both her undergraduate degree and MBA while she worked full-time. Sherry Sherrill, who had been in human resources for 13 years, found her superiors taking a new interest in her career path once she entered an MBA program. To broaden her experience, she was offered a transfer to a different department. She now does contract development, as well as giving expert witness testimony at public hearings. The full cost of a degree—up to $15,000 over two years—is paid by the company, which also gives students time off to attend classes every other Friday. And everyone is eligible for tuition grants of up to $3,000 a year toward an undergraduate degree. "Why do I stay here?" asked Mary Jacobson, who has served on both the board of U.S. West Women and the president's advisory board on pluralism. "Who else is going to pay $400 for my three credit hours? They are paying for my degree. I may be in a nonmanagement job, but I make good bucks. And the benefits are good."

The only glitch regarding benefits has to do with time off before birth. You probably won't be paid disability if you have to stay home before delivery. The company argues that the fetus—not their employee—is usually the one at risk, and disability covers only the worker.

Sexual harassment of the casting couch kind is dealt with swiftly and severely. People have been transferred or fired. However, the issue here is sometimes one of mixed messages. As one female manager explained, the problem is often that women aren't aware they are giving positive signals when they accept a ride home and then, on the third or fourth such ride, stop for a drink on the way. When the man actually makes a pass, it may come after several such encouraging signals, and the man feels that he is merely taking the relationship where she indicated she wanted it to go.

As in all Bell systems, staff reductions are the order of the day. New jobs tend to be in technical areas. The people who succeed have a broad outlook with a focus on the customer. Starting salaries for recent college graduates are in the low to mid-twenties and go up to the mid-fifties for middle management and six figures for senior management. Pay for men and women is equitable, but recently, in a move to encourage excellence, merit bonuses have been instituted, and company women are concerned that unless they are carefully monitored, men will be getting the better bonuses, from male bosses who judge their work more favorably than the women's. A merit bonus can be as much as 20 percent of salary.

Of course this shouldn't be a concern as more and more women move into positions where they are the ones handing out the bonuses. Among the women there's an attitude that says, "We're all in this together." Women in new jobs get plenty of support from other women. Those who have made it at Mountain Bell are mentors for those on the way up. It makes for a comfortable camaraderie, kind of an old girl network.

Linda Malloy, director of customer sales and service, is part of the new female leadership. Commenting on the changes she's seen in the last half dozen years, Malloy says, "This will always be a company in transition. We will never again have a time where our company can stand still as a regulated monopoly can. This represents a golden opportunity for women. Every time you turn around there is some kind of change going on that women can take advantage of."

But for a while at least, you may need a mental hard hat to deflect the brickbats.

MOUNT CARMEL HEALTH

TWO HOSPITALS IN THE HOLY CROSS HEALTH SYSTEM
CORPORATION, A NOT-FOR-PROFIT HEALTH CARE SYSTEM
IN SEVERAL STATES SPONSORED BY THE CONGREGATION
OF THE SISTERS OF THE HOLY CROSS

▲ EMPLOYEES: 3,400; 80 percent are women.

▲ SALES: Not applicable. Operating expenses for 1986 were almost $150 million.

▲ Mount Carmel Health does a spectacular job of recruiting and hiring women. Liberal tuition reimbursement for people who seek further education to advance their careers is available. Six of the seven senior executives at Mount Carmel are women.

▲ Although pay in a hospital cannot be compared to pay at a corporation that manufactures chemicals, women at Mount Carmel consider themselves well paid in comparison to their industry; certainly, they feel at no disadvantage to men in similar positions.

▲ Sexual harassment is not an issue. When the occasional male executive is overly patronizing, he is swiftly set straight.

▲ The two hospitals offer tremendous flexibility in calculating time off, whether the need is for additional maternity leave, care for a sick family member or a vacation. Studies are under way regarding on-site/off-site child care and a resource referral directory for child care services.

▲ This is a company in the throes of the changes all health care facilities are going through.

MOUNT CARMEL HEALTH
793 West State Street
Columbus, OH 43222
(614) 225-5000

Shortly after Sister Gladys took over as president and CEO of Mount Carmel Health in January 1984, when word got around that she was interviewing candidates for a new position, the response was likely to be, "I wonder who *she'll* be." More often than not, the quip was on target, causing somewhat of a stir at these two Columbus, Ohio, hospitals. Indeed, Sister Gladys Marie Martin's reputation as a feminist had preceded her from Fresno, and at her welcoming tea she was asked if she would be hiring men for senior positions. "As long as they're qualified," was her answer.

She's made good on the promise: both of the hospitals—one downtown, one on the east side of town—have women as chief operating officers; the senior vice president for corporate development is a woman, as is the senior vice president of marketing and communications. The senior corporate staff? Six out of seven are women. When a man is hired here, the women said, people sit up and take notice. He must be *very* good.

Or he wouldn't last. When Sister Gladys arrived, it was clear that her assignment had been to revitalize a backward Catholic institution that had been operating pretty much the same for nearly a hundred years and coax it, sometimes kicking and groaning, into today's competitive hospital market.

That meant a move away from acute care to outpatient care, diversifying into subsidiaries that provide different aspects of health care, opening a pharmacy, offering a generous health insurance plan underwritten by Mutual of Omaha to businesses in central Ohio, providing contract management services to smaller community hospitals and other health organizations, initiating programs for the elderly and medically indigent, and cooperating—or merging—with other hospitals in the area as the need for beds shrinks. Procedures that once required days as an inpatient are now done on an outpatient basis, thereby lessening the number of beds a hospital needs to provide the same care. In a local paper, Sister Gladys has admitted that she's got her eye on three to four hospitals in the area that she thinks would work fine under Mount Carmel's umbrella. The story was headlined "The Tough-minded Nun." Sister Gladys is on a career path as definite as any of the people she hires.

In fact, she has already assumed responsibility far beyond Mount Carmel. In 1987 she became regional superior for the Eastern district of her order and moved to a Washington, D.C., suburb. When the new director, Gordon A. Mudler, took over in January 1988, he inherited the senior staff—largely women—Sister Gladys appointed.

Most are from Ohio, but a few have pulled up stakes elsewhere for the opportunities at Mount Carmel and convinced their husbands to follow. Gail Leonard, who was third in line at a hospital in Philadelphia, bit at the chance to run a 500-bed hospital in downtown Columbus. An MBA in health care management, she was in her mid-thirties and pregnant when an executive recruiter phoned her. "It was just the kind of opportunity I was looking for," she recalls. "I told the recruiter I was just about to have a child, and he told me he'd have to get back to me. A day or two later he called and said they were still interested. I was eight and a half months pregnant when I came down here. I had to have special dispensation from my doctor to travel. I could see that Sister Gladys was a visionary. And what she had already done—take a sleepy organization and shake it awake—appealed to me. It seemed like the right next move."

Two months after her baby was born, Leonard reported for work. It was December 1984, and for the next seven months she commuted on weekends back to Philadelphia, where her husband held down the fort with their baby and 12-year-old daughter. By the time school started the following fall, the family had moved to Columbus and her husband, an engineer, had a job there. Leonard frankly says that outside of the obvious move to chief operating officer, she was attracted to the idea of working for a woman, something she had not done before. "I thought that my own personal development would be fostered by working in an organization that was amenable to promoting women," she says.

Other women found the same appeal in working for women, contrary to that old chestnut that women prefer male bosses. Linda Tieman, who moved from San Diego (and brought her husband) to become director of nursing under Leonard, finds the female presence at Mount Carmel a boon. "I don't have to do the defending of myself that I had to do in past jobs," she explains. "I don't have to defend that what I do is as good as what a man might do, or that what I say is as intelligent or that I'm as smart as a man and deserve to be paid attention to. That isn't there. And I find it lots of fun to go to a meeting with ten women and one man."

For Stephanie Fraim Quicksall, who was director of marketing for the East Hospital when we met, working with mostly women is a comfort. "We all speak the same language," she says. One time, she even broke down and cried in front of her boss. "That could have only happened between two women. Our world isn't sophisticated enough to let this happen between a man and a woman. A guy would have freaked. My boss reached out to me."

The bonding that Fraim Quicksall speaks of is precisely the type that connects men at most American businesses and permits them to keep a grip on the positions at the very top. At Mount Carmel, the situation is refreshingly reversed. How do the men handle it? Like everywhere else, the secure ones do just fine.

As for any presumed bitchiness in such a woman's world, the women were quick to deny that stereotype, and most had only high praise for each other and their bosses. Several women spoke of the understanding of their bosses when they had to be away to handle outside responsibilities. Leonard says she feels there's more to be done in this direction, and correspondingly, the hospital is looking into day care options for working parents. "American business needs to be more sensitive to family needs, and not just for women," she says. "Since our work life takes so much of our waking time, we have to integrate family goals and institutional goals."

Leonard should know. She often works 12-hour days, arriving at 7:30 A.M. and going straight through dinner meetings. Long hours are the norm, not the exception. People are expected to give, and then give some more. "It's a busy, demanding place," says Kathy Bennett, vice president of support services for the downtown medical center. "When we recruit, we don't just hire any warm body that comes along. We've always expected and demanded a lot of our employees. There was someone who wanted to work from 9 A.M. to 5:30 P.M. He only lasted a few months."

The expectation that you will give all you've got stems from the old days, when much of the staff was comprised of members of a religious order who worked long hours for benefits not of this world. Since no one could actually fire a nun, this attitude carried over to the lay staff. If you didn't do well in one job, you were given another where you couldn't screw up too much.

While the number of sisters has dwindled and the emphasis is on aggressive salesmanship in a changing market, employees are likely to get their walking papers almost as quickly as they would in any other industry. Mount Carmel is in business just like any other business.

Bennett's list of supervisory responsibilities would sink a less than dedicated soul: dietetic services; maintenance; safety and security; environmental services; telecommunications; distribution; sterile processes; volunteer services; radiology; physical, occupational and speech therapies; EEG and audiology. She's been at Mount Carmel a dozen years, starting as a staff physical therapist. After she became department director, she went back to school and received an MBA in finance from Ohio State University in Columbus. The hospital paid for 80 percent of her tuition, and just about the time she was graduating, Sister Gladys was reorganizing Mount Carmel. Bennett applied for the vice president's job and got it. "There's a lot more accountability today," says Bennett, comparing the present with the past. "Before, you didn't have much of anything to say about how things were done, now you do. Sister Gladys believes in participatory management, and while that takes up a lot of time—you go to a lot of meetings—you can make a suggestion and things move in a forward motion. And if you don't speak up about how something is doing, you'll be asked."

Of course the changes ruffled some feathers. Most of the old management left or retired; some who stayed resent it when their departments face budget cuts while new positions are created and filled by bright young things whose jobs were unheard of when hospitals were charitable institutions. Director of marketing? Who ever heard of a hospital that needed a sales force to sell itself? Indeed, the question came up once when Fraim Quicksall, then in her twenties, was present at a management meeting not long after she joined the hospital. She admits she was shaken, but sees her job as part of a big picture: how to generate income to help support the hospital's outreach program, with its free clinics and soup kitchens for the poor.

The hospital was going through growing pains when we were there, and there was a certain amount of confusion about what was going to happen next. People tended to be wary of changes and on guard to protect their turf. "We're so unsure what the structure will look like in a year," one woman says. "Lots of changes leaves open lots of possibilities if we're on our toes. On the other hand, I would appreciate a little stability." Yet the growing pains allow for input from anyone who wants to be a part of the new picture. "You can make any kind of suggestion that you think will work, and no one looks at you like you're strange or wonders why you said that," comments Linda Tieman. "It's really an open environment."

In more ways than one. Although Mount Carmel is a Catholic institution, religious preference is not a factor in hiring. All that is asked is that you adhere to the philosophy of the Sisters of the Holy Cross: that the primary objective is to relieve suffering and restore health in an environment that respects the dignity of the person. True, abortions are not performed and contraceptive services are not offered, due to the Catholic Church's ban on both. As for the presumed quieting influence of the nuns, employees say they are the liveliest bunch at Mount Carmel. On St. Patrick's Day one year, they organized a parade through the halls with one of the sisters standing in for St. Patrick wearing an old bedpan as a crown. Sister Gladys dresses in business suits and does not resist wearing bright, fashionable colors.

As expected, the medical benefits are excellent: a doctor's visit will cost you $5, a prescription $2. And if you need to stay in the hospital, it's free if you are at Mount Carmel, $100 tops if elsewhere. The pay is competitive with other institutions; some women said it was fabulous, others said they suspected they were underpaid but weren't sure they wanted to find out because they liked their jobs so much they didn't want to leave if it were true. Holiday leave, sick days and vacation time are lumped together, allowing an employee four full weeks off a year, to be taken at the discretion of the employee, as long as staffing needs are met. The plan has worked to the advantage both of the hospitals, which must be staffed around the clock, and of the employees, who have more flexibility than under a traditional system. Adopting parents receive $1,000 toward expenses, and maternity leave depends to some degree on your length of employment and is treated as a medical disability.

Gail Moaney's experience as a new mother may not be typical, but it does exemplify Mount Carmel's attitude to its employees. Like Leonard, Moaney was hired when she was pregnant. To her job as director of corporate communications she brought 14 years of experience in television and an Emmy for a children's program. Six months after she started work, her daughter was born. Moaney took a month off and then began working from her home. She was paid on a free-lance basis. In the third month, she came back to work at full pay, working a half day at home and a half day in the office. In her fourth month, Moaney was still nursing, with the aid of a breast pump and a small refrigerator she had installed in her office. "I can close the door and close the blinds and feel comfortable," she says. "When you're nursing you have to be in an environment that makes you feel relaxed about it. Sure, we're busy and work hard, but you know you're appreciated. I think that has a lot to do with keeping the nervous tension down." Sometimes Moaney brings her baby in on Saturdays, but says that usually people don't have to bring their children to the office. "If your child is sick, you stay home. If you have to leave early because the school has called, you leave. There is an understanding arm stretched out to you." In the midst of her hectic first months as a mother, Moaney was promoted to vice president of corporate communications and public affairs.

Moaney and others say that working at Mount Carmel is like being a member of a big club. Since almost everybody is relatively new on the corporate team, energies and attitudes tend to mesh. "There's a family spirit at Mount Carmel," Moaney says. "When you're new, people go out of their way to meet you and make you feel at home. The men are gentlemen and the women are all gentlewomen. Whether you work in maintenance or the corporate staff or in the laundry room, there's a mutual respect. That philosophy is insisted upon. Any other kind of behavior wouldn't be tolerated."

Administrative secretary Shirley Nebel echoes her thought: "I was a patient here several years ago, and they treated me so nice. I felt they really cared about me. I thought if they were that nice to their patients this would have to be a great place to work. And I was right."

The reception area and doctor's lounge of the new medical staff building are spiffy maroon-and-gray deco. You could be entering a movie studio, not the headquarters of a Catholic medical center. The cafeteria has an unusually large selection of excellent dishes for unusually low prices. In warm weather, a number of outdoor tables provide a sidewalk café atmosphere. Due to an outreach program for the elderly, who can buy their meals at discount, it's an extremely popular place.

The same can be said about Mount Carmel's reputation as an employer. Although the changes are disconcerting to some, Mount Carmel's reputation for taking good care of its employees and the CEO's willingness to hire and promote women are well known in Ohio and nationwide throughout the hospital community. Robin Hutchinson, who's in her late twenties and single, moved from Toledo when she was presented with an offer she thought too good to turn down: director of communications at the East Hospital. "This was a wonderful chance to get in on the ground floor of something new and exciting," she says. "The opportunity for growth and advancement is here."

NEIMAN-MARCUS

HIGH FLYER IN THE FASHION BUSINESS, WITH 22 STORES ACROSS THE COUNTRY AND MORE ON THE WAY

▲ EMPLOYEES: 7,950; 71 percent are women.

▲ SALES: $1.1 billion in 1986; sales average more than $340 per square foot, more than double the national average in retailing.

▲ Neiman-Marcus has no need to actively recruit new employees; more than 1,000 people apply for the executive training program each year. Of the 60 accepted, approximately two thirds are women. The company recruits MBAs only from Harvard. The training program is well respected in the industry. Sales positions are highly prized as well, and well-motivated women can make serious money here.

▲ Maternity leave is the standard six- to·eight-weeks' disability with no other fixed policy. While some understanding bosses allow new mothers to use accumulated vacation and personal time, no standard policy exists. Little flexibility is built into the brutal demands on time placed by this industry, and child care issues are the single area of concern for female employees. It is, however, possible for women to select jobs off the fast track that require less travel during childbearing years. Women who have chosen this route seem confident that they can climb back on the fast track as their children get older.

▲ Other benefits are adequate and vary somewhat as a function of level. All employees receive a 30 percent discount after 30 days' employment.

▲ The company has an explicit written policy on equal employment in which it lists specific stereotypical "reasons" given for excluding women that may not be used. The women we interviewed see no evidence of sexual harassment and feel they are equitably paid.

▲ While 72 percent of Neiman-Marcus employees are women, one third of the 75 employees considered upper management are women. Of 62 vice presidents, 21 are women; more than half the buyers are women, and six of the store managers have been women. Two of the 14 members of the executive committee are women. Both are senior vice presidents.

▲ Major employment centers: Dallas/Fort Worth: 3,300 (four stores, two distribution centers and corporate offices); Chicago area: 950 (three stores); Houston: 500 (two stores); San Francisco and Palo Alto: 625; Los Angeles, Newport Beach and San Diego: 900; also stores in St. Louis; Bal Harbour and Fort Lauderdale, Fl.; Boston; Atlanta; White Plains, N.Y., and Las Vegas.

NEIMAN-MARCUS
Main and Ervay Streets
Dallas, TX 75201
(214) 741-6911

Where can you buy a Baccarat reproduction, featured in *Connoisseur*, of a Baccarat carafe originally made for Czar Nicholas at the turn of the century?

Where would an oil baroness go for a set of seven gold lamé evening bags studded with seven kinds of semiprecious stones in seven different colors, all neatly packaged in a Lucite box?

Where did American Airlines and Mary Martin buy their identically styled smocks, American for their stewardesses to wear during in-flight food service and Miss Martin to wear when applying makeup for her *South Pacific* role?

Where could you get a crystal decanter that holds 12 quarts, in Steuben no less, as one businessman did shortly before Christmas to give a bourbon-drinking attorney?

And of course, *darhling*, we haven't even mentioned the clothes . . . or the furs . . . or the wonderful shoes they send out each season when the new collections come in . . . there's someone there who knows just what I like and she sends me several pairs to choose from twice a year and I've never even met the woman . . .

We are talking, of course, about Neiman-Marcus.

Once a family-run store catering to the Texas carriage trade, it is now a family-run chain of 22 stores catering to America's carriage trade. Richard Marcus, who turns 50 this year, is a grandson of one of the store's founders, and chairman and CEO of Neiman-Marcus. Until last summer, it was Carter Hawley Hale's crown jewel, but it was spun off along with Bergdorf Goodman, the exclusive New York store, and a group of 167 trendy boutiques for juniors, Contempo Casuals, to form a new company, the Neiman-Marcus Group, Inc. General Cinema Corporation, financially in the pink with one of the largest chains of movie theaters and the largest independent Pepsi-Cola bottler in the country, swapped its 49 percent stake in Carter Hawley for 60 percent of the new company. The move left Neiman-Marcus able to control its own budget and turn its handsome profits back into operations rather than have to send money home to poor parents, as Carter Hawley was saddled with $1 billion in debt. General Cinema's earnings in 1986 were $126 million on $1 billion in sales, and return on equity has averaged more than 20 percent for the past 10 years.

Neiman's grew from six stores in 1976 to 22 in 1985, when expansion was halted and the emphasis was put on increasing profits, which the stores did handily. As a division of Carter Hawley, the group earned an estimated $116 million before taxes on sales of roughly $1.1 billion in 1986; sales averaged more than $340 per square foot, well over double the national average in retailing. Carter Hawley estimated that the new company's earnings would grow at a blazing 26 percent annually through 1990. Expansion is on the drawing board at Neiman-Marcus, and a new store is planned for a Washington, D.C., suburb in 1989; Carter Hawley's plans were to add two stores a year; whether this will be heated up by the new management group, which some analysts say is easily possible, is unknown. Whatever the rate of growth, it's clear that there should be a mother lode of jobs in the coming decade with this most tony of retailers.

From bottom to top, women in management are given the green light. Of 62 vice presidents, 21 are women. More than half of the nearly hundred buyers are women, and six of the company's stores have been managed by women, including Dallas's Northpark store, the one with the highest sales volume. Barbara Boettigheimer, who had been manager of Northpark, which rings up some $80 million in sales annually, left in 1987 to become president and CEO of an upscale specialty store with two outlets. Boettigheimer rose at a steady but sure pace once she joined Neiman-Marcus as a part-time salesperson in 1971, after taking 13 years off from retailing to raise three children. Her earlier experience had been as an assistant buyer at Bloomingdale's in New York City. Unquestionably, this is a place where talent will out.

Whether it's more difficult for a woman than a man to enter the very highest circle of senior management is hard to tell. That it is a special club is not denied. But two women belong to the 14-member executive committee. They are Ann Keenes, senior vice president and general merchandise manager, and Rebecca Sharp, senior vice president of merchandise administration and systems. Sharp moved here in 1983 from Macy's, where she felt women were capped and the higher echelons were closed to them; she became part of the Neiman-Marcus inner circle when she was 36. "In all honesty, I'd have to say it wasn't any harder getting on the executive committee than it would have been for a man," Sharp says. "But sometimes I feel my voice isn't heard unless I get really intense about something, and then they tell me to calm down, that I should be less emotional. But that's the only thing they respond to."

But even if Sharp has a hard time being heard, heard she is. She was responsible for getting more computer equipment into the stores to allow for greater control of inventory, and as a merchandise manager she initiated a fine jewelry department that filled a niche between fashion baubles and gems, where prices suit the quality: very, very high. "The best thing about Neiman's is that you can go after something you want, whether it's a new business or a new concept," Sharp adds. "If you have an idea and a well thought out plan, there's a real go-for-it attitude."

Randee Supran, director of employee relations, found the same response to her plan for a new computer-based personnel system, a data base that was expensive to install but has proved its usefulness as it integrates with all other systems that contain employee information. "You are allowed to express your creativity," she says. "You are not inhibited."

Possibly women have little trouble getting their ideas translated into action at Neiman's because one of the founders was a woman, Carrie Neiman, sister of Herbert Marcus. With Mrs. Neiman's husband, the three opened the store in 1907. When Carrie and her husband divorced in the 1920s, the Marcus family bought out Mr. Neiman's share, and when Herbert died in 1950, Carrie Neiman was elected chairman of the board. Along with another woman, buyer Moira Cullen, she is credited with conceiving the Neiman-Marcus style, a high-fashion, high-quality look. Very rich and very Texan.

But it was Herbert's son, Stanley Marcus, who made the store famous for more than its reputation for incredible service. He is the man whose publicity stunts put Neiman-Marcus on the map, figuratively speaking. Take those his-and-her Christmas gifts Stanley originated in 1969. Did anyone ever buy those matching antique mummy cases the store offered in 1971? The store's keeping mum. The store has offered everything from live animals (shar-pei puppies, $2,000) to ice (rare yellow diamonds, one 56 carats, one 21, $2 million for both).

If the flashy style of the father garnered publicity, his more modest son has increased profits handsomely. Under Richard Marcus's reign expansion proceeded apace and operating profits tripled.

It's not surprising, then, that lots of people want to work for Neiman-Marcus. High profits to please the number crunchers the company recruits from the MBAs at Harvard, and Harvard alone. High cachet for the style-conscious recruited into its highly touted executive training program from the liberal arts departments of schools across the country. Retailing or marketing majors aren't exactly excluded, but a more likely candidate would be a well-educated individual with a grounding in the arts. Combine that with a desire to work in retailing, and a large dose of common sense and a certain *je ne sais quoi*—that's what the store is looking for when it hires. Practical art history or classics majors, particularly if you have an interest in fashion, take note. The competition will be stiff. More than a thousand apply each year. Only 60 or so are chosen. Approximately two thirds are women. Three or four of those won't make it through the eight- to 12-week course.

Once in the program, you'll get plenty of math and learn how to be an assistant buyer and run a sales department. Just as in college, you'll be tested on what you learn. For the MBAs, the program is a bit more taxing. For example, you might be put in charge of one or two small boutiques during a special promotion. Your first job will probably be as an assistant buyer, and you will be based in Dallas as all the buying offices are; the next step is likely to be department manager, and at that point mobility is desirable, since opportunities may arise at any one of the company's coast-to-coast locations. Although you might be uprooted, the locale will most certainly be affluent, because that's where the Neiman-Marcus customer is. For those going after the brass ring, a few moves around the country will be necessary and will give you an opportunity to show how well you can perform on your own. But if you don't want to move, it doesn't mean you will always be passed over. It only means you may have to wait longer for the right opening. Once you graduate to full-fledged buyer, you'll return to Dallas and the corporate offices. If store management is the route you're going, you may be able to locate in the part of the country you want, since the stores are located coast to coast, Beverly Hills to Bal Harbour, and more are on the way.

It's not just the spots in the training program that are so desirable. A sales job at Neiman-Marcus is coveted by many, so many that the store gets between 12,000 and 14,000 résumés a year. You can make good money selling at Neiman-Marcus. A handful of women make between $50,000 and $150,000 a year selling precious jewelry or couture fashions at stores in Houston (Galleria), San Diego and Fort Lauderdale.

Although people don't usually move between sales and the executive path, there's lots of movement in management. As a buyer, you can go from shoes to swimwear, from swimwear to couture. Says Debra Barnes, "You are not typecast at Neiman's. You have the opportunity to move as much as you can handle. I started out a shoe buyer and now buy couture. At other companies I would be a shoe buyer forever."

The Neiman-Marcus reputation for service is perhaps excelled by none. There's the story of the woman who ordered 24 gifts, at $5 each, to be gift wrapped. They were to be both table decorations and place cards at a dinner just before Christmas. The gifts arrived the day of the party, *sans* wrapping. Her table setting would be ruined. It was 2:30 in the afternoon. The woman lived in a small town 200 miles from Dallas. Stanley Marcus to the rescue! He chartered a plane and sent a gift wrapper who arrived at 5 P.M. and took care of the problem *tout de suite*. She went out the back door while the guests began arriving at the front.

The Neiman-Marcus reputation for quality is just as deserving. The former head of the precious jewelry department, Dudley Ramsden, once heard that one of his salesmen had lost a sale on a diamond necklace he knew was an exceptional value. Not satisfied with the salesman's explanation, Ramsden flew down to the man's ranch in south Texas. He told the rancher that if the difference in quality between the necklace from Neiman-Marcus and the other necklace—which was the same price—wasn't immediately apparent, he would get back on his plane and quietly leave. The man took out the necklace from the pocket of his ranch coat and laid it on the tailgate of his pickup truck. Ramsden placed the Neiman-Marcus necklace next to it. You can guess who got the sale.

The pace is naturally demanding, the way it is in all retailing jobs, and some of the women approaching the end of the childbearing years wonder how they can fit children in. Some do it, of course, and some find jobs in the company that don't have them negotiating with manufacturers in Hong Kong or going to Europe for the collections twice a year or working Saturdays. Gwen Baum, who had been a buyer making those European trips, wanted to travel less once she began having children and was able to transfer to a job that suited her needs as well as the company's: vice president and director of personnel development and training. She and her husband, also a longtime Neiman-Marcus employee, were expecting their third child when we caught up with her. "I was hired into this job knowing I was pregnant," she says. "There's travel, but I have flexibility and freedom to arrange my time. I get up very early—five A.M.—and work for an hour and a half, and so if I have to leave early for a special karate tournament or a soccer game, I do it." Baum hopes to return to a line job once the children are older and is reasonably confident that she'll be able to.

Not everyone will be able to find the same kind of flexibility, but most bosses are understanding and supportive, even, as Leslie LePore found, if you are leaving them at the busiest time of the year. LePore, divisional merchandise manager of the fabled Neiman-Marcus catalog business, had plans to be gone between Thanksgiving and Christmas. "I was afraid to tell anybody I wouldn't be here to make sure that the epicure cakes and smoked ducks got delivered, but everybody has just been terrific." However, the company has no set maternity leave policy past the six- or eight-week disability period at full pay. Sales people get two thirds pay for a length of time that depends on how long they've been with the company.

In nearly everything besides child care concerns, the women gave their company four stars. (All right, communication from upstairs could be better, but apparently it's being worked on.) If there were more companies like Neiman-Marcus, this book wouldn't be necessary.

Laurel Sung, a Harvard MBA who switched from banking to retailing, joined Neiman-Marcus in 1982. When we met, her husband was working in New York, and she was a men's accessory buyer in Dallas. She says when she decided she wanted a career in retailing, she interviewed with a number of companies and got several offers. "I liked Neiman's very much right from the start. I got a sense that they will treat me right, that they respect people. They are always saying that people are one of the greatest assets of the company, and I think they mean it."

As might be expected with a company this good, people tend to stay a long time. They say they are given plenty of autonomy and more responsibility as soon as they are ready. No one stagnates. The younger women know they can learn much from their bosses, people who are well respected throughout the industry. Eventually, everyone finds they are on many a head hunter's list, as the Neiman-Marcus training is so highly regarded. Some, of course, leave, lured by more money or the chance to head up smaller operations, but many stay, forming strong friendships among themselves and a deep sense of loyalty to the family Neiman-Marcus continues to be. They talk about the "vision" of the store without embarrassment, referring to the company's absolute commitment to quality. And they can't imagine that life could be better elsewhere. "It's easy to be proud of an organization that says, we want to sell quality," says Sung.

For all this munificence, what will you earn? Starting salaries for the training program range from the low twenties to the high twenties; an assistant buyer can make up to $30,000; buyers make between $30,000 and $55,000.

And what will you wear? Whatever it is, it will be chic. After all, this is Neiman-Marcus. Buy it there, and you'll get 30 percent off.

NORTHWESTERN BELL

A SUBSIDIARY OF U.S. WEST PROVIDING VOICE AND DATA
COMMUNICATIONS SERVICES

▲ EMPLOYEES: 15,200; slightly more than half are women.

▲ SALES: Approaching $2.2 billion.

▲ Northwestern Bell is concerned about recruiting, hiring and promoting women. The company provides liberal tuition reimbursement in master's programs and fully sponsored Sloan Fellowships. There are executive leadership programs open only to women. Six of the eight employees now enrolled in the company's management development program are female.

▲ To rectify inequality of pay to women, the company reevaluates individual job descriptions.

▲ Of the 267 employees considered upper management, 16 percent are women. These include the CEO, an executive vice president and two directors of departments, as well as 36 managers of districts or divisions. Of the 15 members on the board of directors, three are women.

▲ In addition to the standard six-week maternity disability leave, both women and men are entitled to a six-month unpaid leave with position assured. Adoption benefits are available as well. In cities where they are available, the company pays for resource referral services for child care.

▲ Charges of sexual harassment (and sexual discrimination) are aired by formal grievance procedure. A training program on sexual harassment includes education, EEO guidelines, self-help and coping strategies, and reporting procedures.

▲ Like Mountain Bell in Denver, Northwestern Bell's pay scale puts it among the most desirable employers in town. In spite of die-hard chauvinists, women can expect to be hired and promoted.

▲ Major employment centers: Minneapolis/St. Paul: 6,359; Omaha: 3,995; Des Moines, Idaho: 3,343; Fargo, N.Dak.: 760; Sioux Falls, S.Dak.:776.

NORTHWESTERN BELL
1314 Douglas Avenue
Omaha, NE 68102
(402) 422-2000

Changing men's minds about women in the workplace never comes easy, but one company in Omaha is succeeding—if not in eradicating sexism, then in seeing that discrimination doesn't hamper women's progress. Northwestern Bell's record speaks for itself: at the level of district manager or above, what the company calls senior management, a full 16 percent of the 267 positions are held by women. Two of the 13 officers of the company are women; one of them is the boss. As CEO, she's also on the board of directors, along with two other women from outside the company.

These gains occurred in the midst of downsizing before and after the break up of AT&T in 1984. Today Northwestern Bell is half its original size. It was able to accomplish so much for women during this turbulent period because the company, or more specifically its former president, Jack Mac-Allister, made a commitment to embrace the essence of equal employment opportunity, not just its stated goals. He determined that half of any new positions in senior management would be filled by women and minorities. MacAllister is now at the helm of Northwestern's parent company, U.S. West, which also includes Mountain Bell and U.S. West Direct, two other companies included in this book. In the end, it always seems to come down to the attitudes and policies of the individual at the top.

Talking with MacAllister, it becomes apparent that his heart is in the right place. Not that he overlooks the business angle. "I want every competitive advantage I can get," he says. "I can't think of anything worse to do if you really want to compete than restricting your options in selecting people for key positions. It just makes good business sense not to do so." But there's more to it than that. MacAllister recalls being chagrined when he saw that the minorities he played football with at the University of Montana—guys he liked and respected—couldn't find decent jobs after graduating. "The fundamental unfairness of that affected me deeply. How frustrating it would be to have your ambitions curtailed because of the way you were born."

MacAllister was at Northwestern Bell when the 1973 consent decree was signed. Intensive workshops on sexism and racial prejudice were mandated for all senior managers. A lot of people wondered why the company was spending money on workshops, since the return in profits was intangible. But MacAllister didn't listen to the nay-sayers, arguing that it was pointless to mechanically meet EEO objectives without dealing with the biases that had made the consent decree necessary in the first place. "You're not going to effect change until you have the whole organization behind it," he says. "Changing attitudes isn't a short-term thing, either. You can't hold a series of workshops for a year and say, 'Wow, we did it. We got rid of all prejudice and bias and now we're home free.' It's a cumulative thing. A lot of people still have trouble dealing with their feelings once they confront them. We still have bias and we still have prejudice, but I think there is a noticeable change in the environment because we dealt with the heart and soul of the matter."

Change yes, but there is still a way to go. Omaha, Northwestern Bell's home base, is a city struggling with a troubled economy, a city where a number of firms have moved elsewhere. Jobs are scarce. Backlash from white males has been considerable. A number of them have complained to the company's EEO manager. "They are saying that the women and people of color are getting all the jobs, but what they are facing for the first time is real competition," says Darlene Siedschlaw. "We have gone on the record as saying that if we have two individuals who are both basically qualified, we are going to go on the affirmative and select the person of color or the woman, and we have the right to do that. I say, 'Hey, that's competition that you didn't have in the past. But you have it today.'" Turning the tables like this doesn't make the men happy. Before, it was the women and minorities who had to be better to get the promotion. Now it's the white males.

This doesn't sit well with the scores of employees who are retired military men—or their sons—from the Strategic Air Command base in Omaha or the Nebraska men who buy into their attitudes, attitudes that are the focus of the workshops MacAllister initiated in the mid-seventies. In the words of one man who went through them, the workshops were "hell on wheels," hitting hard on prejudices you might not have been aware you harbored. For four days, groups of 30–40 people of all races and both sexes met at locations outside the company to confront each other and thrash out their differences. The workshops continue today as new employees join the company, and men and women from all ranks may attend if they choose.

Whether the workshops have succeeded in changing many attitudes is open to question. Some say yes, some say no. But a 1986 company survey found that 90 percent of all employees believe that a pluralistic work force —women, blacks, Hispanics and American Indians, as well as white men —makes for a more competitive business. And Victoria Boyd, a district engineering manager who supervises a total of 30 people—all men except for two—says that the seminars made an enormous difference, that women are now accepted as equals in the technical and operational areas. "I'm not going to say that all women are accepted one hundred percent by all males, but I do not know of any recent discrimination that would inhibit a woman from performing her job or advancing," Boyd says.

However, another woman from another largely male department says, "I've seen a lot of white men come back from the workshops, and if anything has changed it's certainly not visible to the naked eye. One man came back from the male-female workshop and complained that all the women had hit on him. Another man came back from the race workshop and mispronounced the consultant's name just to show his annoyance."

Backlash from the white males rears its head in many ways. One woman told of rejecting a commercial because it did not depict the people of color who work for the company, but the man—we'll call him Joe—who had been in charge of getting the commercial made, her *subordinate*, refused to accept her veto and attempted repeated end runs around her. Finally the woman made it clear this had to stop: kill the commercial, she said. But she knew he would once again go over her head to her boss. True to form, Joe did. However, the woman—his *superior*, mind you—had warned her boss in advance what to expect and told him what had been going on. He put an end to it. Speaking of Joe and others like him, the woman says, "There is quiet acceptance of that kind of behavior here. The company is divided into two camps. One is liberal. The other says, 'All is white with the world and Ronnie's in the White House. We don't have to do anything anymore.'"

Nevertheless, compared to other companies in the area Northwestern Bell is probably the best of the lot. The men might not like the changes, but the company is moving forward. Women and people of color feel free to form caucuses and lobby for their fair share of rights and recognition, as well as helping each other with their own networks. There are organizations for women, black managers, Hispanics and native Americans, all of which have had a tremendous impact. Representatives of the groups meet regularly with Northwestern Bell's officers. A few years ago, U.S. West's advertising campaign was geared around the cowboy: rough and ready, white and male. Complaints from the caucuses squashed that campaign. The company will pay for no memberships to organizations that discriminate, including service organizations such as Kiwanis and Rotary clubs. The policy caused a stir in town when Northwestern Bell announced it would no longer pay for memberships to the Omaha Club, formerly a musty male preserve, until it admitted women. After Northwestern Bell took the lead, other companies in Omaha followed suit, and the club opened its doors to women. The company itself has an open door policy, and it is taken seriously. If your boss is the problem, you go to his boss and on up the line. And no one really forgets that up at the top of the chain, the CEO is a woman, Janice D. Stoney.

Stoney would seem to have had a lot going against her. She joined the company in 1959 before she got her college degree and never went back to finish it. In 1982 she had cancer and had to have major surgery. Yet two years later she was named chief operating officer and in 1987, CEO. Stoney found that the higher she went in the company, the easier it was to gain both visibility and acceptance by male peers. As she sees it, her biggest leap came in 1971, when she was the first woman to be appointed to district-level manager. Several men went to bat for her, but acceptance was not unanimous. However, when she was named chief operating officer a little more than a decade later, she says, "I never felt more accepted by any other group in my life." Times had changed. When she was made CEO, people felt she finally got the title for the job she was already doing while her predecessor was on special assignment for U.S. West.

Stoney, however, is no Pollyanna. Like all women who have made it near the top today, she well knows how tiresome it is to have to prove yourself again and again to be better than the men: "It's exhausting and time consuming, but it sharpens one's skills. When you finally finish the marathon, you know you're competent." She is now amused by what was written on one of her appraisals in the sixties: "It's too bad she's not a man, she could really go far." Happily, it was an assessment she didn't hear of until many years later.

"We have not totally arrived," Stoney comments today. "All those struggles are still going on, but what's changed is that everything is more open. Women aren't afraid to speak up. Women are recognized in the top level of management. The officers review our high-potential a couple of times a year. There was a time when we had to look at our lists and say, 'Where are women and people of color?' That isn't true today. Women and people of color are on all the lists."

Clearly, Northwestern Bell's commitment hasn't slackened. In 1986 Peggy Milford was named chief executive officer of the South Dakota operation and an officer of the company. Milford says of job prospects at Northwestern Bell today, "The kind of people we're looking for now are people who can work with a high degree of the unknown. You need to demonstrate leadership, not just the ability to manage people."

While admittedly there are not a lot of job openings at a company that has downsized radically, they do exist, especially in the technical areas like engineering and computer and data systems. As marketing now drives the company, marketing skills are also in demand. At this writing, the legal department has a few women, but advancement there is blocked. You're likely to be overlooked rather than promoted. In the legal department, at least, the workshops did not make much of a dent.

Starting salaries for recent college graduates range from $22,000 to $28,000. Middle managers can expect to make between $45,000 and $60,000. Senior management goes into six figures. The benefits package is healthy and includes completely paid medical coverage for employees and their families, as well as dental and vision coverage. Counseling for alcoholism and drug abuse is also covered, as is psychotherapy. Prescriptions can be filled through the mail for $2. If you have an accident, your wages will be fully paid for an entire year; long-term disability will pay you 50 percent of your salary until the age of 65, when Social Security takes over. Savings plans for all include company participation: for union members, the company will match dollar for dollar, up to 6 percent of one's pay; for management, the company contributes two thirds, up to 4 percent of one's pay.

Maternity leave is the standard six- to eight-week disability. A six-month unpaid leave, with a similar job and salary guaranteed, is available for both men and women and can be used for absences other than parenting, such as going back to school to complete a degree. The company will pay up to $5,250 annually toward your education. A number of women are getting their MBAs this way. Most managers are encouraging and make allowances for long lunch hours when classes or library research must be squeezed in. For family emergencies, each employee has eight personal days a year. Flexitime is allowed in departments where it can be accommodated. Computer programmers are likely to work four 10-hour days a week. Others might work split shifts, allowing them to schedule college courses or child care around their working hours. Job sharing on a limited basis is being tested. In cities where child care resource referral is available, the service is paid for by the company. How flexible the company is for family emergencies depends, as it does everywhere, on your boss. Sometimes women bosses can be the most rigid.

Northwestern Bell is a company that's operating within a chauvinistic milieu but is doing well by women and minorities despite that. For some like Darlene Siedschlaw, who's been with Northwestern Bell for 35 years, working there has never been more exciting. "It's true that for some, the changes create stress, but for the individual who can accept change, who can be innovative, there is opportunity out there," she says. But the company can't make it happen by itself. Siedschlaw throws the responsibility back onto the women and men who work there. "You can change the corporate culture to a certain extent, you can put in policies and create the environment for change, but we have to take some personal responsibility for making it happen. And I see that happening throughout the organization."

PAYLESS CASHWAYS

A BUILDING MATERIALS RETAILER FOR THE DO-IT-YOURSELFER

▲ **EMPLOYEES:** 13,000; approximately 35 percent are women.

▲ **SALES:** Almost $1.5 billion in 1986. The company is in a growth phase; between 1981 and 1987, 106 new stores were added.

▲ David Stanley, the CEO, is gender blind. His commitment to women is felt at all levels of the company. Payless actively recruits, hires and promotes both women and minorities because it's good business to look for talent from the largest pool possible. A recently installed personnel tracking system should enhance management development and succession planning. Tuition reimbursement is 50 percent.

▲ One sixth of the 49 upper management people are women; three of these are corporate officers.

▲ Although employees in this fast-paced, high-growth company work long, hard hours, Stanley and many high-level managers are active in community affairs, giving the company a high profile in Kansas City.

▲ Family responsibility is an area the company stays resolutely away from, but individual women report that flexibility is there when they need it. Benefits, such as medical, dental and vision insurance and employee stock purchase plans, are excellent.

▲ Although one would not expect a building materials company to rank high on our list, Payless Cashways does. This is a company that makes every effort to let women know they are valued and can succeed.

▲ Major employment centers: Kansas City area: 11,000; in addition to Payless Cashways, the stores operate under the names of Furrow, Lumberjack, Hugh M. Woods, Somerville Lumber and Knox Lumber; stores are located in 23 states in the Midwest, Southwest, Pacific Coast and Boston areas.

PAYLESS CASHWAYS, INC.
1 Pershing Square
2301 Main, Box 466
Kansas City, MO 64141
(816) 234-6000

"You're writing about the best companies for women?" the cab driver asked, to make sure he got it straight.

There was a murmur of assent from the rear seat.

"Let me tell you, Payless is the best—*the best* company. Number one. The top people are the best. Miss Stanton—she's an officer. And David Stanley is someone who doesn't have any prejudice at all—I mean, *at all.*" Sterlyn Garrison, cabbie *extraordinaire*, turned around to make sure he got his point across. "And I'm saying that as a black man—he doesn't care if you're black or female, if you can do the job, he'll give it to you."

Word has gotten around Kansas City that Payless Cashways is an equal employment opportunity company.

It isn't a company that makes a lot of concessions to women. "We do not concern ourselves at this point with familial obligations," came back on our survey. "We do not know who is responsible for parenting, nor do we assume that responsibility. We concern ourselves only if it interferes with job performance."

And it is a company where the pace is grinding. Even in the soft retail market in the Midwest and Southwest, where many of its stores are located, Payless is going through a growth spurt. In the last five years, it has doubled the number of its outlets and tripled sales; hiring seldom keeps up with that kind of growth, meaning there's never enough people to keep up with the work.

But it would be hard to find another group of such enthusiastic women who are so convinced that "the sky's the limit" when asked how far they can go at their company. And these are women selling lumber. Screwdrivers. Faucets. Plumbing fixtures. Fertilizer.

"I've never worked any place where there was so much interest in pushing women ahead," insisted Jan Maloney, who headed up the corporate safety program when we were there. At most companies that's a macho job. Maloney, who's in her mid-forties, has worked for several companies and directed Coca-Cola's safety program on a regional level before moving to Payless three years ago. "I believe in David Stanley's commitment to women," Maloney said firmly.

Stanley is the CEO who came to Payless in 1980 and, to put it mildly, shook the cobwebs out of a chain that was run by men who had spent most of their working lives selling building materials. One of the ways he's made the greatest impact is in the hiring of smart, sassy women. A former anchorwoman on the evening news now handles sales promotion. A young black mother now in the management training program was an assistant manager at Lane Bryant. And the woman who used to run the county jails is now the senior vice president for administration and corporate planning. She's Susan Stanton, whom the cabbie mentioned, and she's not the only female officer of the company. So are Linda French, general counsel and secretary, and Jean Warren, assistant treasurer.

Back to Maloney. Now a consultant for the company, part of her job is telling truck drivers how to navigate the tricky streets of places like Boston. Telling any man—let alone someone who does it for a living—how to drive is a sticky wicket, but Maloney says she goes in low key and tells them she and her husband once owned two trucks and she ran them out of her home while she took care of the kids. Humor is another help. "Sure, they look at me kind of funny when I walk in—these are big, burly guys who are tired at the end of the day when I see them—but I tell them about myself and joke around and it all works out."

At least some of Maloney's self-assurance stems from the backup she gets from Stanley, who, she says, has made sure that managers who might want to bypass her don't. "He's always opening doors and asking questions," Maloney says. One of her responsibilities is working up a strength test for new employees who will be working in the lumberyard, loading cement sacks and two-by-fours into customers' trucks; another is changing some procedures so that more people are able to do them and fewer are injured. For instance, if you raise the level at which 94-pound cement sacks are stored to three feet or so, 74 percent of the female employees will be able to lift the load from that level to a truck bed. At ankle level, where the sacks are stored today, only 40 percent of the women can lift them. At the same time, injuries to both sexes should be greatly reduced.

By making such small but significant changes, as well as coming up with a meaningful measurement of strength, Maloney hopes to open up more jobs to women and minorities who are small in stature (such as Orientals and Hispanics) but still able to do the job.

But hold on now—how many women are going to be applying for jobs in the yard anyway? They are already there. In Addison, Texas, where Maloney went to observe what is actually going on in the shipping yard, she found two women in receiving. She videotaped one of them "who couldn't have weighed more than 110 pounds pulling a pallet loaded with 2,400 pounds of nails." When Maloney asked the guys to name another hard job in the store, they answered, "the paint department." "The next morning I found Maria in the back room throwing around 50-pound cans of spackling." Who says women can't do the job? Or don't want to?

For Darrylyn Swift, a management trainee, beginning in the yard after working in fashion retailing was a challenge she welcomed—even if the guys she had to work with didn't. "I figured it would be great exercise and I'd learn what was going on out there," she says. "I showed up for work my first day at Payless in jeans and T-shirt with my hair in French braids under a hard hat. The guys in the yard told me not to try and show off, and they were glad to help me, but they had some very negative views about women in management." Swift was the second female trainee at the store in Blue Springs, Missouri. After two months out in the yard, she moved indoors to rotate through various departments, from billing to selling on the floor. During that time, she saw some of the men's attitudes begin to soften. "They see who's coming through the program and see that they are staying with the company."

While women at corporate headquarters in downtown Kansas City have an easier time coming up through the ranks than in the male-dominated marketplace, three of Payless's 192 stores are managed by women. Linda Kostic is the manager of a Denver outlet that goes under the name of Hugh M. Woods, a Colorado chain Payless bought in 1984. Kostic admits that the employees' initial difficulty in accepting her as a manager may have made her job a little more difficult than it would have been for a man but adds that she doesn't let it bother her because she, like Maloney, knows she has the support of corporate headquarters. "Conversations would stop at store managers' meetings when I walked into the room," she recalls. "That's re-laxed some. But anybody who thinks she is going to be initially accepted is setting herself up for a big fall. You have to win them over one by one, and if there's somebody who's really opposed to you, don't try to win him over. You just have to do the best you can and run with it."

Regardless of the resistance of some of the male managers, Kostic doesn't let it get in her way. "In operations, it's possible for a woman to succeed," she says adamantly. "No one can hurt you if you do a good job, because in the field it's so measurable." When asked how far she and others could go at Payless, Kostic was equally clear: "The sky's the limit." Kim Silvers, the personnel manager for the Western region, adds, "You can go as high as you want, and I certainly don't think that's true of a lot of companies that are dominated by men."

When Stanley came to Payless, he assembled an almost entirely new management team—young, dynamic and energetic—and let it be known in no uncertain terms that women and minorities were not to be passed over. If necessary, he'd tell someone point-blank that their sexist attitudes had no place at Payless. "David looks poorly on someone who vocalizes their discontent because somebody is female," Stanton says. "He would let him know that. Sure, some people think I'd be better off at home, but I don't take it seriously. My leadership is accepted in the areas I work in, and so there's really no problem."

Stanley looks upon his feminist attitudes as sound business acumen. "You are most likely to get the best candidate for a job if you address the largest possible pool of candidates, without setting up any restrictions," he says. "If the classification is a college degree and five years of business experience, you limit yourself if you also insist that the candidate look like you and went to, say, Notre Dame or Yale."

What made 51-year-old Stanley such a strong supporter of women on the job? His mother. A Phi Beta Kappa from the University of Nebraska, she had a successful career as an investment banker in Chicago and New York before taking off several years to raise a family. When Stanley was 9, she owned and ran a Westchester, New York, newspaper, the *Yorktown Herald*, for a decade. Other competent women he met early in his career reinforced his attitude, he says, as has the success he's had with the women he's hired. Stanley's wife also works and is a vice president of a company that makes office equipment and computers in Minneapolis, to which Stanley commutes on weekends.

Besides carving a path for women at Payless, the energetic Stanley has shepherded the chain from an entrepreneurial operation where a manager pretty much ran his store the way he wanted to a company with fairly strict corporate guidelines on everything from purchasing to hiring. Smaller chains were bought and absorbed, so that acquisitions and new stores account for approximately 20 percent of the company's growth over the past 10 years. Between 1981 and 1986 alone, 76 new stores were added.

Growth like this almost always creates a corporate environment where there's never enough bodies to do all the work. "We have grown so fast we almost outgrew ourselves," comments Stanton. "We have to work real hard to play catch-up ball to support our size." Although retailing is a profession where long hours are the norm, at Payless the pace and intensity are especially grinding. "I've worked nights and weekends up the ying-yang," one woman says. "And you either produce or you're out."

"The hardest part is the stress level around here," remarks Karen Garrison, a former teacher who's now manager of internal communications. "We are asked to do a number of jobs simultaneously, and things are constantly changing. On the other hand, that's one of the intriguing things about working here. You are never bored. But finding a balance between your professional and personal life is a constant challenge."

Garrison is the mother of a toddler. She took two months off (combining six weeks' maternity leave with two weeks' vacation) and kept up with what was going on by phone. For the first few weeks back, her boss—also a mother—let her take work home and ease back into her job by working on fewer projects, coming in late when the baby had been up all night and going home early when she needed to. When the baby began in day care, she was sick a lot, and Garrison was given the necessary time without being made to feel she was a laggard. She even managed to breast-feed her baby for six months by using a breast pump in the ladies' room.

Linda Ward, the understanding boss, says that she would like to think of her handling of the situation as "warm and fuzzy," but that it made perfect business sense. "The fact that we didn't make it so miserable that Karen said, 'I can't do this,' meant we didn't have to start from scratch with somebody new and say, 'We started as a lumberyard in Pocahontas, Iowa, in 1930...'"

While not every new mother has an empathetic woman for a boss, the women who need personal time off say there is never a problem, partly because of the long hours they've put in. When Jari Holland moved by herself from Minneapolis to become director of human resources, her needs were those of a single person setting up a home: time off to be there when the movers came, the phone was installed, the cable TV hooked up. "I took off whatever time I needed, but I had accrued a lot of extra time in the bank so I didn't feel terribly guilty."

How Holland was recruited exemplifies the company's forceful and persistent approach to getting the people they want. As director of training for Target Stores in Minneapolis, she was contacted twice by a headhunter for a similar job at Payless. She turned him down because she could see no advantage in moving to a new city for the same kind of job. Finally, the man who would turn out to be her boss called her directly. "What would it take to get you to reconsider?" he asked. "I knew that they were also looking for a person to fill a human resources position, and I said I would be interested in that or some combination of both jobs," Holland recalls. "He said, 'Get on a plane and come down here.'" Holland assumes what had made her a particularly attractive candidate for the job was her 21 years' experience in retailing, which goes back to when she was 15 and began working for Montgomery Ward as a salesclerk.

Holland's opportunity to stretch—to gain experience in an area of retailing new to her—is also typical of the company. Although no formal posting of corporate jobs to field personnel is done at this point, word of mouth seems to work pretty well, and several people from the field have applied for and gotten jobs at headquarters. A data bank which tracks everyone—women and minorities particularly—and their interests was recently compiled; how much it will be used depends, in part, on Holland, and the women interviewed were confident they would not be sidetracked into dead-end jobs.

Such long-range opportunities were what appealed to Barbara Remkus, who had been an anchorwoman and reporter for the local NBC affiliate. "I had done everything I could possibly do at the station—the only thing left was to begin repeating my schedule," she says. "I didn't want to be an anchor the rest of my life, and the possibilities here seemed wide open." Remkus's job includes dealing with the media, communicating with the shareholders and managing corporate contributions, but she is clearly thinking about gaining wider business experience. "The opportunity is here for you to be thinking about what you would like to do," she says. "They don't say, pick a job, it's pick several jobs that you would like to learn how to grow into. I'm not only thinking in terms of communications. My long-term plan is to be doing something else. I can almost cherry-pick what I'm interested in." As we went to press, she did have a new job: director of sales promotion.

Although it wasn't the reason she left her supposedly glamorous job as anchorwoman, Remkus found Payless's generous benefits package attractive: in addition to regular medical, dental and vision insurance, doctor visits and prescription drugs are covered after a $100 deductible. Part-time workers also receive health benefits, although at a reduced level. A stock purchase plan for management offers an additional share for each two the employee purchases. And all employees are eligible for three months' disability leave at full pay from the first day of work. Women say the pay is good, and no one doubts that they are paid equally to men. One woman whose company was bought by Payless got an immediate $8,000-a-year raise.

Sexual harassment complaints are handled swiftly and have resulted in firings, but a mandatory program for all managers has greatly reduced any problems. Employees who feel they have been unfairly treated or accused, for harassment or any other grievance, can take their case through a procedure that goes all the way up to Stanley or someone he designates to oversee the matter. Linda French, the company's general counsel, is likely to be involved too. French was recruited from the firm that handles much of Payless's outside legal work. She was in her mid-thirties and jumped at the chance to set up a legal department in a growing company. "Any acceptability problems I face have had more to do with setting up a new department —I don't view them as a sex issue," French says.

That may be true, but the corporate culture is a macho one—Stanley's feminism notwithstanding—and the women pay close attention to getting along with the guys. "I work very hard to make my relationships work," says one woman. "It's probably something I wouldn't have to do if I were a man . . . I joke around a lot."

If the women have any complaints besides the crushing workload, it's the lack of communication between departments and between the field and corporate headquarters. To lessen the isolation of the women in the field— they are stretched out among 18 states—women at headquarters have paired themselves up with women in the field. They keep in touch via telephone, and if they are in the same town they usually have a meal together. At headquarters, management women have taken to meeting once a month for lunch. It's one way of trying your ideas out before you present them formally. "When a project goes out on a companywide basis, you already have support for it in the field," remarks Stanton, who acts as a sounding board and mentor to an assistant store manager in a Sacramento suburb.

This informal network, coupled with the we're-all-in-this-together attitude, has bred a keen sense of company loyalty. Remkus finds the atmosphere a far cry from the cutthroat world of broadcasting: "In television, you're out on a limb alone and watching people saw at it. It took me a while to get used to the family atmosphere at Payless. You treat the company like you would your family sitting around the table and talking about what's going on with your mom and your dad and your brothers and sisters. Sure, tempers flare now and then, but they're friendly temper flares."

After all, the women wanted to get across, what company doesn't have problems when it's busting out at the seams?

Fourteen new stores were scheduled to open in 1988.

PEPSICO

AN INTERNATIONAL CONGLOMERATE IN THE
SOFT DRINK, SNACK FOOD
AND RESTAURANT BUSINESSES

▲ EMPLOYEES: 100,000; 46 percent are women.

▲ SALES: $9.3 billion in 1986, a 21 percent increase over 1985.

▲ PepsiCo has no special programs designed to recruit, hire and promote women; they assert that they look for the best and brightest people regardless of sex. Of the 65 MBAs hired in 1987, 25—38 percent—were women. In March 1987, 85 people were taking management development programs; 36—42 percent—were women. Fifteen percent of the company's 60 midlevel executives are women. The company provides 100 percent tuition reimbursement.

▲ At the very top, 21 of the 550 uppermost management—4 percent—are women. They include six vice presidents and two chief financial officers of divisions large enough to be *Fortune* 500 companies. PepsiCo has a strong policy of development and promotion from within and maintains that there are women in the pipeline. One of the 13 members of the board of directors is a woman.

▲ PepsiCo offers standard maternity disability leave and the possibility of more extended leave without pay, negotiated on a case-by-case basis. Part-time work is available for clerical employees as well as professionals. The company offers a resource referral directory for child care facilities and a cafeteria-style approach to employee benefits, with up to $5,000 deductible for child care and eldercare expenses.

▲ PepsiCo handles charges of sexual discrimination by informal hearing. It appears not to be an issue.

▲ Major employment centers: Westchester County, N.Y.: 2,700; Dallas: 1,500; Irvine, Calif.: 850; Wichita, Kans.: 750.

PEPSICO, INC.
700 Anderson Hill Road
Purchase, NY 10577
(914) 253-2000

"It's ten P.M. Do you know where your husband is?" might be what PepsiCo women say to one another in the halls late at night. If they had the time for such chitchat. At work, they only talk shop.

This is a company of nimble managers running hard day after day, especially in the summertime, when it's the busiest. When they're done for the day, they head for home, since it's usually late. As company headquarters is in the suburbs, there's no little bar on the corner in which to stop for a quick drink and catch up on gossip or share intimacies. During the day, if they take a few minutes off from the office, many of them head for the company's physical fitness center or for a jog around the fabulous gardens dotted with museum-quality sculpture that surround company headquarters.

But that doesn't mean they're listening to Bach on the Walkman. "I'll do business with the head of the tax department on a run," says Martha Kenerson, associate tax counsel, referring to James Ditkoff. "He comes down and runs with different people in the department, and you talk business." The talk strays somewhat when senior executives get together on weekends for dinners with their spouses, but at work don't expect to form fast friendships between the hours of 8 A.M. and 8 P.M. You'll be working too hard. One woman said that it hadn't been unusual for her to stay until 10 P.M. when she was single, but now that she's married and a mother, she works from 8:30 A.M. to 6:30 P.M. and doesn't take a lunch. She does, however, take papers and mail home to read many a night.

The killer hours are, in a nutshell, the biggest complaint PepsiCo women have about their employer. Is there life after work? they want to know.

Yet increasingly, high-ranking women are mothers. Two who have children are Peggy Moore, vice president of investor relations, and Pam McGuire, an attorney who's made food law her specialty. Both have two kids. Both are proof that it *can* be done. *If* you plan your life carefully. Both live close to work; both have dependable help at home, supportive husbands and a determination to make the equation balance. McGuire found that it could only work if she had a job that wasn't as inflexible or required the amount of traveling she was doing as head counsel for the Pepsi-Cola division, a post she held briefly after her second child was born in 1983. She had once considered specializing, but didn't pursue it because she loved the challenge of the head counsel's job. It would also have been a move off the fast track. She felt differently after her second child was born.

McGuire took a lateral move to her current post as food law counsel and says it has worked out well for both her and PepsiCo, developing into a bigger job than initially thought. Although the position makes great demands on her time, she has the autonomy to schedule her own hours so that she can manage both jobs—of attorney and mother of two children under seven.

"The company makes concessions where there is a good reason to do so, and I can think of male and female examples," she adds. One man whose wife died after a long illness took all the time he needed during the last six months of her life. Another man won a lengthy battle for joint custody of his two young children, and on the midweek days he had to pick them up from day care or school, he was out of the office at 5:30 P.M. Nor could he travel all the time, since after such a protracted custody fight he could not readily call his ex-wife and ask her to take the children because he couldn't be there on Tuesday. Did he make business calls from home when he had to be there early? You bet he did.

Yet if you are going to make your family or some outside interest your main focus for any length of time, it is difficult to stay on the fast track. People at PepsiCo put the job first. "If it has to get done, you stay up all night, you work on weekends, you do what has to be done, and there is never a question of saying no," said one woman. The pace burns out a lot of people, and turnover is common among junior executives. Yet burnout is not the only reason people leave. Most of the new employees at PepsiCo are brash young managers who are highly trained, very bright, aggressive and, most of all, impatient. They are not going to wait a couple of years for that next promotion. They are going to look for opportunity at another company if it doesn't happen quickly. It can happen quickly at PepsiCo, but don't look to be making $100,000 in two years.

Among senior management the crew is not static, not because they leave the company, but because they are moved from division to division to gain experience. It can create hardships for both men and women whose spouses work and aren't willing to pick up and follow. If you aren't willing to transfer to, say, Dallas, where the Frito-Lay division is headquartered, you might not get promoted as quickly as someone who is. However, should you be toiling at Frito-Lay and find yourself engaged to a New Yorker, requesting a transfer to the East Coast could get surprisingly fast results.

Once you've proven yourself at PepsiCo, plenty of opportunities will come your way, because your name will end up on many a headhunter's list. The company is known for grooming the best and the brightest. Coca-Cola steals from PepsiCo; PepsiCo is more scruffy and gets talent everywhere it can. The recruiting style is not unlike the Pepsi Challenge, the marketing gimmick that the number two soft drink company dreamt up half a dozen years ago to show that a lot of people can't tell the difference between the two colas. Or that they prefer Pepsi.

Overall, Pepsi had at the end of 1986 about 30 percent of the soft drink market to Coca-Cola's 40 percent. But PepsiCo is coming on strong in a new category—soft drinks with real fruit juices added. Slice, now available in four flavors, was unrolled in December 1984; it is now a $1 billion brand. In 1986 *Fortune* named it one of the best new products of any type and the soft drink industry's hottest new entry. As we go to press, Jake's, a new diet cola from PepsiCo now in test markets, was fighting for another piece of the pie: those who like the taste of regular cola drinks but want fewer calories than the real thing. Jake's has 15. In the soft drink war, it's a revolutionary idea. And in the competition for a bigger market share, Pepsi's stock-in-trade is change.

But not by soft drinks alone does PepsiCo survive. The snack division, Frito-Lay, accounts for approximately 30 percent of the company's $9.3 billion in sales. Add to that a lively restaurant division that owns the 5,000-unit Pizza Hut, the 2,400-unit Taco Bell and the 6,500-unit Kentucky Fried Chicken, which joined the PepsiCo clan in late 1986. Flip through the annual report, and new product after new product leaps off the page: Seafood Salad at Taco Bell, Cool Ranch Flavor Doritos, Lay's Jalapeño & Cheddar potato chips, nonfried chicken—yes, really—from Kentucky Fried Chicken, Priazzo, a pizza with bottom *and* top crusts, at Pizza Hut, home delivery from Pizza Hut, Double Beef Burrito Supreme, to name a few. Innovation is the company mantra, and you'd better be chanting it if you expect to last. Just as the company loses people to burnout, Wall Street and the competition, the company doesn't let deadwood dry out for long.

However, a rigorous recruiting process does a good job of eliminating people who aren't willing to work the Pepsi way before they sign on. Pepsi works very hard at getting the best people, and those who make it here say one of the things they appreciate is the savvy of their peers. Those who make it past the first few years are likely to stay for many. And a new management team, installed in 1986 under CEO D. Wayne Calloway, appears to be interested in building company loyalty rather than merely working someone to death for a few years and providing a tough training ground in the meantime.

Happily for women in the pipeline, Calloway is in his early fifties, and many of the senior managers he picked are younger men who don't find the idea of a woman as an equal on the job discomforting. A few—CFO Robert Dettmer, Roger Enrico, president of PepsiCo Worldwide Beverages, and Michael H. Jordan, president of Frito-Lay—are singled out as men who were making sure that good women were promoted on an equal basis with the men. Women who started in the late seventies say that their peers and immediate bosses are typically men who are used to women as peers and form easy friendships with the women at work. Additionally, many of them have working wives, a factor that sensitizes them to the problems of working women. Hearing that his wife is having problems because of her sex makes a man less likely to inflict the same kind of prejudice on someone at his own office.

However, should Pepsi not be the right fit—it won't take too long to find out—you'll be asked to leave unless you figure it out first and depart on your own. No matter how it happens, it shouldn't come as a surprise. Annual performance reviews methodically list your strengths and weaknesses in both personal and technical skills, as well as what your manager thinks would be your best development plan. This goes all the way up the line. The human resources division keeps tabs on both men and women to see that everyone gets all of the various types of experience they need to rise. And to cue you in on how you're doing, a development feedback program asks you to list your pluses and minuses; your boss does the same, and the two of you compare notes. It might sound tough, but it's thorough and ensures that nobody who's hot is going to fall through the cracks. This means nobody gets lost or overlooked.

This means that women are doing as well as men. Amen.

Which is nothing short of amazing for a company the size of PepsiCo. This is no young operation; Pepsi celebrated its 100th anniversary in 1987. PepsiCo ranks 34th in sales on the *Fortune* 500 list and is the nation's sixth largest employer.

We talked to 11 women at PepsiCo, and not one of them said a woman couldn't go just as far as she was able, regardless of the fact that there are no women in the executive suite on the third floor as yet. To these women, it was only a matter of time. Two of the divisions, for instance, have chief financial officers who are women. Both came into those jobs when they were 34. Another woman is vice president of marketing; there are eight female departmental directors.

"There are women in the pipeline, some of them are making it, some of them drop off at different grade levels, but the men do too," remarks Peggy Moore, vice president of investor relations. "Women are doing well, and they are consistently making it."

Both of the divisions that have women CFOs would be *Fortune* 500 companies in their own right. To be the CFO of a *Fortune* 500 company is extraordinary at 34, even more extraordinary for a woman. "If there's a glass ceiling here, it's all theory," Moore says. "You have to give them a chance to mature into their jobs before they are going to have a chance to be chairman." Moore became a vice president in 1987 after 13 years with the company. When she joined the day after Christmas 1973 as a financial analyst in the treasurer's department, she was the only woman professional at corporate headquarters in Purchase, New York. Three years later, she became the first female officer.

She recalls with some mirth the time when invitations to a party honoring two top executives who had been promoted read "stag party." Since it was to be held at a stuffy country club, the likelihood of its having strippers was not high. But whatever the reason, she was the only person who should have been invited—and wasn't. At the time, she was in the process of moving from one of the men's departments to another's. When her old boss asked her if she was going, she told him she hadn't been invited. He went to the executive floor and called down the hall: "Hey, you chauvinists, aren't you going to invite Peggy?" Days passed, and no one heard a word. The guy figured that his career was in shambles. By this time, the place was aflame with rumors that it would be a real stag party, whatever that meant.

But no. The night before the party, the two men being honored came down and insisted that her not being sent an invitation was an oversight—because she was in the midst of a transfer—and she had to come. "I went and wore a red dress, and I had long hair at the time and I wore it down. Those were the days when if the men used a word like 'damn' they would say, 'Pardon my language, Peggy,' and so every time somebody told a joke from the podium they mentioned my name. And everybody made every effort to make me feel part of the group. It was a little embarrassing, but when I talked about it afterward to a guy who was there, he said, 'If I had that kind of press, I wouldn't be embarrassed.'"

Those days are over. Women don't have a chance to stand out like that any more. There are too many of them. Ronnie Miller Hasday, director of personnel administration in the international division, says, "We don't see ourselves as special. The women who are successful here integrate well into the culture." It was a theme we heard repeatedly. As might be expected, women at meetings are no novelty. In a refreshing change, double entendres are sometimes made by the women. That doesn't mean that out in the field in the bottling operations, where marketing people will spend some time, everything is coming up roses. Most blue collar workers in America aren't used to having women as working peers, or what's worse, as bosses, and your skin had better be the kind that can handle walking past a construction site without burning.

If anything at headquarters makes the men uncomfortable, it is pregnant women. One woman says that at a meeting a year ago, the one pregnant woman present heard about her condition every time someone got up to the podium; the woman herself said that she seemed to hear about her own pregnancy at every meeting. "Is this necessary?" she asked. But that's it. Overall, women—and men—are expected to be tough enough to handle situations by themselves.

Ditto, apparently, for sexual harassment. (*But what sexual harassment?* the women wanted to know.)

And ditto, pretty much, for how the company is run. Pepsi managers have a great deal of autonomy and are encouraged to move swiftly, creating a highly charged atmosphere that puts great pressure on people to perform. Hence the late hours, the overwork, the burnout factor. Sign on, and you hit the decks running. One woman was asked to go to Europe to work on an acquisition her first day on the job. This is the kind of place to warm the heart of any type A. This is the place for the class valedictorian who goes to Harvard. "If a woman is ready to go hell bent for her career, this is a great place," says McGuire. "But if someone's not ready for that, this isn't the place, and it's the same for a man. There are plenty of tensions, and the job takes a personal toll. Having said all that, would I want to be in a boring nine-to-five job? No. You make the trade-offs, you have to say, I want an interesting, exciting, fun job, and if I want that, I have to give my all, I have to be prepared to work all hours and travel at the drop of a hat. But the rewards are high if you can pay the price."

One of the rewards is working at a first-class company. The grounds at headquarters are breathtaking. They resemble an English country garden and are the kind that get written up with several full-page color photographs in *House and Garden,* as they did in 1985. The gym opens at 7 A.M. Edward Durrell Stone designed the main building, a strong horizontal structure in white concrete reminiscent of Frank Lloyd Wright. Dense foliage hides the parking lots. A man-made lake is home to ducks and geese. Training, while informal, allows you to make all the right moves you need to gain wide experience. While the benefits are not fabulous, this is one of the companies that pioneered flexible benefits.

"The most impressive thing about PepsiCo is its consistency in offering services and opportunities that are never second rate," sums up Becky Madeira, public relations director for the United States. "While the management philosophy may change and the business priorities vary depending on the administration, I have never been compromised in terms of my needs —training, support, right down to the physical accommodations. They are all first rate."

PITNEY BOWES

THE COMPANY'S NAME IS SYNONYMOUS WITH METERED
MAILING MACHINES; IT IS CURRENTLY MAKING FORAYS
INTO INFORMATION SERVICES

▲ EMPLOYEES: 22,300; nearly 35 percent are women.

▲ SALES: $2.3 billion.

▲ Pitney Bowes's commitment to recruiting, hiring and promoting women—down to numeric guidelines—was stated to the corporate management committee by the CEO himself. Programs aimed at promoting women include job posting, training and development workshops, tuition reimbursement and succession planning. An annual companywide organizational review is aimed at identifying and developing promotable women. The company does not believe it has pay inequities; it employs a formal job evaluation system that it claims is free of sexual bias.

▲ Of the 235 employees considered upper management, 17—8.5 percent—are women. Of these, six are vice presidents. One is a treasurer. Three of the 13 members of the board of directors are women.

▲ Pitney Bowes is one of the pioneers in flexitime. In addition to the standard maternity disability leave, employees have fought for and won up to 12 weeks of unpaid leave with job held. The female general manager—effectively the president of her subsidiary—gives her workers 12 weeks of paid leave, an indication of how much autonomy she has. The company gives monetary support to selected community-based facilities and started a resource referral directory for child care in 1986.

▲ Among its list of excellent benefits is a series of annual jobholders' meetings where every employee can ask questions and air complaints.

▲ Although some sites distant from corporate headquarters (and the CEO) are less progressive in their promotion of women, this is a company acutely aware of the issues and prepared to deal with them openly.

▲ Major employment centers: Stamford and Norwalk, Conn.: 5,000; Fairfield County, Conn.: 6,000; Danbury, Conn.: 1,000; Dayton, Ohio: 1,100; Melborne, Fla.: 800; 130 branch offices; manufacturing in Kansas City and some of the above locations.

PITNEY BOWES
Walter H. Wheeler Jr. Drive
Stamford, CT 06926
(203) 356-5000

Deanna Sokolowski heard that Pitney Bowes was a great place for women when she was on the board of the YWCA in Stamford, Connecticut. "There were three or four women from Pitney Bowes on the board, and I had a chance to watch their careers over a few years," she says. "I watched it happen for these women."

Sokolowski admits to being initially skeptical when she first heard of Pitney Bowes's reputation. Having worked both in academia and in business, she knew that a company could say it was doing a lot for women, but when you got inside, "it was the old boy network running the show." When she went for her MBA at the University of Connecticut, she heard more in the cafeteria: "You would hear women talk so positively about Pitney Bowes, except maybe for one or two malcontents." Now that she's one of Pitney Bowes's boosters, having joined the company in mid-1986, several acquaintances have sent her their résumés.

And well they might. Although Pitney Bowes is indeed a manufacturing company, and in most old-line manufacturing companies women haven't whizzed right ahead, they are doing just fine at this postal and business machine maker. Three women are vice presidents; one is an officer of the company and sits on the management committee; one is a general manager of an operating unit; 11 women are directors, and others have jobs as treasurer, controller and legal counsel. Two women—not just the typical one—sit on the board of directors.

Something is obviously going on here. The person who is making it happen is George Harvey, president, chairman and CEO. George, as practically everyone calls him, would apparently decree that sex and race bias be eliminated. Since that's not possible, he mandated instead that 35 percent of new hires and promotions on the professional staff go to women and 15 percent to minorities. "He once said at a meeting, it's a pile of baloney that you can't find women and minority engineers," recalls Murem Sharpe, who served on the Y board with Sokolowski. "He doesn't do it for sentimental reasons—he doesn't even have daughters. He feels that if Pitney Bowes doesn't make it attractive for women to work here, we're going to be missing out on half of the talent, period." For women, the goal has been more than met. In the summer of 1986, 40 percent of all new hires and promotions were going to women.

Women's opportunities here are likely to grow as the company moves away from the industrial business it has been in since its founding in 1920, and into the service and information areas. "Women are perceived as adept at marketing services," comments Sharpe.

Indeed, the division she formerly headed as general manager does just that. It puts out a time sensitive delivery guide, the industry equivalent of the official airline guide, for transporting packages instead of people. Sharpe discovered a little company that had the concept a few years back, but it wasn't until she was on maternity leave with her second child in 1985 that the negotiations to acquire the company took place. Since she played a major role in them, she was never absent for any length of time. Because information services are a new venture for Pitney Bowes, Sharpe was aware that she was in a high-risk situation, not the usual route for developing management talent. It's the route most women have to take everywhere. "I've got to succeed," she says pointedly. "The first woman general manager *won't* fail." Clearly she didn't. Last year, Sharpe was named a vice president in the mailing systems group.

Sharpe has been with Pitney Bowes since 1979, through a reorganization and, more important, since before George Harvey took over in 1983. She acknowledges that she has been passed over for some promotions and that when new management came in she found herself back at ground zero, even though her track record should have spoken for itself. "When I first interviewed with the guy who came in as my boss, I was seven months pregnant," she remembers. "I thought, here I sit, the quasi-beached whale." She might have had to prove herself again, but prove she did. "In spite of the setbacks, no, I don't think there is a ceiling for women here. At least, I've broken through it, and the simple reason I have been able to pursue this path is because of George Harvey. Maybe I only talk to him twice a year, but for myself and other key women, he plays a very important role."

It always comes back to the CEO. Harvey traces his pro-woman stance to the recession in the early eighties, when he noticed that the people on the sales force who were willing to go the extra mile were largely women. They didn't mind working extra hours and making more calls. "The desire to achieve and the desire to make money were real strong," he remembers. "I didn't see a comfort level set in as it does with some guys, especially if their wives are working and they don't need that discretionary income." Harvey also observed that women could focus on what needed to be done more quickly than many men. Then there was the added bonus of fresh ideas: "You get a lot of ideas out of women that you don't get out of men—women think differently and have a different perspective. I was impressed by that." Add it up, and Harvey decided to go after these women before the competition did. He didn't wait for it to happen by itself.

"If we're going to get the best people, the people who are going to make us a success, we had better make sure that women can have careers here, not just jobs, and I didn't sense that was going to happen by letting things follow a normal course." Hence the recruiting and hiring memo Harvey issued in 1984 that's known here as the 35–15 memo. Everybody knows about it.

But because life isn't fair and George Harvey cannot stamp out sexism by decree, how well a woman fares at Pitney Bowes is once again primarily dependent on who heads up her division. If the general manager thinks women are fine as long as they're barefoot and pregnant and getting the coffee, a woman will find her progress blocked. She might as well not take the job. "Working for some senior executives here would be a terrible place to start," comments one woman. "They might make the job offer—probably because they know 35 percent of their new hires are supposed to be women—but you won't be taken seriously, you won't get a chance to show what you can do." Apparently, it isn't good enough just to know where your direct boss stands regarding women, you need to find out what his boss thinks too. "What do you do if your boss is transferred to another division?" she asks.

The other problem, of course, is that the farther away one is from George Harvey and corporate headquarters in Stamford, the less his influence is felt. However, that is changing. When we first interviewed in the fall of 1986, 30 percent of the sales force in the business systems division was female, yet only two women out of 99 were branch managers. By early 1988 the numbers were quite different. Following a reorganization that did away with the branch manager system, women held 29 of the senior management positions, overseeing sales and administration for 130 regional offices.

To make it easier for women to rise, Harvey changed the rules: it's no longer necessary to transfer to another city to be promoted. While the record isn't anything to brag about yet, the critical point is that women are in the pipeline in sales, an area that's often hard to crack in a manufacturing company.

One woman who started in sales as the token woman in Pittsburgh in 1976 had several promotions in the field before she was brought home to headquarters, where she is a marketing vice president. Kathleen Synnott feels that more than Harvey's commitment to women makes Pitney Bowes a good place to carve out a career: "The larger issue is that this is a company in change, and this presents opportunities for people regardless of whether they are men or women." Perhaps fortunately for her, Synnott is in marketing, an area in which women do especially well at Pitney Bowes. Incidentally, when we interviewed Synnott she was a marketing *director*.

The change that Synnott refers to reflects the company's awareness that it is no longer enough to go out and take orders for postage meters, a market they overwhelmingly dominate, but that new products with innovative concepts and engineering are necessary to stay competitive today. Pitney Bowes generates annual revenues of $2 billion, not only from the marketing of the ubiquitous postage meter, but also from advanced mailing systems that automatically seal and stack envelopes at the same time the postage is added, copiers, facsimile machines that allow printed material to be sent by telephone with a computer hookup, dictation equipment, price marking labelers and a large array of labels and business and computer supplies.

The core of the business remains manufacturing (with a nod to engineering), and that's an area where you don't find many women at any company, for whatever reasons. But Anne Pol, who formerly supervised some 220 people in manufacturing, finds far less discrimination here than she did at previous employers, where she worked in human resources and labor relations. One of those employers was the New York City fire department.

Pol has a five-year-old daughter whom she drops off at a nearby school before going to work. It's not unusual for one of her staff to come along to pick up her daughter if they need to discuss something. "We'll even go to the mall with her in tow and have a beer if we need to talk before I go home to New Jersey," she says.

When Pol's bosses schedule 7 A.M. meetings on days she cannot be there, she doesn't hesitate to say so. Meetings are rescheduled to meet her time frame. She sees it as part of the process of sensitizing company officials to the special needs of working parents. "I got up out of more meetings than anyone else in the boardroom with George Harvey sitting there," she says of a period when she was part of the reorganization team, putting in 18-hour days over a 10-month period. "He got a real education." Making her parental responsibilities known obviously hasn't hurt, even though she had only joined the company in 1984, for when the reorganization planning was over, she was offered the job in operations. Pol is now vice president of personnel.

Pitney Bowes has long been responsive to employee concerns and needs. Stockholders' meetings are usually tame compared with the annual jobholders' meetings. Held in theaters near all the main company sites, these give every employee a chance to ask management about anything or air a personal gripe. Senior officers (often including Harvey) sit on the stage while groups of up to 500 attend. Prizes—$50 U.S. Savings Bonds—are given for the best questions. If a question comes up that can't be answered on the spot, management gets back to the employee later. The meetings date from 1947. Before that, the company had an employee-management council made up of an equal number of management and workers elected by their peers from all divisions. They meet monthly, more or less, depending on what each unit decides. Recent hot topics were child care, the non-smoking area in the cafeteria and parking.

Because of the company's long history of openness, it's no surprise that Pitney Bowes had flexible working hours as far back as 1974, one of the first companies in this country to do so. Workers are expected to be present between the hours of 10 A.M. and 2 P.M., but apart from that, whatever arrangements you and your boss make are fine. A secretary, for instance, might come in a half hour early every day and leave at 2 P.M. one afternoon a week.

Nor should it be a surprise that the company can be unusually accommodating to mothers who need special arrangements, whether that means travel in a job or, in some circumstances, finishing up every day at home. When Mary Maarbjerg interviewed for a new job within the company in 1978, she said that because of her 6-year-old, she would not be able to work a standard nine-to-five day. "I promised to get the job done, but it might not be from three to five," she told him. "It might be from seven to nine. I was extremely confident I could do it, but I was also extremely naive for asking. But this guy was sufficiently persuaded that I would do what I said, and he offered me the job in product planning." Ironically, she ended up working more hours in that job than she has since. Maarbjerg is currently vice president of planning and treasurer of Pitney Bowes' credit corporation, which provides financing for Pitney Bowes equipment and products from other companies. Maarbjerg, who has an MBA from Wharton, says that she has never run into any obstacles based on sex: "I always felt that if I did well, people would give me a chance to do whatever I wanted to do. Life has never proved any different." As for being a woman at Pitney Bowes, Maarbjerg states, "I don't think for any reason I have not been offered the opportunity to succeed because I am a woman. I suppose I might have had even more opportunities because I am a woman. The company bends over backward to give women opportunities."

The pay for very senior women may be excellent, but across the board, salaries are not the reason to join Pitney Bowes, especially in entry-level jobs. It used to be that the company got away with low salaries because of job security, but that doesn't hold as much anymore. People do get fired; however, if one division lets someone go, he or she might be offered another job in a different division the next day. What newcomers gain is the chance to make a mark in areas of the company that are still unsettled, areas where a lot of rules haven't been written about what you can or cannot do. "You can stick your nose into places it normally shouldn't be, but you learn a lot," one woman says.

However, in benefits the company shines, ranking in the top three when an outside consulting firm did a survey of 16 engineering and manufacturing companies. Except for maternity benefits, which are the standard six-week disability, with only partial pay to hourly workers. In 1986 workers argued for—and got—an additional three months' unpaid leave with the same or a similar job upon return. Murem Sharpe, a mother of two, liberalized the policy for the subsidiary she managed; after a year's employment, all workers receive 12 weeks of paid leave. Child care resources and referral services were also made available to all U.S. employees in late 1986.

Sexual harassment isn't an issue with the women we interviewed. The joking and testing of what a woman can handle may go on somewhat more in the field than back at corporate, but even out in the hinterland it's along the lines of everyday flirting and teasing rather than anything more aggravating. A training program implemented late in 1986 includes a videotape and written material for all levels of employees; managers who want to handle things differently are allowed to do so, as long as the message hits home. And leaving no stone unturned, Harvey fired off a memo, covering not only out-and-out advances but also offensive jokes and comments, adding that the company must create an atmosphere where employees feel secure in reporting it. Anne Pol, who previously managed a plant, says, "You don't find any of it at all—either working with the corporate staff or on the shop floor."

While companies that do well with women usually do the same with minorities, Pitney Bowes is having somewhat of a harder time in this area. Doors that might be open to women might not be to black women. The job you interview for might not be the job you actually do. Yet overall, the goal of hiring and promoting 15 percent minorities is being met, a company spokesman said.

Pitney Bowes, certainly not historically thought of as a splashy innovator, moved into splashy new headquarters in 1986. Designed by I. M. Pei, the pink-and-gray granite building overlooks Long Island Sound on one side and a wooded grassy knoll on the other. It's an imposing presence. Inside are two huge atria—one six stories high—and office space designed with state-of-the-art creature comforts and corporate efficiencies in mind. Windowed offices overlook the open spaces of the building, which seem to float into the park. The building cost $100 million. It's a grand statement.

The building is located in Stamford's South End, long thought to be the wrong side of the tracks. It is only a few blocks away from the firm's former headquarters and brings together people who had been spread out in several facilities. Many of the manufacturing employees live in this area. With the new building, Pitney Bowes is sending out a double message. One is, look at us, we're not a square old company anymore, we're on our toes, we're going to do something next that will surprise you. The other message says, we didn't forget our community responsibility, we aren't going to forget the people who make it all work.

PROCTER & GAMBLE

THE ACKNOWLEDGED LEADER OF THE SOAP AND DETERGENT INDUSTRY

▲ EMPLOYEES: 44,400 (in the United States); more than 30 percent are women.

▲ SALES: $17 billion for the fiscal year ending June 30, 1987; earnings were down to $327 million because of plant consolidations.

▲ Since Procter & Gamble adheres strictly to a promote-from-within policy, women have had an equal opportunity to rise since the company started hiring women on an equal basis with men in the mid-seventies. Hundreds of trainees are hired each year for sales management posts and a smaller number for brand management, technical positions and market research. Intelligence, leadership ability and high personal standards are the criteria. Couples are hired. New employees are given on-the-job experience from the start with close supervision, and good performance results in nearly immediate increased responsibility. In management training, P&G is universally respected.

▲ Among 1,139 people classified as upper management, only 53—5 percent—are women; yet women feel their chances to rise are generally equal to men's, and it is only a matter of time until a female vice president is named. The 17-member board of directors has one woman member.

▲ Although P&G does not have flexitime or allow for flexibility of workplace, the corporate attitude is pro-family. Maternity benefits include the standard eight-week disability leave and a six-month unpaid leave with comparable position upon return. Either parent may take the leave, and if both parents are P&G employees, the leave may be split between the two. Other benefits are also outstanding and include two nearby child care centers primarily reserved for P&G parents. The conference board rates P&G as having "one of the most comprehensive corporate responses to child care in the country."

▲ Women attest that sexual harassment is at odds with corporate culture and is practically nonexistent. Should an incident occur, it is handled by the complainant's manager.

▲ Major employment centers: Cincinnati: 12,500; 53 sites in 24 states, and sales offices at several locations throughout the United States.

PROCTER & GAMBLE COMPANY
Box 599
Cincinnati, OH 45201
(513) 983-1100

Around Procter & Gamble you may hear a few low rumbles that no women have been promoted to vice president yet, but then it's not easy for *anybody* to become a VP at the nation's most successful developer and marketer of household products.

And it's not at every *Fortune* 500 company that you'll find a woman in her middle thirties saying with equanimity, "I think I could be president." Fast track she was, and a young mother, who has made it to the level of associate advertising manager, two steps below a vice presidency. She is on her way.

The kind of progress regarding women that P&G has made in the last half dozen years can best be told by the following two stories. In one, Patrick Hayes, associate director of public relations, some eight years ago bet a female coworker a dinner at Cincinnati's best restaurant, Maisonette, that by 1985 at least half a dozen women would be associate advertising managers. Hayes was waiting to collect when we were in Cincinnati. At the end of 1987, 13 women had the title, which means they are responsible for the marketing of several different brands. Three women were even higher; two were advertising managers and one was a general manager. Brand management is definitely the surest route to the "eleventh floor," where senior management spends its days acting much like bankers, funding good ideas relating to the flotilla of products P&G markets. They include a number of the best-selling brands in the country: Pampers, Tide, Charmin, Bounty, Spic & Span, Cheer, Comet, Downy fabric softener, Duncan Hines and Jif peanut butter.

The other story was told by a brand manager who joined P&G fresh out of college in 1981. As far as she's concerned, there's no difference in the way men and women are judged or how far they can go. "I considered going into banking after I got out of school," she says, "but now when I talk to my friends who did—who went to New York—they all say they have encountered a lot more discrimination because they're women than I have. And you wouldn't think of it—a conservative company in the Midwest."

Not surprisingly, a few levels above her, where the competition is keener and fewer women are on track, doubts begin to be heard. Maybe their sex *is* slowing them down. *Maybe.* "I feel I have been evaluated objectively by my managers within their ability to do so," says one woman, "but they have been exclusively male." The question she left hanging in the air, of course, was, do men judge women differently than they judge other men? If it were not for her sex, she wonders if she might have not "moved a little faster," but she was quick to add that only one or two of her male peers are at levels higher than she, and the vast majority are not. And ultimately she says she believes a vice presidency—rare in a manufacturing company—isn't beyond her reach. The bet around P&G is that the title won't elude *some* woman in the next five to 10 years.

The reason there isn't a lot of bellyaching about women higher in the ranks is that the company has a practically ironclad promote-from-within policy, and it wasn't until the early seventies, when women in numbers began pounding on the door with marketing and engineering degrees and asking for jobs, that equal employment opportunities became a reality at Procter. "Sure, we could hire someone from the outside and make her a vice president and look good on paper, but we just don't do that," says Hayes. The few women who have brought suits against the company charging sexual discrimination have lost in the courts, according to a company spokeswoman. Except for two specialized jobs—that of a Washington lobbyist and an attorney who handled considerable P&G business, no one could think of anyone who had joined the company at anything but entry level. It just doesn't happen. Past presidents—as well as the current one, John E. Pepper—started at the bottom.

While women were largely overlooked before the mid-seventies or, in some divisions, offered jobs at a rung lower than their male counterparts, when the company decided to do a turnabout, it did it the same way it pursues the consumer dollar: aggressively. The 25 women who have reached the lower rungs of upper management spend part of their time recruiting women across the country. They are looking for achievement in and out of the classroom and some evidence of leadership. In all, they visit some 200 schools, and women with chemistry and engineering degrees have just as good a chance of being hired as someone who went to business school, since all divisions of the company—including operations—are equally open to both sexes. Overall, nearly 40 percent of the entry-level management positions are filled by women, and close to 19 percent of all managers and professionals are female.

In operations, P&G boasts one of the few female plant managers in the country, Laree Mugler, who shares managerial duties with a man in a food factory in Jackson, Tennessee. Each is in charge of approximately 600 workers, nearly a quarter of whom are female. "We certainly have equal opportunities for men and women here," she says. "It's almost at the point where we don't have to play the numbers game anymore, not like we had to back in the early seventies when there were not enough women and minorities coming out of engineering schools." Mugler says since she came to P&G with a degree in mechanical engineering in 1972, she's never run into any resistance due to her sex.

More women would be running plants, according to management, if it were easier to convince women from other areas of the country to take a job in places like Jackson or, say, Oglethorpe, Georgia. In all, P&G has plants at 45 locations across the country, and it's not unusual for women to constitute up to a quarter of the managerial and technical staff.

Admittedly, corporate headquarters sometimes has the same problem: recruiters say that sometimes it's not P&G they've got to sell to fresh Harvard MBAs, it's Cincinnati. It's a family town, and most of the after-hours socializing takes place at home. For married folks, the town can be ideal. The schools are good, and child care is not difficult to find. "It's safe and easy to get around," was a theme heard several times. And culturally, Cincinnati is not the dry gulch many Easterners think the Midwest is, with P&G making substantial grants to a fine arts fund that is distributed to the symphony, ballet company, year-round playhouse and opera company, to name a few.

Yet Boston, New York or San Francisco it's not, and single women without a network of family nearby sometimes hesitate to come to southern Ohio. One young woman said that if she leaves P&G—and she is thinking of it—it will be solely because "Cincinnati is not a single woman's town."

Finding a husband in the ranks, however, appears to be fairly commonplace, a practice the company looks upon benignly, as long as one doesn't report to the other. P&G even goes so far as to hire couples. Fresh out of Harvard Business School, Nancy Chandler Koglmeier decided that P&G looked good to her—if her fiancé—who *didn't* have an MBA—could also find a good job in Cincinnati. "I called them and said I was interested in the job offer and asked if they would interview my fiancé," she says. "They said they would, but he realized when he was here that they were just doing it to be polite. He had to do a real job selling himself." He succeeded. They started work in brand management on the same day in different divisions. "We both wanted brand management, and here was a chance to go to work for a very good company," she says. "The risk was that it would affect our marriage or that one of us would be unhappy and we would have to leave. But if that were the case, we would have a year or two of P&G on our résumés, and that wasn't going to hurt us." That was in the fall of 1982. Koglmeier says that it's worked out beautifully so far and that she and her husband have more or less kept up with each other's career paths. Koglmeier was promoted to brand manager early in 1986 and was expecting her first child.

Her reference to P&G on her résumé is apt. The company is considered the best corporate finishing school in the country, a fact not lost on P&G. Junior management people are not allowed to be quoted in the press, lest headhunters start phoning with tempting offers simply by dint of seeing their name connected with the company. Neither are titles easily divulged, and even business cards tend to be vague. An exception was made for this book. The people who "graduate" from P&G fill the president's or chairman's post at dozens of major companies. Yet P&G's reputation as the best-managed company in America has become tarnished somewhat in the last decade as newer, younger companies have been quicker to respond to changing consumer preferences. For a few years P&G appeared to be in a slump, and in 1985 it posted a 29 percent drop in earnings, largely due to significant investment in new brands and slow movement on established ones. While P&G appeared on *Fortune's* top 10 of most admired corporations in 1986, it slipped off the list in 1987, although it is ranked number one in its category. And it is regularly cited as a good place for minorities and women to work.

What is so prized is P&G's emphasis on instilling good management skills in its people. Each boss is responsible for training the people directly below and pushing as well as protecting them, making the admittedly competitive atmosphere less than brutal. New people get a lot of nurturing from their managers and are promoted only when they are ready, not according to some absolute timetable. "Basically, I coach the people on the brands I manage," observes Barbara Thomas, advertising manager. "They generate the ideas and do their best to put it together. I'm a combination of a supporter and devil's advocate."

While with coaching you probably won't be allowed to fall on your face, you are given real responsibility as soon as you report to work. Thomas's first assignment in 1974 was to dream up a promotion connected to the reissue of Walt Disney's *Snow White* and convince four different brand managers to pony up their money. She decided upon kids' mugs offered through premiums. "I was told to go figure it out," she says laughingly. "I had to think it up, make sure it was affordable, convince four different brand managers it was a good idea, negotiate with suppliers, get it to the sales force and then figure out how to physically handle the premiums." The promotion came off successfully.

The experience of being the new kid on the block and seeing your ideas implemented is not unusual. Lisa Kremer says that what got her promotion to brand manager was conceiving a brand extension and making it work— in just six months the product was on the shelf. "All of us can list a bunch of things where it was our idea and it got all the way up," she says. "A good idea goes at an amazingly fast pace. People think P&G is so bureaucratic, but I say, 'No, it's not.' But you have to know how to work within the system."

What does that require? Logic, the ability to be persuasive, a sense of what's worked in the past and knowing whom to talk to, not only in brand management but also in product development and engineering. In recent years the company has placed greater emphasis on business teams that cut across disciplines to make decisions about what direction a given product line will take, a strategy that allows for greater input from manufacturing than in the past.

Naturally, any company employing over 44,000 workers cannot escape a large measure of bureaucracy, but the concerted effort to dispense with the old maze appears to be succeeding, albeit not quickly enough for some. However, decisions are now made at lower levels than before. And new ideas, as in Kremer's experience, can be implemented before a calendar year goes by, the usual timetable of the past. Crest Tartar Control formula was test marketed in March 1985 and was available nationally by June, something of a record for P&G. And the hands-down winner in new laundry products introduced in recent years is Liquid Tide. With a revolutionary technology and a bottle top that is a measuring cup designed to allow the liquid to drain back into the bottle, Liquid Tide has become the most successful new brand of its kind in the last 15 years. Crest Tartar Control formula and Liquid Tide represent the kind of leadership in consumer products that has long been associated with P&G, leadership that had slipped in the previous decade. A fat substitute, now dubbed Olestra, is awaiting FDA approval. If it's as good as its advance publicity, grateful dieters could give P&G a sure winner, raising profitability in the food division.

"We don't make decisions to make a fast buck," says Claudia Kotchka, associate advertising manager and the woman who brought out the improved Crest. "We're an ethical company, and we are aboveboard with the consumer. That's one of the things I like best about the company." Other women echoed her thoughts. "I don't spend time worrying about what's right and wrong to do in business," Barbara Thomas says. "You just do what's fair and square, and the company will bend over backward supporting you." True, the statements sound Pollyannaish for any company that does $17 billion in sales annually, but the women say that risk takers who want to make big profits in a short time without worrying about their reputation will do better elsewhere. Risk aversion and the emphasis on thoroughness or, as one woman put it, "the need to know too much before we go to market" were common complaints among the women vying for future office space on the hallowed eleventh floor.

While they are cultivating patience, ambitious P&G people had better learn to master the concise memo that sells itself on the first page, a memo that might eventually wind up on a vice president's desk, even if you are a neophyte at your job. P&G's reliance on tight, refined memos based on hard facts—not instinct—is legendary in American business.

One woman recalled that when she wrote her first important memo back in 1971, shortly after she joined the company, men were just learning how to deal with women on the job. "We had a meeting to go over the memo, and I remember the manager seemed nervous when we started," she says. "What he said was, 'You aren't going to cry, are you?' Those days of special treatment are over." Company women remember that whenever a woman joined brand management back in the early seventies, other women in the company hailed it as a victory of sorts. Now women are so commonplace throughout the company, no one, man or woman, pays much attention to sex distinction when it comes to getting the job done.

That doesn't mean the old sexist attitudes are dead or harassment is nonexistent. "Sure, that's something you run into here," says Susan Mackey, a group manager in market research. "But they know they can't act the way they feel around here. Think of it in terms of smoking—there is the same peer pressure not to smoke as there is not to act like a chauvinist. The chauvinists of the world have been cleared out of P&G, or they change their attitudes here." Indeed, men have been fired for sexual harassment, most often in operations. Mackey supervises six men, some of whom are older than she, and she says that although she's sure that they initially had difficulty with the idea of a younger woman as their boss, it hasn't presented any real problem. This may be partly because of Mackey's sensitivity to their feelings and partly because it is made very clear to everyone that promotions are based on merit, not because the company is pushing women or minorities faster than white males.

Not surprisingly, these liberated attitudes didn't appear overnight. When Leslie Mowry was hired as a research chemist in 1973, she was convinced it was because the company wanted her because of her credentials and ability —not her sex; yet she found in her first assignment that she was treated much like a clerk and spent a lot of time copying reports at the Xerox machine. Eventually she took the matter up with her boss's supervisor, who explained the facts of life to her boss. Today Mowry is one of the highest-ranking women in the technical division, an associate director of product development, and thinks that she can go as far as she would like. How far she would like to go is another question. If she goes too far, she will no longer do hands-on research, which is what she likes to do.

While her beginnings at P&G were inauspicious, Mowry believes that, ultimately, being a woman in the technical division may actually be a plus. "My sex has never held me back and may have helped me more than hurt," she comments. "You have a higher visibility, and since management was anxious to promote women, you at least got noticed."

Mowry has three children under 6, full-time help and a husband who doesn't see child care as her primary responsibility. She works approximately 50–55 hours a week, a number that isn't unusual in any division of the company.

This is not a place for slackers. And while the company once had a reputation for not actually firing anybody, those days are no more. If you want to succeed, you had better plan on long hours and hard-and-fast results. "I get tired sometimes," says one woman. "It's not easy to rack up things you've done, and you have to work hard to make points." One high-ranking woman in her late thirties said that having a baby made her face a decision she hadn't thought about before: was she willing to work hard enough to go to the next rung? She works 50–60 hours a week now. "But if I make the decision and go for it, my being a woman—or a mother—won't hold me back. It will be my decision as to how hard I want to work."

Babies seem to be the norm, not the exception, for P&G people. It's almost as if being a family person makes you one of the guys. Claudia Kotchka, who admits to high ambitions at P&G, says that her boss was delighted when she told him she was pregnant. She was working on an important brand—Crest—and only took six weeks' maternity leave, which allowed her job to be kept open for her. When asked what happens when she can't be there because her child is sick, she recalled the time she was at a meeting on the eleventh floor and motherhood called. "I got up and said I had to take my baby to the doctor and walked out, and I never heard anyone say anything to me. And one day my boss—he's got five kids—called up and said they were all sick and so was his wife and he wasn't coming in."

While Kotchka took only a short leave—eight weeks are given with pay —women *and* men are guaranteed a six-month leave of absence without pay. And many women take the full leave. If both parents work for the company, they can split the leave. Adoptive parents are also eligible for child care leaves when adopting an infant, as well as a stipend of $1,000 to defray expenses, since the medical insurance doesn't apply. Although it's rare, some men do take advantage of the child care leave.

Liberal leaves for dads are emblematic of P&G's benefits package, which is, quite simply, terrific. By nearly every standard, P&G emerges at the top of the list of U.S. corporations when benefits are compared. In 1984 an independent management consulting firm, Towers, Perrin, Forster & Crosby, ranked P&G first in total dollar value of employee benefits, a package estimated to be worth somewhere between $10,000 and $12,000 a year. Twenty major American corporations were evaluated. As one woman puts it, "We've got the Mercedes of benefits, not the Cadillac." Among the goodies:

Preferred placement at two child care facilities near Cincinnati P&G sites. Procter donated start-up money to the privately owned centers with the provision that 75 percent of its openings be held for P&G parents—mothers or fathers. Cost: $90 a week or less for children under 3.

A flexible benefits program that lets employees design some benefit coverage to meet individual needs, whether that be an IRA or child care assistance.

Assistance to employees in dealing with alcoholism, drug abuse and emotional illness.

A communitywide child care resource and referral service funded largely by a $35,000 grant from the company.

A health plan that allows you to pay a maximum of $3.50 for a prescription.

A liberal profit-sharing plan dating from 1887 and thought to be the oldest one in continuous operation in American business. A middle manager who's been at P&G for most of her career could end up with retirement income equal to her final salary.

In addition to the stock set aside for employees, private purchases of stock are encouraged through a payroll deduction plan to the extent that some 20 percent of P&G shares are held by employees and retirees.

Workers enjoy a generous 14 paid holidays a year (including two personal leave days) in addition to vacation weeks; and if you'd rather, some weeks of vacation may be traded for cash.

The only benefits P&G doesn't seem to have for working mothers are part-time employment and flexible working hours, options that are on many women's minds these days. Given P&G's record, it's probably just a matter of time. This is the company that has long believed that its interests and those of its employees were inseparable, a policy the company has implemented since its beginnings in 1837.

As befitting such an old and established company, the offices are serviceable, comfortable and, for the most part, staid. The cafeterias, however, are luxurious, appointed with mahogany-and-slate tables and upholstered chairs that would sit well in many people's dining rooms. The total effect is one of quiet quality.

The architecture underscores this mood: solid, squarish, understated. In the center of downtown Cincinnati, the two stocky P&G towers with pyramid caps have wings that reach out over its spacious plaza. Along with an adjoining central building, they form the largest office complex in the area. The entrance hall is a celebration of retro-deco, and, with its marble fountain and inlaid tiles, Fred Astaire and Ginger Rogers might have used it as a set. Yet the overall feeling is perhaps too serious for a couple of toe-tappers. Women who are looking for excitement and adventure would do best to apply elsewhere.

RECOGNITION EQUIPMENT

A LEADER IN THE DATA CAPTURE INDUSTRY; THE COMPANY MAKES HARDWARE AND SOFTWARE THAT TRANSLATE DATA *YOU* CAN READ INTO DATA *COMPUTERS* CAN READ

▲ EMPLOYEES: 1,927; 17 percent are women.

▲ SALES: $241 million in 1986, a 41 percent jump over 1985. The company has doubled in size in three years.

▲ This fast-growing Dallas-based company is concerned with re-cruiting and hiring women but makes no special effort to single them out in recruitment efforts. Programs aimed at promoting women include liberal tuition reimbursement and a monthly forum for bringing top Dallas businesswomen to lecture and meet with REI women. The Administrative Counseling Team of 15 ad-ministrative assistants and female managers has monthly meetings with the president, ensuring visibility. Although only 17 percent of employees are women, 40 percent of employees enrolled in management training programs are women.

▲ Of the 252 employees considered upper management, 36 are women; one is a vice president, one is associate corporate secre-tary, while the others are directors. One woman sits on the eight-member board of directors.

▲ REI is concerned with the needs of parents. In addition to stan-dard maternity disability leave, new mothers can take additional time off without pay, position assured. New fathers may take a personal leave without pay. The company provides a resource referral system for child care facilities and a cafeteria-style ap-proach to benefits that includes up to $5,000 pretax for child care. A nearby hospital provides day care for sick children at the cost of $25 per day. Part-time work is available for free-lance software people and consultants.

▲ Complaints of sexual discrimination can be handled by informal hearing or by formal procedure. The company is committed to rectifying inequality of pay. It does so by examining what others are doing, through research to establish measures of comparable worth, and through reevaluation of individual job descriptions.

▲ REI has done a study on sexual harassment and issued strong statements on the subject. Women reported that it is not an issue and that if a problem arose they'd have no hesitation reporting it.

▲ Major employment centers: Dallas: 1,000; Washington, D.C.: 50; regional offices in Atlanta, Chicago, New York, Philadelphia and San Francisco; sales and service offices in 200 locations across the country.

RECOGNITION EQUIPMENT, INC.
2701 East Grauwyler Road
Irving, TX 75001
(214) 579-6000

At many companies it's the kiss of death to fall in love with your boss. Or vice versa. But at a high-tech company outside Dallas, such a love story had a happy ending.

Today Tracy Burton is the Midwestern district sales manager for Recognition Equipment, Inc. She and her former boss are married. He's the one who left the company, but not under fire and not right away. They were both still working for REI when they got married one lunch hour.

When he did leave the company a year later to take a job in San Francisco, she decided to follow along. "I thought I would throw in the towel at REI and take whatever I could get in California," she says. "A lot of companies would have been glad to be rid of me, but management here made an effort to find me a job in California where I could make good money. They made a good enough job for me that I didn't even look for work in California."

Burton, who's in her early thirties, was the California sales manager when we met. Keeping her with the company isn't a matter of largesse, as her sales team (four men, one woman) had the highest total in revenues for the year. How much can someone make in a job like Burton's? With salary and commissions, more than $200,000. Last year, she was promoted to district manager in Chicago. Before the move, she and her husband had decided that if she was offered a transfer back to the home office in Irving, Texas, or elsewhere, it would be her turn and he would relocate to suit her. "Last time—when we moved to California—it was his turn, even though that turned out to be good for me," she says. "And he said at the time, 'Next time, it will be your turn.'" He didn't go back on his word.

Burton vividly recalls what happened when their romance was made public, and how it happened. Her boss and soon-to-be husband, against her better judgment, went to tell his boss flat out what was going on. He sounds like a stand-up kind of guy. "It was the same week an article came out in the *Harvard Business Review* about office affairs," she says. "It was written by a woman who said, 'You have to get rid of one of them, or better yet, both of them. It never works out, even if you transfer them. And if you're going to get rid of one of them, it's most likely going to be the woman because she probably is younger and hasn't been around as long as the man, and she isn't as valuable to the company.'" Burton catches her breath, her eyes amused. "Well, all these guys read the *Harvard Business Review*. And my mother sent me a copy of the article, saying, 'Boy, are you in trouble.'"

Happily, sometimes mothers are wrong. Just as wrong as writers of articles with ironclad advice.

As might be expected, Burton firmly believes REI is a place where women can get ahead. In fact, she says, if you are very good, being a woman gives you an edge because it gives you greater visibility. "A woman could go through a quicker succession of promotions than a man because Bill [Moore, the president] and some of the other officers have such a strong desire to have women at higher levels." The woman wouldn't get a job she wasn't qualified for, Burton adds, but she would be given a chance "if Bill was pretty sure she could do the job." It's the kind of risk taking companies have always done with bright young men, almost never with women. At most places women have to have so many tickets punched to advance, they have a hard time keeping up with the men.

But it may be more difficult to have that advantage at REI if you are not the employee who stands out in the crowd; it may be more difficult if you aren't dead serious about your career; it may be more difficult if you don't have the right degrees and background. Burton, for instance, was a math major at the University of Wisconsin and has a master's in computer science from Texas A&M. The right fit for a company that produces the hardware and software that puts data people can read into a form a computer can process. It's called "data capture," and REI is a leader in the industry. Business is booming.

One of Dallas's fastest-growing companies, REI showed an increase in revenues to $241 million in 1986, a 48 percent jump over the previous year. Net income more than doubled, from $4.3 million to $10.5 million. Return on equity rose from 4.9 percent in 1985 to 8.4 percent in 1986. As of last year, the pace had not let up. Net income in mid-1987 was skyrocketing at a 50 percent clip. International markets, less expensive, broader-based products and service and maintenance fees were fueling the rise. Two smaller firms were acquired in 1985, and president Bill Moore was on a roll. "In three years, we've doubled the size of this company," he told the *Dallas Times Herald*, "and we plan to double again in the next 24 to 36 months."

Companies on a roll usually have a certain style. To build enthusiasm and loyalty, they hold lots of management meetings and, frequently, Friday afternoon beer busts. Both of which REI does. Communication from all levels, up and down, is good because stratified barriers aren't yet in place. Senior management is usually highly visible and readily accessible. Also true. You can stop Bill, as everyone calls him, in the hall or see him in his office with a grievance. (But you better realize that he is going to act quickly if you do go to him with a problem. By that afternoon, he is likely to have asked your boss what's going on. And *he* will be taking a new look at you.)

Anyone can sign up for one of Bill's morning management courses, which run from 7 to 8:30 A.M. twice a week. You had better not be late, and while it's one way to make points with the head of the company, it won't help if you appear dull or slow-witted. He isn't likely to forget who you are;

conversely, if you stand out, it's not unlikely that Moore will take you under his wing and see that you get the experience and exposure that you need to rise, as he is doing for a handful of women. Although the company has close to 1,000 employees in the Dallas area alone, Bill knows most of them, as well as the 150-plus sales staff scattered throughout the country.

Top managers go to quarterly meetings off-site at Lake Texoma, where, after the work is done, you *will* play. You will head for the greens or the courts or the volleyball net. You will not say you don't feel like it. Although Jenny Barker, vice president of corporate communications, is the only female VP present, she is not the only woman there. The administrative assistants of senior managers, usually women, are considered to be an integral part of senior management and are included in the meetings and the games. Barker says of Moore's commitment to promoting women, "He is very vocal about his feelings about trying to advance women, but he can't do it alone. What he does do is keep saying the canon."

What he also does is to provide a platform for women's ideas. He was responsible for setting up the Administrative Counseling Team, made up of 15 administrative assistants and female managers. They meet monthly with Moore to alert him of problems and tell him what they would do differently if they were running the company. One of their ideas resulted in the construction of a demonstration room to display company products. Total cost: $1.5 million.

Moore was also the force behind a monthly forum that brings top Dallas businesswomen to lecture and meet with REI women. It's open to all women at the company, secretary to vice president, and is well attended. If a woman doesn't come to REI with well-tuned ambitions, a few rounds of meetings and networking sessions could change that.

But how much of a dent does this make with other men? Of course, there are some laggards in the playing field, some men who can't see a woman's worth until she's proved it three times over. But most of the women agree with Corlis Murray, manufacturing engineer, who says, "Here you are rewarded for your performance. They don't treat me special, and I respect that. I prefer to be handled just like anyone else."

Murray is black, and so her comments have all the more force. She had worked at Xerox, where she felt that she wasn't looked upon so much as a good engineer, but a black engineer, someone to fill an affirmative action quota. "There are no special quotas here, and I don't get special treatment because I'm black," she says approvingly.

Sexual harassment doesn't flourish in an environment like this, but if it cropped up, the women said that they wouldn't hesitate to take the matter up with the human resources division and that their complaint would probably get swift action.

The old glitch in this engineering bliss—it's hard to remember we are at an engineering firm where macho is more than a word from the sixties—is that many, but not all, women feel that their pay is lower than their male peers' and that because they came in at a low salary it's nearly impossible to catch up. However, help is on the way. A companywide job evaluation based on Hay points (a nationally recognized way to rate jobs and assign salaries) was completed in 1986, and adjustments are being made. Engineers fresh from school start at $28,000–$32,000; middle managers make between $40,000 and $60,000; and top officers, well over $100,000 in salary and bonuses.

Although the company can't compete with engineering salaries at giants like IBM and Hewlett-Packard, recruiters here sell the growth opportunities and the breadth of experience someone will get at REI compared to a larger, more compartmentalized company. Engineering students who want to combine work with studies could find a niche here in a program in which they go to school for a semester, then work for a semester. For others, up to $2,000 a year will be reimbursed toward an undergraduate degree; there is no cap for graduate studies. The benefits package is good and includes flexible spending benefits. One of the options is legal coverage, divorce and suits against the company not included. Working parents can deduct pretax dollars up to the allowable $5,000 from their salaries for child care. A tie-in with a nearby school for training child care practitioners was being investigated in the summer of 1987, and a nearby hospital provides day care for sick children at the cost of $25 a day.

The company's savings plan is unusually generous. The company will kick in 70 cents for every dollar, up to 6 percent of your salary. For 1986, when the company had a particularly good year, the ante was upped to 80 cents on the dollar.

As in any company in a growth mode, this is not a place to park if you don't feel like putting out enough to go for the gold day in, day out. Fresh ideas are the company's lifeblood, and enthusiasm is de rigueur. However, when a family emergency demands your attention, you can expect understanding as well as time off from most managers. Pam Guerrero, a senior systems analyst, had to have plenty of leeway with her schedule when her 7-year-old was diagnosed as having a learning disability as well as related problems that required surgery. "I went straight to my boss and explained that Amy was going to take a lot of time in the next few months, and I told him that I was concerned because I didn't want to lose my job. I told him I'd come in at 7:30 A.M. and work lunch hours or do whatever it would take.

He said, 'Pam, I'm not concerned about you working 40 hours right now, take care of your family.' I said, 'But I'm concerned.' He said, 'Read my lips. Right now you do what you've got to do.'"

Although Jenny Barker hasn't needed big chunks of time off, she is the single parent of a 10-year-old son. She's had to be out of town on his birthday and work late nights instead of helping him with his homework. What she likes about REI is not only that family emergencies are taken in stride, but also the way she—and her discipline—are regarded by the senior team. In some companies, the public relations arm is seen as a necessary nuisance. Not so at REI. "One of the things that is important to a PR person is working for a president who understands communications, who understands that you've got to have a lot of knowledge and exposure as to why decisions are made in order to do your job well," comments Barker. "Very few corporate presidents know that, but Bill does. So the complaints and bitches I might have about any number of things are far offset by that."

She quickly adds that none of her complaints has anything to do with sex.

RESTAURANT ENTERPRISES GROUP

MORE THAN A DOZEN CHAINS OF RESTAURANTS, WITH CLOSE TO 700 THROUGHOUT THE COUNTRY

▲ EMPLOYEES: 52,600; 44 percent are women.

▲ SALES: $1 billion (projected for 1987); 679 restaurants, over 300 in California. The company has been bought out by some top executives from W. R. Grace and Company, its former corporate parent.

▲ Restaurant Enterprises Group recruits qualified candidates regardless of sex; at all levels, the company does a good job.

▲ Of the 105 employees considered senior management, nearly 26 percent—27—are women. The figure includes six vice presidents and 21 directors. At the next level, 49 of the 81 managers are women.

▲ Although company policy provides the standard California minimum—usually six weeks—for maternity leave, individual bosses can informally work out more flexible patterns. In line with the industry, benefits and starting salaries are nothing to brag about. Predictably, at the lower levels, turnover is high. However, you can start in operations—and be promoted if you're good—without a college degree. One vice president of operations is a woman.

▲ The company includes a program on sexual harassment as a mandatory part of its training for all employees. Complaints are handled through informal hearings. Complaints of sexual discrimination are handled in a like manner.

▲ The company is committed to rectifying inequities of pay to women. Comparability analyses are conducted by function and job classification. They examine what other companies within the industry are doing, reevaluate individual job descriptions and job functions, and respond to compliance agency complaints.

▲ Major employment centers: California: 22,775; Texas: 2,550; Missouri: 2,460; Arizona: 2,100. More than a dozen chains, in 34 states plus the District of Columbia.

RESTAURANT ENTERPRISES GROUP, INC.
2701 Alton Avenue
Irvine, CA 92714
(714) 863-6300

Nobody ever said the restaurant business was easy. The hours are abysmal, the pay is lousy and the benefits are poor.

Be that as it may, the restaurant business is one of the growth industries of the eighties, spurred largely by the increasing numbers of women who aren't full-time homemakers and have neither the time nor the inclination to put three square meals—or maybe not even one—on the table each day. For them, eating out is not a luxury; it's part of what makes their lifestyle possible.

Stepping into that expanding market is Restaurant Enterprises Group (REG), a billion-dollar operation with close to 700 restaurants countrywide, more than 300 of them in California. They include more than a dozen chains and range from family restaurants such as Coco's, Carrows and jojos to upscale seafood restaurants such as the Bristol Bar & Grill and Gladstone's 4 Fish. Other chains are informal eateries and include Houlihan's Old Place, Darryl's and Baxter's; moderately priced dinner houses, Reuben's, Charley Brown's and Charley's Place, the Devon Bar & Grill, Crichet's, Fedoras and Hogates, as well as a 190-outlet El Torito, a Mexican eating place. The company was formed in late 1986 when W. R. Grace and Company, a New York–based conglomerate largely in the chemical business, agreed to sell a majority interest in its restaurants to a small group of its top executives in a leveraged buyout.

Although W. R. Grace and Company is not known to be friendly to women, its restaurant group is a different story. While the women talk of 80-hour weeks with no time left for boyfriends or children and of medical insurance for some hourly employees that doesn't start until you've been with the company for 18 months, they speak positively about being able to rise to positions of responsibility without a sense of being held back because they are women.

And women appear to be heading for the very top. Six women are vice presidents; one is a VP of operations, responsible for 21 restaurants in nine states and Washington, D.C. In the restaurant business, such a job is the typical route for people to rise to the very top. "I don't feel that I've ever been passed over for a promotion because I was a woman," says vice president and controller of two divisions, Pam Meyer. She's been with the company since 1974, when she started out as a bookkeeper. When we interviewed her in 1986 she'd had a promotion every couple of years. Sometimes she was given the job before she was given the title; whether this would have happened to a man is unknown, but in any event it happened under the previous management.

The new CEO and president, Norman N. Habermann, is more concerned about making the company a nice place to work for everyone than it was under the aegis of W. R. Grace, known for its long hours and little understanding of its employees' outside responsibilities. One of the first noticeable changes was in the company's attitudes to employee gripes. A suspicion that benefits were well below the industry norm led to an outside consulting firm conducting a companywide survey to get to the bottom of the matter; one result was a savings plan (401K) for employees that includes matching funds—50 cents on the dollar, up to 6 percent of an employee's salary—that is scheduled to begin in April 1988.

Benefits were cut back substantially a few years before the buyout as a cost-saving measure, but benefits in the restaurant business are notoriously poor. This is especially true for hourly employees, the servers and bartenders who make up the backbone of the company and account for the vast majority of the 52,600-plus employees. Managers said poor benefits was one of the reasons the company had trouble keeping people, from waitresses to computer programmers. Paltry tuition benefits ($500 a year) were another reason employees left. They don't get any better as one rises, for all salaried employees receive the same benefits package, from supervisor to the very top.

Accounting and finance are areas of the company where women have done extremely well, and that's where the seat of power is at REG, unusual perhaps because this is the hospitality business, but expected since this is a spin-off of W. R. Grace. Company women feel they can do well in these departments, most probably because it's easy to gauge performance when it's based on numbers and charts and nothing so ephemeral as, say, how well you fit in with your colleagues. One former employee who gave up a career as a securities analyst in the East when her husband was offered a good job with the Grace restaurant group was carving out a new career path for herself here also, but left after she had a child. Although she had been initially hired as a consultant while she scoured the territory around Irvine for a position outside of Grace, she was eventually hired full-time. "Everything was wide open in financial analysis," she said. "Although I was willing to throw everything to the winds back East, it worked out well for me. My boss had a great attitude about training and promoting women into management."

The new management's style is clearly evident in finance, as well as throughout the entire corporate staff. Employees no longer have to work crazy hours and cancel plans at the last minute to get out the detailed kinds of reporting required by Grace. It's now possible to have more of a personal life or get out on the links with your coworkers, women invited too.

Yet the hours in operations haven't changed and, given the nature of the business, aren't expected to. Supervisors, who oversee several restaurants, may regularly be out until 2 A.M. checking on the service in their bars. And it's not uncommon to run into one's boss doing exactly the same thing. The long hours have their compensations. Running into your boss at a restaurant at 10 P.M. makes it easy to schmooze and socialize, and since most of the socializing takes place in the company's restaurants, no one needs to be invited to join a group. Yet since the hour is late, you won't be penalized if you don't stay around to kibitz.

However, all this makes having children problematic. Who's got the time? One woman in operations says she is quite sure she and her husband won't have a child because of the demands of her job. "I don't know how I would have time to have a baby," she says. However, if you do have children, that won't hold you back the way it will at some companies where you are perceived differently because you have kids. Get the job done, and you'll get ahead. And working mothers say that when an emergency arises, some bosses are understanding in allowing time off. If you're lucky, you get such a boss; again, under the new management, the number of such bosses seems likely to increase.

But how deeply the new management is affecting lower-level managers and supervisors who don't think women have the right stuff to do the job as well as they do is still a question. You might run into men who tell you to your face that women shouldn't be restaurant managers, let alone area supervisors.

The pay is within the norm for the industry, and the industry tends to pay low. Entry-level positions in the training program range from $19,000 to $25,000, depending on the division and the location. For this, you are asked to work 12-hour days and lots of weekends. Not surprisingly, the turnover rate in the industry is high, and this company is no exception. One woman said that when she hired men for the training program, she was likely to ask them how they felt about not seeing their children for a week. Training programs—which apparently vary in length, since you might be given a permanent position a few weeks after joining—are now filled 20–30 percent by women.

To get ahead here, a street fighter mentality will help; being viewed as a tough negotiator right from the start will be a plus. Not only might you get the extra bucks, management will see you as a possible comer. And you will need to be aggressive about pushing for raises once you join the company, since no formal policy exists to review salaries. Some bosses are conscientious about seeing to their employees' raises and will make them retroactive if they've been delayed for some reason. Others don't bother.

On the plus side of the ledger, this is one company where, for many slots, background and education don't matter much. In finance and accounting, you naturally need the appropriate degrees, but in operations or in some staff positions, such as human resources, you don't have to be a college graduate. Learning by doing will stand you in good stead, and if you can do the job, you'll be promoted into it. Whenever possible, the company promotes from within.

With all the intensity that is part and parcel of this job, burnout is a constant. Women in their thirties who said they loved their jobs didn't know if they wanted to keep working at the same pace for the next 15 or 20 years. But for now, what some of them especially like is the excitement. Laurie Neuse, who joined the company in 1979 for a starting salary of $11,000, had turned down an offer of $20,000 from a chemical company. It was the restaurant business she wanted. "The rewards of working here are in the excitement of being in management and supervision, because basically you run an entire corporation that's doing some two to four million in business," she says. "You are in charge of distribution, manufacturing, marketing and sales, and you control it in a very direct manner. Customers come in and ask for you because you are the manager. It's a hands-on operation and very rewarding when you are successful." Neuse, a Rutgers University graduate from New Jersey, joined the company in St. Louis. She's been transferred to jobs in Kansas City, Phoenix and two sites in California. In 1984 she became her division's first female area supervisor, responsible for five units, which was her original goal when she joined the company.

"We're results oriented," she adds. "If you're good and can produce results, they don't care if you're from outer space, they don't care if you're a woman or an ethnic. That makes it a good place for women because it puts everybody on the same level."

THE ROWLAND COMPANY

A PUBLIC RELATIONS AGENCY THAT IS PART OF THE SAATCHI & SAATCHI WORLDWIDE COMMUNICATIONS NETWORK

▲ EMPLOYEES: 138; approximately two thirds are women.

▲ REVENUES: Annual fee billings, $10.4 million. (Saatchi & Saatchi is a billion-dollar company; first six months of 1987: $579 million.)

▲ The Rowland Company does not need to worry about hiring and promoting women; it already does an excellent job. Word-of-mouth referrals are the best entry, and previous experience is strongly preferred. This small company has no training programs, but it is possible (though difficult) for a college graduate to start as a secretary and move up.

▲ Of the 11 upper managers, seven are women—one executive vice president and six senior vice presidents. One of the four management committee members are women.

▲ The company offers a maternity leave based on years of employment but provides little official flexibility for parenting. However, unofficially the company is very accommodating to family emergencies and allows sick leave for family illness. In addition, the company hires lots of free-lance public relations specialists and people to do media placement, an option for former employees who want more control over their time. It's not hard to get this work if you've done well here and can show results. Some free-lancers work a few days a week on a regular basis, and have offices here.

▲ Because of the numbers of women versus men, and because of the gender blindness of the president, sexual discrimination and sexual harassment are nonissues at Rowland.

THE ROWLAND COMPANY, INC.
415 Madison Avenue
New York, NY 10017
(212) 688-1200

If all companies were like The Rowland Company, the authors of this book would have been out of a job: there would be no need to write it. Asking women about sexual discrimination on the job at The Rowland Company gets a short and sweet answer: it doesn't exist. Says vice president Eileen Smith, who's been with the agency since 1974, "Performance is everything. If you are working hard, if you produce, everything is open to you. If you're not producing, it doesn't matter how high you started or what kind of reputation you brought from somewhere else, you won't make it here."

Promotions are meted out strictly on the basis of results, what you have done for the agency in the last few months and what you can do tomorrow. As for a gratuitous promotion based on sex? "I can't think of one," say Susan Johnson, a senior vice president.

The question, are women taken seriously at meetings? hardly gets a response because at some meetings it's all women, and has been that way since the beginning. You are taken very seriously, you are expected to be smart and you are expected to deliver what you promise. To some extent, it's the nature of the beast—public relations—that feeds the equality that prevails at Rowland. Consumer publicity is what Rowland excels at, and a great number of those consumers are women. So using women to get clients' products mentioned in *Redbook* or on the *Today* show made a certain amount of sense. In addition, many of the editors and booking agents who make the decisions to do pieces about fluoride or easy-care fabrics have always been women. Public relations is sometimes as pleasant as one woman talking to another about clothes that pack well and doing it over a nice lunch at a trendy restaurant. It becomes harried when there are six other editors you need to talk to by the end of the day as well as writing a product fact sheet for a new kind of after-shave lotion.

But at Rowland, women haven't done well merely in the ranks of people who do "placements," which is what it's called when, say, Crest is mentioned editorially; women have also done well at Rowland writing new business plans, making presentations to clients about the results of a six-month or year-long campaign and drumming up new business. At some companies women talk about having trouble making it into the core of the business; at Rowland women are at the very core, responsible for millions in billings. Women have fared so well here that when Herb Rowland, the tireless entrepreneur who started the business in 1961, decided to have a management committee take over much of the detail of actually running the agency in 1981, the women outnumbered the men four to two. The balance has shifted, and it's now five men to two women, but everybody agrees its membership dues are performance, and performance alone.

Back in the sixties, Rowland had a reputation for being largely a company of energetic, attractive women; the women are still attractive, but more men have joined the ranks, possibly because public relations is now solidly established as a profession and both men and women see it as a viable, interesting career, a partner to marketing. The Rowland Company is now one third men.

Clients are the ones who sometimes don't understand that Rowland is a place where women are truly equals; sometimes clients are guilty of saying things that are out of line. When that happens, it won't hurt your standing at Rowland if you make a snappy comeback, and if you get laughter, so much the better. But if you don't, you won't find yourself in the doghouse. One woman who's no longer with the agency recalls that back in the early seventies, when a Southerner made a lewd remark as she walked into a 9 A.M. meeting, she sat down and shot back: "I thought this was a boardroom, not a bedroom." Nobody laughed, and she's not sure whether Herb, as everyone calls him, who was in the room, heard the remark. But in any event, nothing was ever said to her about being nicer to clients. "We went on with the meeting like nothing had happened," she recalls. "The guy sat there with egg on his face, I made my presentation and I never saw him again. We didn't lose the account, either."

Women today say that since the agency is respected for the job it does, and *they* are the agency, they have no trouble being treated like the professionals they are when visiting clients' offices or at meetings at Rowland's Madison Avenue offices. But, they say, they know which clients give women short shrift, and they're glad they are working for Rowland and not the client. It is possible to move from client to agency, and some women have, but it's never done without the agreement of the client.

Not only does Rowland garner respect from its clients—otherwise why would they be clients?—it is highly respected in the public relations field. Rowland people are known for their smarts and their savvy. Say you work there, or once did, and those in the know assume that you are highly capable and experienced. It's not difficult to get a good job elsewhere in PR with Rowland in your background.

One of the reasons for Rowland's stature among the biggies in the business—even though other U.S. agencies have higher billings and employ more people—is that this is the company that pioneered television publicity in the form of what is called a "tour." A spokesperson who is interesting enough in his or her own right to be "bookable" on television and radio talk shows is hired to visit several cities, make radio and television appearances and mention a company or product name in a congenial interview. Noted photographer Jill Krementz, for instance, gave pointers on how to film interesting home videos and, in the process, she explained why a particular Canon camera was the desirable piece of equipment. Rowland has some very big clients—Procter & Gamble has been one for decades; others are McDonald's, E. I. Du Pont, the Louvre, Milton Bradley, Chesebrough-Pond's, Toyota and Puerto Rico. "If I ever left Rowland, I would leave public relations," comments Linda Paternoster, senior vice president and director of the audiovisual and graphics department. "I've had the very best of public relations, and why should I go elsewhere?"

Among the pluses of working at Rowland, Paternoster cited the wide variety your job can encompass. While some agencies compartmentalize their staff into people who do only writing or placement or seek new business, everyone at Rowland really has an opportunity to do everything in time. "You have a chance to explore what you can do in a lot of areas—the creative, the business, the production part of it. It's up to you to make of your job what you want."

As noted earlier, the discussion about whether women are equals at Rowland didn't last long. Instead, it quickly took a turn into a general discussion about whether women market themselves as well as they do their clients' products or, more troubling, as well as the men. The consensus was that women don't, a finding that is repeated in every study of working men and women; Rowland women said that it probably led them to take lower salaries when they began working than they would have had to, thus making less for several years because it's always difficult to catch up. One woman who's in on hiring decisions for account executives said that women applying for jobs often have a hard time even talking about salary when they are interviewed. Yet a check with someone in a position to know brought a vehement disclaimer. Salaries across the board are in line with responsibility, and, she insisted, sex is not a factor in the least.

Not that Rowland is a low payer by any means. Quite the contrary. On the street it is considered one of the high payers in the public relations field; however, public relations is not a high-paying field until you get to the top, where salaries range between $100,000 and $150,000. If you top out in the middle stretch, you'll be making somewhere between $40,000 and $60,000; vice presidents at Rowland, who typically work on several accounts, begin in the $40,000s, and their salaries increase as do their responsibilities, in tandem with the company's desire to keep them happy so they won't jump ship for more money elsewhere. As at banks and advertising agencies, the title of vice president is not reserved for a minuscule few.

While negotiating salary is important, some of your perceived worth could depend on how well you package yourself. Public relations is the image business, so image counts here more than in some places. No little tailored suit from Brooks Brothers for junior account executives; you'll do better buying the most stylish clothes you can afford, and you don't need to shop at stores catering to businesswomen. Rive Gauche and Saks Fifth Avenue (which is nearby) are more like it. Not only are people at the office watching, so is your lunch partner. She could be the decorating editor of *Cosmopolitan*, the beauty editor of *Glamour* or a booker for *Good Morning America*. While other service businesses may feel the need to dress more conservatively, like their clients, this isn't true here. If you're visiting Procter & Gamble in Cincinnati, you are expected to dress like a person who works on Madison Avenue. The clotheshorse will feel right at home.

Although Rowland is hotly competitive with other agencies, within the shop it's best to cool the competitiveness and pull together to make a project work. Because the work is demanding, the hours excruciating (one woman said she had to cancel her long-planned vacation to China), the atmosphere breeds a certain esprit de corps. At a place where the intensity never lets up, there isn't a whole lot of time for politicking, but naturally pockets of it do exist. Yet at least one woman who went to another, larger PR firm, Hill and Knowlton, returned to Rowland because she says it's less bureaucratic and political. In general, the women look upon each other as friends rather than competitors. Helping out on someone else's account is noticed. Being overly competitive with your peers is also noticed and considered disruptive, if it interferes with business, and you'll be the one who gets the ax. It happens here with some regularity.

Service businesses that depend on results can't keep mediocre people afloat, and Rowland is no exception. Rowland was running lean and mean before everyone else was, and it's still small enough not to have any hiding places. At Rowland, if a project fails and a client walks, everybody shares the pain. If you're very good, you won't lose your job; if you are simply an average performer, you might be typing up your résumé that night.

Whether or not Rowland is a nurturing environment is a question the women were divided on; but what is clear is that it's best to come to the company with some experience in the PR field or a related one, such as journalism. Yes, it's possible to make the jump from secretary to junior account executive, but it's difficult. You'll have to do your regular work (typing on a word processor is a must), and you'll work for two or three account people; then you've got to find the time and energy to take on simple projects under a boss's tutelage. And your boss may be so busy she won't have the time to train you. However, most of the account people will teach you the ropes if you make it convenient for them. Incidentally, secretarial pay is pretty good—from $16,000 to 22,000. What you study in college isn't important; a liberal arts degree in history, art or psychology is fine. But as we said, if your degree is fresh and you don't have work experience, you'll be given a typing test.

Part of the reason for the insistence on some sort of business experience is that the clients expect you to understand not only public relations but the client's business as well. "As the value of public relations has become more recognized as an integral part of the marketing mix, we are reporting higher and higher up the executive line," comments Michelle Jordan, an executive vice president and one of the two women on the management committee. "That means we have to know more about the client's business—you have to talk their language, you have to know their consumer, you have to be aware of the competitive products. Some years ago, it was enough to talk product placement with a junior brand manager, but now you're far more likely to be sitting with the president of the company. You're not doing something off to the side. You're in the middle of the marketing arena."

Jordan joined the firm in 1974 and worked her way up through the ranks as a junior account executive. "Nothing is given to you on a silver platter, but it's all there for the taking," she observes. "This is a high-energy place, and if you thrive on that, you are driven to do things you might not think you're capable of."

Are the possibilities limitless? Would a woman have a chance to take over when Herb Rowland retires? Absolutely, say the women. It won't be easy for anyone, but sex won't be the issue. As we go to press, however, Herb Rowland was busy cementing relations with agencies all over the world that are part of the Saatchi & Saatchi group, which is a huge collection of communications (advertising and public relations) businesses as well as consulting firms. Rowland, with 138 employees, is the largest of the public relations firms, and that's one reason why Saatchi & Saatchi's public relations arm is now named the Rowland Company Worldwide.

How do children fit into this equation? Some women leave when they have a baby. Others say they don't see how it's possible. Yet Mary Trudel-

Woolley, the other woman on the management committee, has a 10-year-old son. She joined the agency as a vice president when he was less than 3 months old. She is blessed with a reliable full-time housekeeper. "We are understanding of emergencies," she says, "because everyone is working so hard you have to be. That's the flip side of expecting people to give their all. But emergencies better not happen too often." Kids are not welcome at this office, no matter what, but business plans and releases can be written at home.

As for personal emergencies, Susan Johnson found the agency unusually accommodating when she was laid up for three weeks after a skiing accident required surgery. "I was convinced I would be fired because this place moves very fast," she says. "But they were fantastic. I was in the hospital almost two weeks, out of work three, but once I was ready to come back they sent a car service to come get me and take me home."

Nobody is saying the pressure isn't high at Rowland, but for some people it's the kind of energy they thrive on. It is exciting. It can be fun. Your peers are quick and lively. The difference between working at the Rowland Company and, say, the public relations department of a major corporation is the difference between the *1812* Overture and *Swan Lake*. It may not be the right fit for everybody, but listen to why Trudel-Woolley thinks it's the best of all possible careers for her. "My thrill in PR and at this company specifically is that I didn't want to spend my life trying to break into something, trying to be allowed to do it. Here it's for the taking. It's, yes, you can do this. What else can you do? And what about this? When you treat people that way and reward them with money, and give them a bigger plane on which to operate, often they surprise themselves. I've enjoyed the kind of opportunity that women in the past didn't have."

SAKS FIFTH AVENUE

A CHAIN OF UPSCALE SPECIALTY SHOPS FOR MEN AND WOMEN

▲ EMPLOYEES: Approximately 10,500; more than 78 percent are women.

▲ SALES: Close to $1.1 billion in 1986.

▲ Saks does a super job of recruiting women; 80 percent of the people recruited twice annually at major universities for the entry-level executive training program. The minimum starting salary is around $20,000. Approximately 68 percent of the people who enroll in management training programs are women.

▲ Saks, owned by BAT Industries of London, is in an expansion mode—plans are to open five new stores, in Denver; Portland, Oreg.; Minneapolis; North Palm Beach, Fla.; and Tyson's Corner, Va. Additionally, the New York store will be expanded and more than 20 others will be remodeled. Total number of stores is 44.

▲ Of the 58 employees considered upper management, 21 are women; four are senior vice presidents and 17 are vice presidents.

▲ In addition to the standard maternity disability leave, women can take up to 13 weeks of unpaid leave. Some women start back part-time; many report that informally, bosses are flexible about parenting needs.

▲ Employees get a 30 percent discount on all merchandise.

▲ Saks is a genteel company whose corporate culture strongly discourages sexual harassment. All managers and professionals attend a training program on the subject.

▲ Charges of sexual discrimination are investigated by a representative of the corporate personnel division. Although the company did not specify how it follows up in its commitment to rectifying inequality of pay, one senior woman reported that when she was promoted, her salary was doubled to bring her "more in line with executives at her level."

▲ Major employment centers: Greater New York area, including New Jersey and Connecticut (five stores, a service center, distribution center and corporate offices): 4,000; Chicago (three stores): 725; Detroit area (two stores): 500; Los Angeles area (two stores): 425; San Francisco/Palo Alto: 425; Miami (two stores): 370; Houston (two stores): 295; Fort Lauderdale/Palm Beach, Fla.: 270; as well as stores in Arizona, Georgia, Louisiana, Maryland, Massachusetts, Missouri, Nevada, Ohio and Pennsylvania.

SAKS FIFTH AVENUE
611 Fifth Avenue
New York, NY 10022
(212) 940-4000

Is there a woman alive who doesn't like saying "I got it at Saks" when asked where she bought something she's wearing? Such a simple statement. Such a lot of class it implies.

And to listen to the women who work there, Saks itself is a classy place to work.

"To understand the culture of this company, you have to understand that you are dealing with the *crème de la crème* at every level," says Jane Scott, vice president and divisional manager of home furnishings. "In the marketplace we see ourselves reaching the *crème de la crème*, and that gives us an intrinsic pride about Saks. It penetrates into every relationship—the way the company treats its employees and the way the employees respond." Men and women call each other Mr. and Miss here. People are nice to one another.

The politesse stems not only from the good breeding of Saks's clientele, but also from the old days when Saks was a family business headed by Adam Gimbel. He retired in 1969 after heading the company for more than four decades. Apparently not only was Mr. Gimbel polite, he was caring. And although the chain of upscale specialty shops went from a family-run business to a cog in a corporate wheel in 1974 when a British conglomerate, BAT, bought Saks Fifth Avenue, the attitudes Mr. Gimbel instilled remain part of the milieu.

Anne Maddox, a senior vice president and director of stores for the Midwest, says that when she recruits, she tells prospective employees that they most probably will find Saks unlike any other retail company. Individual talents are coddled, not ignored. "Care and attention are paid to individual potential at every level," she says. "It's not just at the executive or senior level."

Maddox herself is an example of that kind of nurturing. Although she came to the company with solid retailing experience in 1964, she lacked a college degree. Her first job at Saks was as a department manager in San Francisco, where she'd gone on a whim; when family needs required that she move back East, she was hired as an assistant buyer in New York. When her boss retired a year and a half later, Maddox got her job. While once a senior buyer's job was an end in itself, by the seventies it wasn't. When women took a new look at themselves and their ambitions, Saks responded in kind. (A class action suit in California for equal pay around the same time helped focus management's attention.) Maddox became a regional vice president in 1975, and during a reorganization the *senior* was added to her title. Three other women are also SVPs, out of a total of 16. Maddox lives in Chicago but is gone a few days most weeks to travel to New York and stores throughout the Midwest.

"All along I found people who were not only willing to let me grow, but helped me do it," Maddox says. "It's what is unique about Saks."

While Maddox thinks it still might be possible to rise in the hierarchy without a college degree, it is assuredly more difficult today than when she did it in the sixties. A college degree of some sort—not necessarily in merchandising or retailing—makes it infinitely easier.

Recent college graduates usually take all the 30 or so slots in the executive training program, which starts in June, but another, which begins in February, will include trainees who began at Saks in clerical or sales jobs without a degree. Approximately two thirds of the trainees are women. Although the usual program is to rotate through the various departments in eight-week stints at the flagship store on Fifth Avenue in Manhattan, even here, exceptions are made, and the program is somewhat tailored to suit ability. The starting pay, $20,000 in 1987, is a few thousand less than what you might make at other retailers, but the company has no trouble attracting employees. Part of the compensation, you see, is in being able to say you're with Saks, not Macy's. It undoubtedly wouldn't hurt to walk into the interview looking as if you've been shopping at Saks all your life.

It is an unwritten code that employees are expected to dress as well as their customers, making the 30 percent discount on merchandise more than a piffle. An attorney who came from another industry said that it took her a while to realize everybody was noticing what she was wearing, down to her earrings. Her wardrobe soon was spiffier than it had been before.

But nice clothes and good manners aren't all that you need to get ahead at Saks. This is retailing, remember? And every night the sales receipts are tallied. As one woman said, it's like getting a report card every day, week after week. The pressure never lets up. And because safari neutrals and snakeskin moccasins can go out of style while you're waiting for them to be shipped from the Orient, the ability to handle pressure with grace is a prerequisite. "I have people who are at the buyer level or divisional level and who won't go any higher, not because of their ability to do the job per se, but because of their inability to deal with the pressure, and that affects their management of people," says Mara Urshel, a senior vice president and general merchandise manager. "In a large corporation like this, you are responsible for many factors you don't have great control over. We have nearly 50 stores, and you're always thinking about the goods—are they going to flow in or are they on the road somewhere? The people who make it are the people who can deal with those pressures."

Urshel herself understands pressures that come from more than the job. She achieved her career climb at Saks while being stepmother to three children who lived with her and her late husband. There would be times when she would be dealing with a vendor and the school would call, informing her that one of her sons had hit another student over the head with a wet balloon. Urshel was also the good corporate wife. Sometimes the going got sticky. One time, before all merchandise was computerized and inventory literally took most of the night, she had a command appearance at a black tie dinner of her husband's at the nearby Rainbow Room. She slipped out of the building through the back door in formal duds around 9 P.M. and thought she was home free. She ran into her boss going through the revolving door at the Rainbow Room. The next morning she explained what she had been doing, but realizes now she should have gone to her boss in the first place and explained her predicament. The company, she says, was always understanding.

"If I had a problem at home, I often came in anyway because I felt I had to get my work done," she says. "But it wasn't unusual for the president to find out, and then he would storm into my office and ask, 'Is this where you should be?' This has always been a company sensitive to people. The management changes, but the attitude stays the same." Urshel added that when people—men or women—can't be at meetings because they have to pick up kids or take them to the doctor or whatever, the meetings will be rescheduled.

Maternity leaves are common, and although you can have up to 13 weeks of unpaid leave after six weeks of disability leave with the guarantee of your job or a comparable one upon your return, it is difficult to take that much time off at the vice president or store manager level. You might be asked to start back part-time, such as just going to the fashion shows, says Carla Slocum, a vice president and merchandising manager, "but you get sucked back right away—you get driven by the flash and glamour. When you go home to have your baby, you feel like the plug's been pulled, and you miss the electricity of the job." In any event, if the children don't slow you down or lower your ambitions, Saks won't change its attitude about you. But live-in help might be needed.

So what we have here is a slightly schizophrenic corporate style: white-gloved manners and familial nuturing, right along with the pressurized atmosphere of retailing. "One day you're a hero, the next day you're a bum, and you've got to explain why," remarks Urshel. However, a single slow season won't mean your department's budget will be cut back and you'll be cut loose; women who came to Saks from other stores say you're given a chance to recoup from a poor season, when you wouldn't be elsewhere. "Management is sensitive to the fluctuations of the market, as well as someone's weaknesses and strengths," remarks Ellen Levin, divisional merchandising manager. "Everybody wants everybody else to succeed."

The long hours in retailing are legion throughout the business world, but apparently this is changing somewhat at Saks. Data processing and a different attitude on the part of the younger workers, i.e., men and women with family responsibilities, have made the nights until eight nearly a thing of the past in the merchandising and buying offices. For the store manager, it's a different story. At that level, 60 hours plus is the norm, and department managers don't get away with much less.

While a department manager's job in, say, Dearborn, Michigan, is not as glamorous as that of a buyer in Manhattan, it is a highly responsible position. Annual sales in a single department can top $2 million. In effect, the manager operates as if she were running her own little shop. She may have six or more people reporting to her; she has to get the merchandise into the store, display it well, answer the buyers knowledgeably, and motivate her sales force, managing their schedules and keeping them happy. And then she has to answer to the store manager who will come along and say, "How come these sweaters aren't displayed better?" Since many of the stores are open seven days a week, she'll work some weekends, including Sundays. On top of all this, she has no definite career path, especially the farther she is from the home office in New York. Starting salary for this job? Somewhere between $19,000 and $20,000. However, for someone who doesn't have a college background, there are worse things one could be doing in Dearborn—and you will probably be better dressed than your neighbors. The job could also be the ticket to the executive training program in New York and an entrée into the buying or merchandising departments. Admittedly, the move from suburban store floor to training program is somewhat easier if you are located in one of the half dozen stores in the New York–New Jersey–Connecticut area. After completing the program, you will most likely have to relocate a few times, but the women say the demands aren't excessive.

While the nature of retailing is intense and the return not great until you enter the ranks of senior management, where salaries top $100,000, the business in general and Saks in particular have no trouble attracting people. Comments Jane Scott: "This business allows you to express so many talents that other businesses don't. You can be creative and business minded. It's fast paced, and you do something different every day. You can be a manager, a motivator and a role model."

Whether or not salaries for men and women at the top are equitable is something of a mystery. The company doesn't reveal figures, and the women didn't know. After all, talking about money is *déclassé*. One senior woman recalled having her salary doubled "to bring her more in line," she was told, with executives at her level; another woman said that in the late fifties, when she started in the training program, she learned that she was making $10,000 a year less than the men. When she asked why, she was told, "Oh, well, the men . . ." Today she's chagrined that she didn't make an issue of it and believes her pay is comparable to what male store managers make. One expects—or, at least, hopes—that those unequal days are long gone.

Is there a topping-out for women at Saks? It depends on what you mean. Yes, the president, CEO and chairman of the board are men, and just below them is an executive vice president, also a man, but women are right below that as senior vice presidents with bottom line responsibility, like Maddox and Urshel, who says, "If a person is capable and has all the necessary management skills, I don't think being a woman would be a problem." Yet it is not lost on the women that Saks is owned by a company headed by a WASPy group of men. At least one senior woman was dubious that they "would tolerate somebody as chairman or president who wasn't one of them." But considering corporate America, who's surprised?

It isn't just at the very top that your progress might be impeded, and it's not just sex that gets in the way. Because Saks is such a nice place to work, people tend to stay a long time. Where do you go once you become a vice president and your boss isn't retiring for at least 20 years? It's possible to find yourself in this quandary at the age of 35. "This is the top of the heap in prestige, in working conditions, in benefits and in the caliber of people you work with," says Jessica Mitchell, vice president and fashion director for sportswear. "But if there isn't an opening in your career path in the foreseeable future, where do you go from here?"

Maybe to Neiman-Marcus. See page 256.

SALOMON BROTHERS

WALL STREET'S LARGEST INVESTMENT BANKING HOUSE

▲ **EMPLOYEES:** 4,800 (in the United States); more than 45 percent are women.

▲ **REVENUES:** $6.8 billion in 1986. Expected post-tax earnings for 1987 are $100 million, a steep drop from $332 million the previous year and the peak of $557 million in 1985.

▲ In October 1987 Salomon Brothers closed its municipal bond department and dismissed approximately 800 employees throughout the company. Yet recruitment at top business schools for the best and the brightest people continues, although fewer jobs are available than before the stock market crashed last fall.

Recruitment teams on campuses include enthusiastic female employees. Promotion programs include tuition reimbursement, specific training and workshops, tracking, succession planning and management development.

▲ Of 790 vice presidents, 111—14 percent—are women. At the next level, nine directors out of 141—6 percent—are women. Of the 114 managing directors (which we would define as true upper management), three—2.6 percent—are women. None of the 18-member board of directors is a woman.

▲ The company provides standard maternity disability leave. Although flexible work hours are offered, all professionals and managers work incredibly long hours. Many said they'd never contemplate taking more than a week off for any reason. The company has a resource referral directory for child care facilities and a cafeteria-style approach to benefits that includes subsidies for child care.

▲ Salomon is committed to rectifying inequality of pay to women. To do so, it examines what other companies are doing and re-evaluates individual job descriptions.

▲ The company has done a study on sexual harassment and has issued statements on the problem. Attendance at the program on sexual harassment is mandatory for all managers and professionals. Complaints are handled by informal hearing.

▲ Major employment centers: New York: 4,240; Chicago: 225; San Francisco: 125; Los Angeles: 50; Dallas: 45; Atlanta: 55; Boston: 60; in addition, there are 250 people in London and 60 in Tokyo in three-year expatriate assignments.

SALOMON BROTHERS, INC.
One New York Plaza
New York, NY 10004
(212) 747-7000

Until Black Monday, that October 19 last fall when the stock market plunged 508 points, many businesses lost a number of the best and brightest to "the Street." Wall Street still might be to business what Hollywood is to the rest of the country, but the aura of limitless possibilities that it gave off during an unprecedented five-year bull market has evaporated. Wall Street is still unquestionably where the most money can be made—and lost—the most quickly, but the trade-off is high risk.

All investment houses were hit hard last fall. E. F. Hutton was put up for auction and sold to Shearson Lehman Brothers. Things didn't get that desperate at Salomon, but last year was a difficult one for the investment house that had become a powerful player in the international financial market. In

September, after months of dwindling profits, the firm was forced to fend off a hostile takeover. A few weeks later, its municipal bond division, once the largest underwriter of municipal securities, was shut down; so was its commercial paper division. Eight hundred workers were let go.

Naturally, there aren't a lot of jobs for anyone—at Salomon or elsewhere. All securities firms have scaled back in the past year, and as we go to press a volatile market has left Wall Street bearish on hiring at the same time several thousand laid off workers are flooding the marketplace. In spite of this, Salomon is still recruiting at top business schools and college campuses. The pay is anything but shabby.

New associates in, say, the corporate finance department—people with an MBA (a good school helps) and two years of experience—typically start at $80,000 and go up from there. In five years, with "vice president" on your business card, you will probably be making over a hundred grand— between $200,000 and $250,000 is not all that unusual. Assuming you're good, it keeps on going up. As it goes up, an increasing percentage of your income is bonuses. VPs are paid a base salary, for instance, but their compensation varies wildly because so much of it is tied to a bonus for business brought in during the previous year. Remember *Esquire*'s gee-whiz piece a few years back about "The $100,000-a-Year Woman"? For a sizable number of Wall Street women, the numbers were off by a few hundred grand. However, last year Salomon's financial health dictated that everyone take a major cut in compensation. Bonuses were down dramatically—and the more money you made, the more dramatic the cut. Typical was a 25 percent cut in bonus over the previous year and no raise in salary.

Wall Street has been historically cool—frigid is more like it—to women. In 1967 Muriel Siebert, who now runs her own discount brokerage firm, caused a furor when she became the first woman to buy a seat on the New York Stock Exchange. The ratio was daunting: 1,365 to 1. (Siebert was originally denied a seat on the NYSE because there was no ladies' room on the exchange floor. Talk about a men's club.) And as recently as 1985, a group of anonymous women at Goldman Sachs sent a letter to the deans of the best business schools urging them to warn their women away from the firm: "Compensation of the top women is a fraction of that of the top men. . . . Women will be treated unfairly," the letter said. In another infamous incident, a Goldman Sachs recruiter at Stanford University seemed to be asking women if they would be willing to have an abortion to stay on the fast track. After the *Wall Street Journal* created a ruckus by recounting this episode, Goldman reprimanded, but did not dismiss, the young banker.*

*In fairness to Goldman Sachs, the firm has at least one female partner, Jeanette Loeb, who is in her mid-thirties. She was appointed in 1987. Nevertheless, the firm's reputation as a place where women meet obstacles to getting ahead still holds.

So why is Salomon Brothers unlike the rest? Why is it in this book?

"We've got John Gutfreund," says one woman who chose anonymity because she didn't want to sound too rah-rah about her firm. "If he gets interested in an account, he doesn't care if you're a zebra or someone from a small area of Tibet, you're the person he'll call if anything gets screwed up or he's got an idea he wants you to think about. And if you need to find him, you just walk over to his desk, you don't have to go through a secretary. He is color blind and sex blind. He's not interested in you personally, he's only interested in what you are doing to make money from your accounts. It may sound mercenary, but there it is."

Certainly, according to the women we spoke to, there's no discrimination visible to the naked eye at the entry- and midlevel positions. Women, just like men, are expected to be quick witted, daring and tireless. Both are also expected to make vice president within four or five years of joining the firm. After that it's anybody's guess what will happen to the women, because professional women in any number didn't start joining the firm until the grown-up Baby Boom generation, highly educated and ambitious, came knocking on the door. Salomon gave some of them jobs. As they are moving up the pipeline, they are making their presence known: out of 790 vice presidents, 111 are women. Beyond that, there's a relatively new level of director: Salomon has nine female directors out of 141. And then there's managing director, that elite circle at the top. Salomon has 114. Three are women.

In 1986 Barbara Alexander was the first woman to be so anointed. (Two more were named last year.) Sheer competence was Alexander's ticket. For a number of years, she has won first-place rankings on *Institutional Investor*'s prestigious "All-American Research Team," the listing no one in the business ignores. Although typically the most direct route to the top is by being a trader, Alexander's area, research, is up and coming, which should help other women, since it is an area where women have traditionally clustered. "While the perception is that Salomon is a bond-trading firm, in the last few years, finance and equity—of which research is an intrinsic part—have become important profit centers," she says. In fact, Salomon's unwavering commitment to research was what increasingly separated Salomon from its rivals during the growth of the seventies and gave it some of the clout it has today. And while research might not provide high visibility at other Wall Street firms, that's not true at Salomon, and several male managing directors have come up through that route.

Alexander's credentials are impeccable. She has a master's in theoretical mathematics and taught at the University of Arkansas for two years before she stumbled into securities analysis at a Southern bank. She joined Salomon in 1984 with 11 years in the business.

Arkansas-born Alexander was quick to realize that success often hinges not on how well you do your homework, but on how you relate to different types of people, even die-hard male chauvinists. "I grew up in the business learning how to cope and succeed with people who had very different personality traits," she remarks. The lesson has served her well. Although the task of a securities analyst is to study a particular industry or two and predict which companies will prosper, which stock prices will rise and which will fall, part of the job is gaining the client's confidence. That often means dining at the best restaurants in whatever town their business is in, convincing them that it will serve them well to introduce this relatively young (Alexander is in her late thirties) and not terribly fragile-looking woman to their board. To avoid any potential embarrassment to the senior executives (who is that young woman with Joe?) and to avoid getting into tricky situations herself, Alexander usually arranges for a group of them to have dinner at the end of the workday. Failing that, she often asks wives to come along, making allies of them whenever possible.

Alexander's clients call her one of the most thorough students of the industries she covers, home building and home furnishings. But because Alexander is so clearly deserving of being a managing director, does it mean that women still have to be better to be equal? No one knows yet. The general feeling is that the reason only three women are managing directors is because they haven't been around in any number long enough. "I don't think there's a glass ceiling—but maybe a cellophane one," says one woman. It's also possible more women haven't been elevated to the managing director level (analogous to partner at a law firm) because they are underrepresented in those areas that yield a high number of managing directors: sales and trading.

Unquestionably, the surest route to managing director is as a trader. A number of hotshot men jump up there without seemingly putting in the time as do some of their peers—and all of the women. But there aren't a lot of female traders or bond saleswomen yet.

"The power is on the trading floor," says one woman. "You get more kudos for something that ties into the floor than the sweetest analysis or best-organized presentation of results. And those trading operations are still male dominated."

It takes a tough stomach and a street fighter mentality to make it as a trader. It takes an addiction to hard work and a fast pace for anybody to be happy at Salomon, no matter what the job, line or staff, or, as they are referred to here, front and back office. It doesn't matter if you aren't going to be trading when the board opens at 9 A.M. Monday, you are expected to know what's going on in the market at 8 A.M., when most have already been at work for half an hour.

The hours go on long after most business have shut down for the day. "You don't feel that you have to stay until the geeks down the hall or the managing director in your area leaves, but I'm on the phone all day long talking to all of our organizations—you don't have the excuse of not knowing what's going on—so when do I get things done?" asks one vice president. "At the end of the day, that's when you get thinking time, that's when I'll go find someone in a department where we've got to work out something. And it starts at 6:30 P.M." It can go on until 11 P.M. and run through the weekend. Glamorous the Street can be, but it's glamour at the expense of a personal life. Traders and people in capital markets, at least, get evenings and weekends off. Despite the demands, the women are seemingly not fazed by it. Our focus group met at 7:30 A.M. at Fraunces Tavern, across the street from company headquarters. One woman from Connecticut was early. An hour and fifteen minutes later, the women were raring to get across the street and plunge back in. You get the idea that they love it.

Most Wall Street firms are volatile, highly charged places, and Salomon is more so than many. It has a reputation for being aggressive but fair, with an appetite for risk unrivaled among financial middlemen. It is the one competitors fear most. It is not a place for the faint of heart; it is a place for men and women who are shrewd, supremely intelligent and cosmopolitan, characteristics that *Business Week* attributed to leader Gutfreund a few years back. In the seventies, Salomon Brothers was thought of as a tribe of brutish traders lacking the style to be admitted to the investment banking elite. But sheer competence and loads of capital made them full members of the club. The five-year bull market in stocks and bonds that came to an abrupt end in October 1987 transformed Wall Street investment houses, Salomon among them, into powerful international corporations. Salomon's capital, for instance, has surged to more than $3.5 billion from only $200 million in 1980. Employee ranks have more than tripled to over 6,000 worldwide; the number of U.S. employees was 4,800 at the end of 1987.

However, a certain eclecticism is still evident among the employees, especially when comparing Salomon to others like Goldman Sachs or First Boston Corporation. You don't have to be an old-line WASP whose father belonged to all the right clubs or all wear the same kind of suits. Catholics, Jews, women are all welcome, just as are all personality types, with all kinds of backgrounds. You just have to have the fire in the belly.

Certainly an MBA won't hurt, but it doesn't have to be from Harvard or Wharton for you to gain acceptance into the six-month training program. The door is open to exceptional people from any good university with any academic background. The 1986 class included 13 J.D.s, eight Ph.D.s, seven M.A.s, and 54 B.A.s, in addition to those trainees with business- or quantitive-oriented degrees—B.S.s, M.S.s and MBAs. Katherine Moynes, an analyst who specializes in insurance, has an undergraduate degree in anthropology from the University of Michigan. After traveling around for a few years, she decided on the investment business for a career, and went to work for Salomon in 1981. She was hired to work on statistics for the insurance team, learning the industry from the bottom up. Last year she became a vice president.

"Your goal as an analyst is to become known among your clients so that you have a certain following," Moynes observes. "Another one is to work with your counterparts in the industry to sell other aspects of the firm. Hopefully, the work you do through research could bring in business, and that's the bottom line."

What Moynes particularly likes about her job is her interaction with different people in the firm, a characteristic that apparently cuts across department lines and job levels. Although some people have offices with doors that shut, a lot of the offices have glass walls. All the arguments are out front; there aren't dark covens of people figuring out plans of succession, because everybody already knows what's going on. Everybody is aware when you've got a problem. And if you've brought in a big piece of business, you can walk around and take a victory lap. Nobody will need to be told why you're beaming.

Unlike a corporation, the firm's hierarchy is flat. There is a vast corps of revenue producers coached by a few senior executives. The company likes to think of itself as "top led but bottom driven." The deal is what counts. "If I am making a junk presentation, I make up the team I need for that call," observes Diane Price Baker. "Maybe I get somebody from the trading desk, somebody from corporate bond research, an analyst associate to get the grunt work done, my secretary. Then I have to go to the screening committee to let me do the business. Some other account may have a totally different mix."

Because you interact with so many different people, compensation is not based only on one person's assessment of you—there is a lot of input from other areas of the firm. In the beginning, of course, it's what you bring to the party that counts. In corporate finance, undergraduates without prior experience are hired as financial analysts. The first step (as it is for anybody) is the extensive, broad-based training program; like all of Salomon, it's not for slouches—sessions that begin at 7:30 A.M. will continue throughout the day for 10 or 12 hours. After the program, they spend a month rotating through several research areas of the firm, settling on an area that suits the company's need and the employee's interest. Pay is in the high $20,000s to low $30,000s, and skills with Lotus software are a big plus. You'll work 60- to 90-hour weeks, always with demanding deadlines. The best of the lot can make from $35,000 all the way up to $72,000 by the time they're ready to leave for business school two years later. If that's their choice. Not everyone does, but many do.

When you come back, you typically start at around $80,000, as noted elsewhere. Compensation varies by area. In research, for instance, MBAs start at around $50,000. In the first year, associates are likely to move around a lot, working on a variety of projects with more experienced people; by the second year, they should have selected a speciality, such as media, aerospace or consumer goods. But nothing is written in blood. Even people at the managing director's level move from one area to another depending on their interests.

As one moves up in experience and years, an increasing percentage of income will be bonus, which is tied not to a percentage cut but purely to management's assessment of one's overall contribution. And last year there was a movement afoot on Wall Street to keep salaries in check. Not that people aren't making a lot of money today. They are. Major money. Managing directors at Salomon are earning several hundred thousand dollars. The top is in the millions.

And where do children fit into this pressure cooker? No one is quite sure yet. The women we met who had children were in back office jobs, and that seems to be typical; however, some women hitting their mid-thirties who joined the company a half dozen years ago are beginning to plan for families. Marriage is manageable, say the women, but children? Without a retired husband and/or live-in help, it may be nearly impossible. But it can be done, as the appointment last year of Jessica Palmer to managing director shows. Palmer, the mother of three young children, specializes in capital markets, where the hours and pace are not nearly so frenetic as in other areas. To manage children and a Wall Street career is possible, then, but you need to pick your area carefully.

However, some women take leaves beyond the standard disability period and come back to their jobs. "If you're good at what you do, you'll be back and they'll be waiting for you," says Jane Metzroth, vice president of human resources. "If you don't really care one way or the other, the company will adopt that attitude about you." You may not find a job waiting.

But many women can't imagine taking more than a week off to do anything. "The markets are open every day," says one vice president. "I start to get itchy after a few days." Addiction is the word that comes to mind.

In this rough-and-tumble atmosphere, sexual harassment is a nonissue. So are sexist put-downs. These are tough, aggressive, confident women who don't brook a lot of flack from anyone. "You have enough freedom to say, 'Shut up and get the hell out of here' without thinking twice," says a director. To no one's surprise, some traders are obnoxious, but they are obnoxious to everyone. They can have egos as big as the sun. Egos out of control frequently belong to star performers.

"If you are a star, Salomon is a great place to be," concludes Metzroth. "No one pays any attention to whether you are a man or a woman if you get the job done. If you're good, you can design the deal the way you want and run with it." And if you screw up, you're dead, but only for a day. Somebody who's the goat today will be a star tomorrow. It's, what have you done for me this afternoon?

Some of that may be changing. Firms like Salomon found out last year that stars left unchecked cost the company more than they are worth. A tightly run company with costs under control seems a lot more appealing to CEO Gutfreund than a stable of Wall Street superstars these days. Last year one of Salomon's major superstars got the boot. Forewarned is forearmed.

SIMON & SCHUSTER

A LEADING PUBLISHING AND INFORMATION COMPANY

▲ EMPLOYEES: 9,000; 67 percent are women.

▲ REVENUES: As the publishing and information unit of Gulf + Western, Inc., Simon & Schuster reported 1987 revenues of $1.074 billion, breaking the billion dollar mark for the first time in its 64-year history.

▲ Simon & Schuster is concerned about recruiting, hiring and promoting women. Although it has no special programs to do so, its numbers are excellent. Of the 276 employees considered upper management, 59—21 percent—are female.

▲ In addition to the standard disability maternity leave, S&S allows flexible work places and sick leave for family illness. Subsidy for child care is one of the choices on the cafeteria approach to benefits. Part-time work for managers and professionals is available.

▲ The company handles complaints of sexual discrimination through informal hearings by human resources. S&S has issued statements regarding sexual harassment, but has no training program. Complaints of harassment may be handled informally or through a formal grievance procedure.

▲ The company is committed to rectifying inequality of pay to women. It does research to establish measures of comparable worth, reevaluates individual job descriptions and makes grade level adjustments where necessary.

▲ MAJOR EMPLOYMENT CENTERS: All in the Manhattan/Bergen County, N.J., area.

Simon & Schuster, Inc.
Simon & Schuster Building
1230 Avenue of the Americas
New York, NY 10020
(212) 698-7000

Simon & Schuster was nominated eight times in our initial phase of research, and thus was an obvious candidate for inclusion in the book. Since S&S is our publisher, however, we felt it inappropriate to provide anything more than the factual summary.

SOUTHERN NEW ENGLAND TELEPHONE

THE CONNECTICUT TELEPHONE COMPANY

▲ EMPLOYEES: 13,900; more than half are women.

▲ SALES: $1.43 billion; net income, $139.2 million. A vigorous business climate in Connecticut spurred a substantial 8.6 percent increase in toll calling volumes and a 21 percent increase in directory revenues, to $103 million.

▲ SNET is concerned about promoting women. Progress includes their advanced management development program, an external middle management development program and various organizational development courses. Fifty-seven percent of those enrolled in management training programs are women.

▲ Of the 71 employees considered upper management, 10 are women; they include one vice president, two department directors, and seven division-level managers. Two of the 16 members of the board of directors are women.

▲ SNET is clearly a family-oriented company. The child care center, originally sponsored by SNET, is run by employees. Paid parenting (male or female) leave of up to six months is a standout benefit. Flexible working hours, adoption benefits and sick leave for family illness are others. Under the cafeteria-style approach to benefits implemented in 1986, subsidies for child care are an option.

▲ The company handles sexual discrimination complaints through informal hearing, formal procedure or, when necessary, through lawsuit. The company has no training program on the subject.

▲ To rectify inequality of pay to women, SNET examines what other companies are doing and reevaluates individual job descriptions and jobs held predominantly by women. Where necessary, it makes grade level adjustments and gives retroactive pay.

▲ Major employment centers: New Haven: 7,300; the remaining 6,600 are at four sites throughout Connecticut.

SOUTHERN NEW ENGLAND TELEPHONE (SNET)
227 Church Street
New Haven, CT 06506
(203) 771-5200

The telephone company that traces its origins to the first commercial telephone exchange in 1878—and that has been a technological leader since —is also a pioneer in the work/family arena. After 1977 the old Bell system granted all employees a six-month leave of absence following childbirth, but Southern New England Telephone also pays benefits during those six months. Very few other companies do this.

SNET's child care leave is one of the most liberal in the nation, and its benefits director, Jeanne Kardos, has become a national spokesperson on the issue. Kardos is largely responsible for SNET's current leadership in the area of corporate health policy, although this is a company with a long history of social responsibility toward its employees. In 1986 the Washington Business Group on Health, a national organization supported by 150 of the largest corporations in America, honored the company for outstanding contributions in the area of health policy.

The policy Kardos has fashioned for SNET should warm the heart of any woman thinking about becoming a mom. Following the disability period (typically six to eight weeks), a parent, man or woman, may take a six-month leave. You'll be guaranteed a job of like status and pay upon return; in practice, you may have to be responsible for making the most out of a position that doesn't initially seem challenging, since good jobs don't go begging for any length of time. Full health benefits are extended during the leave. During those six months, managers sometimes arrange for part-time work for new mothers. PCs have been installed at home. Typically, a woman might work at home and come in for meetings. Even some supervisors have been able to ease back into full-time by working part-time for the first few months.

Parents who want an additional six-month leave can extend their health benefits by paying at the reduced group rate; although they are not guaranteed a job upon return, several women have done so successfully. Their years of service are added together so that they do not lose pension or vacation benefits. A few men—Kardos could recall only two—have taken parental leave. Parents who adopt a small child or who have a seriously ill child are also eligible. "This is not so much a benefit as it is a social issue," Kardos says, "and the rest of the world has already dealt with it. The United States and South Africa are the only industrial nations that haven't—even the Philippines and Haiti have parental leave policies. The company feels strongly about this for its employees and allowed me to become an advocate."

It isn't just parents who benefit from SNET's tender loving care. Retirees are not forgotten. The New Haven chapter of the Telephone Pioneers, a national organization for retired telephone company employees, was allotted space in a company building as well as free telephone lines to call people who can't leave their homes, to chat and to make sure that they are getting the kind of assistance they need.

And then there's the day care center. SNET contributed more than $100,000 to transform an oak-paneled dormitory on the nearby Albertus Magnus campus into a day care center for children of SNET employees. The center came about when the company's Management Women's Association lobbied for one. The company reacted as it does to all new business proposals: a feasibility study was ordered. The report convinced SNET officials that the company would recover its onetime initial investment in the center many times over in improved morale, greater productivity and reduced absenteeism among participating parents. The center takes infants from 3 months old up to kindergarten. For kids under 3, the cost is $113 a week; over 3, $85 a week. The center opened in January 1985 with 14 tots; now it's self-supporting and operating at full capacity with 59 children.

"It's an excellent-quality center, and it's five minutes from downtown," says Beverly Schirmeier, a staff manager whose 3-year-old has been enrolled since it opened. "The advantage to having a corporate center is that the days and hours correspond to mine. There aren't any holidays that I don't have off too."

Given the above, it's not surprising that "family" is a word workers often use in reference to their employer, even though they say that the emphasis has shifted somewhat to profits since the breakup of AT&T in 1984. But not so much so that having children here isn't almost a plus. "The reaction I got was something like, 'Good, now you're one of us,' " remarks Fay Kandarian, a district staff manager in customer relations. "Family is a value at SNET." Kandarian took the full six-month leave in addition to eight weeks of disability leave following the birth of her son last year. She came back to a new job. Kandarian found that the time away from the company—she had been with the firm since 1969—gave her a fresh perspective and renewed enthusiasm for her job.

Kandarian is not concerned that having children will hurt her career and points out that high-level women often got their promotions just before or after they had a child. One of those women is Noreen Haffner, a general manager in corporate planning. She has four children ranging in age from 4 to 15. Haffner jokes that when she joined the phone company nearly 20 years ago, it was considered the right thing for a good Irish Catholic girl from New York to do. "The attitude was, if you're not going to be a nurse or a nun, you should work for the phone company." It's doubtful that Haffner's family thought she would wind up being one of the highest-ranking women at the company, one of the women who is being closely watched by women beneath her. Will Noreen have a shot at being a vice president, the next move up? Or will she be passed over because the boys in the boardroom feel more comfortable with one of their own kind, another white male?

Passed over possibly, but not ignored. Haffner makes sure of that. She was a district manager in information systems a few years back when the division was to get a new building, and she and another woman were to be the liaison between IS and engineering, which would supervise construction. Haffner's job was to see that the building's design met IS needs. Haffner mirthfully recalls that the man she had to deal with was an ex-Marine, the kind who proudly sports a big tattoo on his arm. He was a real man. And he was not about to take an advice from a f——— woman. Whenever he returned her calls, it would be at 4:10 P.M., and he would begin the conversation by saying that he had a bus to catch at 4:20. At the end of their fourth or fifth meeting, he suggested that Haffner and the other women go back to their offices and he would call them when it was time to pick out the curtains.

Finally, a meeting was scheduled with a consulting engineer from New

York. He was another Mr. Macho type, Haffner says, big and roseate. Haffner, tall herself, tried to look imposing but wound up listening while the men talked around her. However, she had her ace in the hole. She had final approval on any construction plans. Finally, Haffner spoke. "I sat up straight and said very calmly, 'You can work with us now on the design and we'll work it out together, or you can get it all done and bring it to us for approval. But what you have to understand is that this building doesn't move forward until I say so.' There was dead silence in the room. The guy from New York looked at Mr. Marine and said, 'Can she say this?' With great strain, he said, 'Yes.' It all changed after that."

Haffner was able to turn that situation around, but whether she or any woman will be able to change the ratio of men to women on the officer level anytime soon is questionable. A female vice president? They already have one. She's Jean Handley, vice president for personnel and corporate relations. But what the women want to know is, is she going to be the only one? When she retires, will they appoint another woman just to have *a* woman? Is there room for only one woman at the VP level, no matter how talented another woman might be? Will comfort level supersede all other concerns, competence included? The women at the company are keenly tuned in, and if they had to place bets, they wouldn't bet that talent would win.

"The higher up you go, the more the pendulum swings to comfort because competence is assumed," observes Karin D. Mayhew, a district manager. One discouraging note was the 1985 replacement of one of the two women on the board of directors with a white male. Women say they must have more tickets punched to move up than white males, that the rules are like constantly shifting sands. Women are told they don't need a certain kind of experience—field, for instance—to go to the next level; but when a job opens up that they want, they are then told that they don't have the experience that Joe had, because he has field, or line, experience. One senior woman says that getting field experience doesn't really help your career because women assuredly will not get a good appraisal of their performance from male superiors, no matter how well the job is done. For minorities, it's an even tougher game. They stay in positions longer than whites, they have to take one slow step after another. You don't ever go very high that way. Too much time and energy get spent at lower levels.

As in all companies with good intentions, something is being done to try to shift the balance of power. Workshops on male-female issues in the workplace have been offered to managers since 1978; on race relations, since 1981. Several hundred managers have gone through the three-day off-site workshops, and a follow-up survey on the race workshops shows that they have had a lasting impact. (No such follow-up study has been done on the male-female workshops, but the women say they have no trouble making their points in meetings.) More than half of the 90-plus people in an advanced management development program are women; a third are minorities. Continuing education is part of the plan. A program at Smith College, which is spaced over two years and costs $10,000 per individual, has been completed by several SNET women. According to Handley, and probably because of her, succession planning carefully looks at women and minorities. Personnel planning committees, made up of four to six people from each department, have some leeway in moving people around and could be helpful if you're stuck professionally between a rock and a hard place. But you would be advised to sharpen your political skills. This is a bureaucracy, never forget that.

Bureaucratic it may be, but this Bell company went through considerably fewer growing pains at divestiture in 1984 than others did. The only employees who had to be laid off were recent employees who formed a new business group, a venture that proved unprofitable. Downsizing was never an issue here, largely because the company was already an independent, moving in the AT&T orbit only by virtue of a 24 percent stock interest that AT&T obtained in exchange for some patents a century ago. So when AT&T was broken up, SNET went on doing what it had been doing and didn't face a morass of disruptions. The company's emphasis on service and technology dates back to its founding. SNET was the first to convert to all-dial service and the first to serve residential customers with clear-as-a-bell optical fiber technology, as well as the first to install such a network for statewide service. Now the battleground for SNET is retaining its statewide monopoly past 1988.

Considering the company's bent toward technology, engineers might do well to find jobs here. Other areas where jobs might be found are marketing and finance. Since divestiture, a few people have come in at fairly high levels, but not all of them last, as they have trouble adjusting to the company's way of doing things. SNET is a company of low-key team players. Glamour doesn't go. You'll be handsomely paid for your conservatism; new hires right out of college could come in in the low thirties, although a more typical salary would be in the twenties. Middle management makes from the mid-forties to $70,000; senior management into the healthy six figures.

Sexual harassment is a tricky issue. One high-level man who hadn't grown up in the company was flat-out fired when his proposed dalliances became known. Another man, who had lots of friends by virtue of having been an old-time employee, was quietly asked to retire early. The women say bosses who make unwanted passes are not easy to deal with, especially when it happens where it most often does, at the middle management level. Friends in high places are your best resort.

A flexible benefits program lets employees choose how to spend their benefit dollars. Although the company now has a deductible payment tagged to its medical insurance (the amount varies depending on the kind you select), the company picks up the full tab of the coverage for employee and family. If coverage is lost for any reason, such as a divorce, the spouse who would otherwise lose the insurance is able to buy it at group rates for up to three years. If you don't want any of the benefit packages because you're covered elsewhere, you can walk away with the cash, somewhere in the vicinity of a thousand dollars annually.

One acid test of any company's attitude to advancing women is how it deals with private clubs that don't allow women members. When large corporations decide to stop paying for memberships and stop holding functions at such clubs as long as they deny women membership, many clubs rethink their policies and admit women. It happened in Rochester, New York, when the Gannett Company walked out of the Genesee Valley Club, and it happened in Omaha when Northwestern Bell did the same to the Omaha Club. Both clubs now admit women as full members.

In New Haven, the tactic was different. The first day Jean Handley reported to work as a vice president in 1978, she was notified of an officers' luncheon meeting to be held next door to downtown headquarters at the all-male Quinnipiack Club. The by-laws of the club, which dates from 1871, did not specifically deny women memberships, but none had ever applied and it was generally understood that this was a man's club. Women could attend certain functions, and wives could eat in ladies' dining rooms. "I told the man who was chairman then that I was sorry I had to make an issue of this so early, but I wouldn't be going to the lunch, since the club didn't admit women," Handley remembers. "He said that he hadn't meant to bring it up so early either, but since I had, would I consider being put up for membership?" He explained that there was a movement afoot to admit women. He assured Handley there would be no problem. Handley figured otherwise but agreed to be their test case. As Handley predicted, there was a general uprising among the ranks. Newspapers splashed the story over their front pages. Lawyers who were members selected sides and wrote briefs. A general election was called.

The vote was close, but Handley got in. She says no one has ever been unfriendly. The only sour grapes came in the form of a postcard depicting Iranian women wrapped in veils. "Why don't you go where they know how to treat women?" the anonymous sender wrote.

Jean Handley has. And it's not Iran. It's SNET.

The question remains, is there room for more than one woman at the officers' meetings?

SYNTEX

A PHARMACEUTICAL COMPANY THAT WAS INVOLVED IN
THE DEVELOPMENT OF THE
BIRTH CONTROL PILL

▲ EMPLOYEES: 4,900; nearly 48 percent are women.

▲ SALES: $1.1 billion.

▲ Syntex has always been a research-driven company, allocating 13.5 percent of its annual budget of slightly more than $1 billion to research. To date, women in R and D have risen higher when they join management rather than as individual contributors in the laboratory, but this appears to be the result of personal choice and not discrimination.

▲ Syntex recruits women through advertising and executive search firms. It is also an active presence in the Palo Alto Resource Center for Women via contributions, employee speakers and board membership. Syntex supports other groups as well, including the Center for Research on Women at Stanford University and the National Hispanic Women's Network.

▲ Job posting, additional training, tuition reimbursement and succession planning ensure that qualified women get promoted. Of the approximately 243 employees considered upper management by Syntex, 32—13 percent—are women; of these, five are vice presidents, 37 are department directors, and one is a general manager. The 13-member board of directors is all male.

▲ Discrimination and sexual harassment complaints are handled informally or through a formal grievance procedure; the company has no training program on harassment.

▲ Syntex is aware of past inequities in pay to women, and to rectify them studies what other companies are doing, reevaluates individual job descriptions, reevaluates job categories held predominantly by women and makes grade level adjustments when needed to bring women up to par.

▲ Syntex is a flexible place to work. In addition to the relatively liberal 10 weeks of maternity disability mandated by California, you may hold your job, without pay, for up to four months. Sick leave may be used for family illness. And Syntex is one of the few companies to offer on-site child care. Other attractive benefits include physicals every six months for employees and their families, exercise classes and a fitness center, as well as excellent medical and life insurance plans. The company is strongly committed to excellence in its products, and pride in one's work is one of the tacit benefits.

▲ Major employment centers: Palo Alto, Cupertino and Mountain View, Calif.: 3,550; Boulder, Colo.: 240; Springfield, Mo.: 76.

SYNTEX (USA), INC.
3401 Hillview Avenue
Palo Alto, CA 94304
(415) 855-5050

Approaching the headquarters and laboratories of the Syntex Corporation in northern California is like coming upon a gorgeous college campus: low, modern buildings set among the rolling Los Altos foothills, lawns speckled with sculptures by people such as Henry Moore, a reflecting pond stocked with fish, joggers in the noonday sun. Stop and have lunch in the company-subsidized cafeteria—a healthy meal of sprouts, veggies and fruits—and eat outside if you choose. Come after work and see people playing volleyball. This is big business in the Silicon Valley.

The 106-acre industrial park in Palo Alto, where Syntex is located, belongs to its nearby neighbor, Stanford University, adding to the campuslike atmosphere. And although Syntex employees tend to put in workaholic hours, they manage to do it without looking brutalized.

Maybe it's the air.

And maybe, in part, it's the corporate attitude. "People feel good about working here," says Fran Safier, director of human resources. "It's not just the products we're making, although that's a part of it. The work is interesting, and the people are treated well. And if something is not going well, you can go tell somebody because there's a lot of ears out there to listen. Even the employees who are the biggest complainers will come up to you at an anniversary luncheon for somebody who's been with the company for 20 years, and they will say, 'I just love being at Syntex.' "

Vice president of public affairs and communications Kathleen Gary feels that much of the good attitude about working for Syntex comes from the kind of business it is. Gary should know. She spent 13 years working in the steel industry. "There is something remarkable about working here," she says. "People believe in what we are doing and know what we are doing is important. One of these days we are going to be marketing drugs that keep people alive, not just improve their lives, and you can't measure what that means in a job. The feeling is that we can really be proud of what this company does, and for me that is an exciting thing to be part of. You don't have to apologize for picking a career with Syntex the way some people have to when they pick a career with a utility or an oil company."

Vice president of business development Jackie den Boer believes that the atmosphere at Syntex is one that allows employees to make a psychological contract with the company. "There's an altruism here people can hang on to," she says. Consequently, she adds, people tend to stay at Syntex a long time, and not because of the high salaries or fabulous benefits but because of this psychological connection to a company they believe in.

However, just as it's easier to love a rich man over a poor man, Syntex makes it easy for employees to stay psychologically committed. The company offers a better than average salary and benefits package, setting the compensation at 105 percent of the industry average and allowing it to outshine its benefits-rich neighbors in the Silicon Valley.

For working parents, that means access to a child care center to which Syntex provided $145,000 in start-up costs and which the company continued to subsidize for the first few years. The center is three miles down the road from Syntex at a former high school, and parents can drop off their tots as early as six weeks after birth. A high teacher-to-child ratio is maintained, and a registered nurse is on the premises. More than a hundred children are enrolled. Parents who need financial help in meeting the fees, which range from $75 to $105 a week, can apply for company-funded scholarships. Fees can be paid with pretax dollars through a payroll deduction plan.

Standard California maternity leave is 10 weeks—four before birth, six after—and California law also dictates that your job be kept open for four months. Since this means that the other workers in an absent employee's department have to pick up the slack, extensions are not easily granted. For pregnant employees who work with chemicals, a job change to an office atmosphere can be arranged, but managers have found most women don't want to make the move. Flexitime is offered at the discretion of the manager, but the practice appears not to be widespread.

Although Syntex has the outward signs of being an accommodating company for parents, in the office it's business as usual—children or not. "You are expected to do your job to the same degree as someone who does not have a child," says one mother. "And whether you are a man or woman, no concession is given. If you want to move ahead, you cannot allow your family to impact on your time or your work." Another mother told of being called to an impromptu evening meeting and having it pointed out to her that all the people who would be present were giving up personal time. The implication was that she had better be willing to do so also, children not-withstanding. She was there. Long hours and weekend work appear to be routine in the valley, where a badge of your success is how many hours you work. Syntex is by no means a laid-back California company. The idea is that when you want to succeed in industry, you have to make trade-offs. Men have been doing it for years.

What may eventually alter the workaholic mentality at Syntex is a new breed of involved fathers, dads who must pick up their kids from the day care center because Mom's out of town or at a late meeting, dads who want to be at their daughter's track meet or their son's Little League game. "Men feel comfortable walking into a room and saying, 'It's four-thirty, I'm out of here at five-thirty because my son's got a game,'" one woman says. "Women who aim for the top don't feel comfortable saying that."

"Male colleagues with young children and working wives are what's going to change things," another woman adds. "Then it will be perceived as people's issues, not, what concessions must we make for women?"

Syntex is a relative newcomer in the pharmaceutical field, one of two U.S. companies started since World War II that have become major drug manufacturers. Syntex is both a role model for would-be pharmaceutical giants and a mirror of the opportunities and hurdles facing established leaders in the field.

What got the company off the ground was the discovery that a scraggly yam called *barbasco*—which Mexican people rubbed on their hands and feet to heal wounds—could be synthesized and used as a cheap source of a substance to make sex hormones. Hence the company's name: *Synt* from synthesis, and *ex* from Mexico. While the scientists could make the steroid extract from the plant, they lacked the resources to make a birth control pill but were responsible for developing three of the first four oral contraceptives that became available in the United States.

Although later Syntex marketed its own oral contraceptive, the company was never able to take a leader's share in that market and today comes in third. However, the profits from the early research have made it possible for the company to develop and market other drugs under its own label, and today Syntex competes in many therapeutic and diagnostic areas.

One of its most successful products has been Naprosyn, which is the best-selling brand of prescription drug for arthritis and related conditions in the United States and the fifth best selling of all prescription drugs in the United States. Cumulative sales of Naprosyn and Anaprox (a closely related drug) have reached $1 billion since Naprosyn's introduction less than a decade ago, which makes possible Syntex's large investment in research.

Consequently, Syntex is a company with a scientific elite and a CEO who's a scientist himself. Nonscientists, no matter how well educated or recognized outside of Syntex, will have a hard time getting to the top here unless the company changes direction radically in the future. Syntex, for instance, does not sell any over-the-counter drugs, which is why its name is not better known.

In that scientific haven at the top, it's a men's club. At middle and entry levels in the laboratories, the ratio of men and women is evenly split. A number of female chemists and biologists from other companies have come over to Syntex for what they see as expanded opportunities. But the higher you go in the labs, the more predominately male they become. While the company has dual career ladders—one scientific, one management—no women have progressed on the scientific career path to the levels that are open to men. Women who have gotten ahead in research have moved into management and left the laboratory.

One of them is Ruth Havemeyer, a director of research administration who started with the company more than 20 years ago as a group leader in the laboratory. She's seen Syntex through the changes that have made the place a more open environment for women. Little more than a decade ago, when women were not considered seriously committed to their careers even if they had Ph.D.s, a peer advisory board on which Havemeyer served was set up to determine what the barriers were to women getting ahead. They talked to women throughout the company and brought back recommendations to senior management. "The recommendations were not received very well, but management had made a commitment that they were going to act on them, even if they surprised them or if they didn't agree wholeheartedly," Havemeyer says. "Now it's neutral to be a female here, while before it was a disadvantage."

The willingness of top management to admit they are wrong has been a big plus for the company, since it allows in the fresh air of new ideas. "One of the exceptional things about Syntex is that the people at high levels have always been accepting of different ideas," says Jackie den Boer. "It might be hard to get them across, but they are willing to listen. It's a company that's willing to do things differently, and that's why we are where we are. When I started in 1972, we were $200 million in sales. Now we're over a billion, and you don't get that way by being pedantic." By her own admission, den Boer is "irreverent, not traditional," qualities that gave her visibility as she rose from an entry-level job in accounting to her current vice presidency.

To be a woman and successful at Syntex it seems to be imperative to be able to get your ideas across with the forcefulness of the Furies. It's not enough to present a good idea and hope that it will be accepted. You'll probably have to repeat it a few times and work like hell to make it succeed —and quickly, because everybody will be watching over your shoulder, waiting for one false step. "Even somebody with strong convictions and a strong track record is going to be watched," one woman comments. "I'll say, 'This is what I want to do and here's how I'll make it work.' If a man said it, they would believe it and maybe comment on it and leave it alone. But with somebody like myself [a woman], it's going to have to be validated, and they will make sure there's a safety net." Another woman suggests that men are seen as more knowledgeable and competent largely because they act as if they know all the answers.

"I've watched several settings where women have had skills at least as good as men but were not promoted up, not because they weren't good, but because they presented themselves in a fashion that did not appear to be as competent," she says. "Whereas men will bullshit their way through and actually half the time they may be wrong, but by George, they know all the answers." To help women enhance their credibility, Syntex organized a program some years ago. Videotapes were made on the first day and again on the second day at the end of the sessions. For many, the improvement was immediate. When men asked to be admitted, they were. But the women stopped coming soon after, and the seminars were discontinued.

But with or without special training and regardless of how they communicate, the women in our discussion group wondered if men at Syntex—or men in general—were ready to deal with women who did not begin sentences with "In my opinion . . . " or "Let me offer this for your consideration . . . " They also concurred that women who appeared to be too competent, confident and ambitious were likely to be viewed as too intense, too striving or too "perfect," as one woman stated. As a result, qualities that would be seen as positive in men are viewed negatively in women, an attitude that leaves its stamp on performance reviews. "Men always agree with me in public, but when it comes to performance reviews, it's a different story," one senior woman says. "Men are still judged on results, and women are criticized on aspects of their behavior."

The generation gap between senior management men who are doing the reviewing and working women 20 years younger creates a gulf that probably won't be crossed until the older men retire. "Although they have daughters who are entering the work force, they haven't really experienced what's going on with women or how to deal with them as business equals rather then in terms of male-female stereotypes," she continues. "Only two of the corporate officers have working spouses. These men have wives who stay home and take care of the social obligations, talk to the children and buy the Father's Day cards." The likelihood of their changing their attitude is probably small.

The human resources division is watching to see that women are given management opportunities and not overlooked in the succession planning. Every spring, workers and their superiors go through an evaluation process, discuss where the subordinate wants to go and work out a course of action, whether that includes additional education or a lateral move to broaden one's experience. The plans are written up and go to the corporate operating committee, which decides who's ready to be considered for various moves. But how well you fare depends to a great degree on your direct superior's willingness to embrace the concept. "If your manager thinks of it as a paper-and-pencil exercise that must be done to satisfy the company, it can be useless," one woman states. "If your manager makes it a real exchange, it can be outstanding. I see both types of managers, and I don't see the manager who treats it as a useless exercise being penalized." The message is, if you want to move up or transfer to a different division, you have to see to it yourself.

Syntex offers a number of educational possibilities to facilitate the process. Seminars on a variety of topics from goal setting to how to be a working parent to premenstrual syndrome are held noontimes and evenings; on-site classes for credit are offered at Golden Gate University; and tuition reimbursement makes it possible for an employee to complete a college education at the company's expense. Fran Thompson, now a personnel representative, received her B.A. degree at the age of 39 with the company picking up the cost for her last two years at the University of San Francisco. The first two years were at a nearby community college. Once she received her degree, she moved from executive assistant to executive recruiter. "I've been here nine years, and if I can be as happy in the next nine years as I've been in the previous, I'll be here," she says. "This is a stable company with opportunities for promotion and nice regular increases."

Stability is a double-edged sword for women at Syntex. Senior management is likely to be around until they retire. Now jobs at high levels don't open up often. And because many of the senior men have been with the company for such a long time, some of them get away with a certain amount of sexual harassment, seemingly because no one wants to tell them they can't.

"The old guard that's part of the original group who founded the company are more or less protected," one woman says. And although a formal policy regarding harassment is on the books, the policy isn't well known and many women are still afraid to speak up, according to the women we interviewed. However, people have been fired, indicating the company's commitment.

Short of filing a formal charge, some women talk over with their personal representative how to handle a sticky situation on their own. They can also use a "speak out" program for harassment charges, as well as anything from a leaky roof to a sexist boss, which brings the complainant—if she chooses —face-to-face with whoever can best solve the problem. All such complaints are funneled through employee communications, and while someone there knows the identity of the person with the problem, it need not be revealed to the person causing the difficulty.

What constitutes harassment and what is simply kidding around has not yet been settled to anyone's satisfaction, and Syntex is no exception. While the research and corporate divisions are models of decorum, a woman in marketing or sales would be better off enjoying an occasional foul joke then finding her skin burning each time one is told, for the boys in these departments like to fool around. They're just getting used to having women in their meetings, and so a locker room quality still prevails. "We need to make distinctions about what is offensive and what is simply kidding around," says Diane Feldman, a product director for new products. "The men are used to doing it because there haven't been women around. You'll be in a meeting and the remarks will be flying fast and furious and some women will get offended when it's not meant personally. That's a distinction we have to learn to make."

Just as women are struggling to decide what's kosher and what isn't when it comes to sexual innuendo, Syntex is struggling to find ways to keep its employees—men and women—content. The women we met say Syntex is doing so within a framework of high ethical standards, both in how it treats employees and in how it competes in the marketplace. Ruth Havemeyer, who's been with the company since 1966, speaks for many when she says, "For all the things that are wrong, why have all of us stayed here? Because you are treated very well as a human being, as an individual. You don't have the feeling that somebody is going to stab you in the back. And we like one another."

TIME INC.

THE WORLD'S BIGGEST MAGAZINE PUBLISHER; OUR REPORT DEALS WITH ITS SIX CORE MAGAZINES AND CORPORATE STAFF

▲ EMPLOYEES: 3,400; approximately 54 percent are women.

▲ REVENUES: $3.7 billion, up from the previous year's revenues of $3.4 billion; net income was $376 million.

▲ Time Inc. is a company concerned with recruiting and hiring women. Division-level executives are held accountable for meeting affirmative action goals.

▲ Programs aimed at promoting women include job posting, training programs, tuition reimbursement, management development and succession planning. In 1987, 47 percent of the 171 people enrolled in management training programs were women.

▲ Of the 183 employees considered upper management, 74—24 percent—are women. These include six vice presidents, 31 directors, the publisher of *Life,* the managing editor (who functions as editor in chief) of *Life,* two assistant managing editors and an assistant treasurer. One of the 20 members of the board of directors is a woman.

▲ Time Inc. offers an impressive array of benefits for parenting. In addition to the standard maternity disability leave, parents can take up to a year of unpaid leave, retaining full medical benefits and seniority. The company offers flexible work hours and workplaces where department needs permit, and limited part-time work is available for managers and professionals. In 1987 the company introduced a flexible benefits plan, including the option of tax-deductible child care, and purchased a resource referral service for child care facilities. Other impressive benefits include a liberal vacation policy and sabbatical allowances.

▲ Complaints of sexual discrimination are handled either by the director of affirmative action or any other manager for informal resolution. Union members can use formal grievance procedures. A class action suit in the early 1970s, settled out of court, resulted in some important changes in the company's policies and practices toward women.

▲ Time Inc. issues periodic strong statements on sexual harassment, and the women we interviewed felt it was a nonissue.

▲ Time Inc. has taken aggressive measures to rectify inequality of pay to women. They examine what other companies are doing and do research to establish measures of comparable worth. Every year they reevaluate women and men in the same jobs to ensure comparable pay and equal treatment.

▲ Major employment centers: New York City. Bureaus and sales staff throughout the country and the world.

TIME INC.
Time & Life Building
New York, NY 10020
(212) 522-1212

From a woman's point of view, Time Inc. is two distinct places. On the business side of the six magazines Time Inc. publishes—*Life, Fortune, Sports Illustrated, Money, People* as well as *Time**—it is excellent for women. Women are getting ahead. And although it takes some doing in the go-go atmosphere of magazine publishing, many are managing to have both rewarding careers and families. On the editorial side, it's another matter. You get a lot of mixed messages. Some magazines seem to promote women into important editorial positions, others clearly do not and are fortresses of male chauvinism. The newsweekly, *Time*, is a terrible place for women writers and editors. More about that later.

First the good news, and it is very good news. Women on the business side at Time Inc. are going gangbusters. Affirmative action and a lawsuit for sex discrimination in the early seventies (settled out of court) might have been the impetus that got them hired, but once Time Inc. had a crop of bright young women with degrees from the very best schools, it didn't let them go to waste. They started marching right up the pipeline and now hold a number of important positions on Time Inc.'s magazines, as well as in the corporate offices. Carolyn K. McCandless is vice president of employee plans and benefits; Bonnie Blecha is an assistant treasurer; both are corporate officers. Ruth Shields is magazine group circulation director. *Life* has both a woman publisher and a woman editor. The general managers of *Time* and *Sports Illustrated* are women. Both are mothers of young children.

When Barbara Mrkonic is asked if being a mother has slowed down her progress, she laughs, "I kind of wish it would a little." Since she had a child in 1983, she has been general manager of *Money*, general manager of *Discover* (since sold), then general manager of *Time*. She is responsible for finances, personnel and administration, as well as advertising production and records.

"Being a woman here is neither a help nor a hindrance," she says matter-of-factly. "It's neutral. People have not been shy about promoting women." Mrkonic credits much of the success of the women to the fact that some men in senior positions are in their thirties and forties and do not have noticeable biases against women. *Some* men.

J. Richard Munro, chairman, CEO and ex-marine, happens to be in his late fifties, but he is generally credited as the man at the top who made it

*Time Inc. also owns other properties that include a publishing division with several companies; a telephone subscription operation; a subsidiary, Southern Progress Corporation, which publishes five magazines; and interests in *McCall's*, *Working Woman*, *Working Mother*, *Parenting* and *Asiaweek* magazines. Home Box Office (page 194) is also part of the Time Inc. family.

happen for these women. "The clichés are that we can't take them to the New York Athletic Club—they don't fit in . . . women fit in everyplace," Munro has stated. However, outside pressure perhaps made him see women's worth clearly—specifically, a class action suit filed with the New York State Division of Human Rights. Time Inc. settled out of court and promised to do better by women in the future. A few promotions followed, and *Time's* corps of researchers, up till then a female ghetto, were upgraded to researcher-reporters, which turned out not to mean a great deal. More important, female MBAs were hired as they came out of business schools such as Harvard and Columbia and given the green light. Time Inc. was out of the hot seat. So it would seem.

Mrkonic, Harvard '78, like a number of Time Inc.'s best and brightest, has an MBA from an Ivy League school. Time Inc. is so well known for its penchant for Ivy Leaguers, male and female, that when someone reaches a top job without a swell background, it's likely to be noted in print. Hotshot editors are likely to have been Rhodes scholars. Nicholas J. Nicholas, Jr., heir apparent to Munro and chief operating officer, went to Phillips Academy and Princeton. One woman said that the first serious conversation she had with Dick Munro was after he learned that both their families summered on Fishers Island in Long Island Sound. WASPier than that you don't get.

However, if you arrive on the doorstep as a youngster without the right background but show promise, Time Inc. will help you get the credentials you need. Linda Plevrites joined in 1964, when she came to New York from Washington State on a lark halfway through college. She was hired for $76 a week as an accounts payable clerk. Like many women of that era, she didn't seriously think about having a career for many years, although she was promoted into a number of different supervisory positions. Plevrites took a year's leave in 1975, and when she came back took stock of her chances for advancement. She knew her lack of a degree was holding her back. When she was offered the opportunity to get a master's from Columbia University, she jumped at the chance. For four terms, she attended classes for a week at the beginning of each semester and every Friday. Time Inc. paid the bill and not only gave her the time off, but, more important, made her education a priority. Only a real crisis could pull her away from school. Meetings or trips were not scheduled for Fridays. "It was a tremendous gift," she says.

It was also the ticket to the second stage of her career. As she was finishing her degree, one of her projects was to restructure the magazine group's financial operations. In doing so, she unwittingly created the perfect job for herself. At one time or another, she had supervised all the departments that would be reporting to whomever held that position. But she knew she would get it only if the man who would be her boss wanted *her*. It turned out to be someone she didn't know well, but she got the job—magazine group controller—anyway. Like other women at Time Inc., Plevrites says she hasn't run up against sexual bias, but she keenly felt her lack of academic credentials. "For years I was treated differently because of my education, but nothing was ever spoken," she says. On the issue of being a woman, she, like Mrkonic, joined the chorus of women who said they had not been held back because they were women: "I'm a woman, but that doesn't have anything to do with anything here."

Of course, that doesn't mean that there are no died-in-the-Paul-Stuart-wool male chauvinists roaming the halls in the Time & Life Building or swimming in the buff at the men-only New York Athletic Club. There are. Another woman who has been with the company for two decades said that she had "worked for the absolute chauvinist pigs" as well as "those who hardly knew if I was a man or a woman, it made so little difference." Yet Plevrites and others said that blatant abusers would usually make some other mistake and get the ax in the end. Remember, we are talking about the *business side only* here.

Several up-and-comers on the business side have young children. Ann Jackson, business manager of *Money*, has two. Jackson says she sometimes feels guilty walking out at 6:15 each evening to catch the train to Westchester, but that overall the company has been very supportive. "People say, 'How do you do it? It's so great that you are coping with kids. . . .' It's not like a place where you are afraid to say anything about your children or home because that diminishes your professionalism. Obviously, you keep a lid on it, but you feel that kind of freedom and support, and it makes a huge difference."

Management's accommodation to Jackson's personal needs also made the difference between her staying or leaving the company when her banker husband was transferred to London. Time assigned her to its London office for the duration and brought her back when he was transferred back, asking only that she come a few months early because a job was waiting. That kind of flexibility is rare indeed. When she returned to the States with two babies and a nanny, she was given the kind of support she needed to make the move work. She got financial aid to cover relocation expenses and time to find a sublet, as well as the understanding that is the most important part of it all.

Time's maternity policy is, on paper, one of the best in the country. Following eight to 12 weeks of paid disability leave for normal births, new mothers can take a year's leave of absence, during which time they are extended their full health benefits and no loss in length of employment. A job of equal status is guaranteed upon return. Men can take the same leave, but few do. Yet the policy is not without its problems, according to Ann Moore, general manager of *Sports Illustrated* and the mother of a 3-year-old. "The policy was written at a time when we never assumed any women were going to occupy any positions of power in the magazine group," she notes. "Certainly it's a little insulting to imagine that we can go without a general manager for a year. Or a publisher. If women want equality, let's start admitting there's a price you pay for it."

Moore had her son when she was in her current job. She went directly from work to the hospital. She had an easy delivery and a healthy baby, who, at two and a half weeks, went with her to Dorado Beach for a business meeting she had helped plan. Eight weeks after he was born, she was back at work full-time.

Moore has made it possible for Gretchen Teichgraeber, a mother of two, to work four days a week instead of five as the person in charge of magazine development and acquisitions for *SI*. Incidentally, last fall, *SI*'s Eastern sales manager was pregnant with her second. It may be a jock's magazine, but the business side is replete with women.

Yet whether or not women admit they are taking time off to take their child to the doctor or because of illness seems to depend on one's status. The higher up you go, the less worry there is over telling the truth. Women in lower positions are more likely to say they are ill themselves.

However, the extremely generous vacation policy makes life a little easier for parents who need time off. Salaried employees get four weeks plus two personal days a year; the hourly workers (in this business, hourly workers are found in a number of job categories) get three weeks, and everybody gets four weeks after five years. The policy may be the most liberal in the country. We haven't heard of anything that matches it. Actually taking the time allotted is another story. "It's catch-22—they say, here, we'll give you four weeks vacation, but you'll be so busy you won't be able to take it," Moore adds wryly.

Be that as it may, all of Time's benefits are deluxe, and although the company has been in a cost-cutting mode in the last few years, the employees still remain the most cosseted in journalism. Benefits were scaled back a fraction last year when flexible benefits were introduced. Yet when Time's total package—comprehensive medical plan, generous pension and profit sharing—was compared with others in the industry and a few large corporations known for good benefits, the consulting firm of Hewitt Associates found that Time was still way ahead of the pack. If average is given a value of 100, Time was 147. The next highest ranking firm was at 117. And after the benefits were scaled back in 1987, Time still ranked at a lofty 145. A major change was that the deductible on medical insurance was raised from $50 to a sliding scale ranging from $100 to $350 per individual; the higher an employee's compensation, the higher the deductible. Compared with others in the industry, the working conditions and benefits are positively sybaritic.

For many, the new benefit package is a better deal, since it offers options such as a 401K plan and allows up to $5,000 pretax to be set aside for child care. Last year, a child care resource referral service was purchased for workers in New York, and it will be expanded to other cities if it is a success. Time Inc.'s well-known sabbatical policy remains untouched. After 15 years of service, an employee can take off six months at half salary, or two three-month periods; after 20 years, you can take three months off at three-quarters salary. For people wanting to write a book, it's a honey of a deal.

If you're working late, you're allotted $12 for dinner. If it's after 8 P.M., you can take a cab home and turn in the chit for reimbursement. What some old Time staffers on the editorial staff remember fondly is taking a cab in the wee hours of Saturday morning to Sag Harbor, where a number of them spend summer weekends. That way, they could turn up at the 9 A.M. writers' and editors' softball game on Saturday and brag about the macho hours they had put in the night before. The fee for the 200-mile round-trip? A few years ago it was $170. Although the different magazines still have some leeway with their budgets, taking a cab to the Hamptons is now *verboten*. Those who did it last year were told that the next time, they would pay. When management first announced that it was slashing expenses, the joke that made the rounds in the building was that Time Inc. could save $75 million a year by eliminating Dial-a-Cab. In 1985 the Christmas lunch for senior editors was at Lutèce, one of Manhattan's best and priciest eating places. The Christmas lunch is no longer at Lutèce. Nor can liquor be requisitioned, as it once was, except by the most exalted.

Most of the cost cutting has come in the form of layoffs, and hundreds of writers, editors and production people at Time Inc.'s core magazines have been laid off in the past few years, raising howls heard as far as Sag Harbor. Many were offered generous packages to retire, and many took them, since for some, the walkaway money was as high as $100,000. A few took deals to write on a contract basis.

Sexual harassment appears to be history, and simply having a no-nonsense policy in place appears to have kept the lust in men's hearts, not in their actions. "Women feel strong enough to confront an individual, and he would know that if they complained, it would be dealt with swiftly," says Linda Plevrites. "All a woman has to do is point this out, and it would stop."

Sexual discrimination is another matter entirely. If MBAs are having a grand time making their mark, women writers and editors are having a much harder go. At *Time*, for instance, a lone woman had the rank of senior editor from 1974 until December 1988, when Claudia Wallis was promoted. The other female staffers heaved a collective sigh of relief. The promotion for a woman had been a long time in coming.

One male writer at *Time*, upon learning that his company would be included in this book, shook his head incredulously. "It's got to be one of the worst places in America for women," he stated unequivocally. One woman writer said that while some men in high places treated women fairly, a whole slew of the younger generation didn't share their attitudes.

"Many women at *Time* comment about this," she notes. "A lot of the younger men have very old-fashioned ideas. We look at each other in wonderment and say '*Where do they get these dinosaurs?*' Or does the environment make them this way?" Does it happen when they are rubbing shoulders for a few years with the old boy network? While having drinks after work at Uncle Sam's in the building, a Time & Life hangout?

However, the staff reductions of the last two years, while hard to live through—*Am I Next?* is the question that plagues everyone—are likely to have a positive effect on breaking down old barriers. When old boy networks crumble, raw talent makes headway. As the numbers dwindle, sex discrimination becomes weighty baggage that holds back excellence. Who's there to pass the flame on to becomes an open question, particularly as the managing editor named last year, Henry Muller, is one of three men credited with bringing equality to the bureaus. It appears that he may do the same for the editors and writers who toil at the Time and Life Building.

To be fair, Time Inc. has made some improvements over the years in women's lot, however minuscule. Management promised to be good when 147 women from all the magazines—possibly the largest group of women ever to charge an employer with sexual discrimination—brought a class action suit that was settled out of court. *Time* magazine agreed to hire men as researchers, not just women. Previously, the category had been an all-female ghetto, and women, regardless of their experience, were offered jobs as fact-checkers. The whole category was then upgraded to reporter-researcher, although the job itself remained the same. Now reporter-reseachers are much more likely to be given writing tryouts than in the past. And occasionally, people do move up. While theoretically it was always supposed to be possible, in reality it almost never happened. Even today, although the research staff remains three-quarters female, it's largely the men from this group who actually get the tryouts. And women who move up from this category have a hard time shedding their image of handmaidens who are there to take care of the details and tell the editors what a great job they did.

It is worth noting that some women like the lack of responsibility and don't want to make the sacrifices moving up would mean. It's not difficult to be a part-time researcher. Some mothers like the job for that reason, and one woman works on Saturdays only.

To prove its good intentions, in the fall of 1971 *Time* had one woman listed at the associate editor level. She was the lone woman among 20 men. She was also the chief copy editor. She was not there as a stop-off point before she became a senior writer or senior editor like her male peers. Today, the crop of associate editors is approximately one-third female, a fair if not admirable number. Yet men are often hired directly into this category; women almost never. But since no woman in this group has yet made it past this level, *Time* women are beginning to wonder if it is a launching pad for men, a holding pattern for women. That's what it was beginning to look like until Wallis's promotion.

Management did promote two women to senior editor between 1972–87. One became Henry Grunwald's assistant and has since retired. The other is Radcliffe graduate Martha Duffy, anointed in 1974, whose bailiwick is the arts. Wallis's appointment to that elite circle of power—where one has a say about how the news is covered, how much space will be allotted, if a story will be assigned at all—was the first for a woman in 13 years.

It's not as if *Time* hadn't hired talented women. They had. But not being fools, many of these women went elsewhere to make their mark. Above all, journalism is a star system. If you write sparkling copy or ferret out scoops nobody else does, you can take your wares just about anyplace. You will be sought after. *Time* women, with pride and a rueful irony in their voices, rattle off the names of women who have left: Michiko Kakutani, now a powerful literary critic at *The New York Times*; fellow *New York Times* staffers Lydia Chavez, who covered El Salvador and is now assigned to the metropolitan desk; Maureen Dowd, whose witty copy from Washington often graces the front page; and Annalyn Swan, who achieved a rank comparable to senior editor at *Newsweek* before leaving to become editor in chief of *Savvy*. "If Time Inc. had been good for women, all these people wouldn't be gone," one writer states. "And Jason McManus [editor in chief of all the magazines] worries and wonders why." Odd that he couldn't figure it out.

It's not that *Time* promotes only from within. Men are regularly hired from outside as senior editors. When an effort was made to recruit minorities into this rank, one writer asked someone in management why women couldn't be found to hire as senior editors. "Any woman smart enough to be a senior editor is smart enough not to work here," was the off-the-cuff comment. At least the speaker was aware of how the cards are stacked. One female writer, assigned temporarily to the magazine's "Nation" section, says, "It's a totally male environment. You feel like an alien species. The men have lunch together, they are chatting all the time. There was a whole culture going on that I wasn't a part of. Generally, the only women in the section are researchers, and they are there in a subordinate position." The "Nation" section, incidentally, is where the fast trackers congregate.

Women correspondents, who report the news from bureaus in every major city in the United States and throughout the world, have fared remarkably better because the men in charge for the last 10 years have broken away from *Time's* inbred chauvinism and given able women a chance. For years women have been assigned to hot spots and major bureaus, sometimes running them.

Bonnie Angelo is one such woman. Bureau chief in London for more than seven years, she now heads a staff of five women and five men in New York City. She joined the Washington bureau with solid credentials in 1966 but decided to quit a year later after being assigned one too many silly trend stories. When she complained, she was told there was nobody else to do them. She figured there never would be. Only when *Newsday* offered her a job as a columnist and she was ready to take it did things improve. And they never slipped backward. "I've had a wonderful career with *Time,* but I credit the women's movement for making everybody aware what the problem at *Time* was," Angelo remarks. "Yet once they were made aware, *Time* was very good indeed." *Time's* man in Peking is Sandra Burton, in Jerusalem it's Johanna McGeary; Miami, Cristina Garcia; Rio de Janeiro, Laura Lopez. The person on the Philippine scene as the Marcos regime toppled was Burton.

And for every rule, there are exceptions. Yale graduate Claudia Wallis, for example. Wallis, who wrote the cover story on child care in America last year, writes on medicine in the back of the book, where it is generally easier for women. She has few complaints to date. Her move up the ladder from writer (she was hired as a writer after a year on the company's internal publication, *FYI,* but that was in 1978 and no one's done it since) to associate editor has mirrored that of a man who was hired around the same time as she was. She feels she may have lost a bit of ground in taking a six-month maternity leave in 1987. "I have not been penalized for being a woman," Wallis says. "I can't tell if I'm a special case or if I've been very lucky. Many of my female colleagues have horror stories to tell." The mother of a young son, Wallis is happily experimenting with a four-day work week. Naturally, she puts in an extra day when she's working on a cover story.

Not all is *Bleak House* on the Time Inc. editorial side. Time Inc.'s six magazines are run as fiefdoms, and each has its own distinct culture. At the top of each is the managing editor, and his—or *her*—attitudes determine policy, by and large. What's going on at *Time,* the newsweekly, fortunately isn't the whole story. And you're right, we did say *her.*

She's Pat Ryan, who was M.E. of *People* up to last year, when she moved over to *Life*, where she replaced another woman, Judith Daniels. Although there had been some criticism that Ryan didn't promote enough women up the editorial ranks at *People*, Ryan says she couldn't get a woman to take the job of editor of the news section, traditionally a male stepping-stone position that requires grueling hours. She had offered it to three women. At *Life*, she inherited a staff well integrated with women.

At the other magazines, it's no more or less difficult for women than it is most places in big cities: possibly tougher if you are a woman, but not impossible. *Money*, which wasn't even around when the sexual discrimination settlement was negotiated, is receptive to women, and its writing staff is split evenly between the sexes. One writer, following a maternity leave and signing a book contract, negotiated a deal whereby she works half-time. She is assigned half as many stories as a full-time writer and is able to set her own hours. *Money* had two female senior editors until Julie Connelly left in 1986 to join *Fortune* on the board of editors, a position analogous to senior editor at *Time*. She's one of a half dozen women to have that rank at *Fortune*. *People* has a number of women writers and associate editors. The assistant managing editors of *Fortune* and *Life* are women. *Sports Illustrated* has a stable of star writers and may be a tougher nut to crack unless you have special knowledge or an inside track to a sport they focus on.

Yet making it to the top jobs editorially has meant forgoing children. Most senior editorial women are childless. One editor with a 3-year-old says that to rise, "You have to be willing to put your life on hold and put in a lot of hours." Voicing what several women said, she adds that while one is judged by one's copy, how late you stay at the office also counts for points. "Productivity is not totally measured by results," she says. "Time Inc. is a labor-intensive company. It's not enough to work smart." While motherhood alone appears not to be a stumbling block, it's necessary to prove that you can put in the hours just like you did before. Without around-the-clock help and take-charge husbands, that could prove impossible. At *Time*, for example, on the nights that sections close—Thursdays and Fridays—it's typical to work until well after midnight, sometimes as late as four in the morning.

Time Inc. pays well, as do most big city and national publications. The salaries are generally not out of line with what the competition pays. The average for a writer or a correspondent on all the magazines is in the fifties but can increase significantly with experience and area of expertise. The same is true of editors—salaries vary from $40,000 to well over $100,000 —which is a jump into the stratosphere as far as most journalists are concerned. If you're good and you're ballsy, you can probably make a lot more at the writer and associate editor level than someone who quietly does a good but not outstanding job. The general managers and business managers we interviewed say they watched the salaries of people who worked at their magazines, and no inequity existed between men and women. One woman recalls making $50,000 as a senior editor on a magazine other than *Time* and suddenly "getting a gigantic raise" a few years back. She speculates it was to bring her salary in line with the men's. Now she believes she is as well paid as men in similar jobs.

This pay parity push, if that's what it was, may have been sparked by a guild survey of male and female salaries in which glaring discrepancies were found at *Time* magazine. At that time, 1984, the average for men in the writer-editor category was $48,620; for women, $35,828. At the higher end of the scale, for people with 15 years' experience, men were earning $1,200 a week on the average, while women were making significantly less. Because of the small number of women with more than 15 years' experience, the figure was not published in the guild's newsletter. Susan Geisenheimer, vice president of human resources for the magazine group, says a salary survey in 1986 found some disparities in salaries—of both men and women—and they were corrected. Any differences now, she claims, are due to performance, responsibility and length of service.

On the business side, only a few undergraduates are hired for positions in finance, marketing and production at salaries starting between $20,000 and $28,000. New MBAs start in the mid-forties; at the general manager level, salaries top $100,000 and go as high as $200,000, higher in years when incentive bonuses are paid out.

Women, incidentally, are doing well in sales, and a number of them are among the company's top performers, where they are earning more than $60,000. More than a third of Time Inc.'s sales force is women. There's still a certain cronyism among some old-timers in the sales force, but that is changing, and changing rapidly. To succeed, you don't have to be a back-slapping male; the proof is in the numbers, and that's enough for management. Over 16 percent of the sales managers are women, indicating there are few, if any, barriers to women getting the jobs where compensation can exceed $100,000.

Time Inc. has always prided itself on separation of church and state. Editorial will not be influenced by advertising. Business concerns are not editorial's, and vice versa. It is ironic that the very formula that produces excellent and successful magazines should also produce separate cultures that treat women so differently.

U.S. WEST DIRECT

THE PUBLISHER OF THE WHITE AND YELLOW PAGES FOR
MOUNTAIN BELL, NORTHWESTERN BELL AND PACIFIC
NORTHWESTERN BELL

▲ EMPLOYEES: 2,400; nearly 70 percent are women.

▲ SALES: approximately $600 million.

▲ U.S. West Direct makes no special efforts to recruit and hire women, since nearly 70 percent of its employees are female. Because of downsizing, the company is not actively recruiting managers but has taken aggressive action to increase its pool of promotable female. managers. Methods include job posting, tuition reimbursement, active tracking, succession planning and management development training.

▲ The company's aggressive action has bred results. From January to September 1986, the number of women in upper management doubled. Now 13 of the 51 upper managers—one quarter—are women.

▲ The company feels that any past pay inequities were rectified by the 1973 federal consent decree with AT&T.

▲ U.S. West Direct is a company sensitive to the needs of parents. In addition to standard maternity disability leave, employees make active use of flexitime. The company provides paternity benefits, adoption benefits and sick leave for family illness. Part-time work for managers and professionals is available, and the company has a cafeteria-style approach to benefits. Benefits are liberal and include an employee assistance program as well as medical, dental and vision insurance.

▲ Salaries are competitive, and a lump sum bonus is available to all employees, based on company financial performance and individual performance. To encourage innovation, suggestions that save money or increase revenues are awarded $50–$5,000, based on 10 percent of the first year's gains.

▲ The company has issued strong statements on sexual harassment and done a study on the issue. A training program that includes education, EEO guidelines, reporting procedures and self-help coping strategies is mandatory for all employees.

▲ Major employment centers: Denver area: 770; Portland, Oreg.: 385; Omaha: 300; Minneapolis: 280; Phoenix: 200; Seattle area: 140; Des Moines: 50.

U.S. WEST DIRECT
2500 South Havana
Aurora, CO 80014
(303) 337-8888

If any company exemplifies the changes brought about by the breakup of AT&T in 1984, it is U.S. West Direct, publisher of approximately 300 telephone directories for U.S. West's 14-state region. The old Bell system was a stodgy, slow-moving gargantuan bureauracy, more concerned about policies and procedures than meeting customer needs. The marketing premise went something like this: You want to be in the Yellow Pages? Fine. You don't? That's fine too. There was no need to be concerned about customer preferences because there was nowhere else for customers to go.

The breakup of the system—and the floodgate of competition it opened—changed all that practically overnight. In a competitive marketplace, hidebound rules no longer apply and whole new strategies have to be put in place. And that's what's happening at U.S. West Direct, a progressive, aggressive, customer-driven organization. The order taker who worked in low gear no longer has a home at U.S. West's publishing arm. "We're looking for people who are innovative, creative; people who can see a different way of doing things," says Patricia Lingeman, director of production and operations. "We don't want people who do things according to the procedures if the procedures don't make sense," she says, referring to the old days, when simply following orders was the way to get ahead.

While the company is in the midst of reinventing itself, chaos has become a by-product. Thriving in the midst of it is a requirement to do well. "Some people are freaking out," Lingeman admits, "especially the ones who can't cope with responsibility and accountability and the freedom to be creative."

But these "Bell-shaped heads"—a reference not to physiognomy but to management style—are lessening in numbers and influence, in spite of the fact that most of the employees came from the old Bell system and most of them are doing roughly the same job they did before divestiture. "The thinkers are going to drive the company," Lingeman adds. With people like her running major departments, along with other highly placed women such as vice president Carol Johnson, who runs the sales division, it's certain that a lot of those people are going to be women. Lingeman, for instance, had four people reporting directly to her when we met in 1987. Two are white men; two are women, and one of them is black. She hired all of them.

Building diversity in the work force is taken seriously here. When a 1985 task force report on pluralism at U.S. West Direct included strong words about what needed to be done, the president sent a copy to all employees stating that he endorsed its recommendations and the company would be implementing them. It has. Before January 1986, you could count on one hand the number of women in senior management; by the fall of that year five had been added. Senior management is now more than a quarter women, one of the best records around anywhere. Minorities are also making inroads into senior management, although the company is having a harder time finding individuals from minority groups to promote than it is women. Not only is the concept of pluralism morally right, but also a diversified work force can be more attuned to a marketplace increasingly made up of people of all colors and both sexes. "We are looking to diversify ourselves because we know it is good business," comments Donna Newlun, who's of Japanese ancestry. "I don't know if I would have been promoted, not so much as an Asian but as a woman, if the task force [on which Newlun served] had not specifically said, close to 70 percent of our employees are female and only 17 percent of our senior management is, while 85 percent of our lower management is female. Something is wrong here."

Progress has been slower in some departments than in others. Sales, although it has a female vice president, is chockablock with men who aren't thrilled to have women joining their ranks as premise salespeople, sales reps who visit customers on site, usually for bigger ads and fatter commissions than the women who sold advertising space over the telephone. Most of the men who traditionally had these lucrative jobs have wives who don't work; they're at home taking care of the kids. And while VP Carol Johnson heads the sales division, right below her are men who don't help their female salespeople but seem to enjoy seeing them struggle. "The harder they struggle, the easier it is to say, 'I told you so,'" one woman says. As we noted elsewhere, we are in cowboy country here in Denver, and feminism is just another dirty word to a lot of men. Be that as it may, the men have had to make room for the women, and the women are coming on strong.

While more men than women still work in premise sales, the staffs are becoming increasingly integrated. More than half of the high performers in both premise and telephone sales are women. The average salary for a premise sales rep is approximately $76,000; some are topping $100,000.

Last year the company began trying out a system whereby a single sales rep would service a customer, however the customer preferred, by phone or an on-site visit. The move will blur the distinction between premise and telephone sales and should ultimately result in more women being give a shot at the bigger sales.

Although the numbers are changing in the customer service area also, women still tend to be clustered in this division, where the top salary one can make is around $24,000 after five years, unless you are a manager. An attempt to move customer service reps into sales met with initial resistance, but as the strategy boosted profits, reluctance gave way. Customer service reps called on businesses, not to make a sale, but just to say, "Hi, I know there is competition in the area, and we just want you to know that U.S. West Direct people are available for you and here's a packet of information."

Sales is a job where motivation and long hours are directly proportional to success; flexibility, or a lack of it, for parenting is up to the individual. Elsewhere in the company, flexibility is an accepted fact of business. While you have to get your job done, the company doesn't even have a firm attendance policy. Employees who would have been considered attendance problems at some companies aren't considered so here because some bosses don't insist that the work be done at the office. In finance, for instance, where the bulk of the work is paperwork, it's permissible to do it at home and not be "absent" from work. "People want a half day to attend their child's school play or because somebody's sick, so we allow them to work at home," explains Kim Whitehead, formerly a director in budget administration. "We get better productivity this way. They are not at the job being frustrated because they are concerned about the child."

Having children here is no hindrance, and the company is in the middle of a baby boomlet. Whitehead was able to override male fears about working mothers' commitment to the job when she hired a woman who was seven months pregnant for a responsible position. The woman came to work after her child was born. To Whitehead's delight, she has worked out extremely well. (Whitehead now works in strategic planning for U.S. West Direct's parent company, Landmark Publishing, and other people we met also have transferred elsewhere within the corporate family. Obviously, it's not all that difficult to do.)

A widely used flexitime policy also eases the burden for working mothers. Some divisions allow employees to work four 10-hour days a week, rather than five eight-hour days. Attorney Roseanne Hall, who works from 9 A.M. to 3 P.M. three days a week, feels that she has one of the best part-time legal jobs imaginable. "I get to do meaningful work, I set my own hours, and I work on the thing I want to work on," says this mother of two. "I know the marketplace, and I know there aren't a lot of jobs like this one."

Socializing among employees is common and appears to make it easier to be an insider. Work decisions often get made when employees get together on weekends, but women are not excluded. Women golfers join men on the links, and Hall occasionally sets up golf dates with men in her department. Minority women have a somewhat harder time making inroads into closed circles.

On most sales forces, boy will be boys, and U.S. West Direct is no exception. Derogatory statements about women are not unheard of in sales, which makes up about 40 percent of the work force. However, that's as far as it goes. Women here unanimously stated that the men know better than to be so stupid as to make unwanted advances on women who work for them. If they did, the women said there would be no problem filing a complaint and getting quick action.

Salaries are competitive with the marketplace, and any discrepancies are due to longevity or status. All salaried employees are eligible for annual lump sum bonuses. Rewards for employee suggestions that save the company money or increase productivity are figured at 10 percent of what the company saved in the first year.

U.S. West Direct is located on a busy highway in a suburb outside Denver, but the view from at least half of the offices is of a large pond with a huge fountain shooting up 50 feet or so. On a clear day, you can see the mountains in the distance where the sun goes down. A grass roots movement from employees has restricted smoking to two lounges on the premises. Groups such as Weight Watchers and Toastmasters meet in the building. The building is modern, the colors are trendy muted tones of blue, mauve and wine. It's an inviting atmosphere. And women are definitely welcome.

WHY JOHNSON & JOHNSON AND CONTROL DATA AREN'T INCLUDED

Two companies we investigated because we thought they were good for women, to judge from their publicity and previous reputation, turned out not to be places we can recommend: Johnson & Johnson and Control Data Corporation. Both companies have glass ceilings so firmly in place that getting ahead is nearly an impossibility. We leave open a little loophole because there is always the exception to the rule. There are usually a few women who can be found who appear to be doing well and do not feel blocked.

But at both places, we were not given real numbers of senior management. Control Data insisted that the top group about which they would release information consisted of 4,466—not a number most people consider upper management. Of this group, a paltry 11 percent are women. Since the smaller number of senior management was not disclosed, it can only mean that the vast percentage of these women are clustered at the lower end of "upper." At Johnson & Johnson, the pattern was the same. Their top group of managers of more than a thousand (which is at least a few thousand less than Control Data's numbers) has 7.8 percent women. Not numbers to inspire anybody. Both of these companies, incidentally, have roughly the same number of employees: Control Data has 26,500; J&J, 30,000.

J&J regularly makes lists of places that are good for women. When we investigated in depth, we heard depressing tales of old boy networks calling the shots, of women whose careers had been going well for the first eight or nine years but who then had topped out and been told they ought to accept reality rather than fight it. "There were at least two times when I was not considered for moves but was more qualified than the men who got them," says one woman whose function and division will remain anonymous to protect her. "I was simply not a part of the old boy network, and in fact that's how it was explained to me when I challenged the situation. 'That's the way it works,' he told me. And there was nothing I could do about it."

As for a career-tracking program that supposedly exists, one woman said that it is dangled out as a carrot in front of you during the recruitment process, but "it's all talk and no action." The woman said she had no confidence that anybody was actively managing her career path, much less doing it fairly or seeing that she got the experience she needed to continue moving up. Another woman bluntly stated that she had been denied certain jobs that would have put her in competition for promotion past her level, and that when she asked to gain that experience, say in sales, she did not get a response and didn't feel she had much of a chance to get it, since she would be competing with men in sales who wanted those promotions too. At other companies, we met women who had left J&J for what they said was a lack of opportunity to move up. Some younger women appear to be doing better, particularly in marketing, but it is too soon to tell whether they too will top out and become disillusioned. Women with important titles tend to be clustered in personnel and public affairs, traditionally dead-end staff jobs; marketing is a possibility until you hit the glass ceiling. Research and development and operations are no good for women wishing to rise.

On the child care front, J&J looks upon children as a woman's problem. (If *she* wants to have a baby, *she* had better be able to manage it herself.) When we last talked to someone at J&J in the late summer of 1987, the company had recently hired someone to study the possibility of a day care center near their corporate headquarters in New Brunswick, New Jersey. Managers had already been talking about doing such a study more than a year earlier, indicating the degree of urgency the company feels about the issue. Here we met a number of women with children who felt they really had to prove themselves—to have the baby and be on the phone with the office within days.

The company is known for great benefits, and its wellness program is considered one of the most comprehensive around. In short: a great place if benefits are a main reason for working and if the idea of exercising during your lunch break turns you on. If you want to move ahead, look elsewhere.

Control Data has had so many financial problems in the last few years that many of the social welfare programs for which it became famous in the seventies have been severely cut back or gotten rid of altogether. Many of its diverse businesses have been cut loose under a new CEO, Robert Price, who is desperately trying to rescue the company from the nosedive it took in

1985–86, when the company lost $832 million. In some such situations, talent will out and women fare well, as they did at, say, Fidelity Bank, but that doesn't seem to have happened here, and there were no signs that it was going to when we visited there in the spring of 1987. While Price was holding periodic meetings with employees at all levels to hear their concerns and women were included, little or no progress is apparent. Two women hold high-level positions in the company—one is Jean Keffeler, vice president of strategic and operations planning for data storage, one of Control Data's bread-and-butter businesses; another is Lois Rice, senior vice president of government affairs, who mainly works out of Washington, D.C. But as both women were brought in at senior positions, it does not speak well for movement up the pipeline within the corporation. Yet in Rice's department, we found one woman, Judy Alnes, who is pleased not only about her movement in the corporation, but also about how her having babies—she has two—was treated. "I've always had spectacular bosses who have given me the room I need to have babies and deal with sick kids and go to class plays and T-ball games." Yet from conversations with other women, she certainly seems to be the exception.

Women are in sales (again, we have no percentages), but making it to a managerial position is very rough. The men don't want women there and make life uncomfortable for them. One woman said that for every man who was supportive of her in sales there was another waiting—hoping—for her to fall flat on her face. On sales trips, she is regularly excluded from the informal talk, where, as she puts it, "a lot of stuff gets talked about."

The company has somewhere in the vicinity of 300–350 vice presidents. We guess, with some help from an inside source, that approximately five of them are women. Yet only the two mentioned above have any real clout—the others are VPs without much power. One woman in the legal department went with one of the businesses as general counsel when it was sold; when it was reabsorbed, she was let go. The legal department, in particular, seems to be a bad place for women as a number of them have left in recent years—we ran into them at Honeywell, also located in Minneapolis.

Control Data has kept its extensive educational programs to maintain a technical edge, and through the use of monitors it's possible to sit in on classes at the nearby University of Minnesota and even ask questions as if you were sitting in the classroom. An Employee Advisory Resource service provides professional counseling, and the company maintains a staff of 15 psychologists who serve not only Control Data employees but outside clients who buy the service from the company. But these fringes are not enough to change the overall attitude of the company toward women.

"Progress for women in this company is horseshit," says one woman the company had not arranged for us to talk to. We thanked her for her candor.

WHAT WE LEARNED

Women are through the starting gates and into the lower to middle levels of management. But even in the best companies, women are just beginning to penetrate the uppermost levels of senior management. With the exception of five companies—each a special case—the inner circle is virtually all white and male.

Where in this country will the barriers tumble first? Probably at some of our companies. Not surprisingly, opportunities are greater in industries where enormous changes are taking place. Women are making strides in computers, telecommunications and financial services, where fresh talent is sorely needed. Women are also, finally, beginning to break the last barriers in industries that have traditionally hired many women: retailing, publishing, advertising and commercial banking.

As a group, here's what our best companies look like:

RECRUITING, HIRING AND PROMOTING WOMEN*

73 percent of respondents have an active plan aimed at attracting women. The companies that don't have a high percentage of women already.

Ten companies geared special advertising to women's media. Nine specifically requested women from executive search firms. Four

---

*When Title IV of the Education Amendments of 1972 opened fields to women that had previously been virtually closed, the era of equal opportunity began in earnest. The Equal Pay Act of 1964 required employers to pay the same wage to employees performing the same job. Title VII of the Civil Rights Act of 1964 prohibited wage discrimination on the basis of sex, race, religion or national origin. The Equal Employment Opportunity Act of 1972 prohibited companies from discriminating against women and minorities in hiring. But until women had the educational credentials necessary to obtain jobs in traditionally male fields, these acts had little bite.

used networking. Five used employee referrals. Thirteen used campus recruiting and brochures.

75 percent of these companies are actively engaged in programs for promoting women. Methods used included job posting (47 percent), training and workshops (47 percent), tuition reimbursement (56 percent), active tracking (20 percent) and succession planning (39 percent). Only two companies have a structured mentor program.

51 percent of the companies have written politics on recruiting and hiring women, and 73 percent have a grievance procedure for resolving complaints of sexual discrimination. Twelve percent have been involved in lawsuits at some time.

63 percent of the companies are committed to rectifying inequality of pay for women. Of those 32 companies:

▲ 23 examine what other companies are doing.

▲ 6 do research to establish measures of comparable worth.

▲ 25 reevaluate individual job descriptions.

▲ 11 engage in systematic reevaluation of descriptions of jobs held predominantly by women.

▲ 16 do grade level adjustments.

▲ 5 have given paybacks for past inequities (these five have, of course, done so as a response to lawsuits).

Most of the 37 percent remaining did not answer the question; a few, mostly smaller companies, stated that pay inequity was not an issue.

NUMBERS

The size of our companies ranges from a high of 300,000 for AT&T (after divestiture) to the tiny Drake Business Schools (88).

The percentage of employees who are women ranges from a low of 17 percent at Recognition Equipment to a high of 80 percent at Mount Carmel Health. The average for all companies is 45 percent.

The percentage of upper managers who are women ranges from a low of 2 percent at GTE to 54 percent at Hearst Trade Books and 100 percent at Drake Business Schools.

▲ 13 companies have at least one female president.

▲ 10 companies have female executive VPs.

▲ 18 companies have female senior VPs.

▲ 39 companies have female VPs. Financial institutions and retail firms, in particular, have *many* female vice presidents. The title has a different meaning in manufacturing firms.

▲ 8 of the companies have a female treasurer.

▲ 32 of the companies have at least one woman on the board of directors, up from 20 in 1980.

POLICIES AND ATTITUDES ABOUT TWO-CAREER COUPLES

These responses are particularly interesting when combined with the responses of corporations to Zeitz's Catalyst survey, run in 1980–81:

	1980–81 (%)	1986–87 (%)
Forbid couples in same company	17	2
Forbid couples in same department or function	72	37
Attitudes about married couples pursuing careers in the same company:		
A great idea	5.6	20
Company gains overall	22.8	45
Creates more problems than it solves	28.7	18
A bad idea	8.4	2
Wouldn't allow it	6.6	2

The percentage of companies that have, and human resources heads who favor, a variety of benefits important to women are also particularly interesting when contrasted with the percentages found in the 1980–81 Catalyst study (Table 1). In general, *more* companies in the present study now offer benefits ranging from flexible work hours to paternity benefits to a variety of child care options and subsidies.

TABLE 1

	DO HAVE SUCH A PRACTICE (%)	CATALYST SURVEY 1980–81 (%)	DO FAVOR SUCH A PRACTICE (%)	CATALYST SURVEY 1980–81 (%)
1. Flexible working hours	59	37	71	73
2. Maternity benefits	91	96	84	94
3. Paternity benefits	37	9	49	26
4. Adoption benefits	49	10	69	42
5. Flexible workplaces	37	8	51	35
6. Sick leave for family illness	59	29	61	44
7. Leave without pay, position assured	75	65	69	69
8. On-site child care	6	1	22	20
9. Subsidies for child care	22	0.8	33	9
10. Monetary support of community-based child care facilities	27	19	41	54
11. Resource referral directory for child care facilities	47	N.A.	73	N.A.
12. Cafeteria-style approach to employee benefits	30	8	69	62
13. Part-time work for managers and professionals, with proportional benefits	49	N.A.	63	N.A.

With all their faults (and we've pointed them out in the profiles themselves) these companies really *are* the best. However, we are fairly certain that some of the companies nominated that refused to participate are good companies for women. You can find a list of those companies on page 384.

Curiously, many companies essentially run or owned by women refused to participate in spite of letters followed by repeated phone calls. Among them were:

Liz Claiborne
Esprit
Stop & Shop
Bergdorf Goodman
Omega Engineering
W. L. Gore

The answer we got from these women was "We're too busy" or an out-and-out refusal with no explanation, although we were not, of course, asking the heads of these companies to spend the time. We hope that this response—or nonresponse—is not reflective of how women in general are doing at these companies. And we regret that women who are themselves leaders would not share their knowledge with an audience of career-oriented women.

WHAT THE WOMEN SAID

The baby boom generation is now fully absorbed into the workplace. In the 1990s the number of adults in their late twenties and early thirties in the United States will diminish by about 20 percent. Even if companies recruit, hire and promote from the entire potential pool of qualified applicants, they will have a more difficult time than ever before. The best companies already know that they can't afford to undervalue the 52 percent of undergraduates or the 33 percent of MBA candidates who happen to be women.

The policy-making people we talked to about recruiting, hiring and promoting women do so for varying reasons. At companies that are less good for women, the reasons are "We're required to by law" or "It's the right thing to do." Those were acceptable reasons in the seventies, but the heads of the very best companies for women have moved beyond that. Their reasons are "Because it's good business" and "Our survival depends on it."

They are right. But in many companies, the promoting is not happening yet. At the very top, corporate America is run by white males. *Business Week* and *Fortune* have noticed and commented. In 1986 *The Wall Street Journal* coined the phrase "glass ceiling"—a description the women we interviewed, many of whom hadn't read the articles, understood immediately.

Among our 52 companies, which are by no means limited to the *Fortune* 500 or *Business Week*'s 1,000 most valuable, only two—Barrios and Drake Business Schools—were started by women and continue to be run by women. And these 52 companies are the *best* out there for women. We did find a president here, a general manager there and a number of EVPs who are women, and we believe that women will eventually shatter the glass ceiling. But it will take some work, and legislation isn't likely to help it along. The impetus will come from the top.

THE MEN AT THE TOP

Our most important finding as we researched *The Best Companies for Women* is that it is the person at the top who determines how fairly women are treated. In all cases in the largest companies, and in most cases in the smaller companies, this person is a man. Never mind how he got to his gender-blind philosophy. Sometimes he had a mother who worked. Sometimes he has a wife who works. Sometimes it's a daughter who he thinks should be treated fairly in business. Sometimes no personal reason seems evident. The why is not important. The commitment—both the knowledge and the follow-through—is what counts. When the message from the top is loud, clear and unequivocal, it happens.

Jack MacAllister, CEO of U.S. West, wants "to get the best competitive advantage I can get." MacAllister remembers, from his earlier management days at AT&T, "I was outraged that I was part of the management team that misfired in such a sensitive human issue." U.S. West companies have excellent recent records in promoting women, in spite of their cowboy country geography.

Al Neuharth at Gannett has for years tied publishers' bonuses, in part, to how well they met specified goals regarding hiring and promoting women and minorities. Neuharth, renowned as a tough-minded businessman, says, "I don't care about sex or age or family name. We think companies that do penalize themselves. Let's face it. Middle-aged males like myself are in the minority. And women represent the majority—51.4 percent of the people in this country. Why should a minority of us white males make the decisions in a media company that tries to reach the vast audience out there? It's good business to hire women and minorities."

David Stanley at Payless Cashways has, in six years, convinced women that the sky's the limit in every aspect of that building materials company. "You are most likely to get the best candidate for a job if you address that largest possible pool of candidates without setting up any restrictions," he says. Relatively small changes in requirements have enabled women to assume jobs never before held by women, and to excel in them.

At Pitney Bowes, CEO George Harvey issued a recruiting and hiring memo in 1984 that mandated that new hires and promotions include 35 percent women and 15 percent minorities. "If we're going to get the best people, the people who are going to make us a success, we had better make sure that women can have careers here, not just jobs, and I didn't sense that was going to happen by letting things follow a normal course," says Harvey in a masterpiece of understatement.

In the last few years, Dick Schlosberg, former publisher of *The Denver*

Post, and Daniel Hall, former editor in chief,* have made it possible for bright, competent women to be rewarded with major promotions. These women were smart before Schlosberg got there; he was simply able to give them the recognition they deserved.

When Raymond Dempsey came to Fidelity Bank in the early seventies, it was foundering. Part of the turnaround involved changing the rules from an old boy network to meritocracy. When Dempsey left in 1984, Harold Pote, 42, the new chairman and CEO, further strengthened the message that talent, and only talent, determines success.

At all these companies, women are doing well.

ON ORGANIZED ACTION

Some companies we visited have active women's groups, varying in organization, formality and purpose.

CBS women have been meeting for 15 years—it's among the oldest corporate women's networks.

At Home Box Office, Shelly Fischel, senior vice president for human resources, and other high-ranking women began to hold forums for women to find out what women thought was wrong at HBO. What the women talked about was the glass ceiling. When we interviewed Michael Fuchs, CEO of HBO, he conceded that his young, aggressive company teeming with talented women is still run by an old boy network at the very top. At least he is sensitive to the fact and knows that these highly talented, vocal women are aware of it and are watching for further developments.

At Honeywell, an active women's council, formed in 1981, is a formal, 30-member group with direct input to upper management. Vice presidents are frequently members of the council.

At Southern New England Telephone, a day care center came about because the company's Management Women's Association lobbied for one.

Jack MacAllister, who heads the U.S. West companies, stresses the value of the support the women get from the support groups, as well

---

*As we go to press, a new owner of *The Denver Post* has replaced both Schlosberg and Hall; however, the new man, Maurice L. Hickey, is a veteran of Gannett who sees no problems in continuing the same gender-blind philosophy.

as the input he gets from them. U.S. West Women is an active support organization that regularly meets with top officials and includes high-ranking company women in its membership.

INDIVIDUAL CONTRIBUTORS

Women in some companies have stood up for themselves and one another individually, thereby causing important changes. At Hewitt Associates, Susan Koralik opened the door for women to be account managers in 1975 because she refused to accept the stereotype that "Girls can't be account managers." The man who originally said that, and eventually became her strongest supporter, also said, "You've got to understand that I've had the feelings I've got for years, and it's going to take time for me to change."

He did. And others will too. But women have to take some risks, singly and as part of a group, in order to be heard. And many have taken a stand on some issue, at the risk of standing out *as a woman:*

> Murem Sharpe, general manager of a subsidiary of Pitney Bowes, gives her employees 12 weeks of paid maternity leave, rather than the standard disability allowed.
>
> In the spring of 1982, U.S. West women invited officers of the company (at that time, all men) to a dinner meeting. George Ann Harding gave a speech about the backsliding that had occurred since the consent decree had expired. "Women and minorities were going down the tubes," she told us. An attorney in the legal department then, she is now Mountain Bell's highest-ranking woman and only female officer, vice president and chief executive officer for Wyoming.
>
> Judith Norton, senior vice president and director of human resources at Manufacturers Hanover Trust, talks about her matter-of-fact persistence of returning every year to managers who are not promoting women and reminding them repeatedly of women in their groups who are qualified.

SEXUAL HARASSMENT

Lots of people feel that with the surge of women into the work force, sexual harassment is no longer an issue. In some industries, that's actually true. In most, it's not. Furthermore, it's easy to get a false sense of peace if you spend most of your life at corporate headquarters, where manners tend toward the genteel. Management women with some degree of power are more likely to have the skills to handle a budding problem themselves or to blow the whistle on the offender. The cases that reach lawsuit stage tend to involve relatively powerless women.

A short paragraph in the employee handbook usually will not suffice to deter harassment. Most large companies have had someone step over the line, and how swiftly and seriously the matter has been treated gives you a clue as to how the company looks upon harassment.

At General Mills, word quickly made the grapevine that a high-ranking man had been fired for sexual harassment. Men were on notice that known offenders would be out, and women felt assured that their complaints would be taken seriously.

At Avon, a man who had been with the company for a long time was fired but given a healthy financial package to provide for his family. Still, the message to employees was loud and clear.

At companies where offenders are transferred, that action may be deemed appropriate, especially if the harassment is a borderline case. If the harassment is clear-cut and serious, a transfer is deemed an ineffectual response, and the women feel abandoned. The punishment needs to fit the offense.

At Barrios, a complaint about a NASA worker—the company's client— also got swift attention and a public apology for a wisecrack said in front of several coworkers, embarrassing the woman to the point where it was difficult to continue her job with dignity. The message is so strong at Barrios that women think twice before making a complaint but have no compunction when it is necessary.

At companies where only one reporting procedure is in place, filing a complaint can be problematic in some cases. The individual the woman is to complain to may be the offender, or the offender may be the boss of that person.

It may be difficult, if not impossible, to find out all of these things about a company when interviewing, but asking about policies, and whether there is a program on sexual harassment, will not be out of line and will give a clue as to the depth of the company's commitment.

SEXUAL DISCRIMINATION

Discrimination in the eighties is more likely to be subtle than blatant, yet we all bring our socialization with us to work. If a company has managers who are discriminating against women—talking in insulting ways, holding them back from promotion, underrewarding them with skimpy raises—it may not become known until the rapid turnover in that person's department becomes noticeable. Long before then, however, morale will be low and productivity will decline.

At Federal Express and Herman Miller, employees are given an opportunity to evaluate their managers, and the process quickly exposes sexism. At Federal Express, the review is anonymous; at Herman Miller, it takes place in peer group meetings without the boss's presence. And Gannett was among the first of several companies to tie managers' bonuses to their hiring and promotion of minorities and women.

Another method, less direct, perhaps, but still effective, is to use sensitivity sessions.

In 1979 Merck, a leader in how it treats its employees, launched a massive program that started with top managers, who in turn were trained to be group leaders. All 15,000 employees have attended the full-day training, which includes film, videotaped vignettes, presentations of case studies and discussions.

Levi Strauss put its executives through an intense three-day, off-site exercise specifically on attitudes toward women and minorities. The next year similar programs were held for people in the field, and the first group was scheduled for follow-up sessions. This is a company in an industry sorely pressed financially and structurally that thought the investment was worth it.

At the insistence of several top women at Home Box Office concerned with the sexist atmosphere, one male manager scheduled dinners with small groups of female employees to hear what they had to say. Afterward, the company hired a consultant who came in and ran sensitivity sessions. The atmosphere changed dramatically.

Companies that make it plain that discrimination of any sort is intolerable do not reimburse employees for membership or activities at clubs that don't admit women. Some examples from among our best companies:

Levi Strauss will not reimburse entertainment of buyers at clubs that discriminate against women, blacks or Jews.

Northwestern Bell announced that it would no longer pay for memberships to the Omaha Club until it admitted women. After Northwestern Bell took the lead, other companies followed suit; the club opened its doors to women.

Gannett left the Genesee Valley Club in Rochester, New York; the club now admits women.

In 1980, when Philadelphia's Union League voted on admitting women, it was defeated. Then head of personnel and a senior vice president (now president) of Fidelity Bank, Rosemarie Greco, told

CEO Ray Dempsey that this was a good place to make a statement about women's equality. Within 20 minutes after the vote count, Dempsey had delivered his resignation. Officers' memberships that had been paid by the bank were canceled, and no bank functions were held there. It took six years, but other companies followed suit, and in 1986 women were admitted to the club.

At Southern New England Telephone, a female vice president was put up for membership by a company peer at the all-male Quinnipiack Club and, in spite of the furor, got in and broke the tradition.

CHILD CARE AND FLEXIBILITY FOR PARENTING

Some of the companies profiled in this book offer unusually flexible arrangements for childbirth and the early months of a new mother's life. A few even offer paternity benefits, although practically nobody takes advantage of them. The flexibility reported by women from some companies is commendable. Some examples:

Merck started an off-site day care center that is now run by parents.

First Atlanta, Proctor & Gamble, Southern New England Telephone and Syntex have on-site or near-site centers.

In 1984 IBM funded one of the first and most comprehensive national resource referral services, which is used as a model for other companies.

To date only about 150 companies have made the expensive commitment to on-site day care, but approximately 3,000 have made some response, from resource referral services to including child care in their cafeteria-style approach to benefits, a jump of 50 percent since 1984.

There are no clear conclusions about what kinds of company responses to child care needs are best, because much depends on location, the demographics of employees at various sites and the availability of existing alternatives in an area.

At many companies, flexibility is built into the rules. At Fidelity Bank, one woman was able to have a computer terminal installed in her home and go back to work full-time, although she came into the office only one day a week for four months after the birth of a child; at Honeywell, one manager kept track of the days one of his workers came in during her maternity leave, and when she needed time for visits to the doctor or whatever in the first year, she went into the bank of days she had accumulated during her leave. At U.S. West Direct, women managers are unusually flexible if work can be done at home and a child is sick. U.S. West also allows a female attorney to work part-time. These are but a few examples of how flexibility for parenting makes it easier for women to keep up their jobs and not feel guilty about not having time for their children. It makes for loyal employees with high morale.

SO YOU'RE LOOKING FOR A JOB, OR, WHEN YOU'RE POUNDING THE PAVEMENT

If you're just entering, or reentering, the work force, or if you're already in place and aiming for the top, what should you be doing? While you are doing research for interviews at any company, keep in mind the criteria highlighted in our summaries. As you read through the annual reports, take notice of the pictures. Are there women portrayed as professionals and managers? Look at the list of corporate officers, the board of directors. Are there any women listed? Don't look for hordes of women—you won't find them. A few will do.

Know what you're after. Some companies are noted for their training programs. It's up to *them* to make it worth your while to stay after you've been trained.

Some companies are known for their benefits. If you want or need that at this stage of your career, that would be the deciding factor. Munificent benefits are *not* related to upward mobility. In fact, in companies like Merck, universally admired for the way it treats people, there are few women in upper management. Turnover is low; if nobody leaves, women in the pipeline don't move up. On the other hand, a company like Conran's, where benefits are not great, is wide open to women at the very top. Southern New England Telephone is an example of a company where benefits are excellent and upper management has a good ratio of women.

Read the profiles to find out what to expect in each company. We found out what we could about everything from corporate culture to starting salaries to where the best opportunities are. Ask yourself the same kinds of questions about any company where you're interviewing. Keep them in mind as you're being shown around. But be careful about asking some of the hard questions until after you've gotten a firm job offer.

Think through the issues raised in the profiles. Most important, if you want to be successful in business, get a sense of the characteristics of the women we interviewed. Some of the simplest advice is also the best.

FOCUS ON LINE JOBS.   Think twice about what Ruth Schaeffer, a senior research associate at the Conference Board, calls the "velvet straps" of staff jobs, if you want to rise to the policy-making ranks of your company. Understand that this frequently means you must have the flexibility to move.

> Paula Gavin, the AT&T vice president who manages the 40,000 person Operator Services Division, took transfers to sites throughout the company during her 20 years with AT&T.
>
> Laurie Neuse, who became the first female supervisor in her division of Restaurant Enterprises Group in 1984, joined the company in St. Louis in 1979 and has taken transfers to Kansas City, Phoenix and two sites in California during her 11-year career.

Some companies, like IBM, have a carefully thought out career development plan in which people are moved from line to staff and back again; most companies merely pay lip service to the concept. At IBM, being assistant to the president for *a predetermined length of time* is a coveted assignment that has helped women. In many other companies, that assignment can be the kiss of death.

KEEP YOUR EYE ON INDUSTRIES IN A HIGH GROWTH PHASE.   You'll have better opportunities in retailing or computer software, where the need for talent is at a premium, than in most traditional, hierarchical manufacturing firms.

REGARDLESS OF THE INDUSTRY, WOMEN FARE PARTICULARLY WELL IN SALES, WHERE THERE IS AN OBJECTIVE MEASURE OF "HOW'M I DOIN'?"
It's difficult for even a sexist boss to ignore dollar-based performance. Particularly if you're coming in with an undergraduate degree, sales is an excellent place to start. Whether you move up into sales management or jump to marketing, for example, you will enjoy a well-earned reputation for learning what it's like in the trenches.

LOOK AROUND.   Whether you're contemplating your first job or a move from your present job, don't ignore the marketplace. Although the training in large, traditional companies like IBM and AT&T is unsurpassed, opportunity may be greatest at a company like Lotus or Recognition Equipment that is undergoing explosive growth. Do thorough research on recent and projected growth rates at companies you're considering.

LOOK AHEAD. If you want to stay with your company, you also need to assess whether your company will stay in the product or service you're in now, or whether they're likely to refocus. You can't wait around passively. Ask to be moved to an area that is about to become more important.

> Our telecommunications companies are prime examples of where large-scale decisions to get out of one area and into another in order to gain the competitive edge can offer unusual opportunities.
>
> Murem Sharpe at Pitney Bowes saw an opportunity for this traditional manufacturing company to form a service-oriented subsidiary; it was a high-risk operation that has been a key to her visibility and success.

TAKE ADVANTAGE OF YOUR COMPANY'S MANAGEMENT TRAINING OPPORTUNITIES.

> Dana Becker, who was certainly doing well in a primarily technical career at AT&T, found that her year spent (at the company's request) at MIT on a Sloan Fellowship meant that management looked at her differently.
>
> And Deanna Hormel started as a dietitian at Hallmark. After her management development program, she was given the chance to run the food service, which serves some 4,800 meals a day. She also sits on an employee relations staff that's part of the personnel department, and she sees all kinds of growth opportunities in her future.
>
> Bonnie Osborn, now one step away from a vice presidency at Mountain Bell, started 28 years ago and got both her undergraduate and MBA while working full-time. Sherry Sherrill, also at Mountain Bell, found that management took a new interest in her career path once she entered an MBA program.

Most good companies do reimburse for tuition. Even if they do not specifically sponsor you in a program like the Sloan Fellowship, make it your business to find out what it takes to be considered promotable. Frequently it means an MBA.

IS TOP OF THE HEAP WHAT YOU REALLY WANT? HOW BADLY DO YOU WANT IT?

Helen Axel, a senior research associate at the Conference Board and director of the Career and Family Center there, says, "There's a need for ultimate optimism, the anything is possible approach, when you're intent on breaking down cultural barriers. There's also a need for systematic realism when accomplishment falls short of expectation."

Statistically—realistically—the work environment even in the same company is very different for a 28-year-old woman than it is for a 38-year-old woman. When Carol Green joined the *Denver Post* in 1968, she had had years of solid experience, yet she had to start in the women's department, typing times and dates of social gatherings, before being transferred to the city desk—a job she was indisputably qualified for. The transfer came when she did a series on false claims of health clubs on her own time. Eight years later, when Gay Cook joined the paper with good credentials but less experience than Green, she went directly to the city desk. Women who, regardless of educational credentials, used to start as tellers in banks and as clerks everywhere else, now start at the same place as do men with similar qualifications.

This means that, for the most part, older women had to work longer and harder just to get to the starting gate. For many of these women, it is unrealistic to demand of themselves that they reach the very top.

In spite of all odds, some of them have had spectacular rises, some with educational credentials, some without.

> Rosemarie Greco, president of Fidelity Bank, started fresh out of the convent, without a college degree, as a secretary.
>
> Beth Styer of Fidelity Bank is a senior vice president who started as a teller and got her degree while working there.
>
> Carole Presley, a senior vice president at Federal Express, never went to college.
>
> Karen Bachman, now vice president for investor relations at Honeywell, was an English major whose first job at Honeywell was opening customer mail.
>
> Anne Maddox, senior vice president at Saks Fifth Avenue and director of stores for the Midwest, went to work for them with a high school degree. She came to Saks at 18 with retail experience but no college degree, and has moved steadily up throughout her 22 years with Saks.

What do we mean by overcoming great odds? Lest you think that sexism is a dead issue:

> Janice Stoney, now CEO of Northwestern Bell, reports that on one of her appraisals in the 1960s, her manager wrote, "It's too bad she's not a man; she could go really far."
>
> In 1976 Sara Dickinson, with her brand-new engineering degree, chose Hewlett-Packard for her first job because they gave her a seri-

ous, rigorous interview. In the decade of her career at HP, this fast-track engineer was promoted approximately once every two years. Yet after she joined the company, she saw the recruiter's summary of her rigorous interview: "Pretty good for a girl."

UNDERSTAND WHEN TO LEAVE.   Women leave jobs for the same reasons men do: because they've plateaued where they are, because the opportunity is better elsewhere or because they decide they'd rather do something else. The only difference from men is that sometimes opportunities in their present job are limited by sexual discrimination, and sometimes the something else women decide to do is become a full-time mother. In our view, if you've realistically assessed the situation in your company and you honestly feel that sexual discrimination is the only thing holding you back, then you should leave. Find a place where you are evaluated for your talent.

Those who leave large companies because they have topped out frequently leave in the same way men do—for smaller, younger, riskier companies. One marketing executive at IBM, with 17 years of arguably the best training and experience in the country, left. IBM's loss; Cognos's gain. She is now president of the U.S. division. Another recipient of IBM's training and experience is now at Lotus.

Others will leave to start their own firms, just as men have done. This phenomenon has been portrayed negatively in the business press; we're not sure why. Three kinds of women leave for greener pastures of some sort: those who've topped out and seek more challenge elsewhere, those who decide that they prefer entrepreneurship to corporate hierarchies, and those who find they want to spend more time with their families than their current careers allow. We see these as growth reasons to leave.

Sadder is a particular group of women who do *not* leave. The most bitter women, those with the biggest ax to grind, are those in their forties and fifties, the groundbreakers who clawed their way up in environments totally unreceptive to women and plateaued out for lack of proper educational credentials or management skills, or because of out-and-out discrimination. In return for their truly heroic efforts, they do have a job, but they are grossly underpaid in comparison to men at their levels. However, they are paid enough so they're afraid or unable to leave. Additionally, they are infuriated by the current group of highly qualified, young entry-level women who arrive bright eyed and bushy tailed, who truly believe that being a woman is a total nonissue.

The hallmark of these women is that they dislike what they are doing. In contrast, the successful women—the ones who've moved ahead, or who have reached the place where they want to be, love what they are doing. Did they get ahead because of their enthusiasm, or are they enthusiastic because they got ahead? One suspects the former. But one part of the enormous enthusiasm of the successful older women has to do with the gap between what they expected to achieve and what in fact they *did* achieve.

> Rosemarie Greco started at Fidelity as a secretary, so she could earn enough money to go to college and get a degree in teaching. She is now president.

> Irma Wyman, now vice president of corporate information management at Honeywell, manages an organization of 540 people. In the sixties, a vice president told her, "You would have a great future if you were a man."

> Betty Jones, now a senior vice president at Citizens and Southern Bank, thought in the sixties that she would work for a few years before beginning a family. "It wasn't until I decided I wanted a career that I had one," she said.

MAKING CHOICES.   Betty Jones and her husband decided not to have children, a decision shared by many of the senior-level women, although certainly not by all.

The talented, well-educated women who have left their careers for full-time motherhood that have popped up in magazine articles are interesting, but they are aberrations. The vast majority of women take short periods of time (ranging from two weeks to a maximum of six months, the average being 12 weeks) and return to work. Most women couldn't afford to choose full-time motherhood even if they wanted to; most women wouldn't want to. What most women want is a reasonable amount of time off. Once fathers see that option as socially acceptable, we believe that more of them will want the same thing.

Many of the single, high-level women we talked to listened in amazement to colleagues in focus groups describing how they combine career and family and told us that they couldn't imagine how one *could* have both.

The answer is, we think, that you *can* have both, but serially, not all at once. Many of these best companies make it possible to have a baby, even take a few months off, and return to the same job. Yet many senior-level women told us they had gone into labor at the office, or went straight to the hospital from the office. One said she was on the phone with the boss telling him what to say at a meeting while she was in labor. Some had meetings in the hospital, or came in for a special meeting within a week. These women barely missed a beat. Many of them, to their company's credit, came back to a promotion and more responsibility.

We don't believe those dire predictions of "the baby will pay." These women had the wherewithal to hire full-time, caring help. We wonder whether, 10 years from now, these mothers will feel that they themselves have paid. If you have a high-powered career and make the decision *not* to step back at all when your baby is born, you will pay the same price in your personal life that men do. Just be aware that you *are* making trade-offs.

To the women who worry that taking any time off to have a child will hold them back in their careers, we say, it well may. So what? Men and women can expect to have careers—possibly two or three different ones— that span 40–50 years. In the overall scheme of things, so what if you get where you are going a little more slowly?

Of course, once the issue is seen as the people's issue it is, rather than a woman's issue, once parental leave of reasonable length is mandated by law, as we believe it should be, presumably both male and female parents will be equally slowed in their careers and richer for it.

Pursuing a career, or a relationship, is a reach—a risk. Pursuing both is a double reach. The happiest women seem to be the ones that regard career —and/or relationship—more as a process than as a product. They don't focus much on what it will be when it's done. They work at it and thoroughly enjoy the everydayness of it, moving toward the next step and then the step after that, but taking primary pleasure in the doing.

The best companies for women are the places that make it possible to do just that.

WORTH INVESTIGATING: 60 ADDITIONAL COMPANIES

Many of these 60 companies were nominated by key executive recruiters or professional women's groups. The nominators judged the company to be good for women in the benefits it offers, in the potential for upward mobility, or both.

Informally, we heard some good things about each of them. But one not-so-good thing is that the companies either refused to participate outright or failed to return a minimum of five phone calls following the initial letter and questionnaire. Companies refused for one of three reasons:

(1) We're not good enough.
(2) We're too busy to be bothered.
(3) We're undergoing massive restructuring.

We'll never know the reason for the companies whose representatives refused to return phone calls.

Some of the companies below did not refuse to participate, but we came upon them too late in the course of our research to investigate them.

We suggest that if you interview at these companies, you use our criteria to judge for yourself. We have listed the companies alphabetically and indicated their primary business.

WORTH INVESTIGATING

American Savings & Loan
77 W. 200 South
Salt Lake City, UT 84101
(801) 483-5800
Banking

ARA Services
1101 Market Street
Philadelphia, PA 19107
(215) 238-3000
Consulting

Atlantic Richfield Company
515 S. Flower Street
Los Angeles, CA 90071
(213) 486-3511
Petroleum

Bank of America
555 California Street
San Francisco, CA 94104
(415) 622-3456
Banking

Bankers Trust
280 Park Avenue
New York, NY 10017
(212) 250-2500
Banking

Bergdorf Goodman
754 Fifth Avenue
New York, NY 10019
(212) 753-7300
Retailing

Boston Consulting Group
Exchange Place
Boston, MA 02109
(617) 973-1200
Consulting

Cable News Network
CNN Center
Atlanta, GA 30348
(404) 827-1500
Broadcasting

Calvert Group
4550 Montgomery Avenue
Bethesda, MD 20814
(301) 951-4800
Financial

Campbell Soup
Campbell Place
Camden, NJ 08103-1799
(609) 342-4800
Food

Cardiac Pacemakers
4100 N. Hamline Avenue
St. Paul, MN 55112
(612) 638-4000
Health Care

Carter Hawley Hale
550 S. Flower Street
Los Angeles, CA 90071
(213) 620-0150
Retailing

Chemical Bank
277 Park Avenue
New York, NY 10172
(212) 310-6161
Banking

Christian Dior
1372 Broadway
New York, NY 10018
(212) 221-4744
Apparel

Citicorp-Citibank
399 Park Avenue
New York, NY 10043
(212) 559-1000
Banking

Condé Nast Publications
350 Madison Avenue
New York, NY 10017
(212) 880-8800
Publishing

Connecticut General
Hartford, CT 06152
(203) 726-6000
Insurance

Contempo Casuals
5433 W. Jefferson Boulevard
Los Angeles, CA 90016
(213) 936-2131
Retailing

Dayton Hudson
777 Nicollet Mall
Minneapolis, MN 55402
(612) 370-6948
Retailing

DDB Needham Worldwide
437 Madison Avenue
New York, NY 10022
(212) 415-2000
Advertising

D-A-Y
40 W. 57th Street
New York, NY 10019
(212) 977-9400
Public Relations

Encyclopedia Britannica
310 S. Michigan Avenue
Chicago, IL 60604
(312) 347-7000
Publishing

The Equitable
787 Seventh Avenue
New York, NY 10019
(212) 554-1234
Insurance

Esprit
900 Minnesota Street
San Francisco, CA 94107
(415) 648-6900
Apparel

Estee Lauder
767 Fifth Avenue
New York, NY 10153
(212) 572-4200
Cosmetics

European American Bank
EAB Plaza
Uniondale, NY 11555
(516) 296-5000
Banking

Exxon Corp.
1251 Avenue of the Americas
New York, NY 10020
(212) 333-1000
Petroleum

Federated Department Stores
7 W. 7th Street
Cincinnati, OH 45202
(513) 579-7000
Retailing

W. L. Gore & Associates
551 Paper Mill Road
Newark, DE 19714
(302) 738-4880
Manufacturing

Hoffman LaRoche
340 Kingsland Street
Nutley, NJ 07110
(201) 235-5000
Pharmaceuticals

Liz Claiborne
1441 Broadway
New York, NY 10018
(212) 354-4900
  Apparel

R. H. Macy's
151 W. 34th Street
New York, NY 10001
(212) 560-3600
  Retailing

Marriott
10400 Fernwood Road
Bethesda, MD 20058
(301) 380-0000
  Hotels

Mary Kay Cosmetics
8787 Stemmons Freeway
Dallas, TX 75247
(214) 630-8787
  Cosmetics

Mattel
5150 Rosecrans Avenue
Hawthorne, CA 90250
(213) 978-5150
  Toys

McKinsey & Company
55 E. 52nd Street
New York, NY 10022
(212) 909-8400
  Consulting

Merrill Lynch & Co.
World Headquarters
North Tower
World Financial Center
New York, NY 10281
(212) 449-1000
  Financial Services

Mervyn's
25001 Industrial Boulevard
Hayward, CA 94545
(415) 785-8800
  Retailing

Montgomery Securities
600 Montgomery Street
San Francisco, CA 94111
(415) 627-2000
  Financial Services

Morgan Stanley
1251 Avenue of the Americas
New York, NY 10020
(212) 703-4000
  Banking

New Jersey Bell
540 Broad Street
Newark, NJ 07101
(201) 649-9900
  Telephone

Newsday
235 Pinelawn Road
Melville, NY 11747
(516) 454-2020
  Publishing

New York Times
229 W. 43rd Street
New York, NY 10036
(212) 556-1234
  Publishing

Nordstrom
1501 Fifth Avenue
Seattle, WA 98101
(206) 628-2111
  Apparel

Northwestern Mutual Life
720 E. Wisconsin Avenue
Milwaukee, WI 53202
(414) 271-1444
Insurance

Ogilvy & Mather
2 E. 48th Street
New York, NY 10017
(212) 907-3400
Advertising

Omega Engineering
1 Omega Drive
Stamford, CT 06907
(203) 359-1660
Engineering

Polaroid
549 Technology Square
Cambridge, MA 02139
(617) 577-2000
Photographics

Port Authority of New York &
New Jersey
1 World Trade Center
New York, NY 10048
(212) 466-7000
Transportation

Publix Supermarkets
P. O. Box 407
Lakeland, FL 33802
(813) 688-1188
Food Markets

Quaker Oats
P. O. Box 9001
Chicago, IL 60604-9001
(312) 222-7111
Food

Rainier National Bank
P. O. Box 3966
Seattle, WA 98124
(206) 621-4111
Banking

Sara Lee Corporation
Three First National Plaza
Chicago, IL 60602-4260
(312) 726-2600
Food

Security Pacific Bank
333 S. Hope Street
Los Angeles, CA 90071
(213) 345-6211
Banking

Shawmut Bank
1 Federal Street
Boston, MA 02211
(617) 292-2000
Banking

Stop & Shop
1776 Heritage Drive
North Quincy, MA 02171
(617) 770-8000
Food Markets

Tenneco
1010 Milam
Houston, TX 77002
(713) 757-2131
Conglomerate

3M Corp.
3M Center
St. Paul, MN 55144-1000
(612) 733-1110
Manufacturing

Weinstocks
600 K Street
Sacramento, CA 95814
(916) 449-8888
Retailing

Xerox
P. O. Box 1600
Stamford, CT 06904
(203) 968-3000
Office Equipment

COMPANIES LISTED BY GEOGRAPHIC LOCATION:

NORTHEAST

CONNECTICUT

American Express
American Telephone & Telegraph
Avon Products
*Conran Stores
Digital
Federal Express
*Gannett
General Mills
**GTE
*Hallmark
*Hewitt Associates
Hewlett-Packard

IBM
Levi Strauss
*Manufacturers Hanover
Merck
**Pitney Bowes
Procter & Gamble
*Restaurant Enterprises Group
*Saks Fifth Avenue
Shearson Lehman Hutton
**Southern New England
 Telephone
Syntex

MAINE

American Express
American Telephone & Telegraph
Avon Products
Digital
Federal Express
General Mills
Hewlett-Packard

IBM
Levi Strauss
Merck
Pitney Bowes
Procter & Gamble
Shearson Lehman Hutton
Syntex

**Indicates corporate headquarters
*Indicates major employment centers. Some larger companies maintain a presence, such as sales
and/or support service offices, in every state. Number of employees in these offices may be small.

MASSACHUSETTS

*American Express
American Telephone & Telegraph
Avon Products
*CBS
**Cognos
*Conran Stores
**Digital
*Federal Express
*Gannett
General Mills
Hewitt Associates
*Hewlett-Packard
*Honeywell
IBM
Levi Strauss
**Lotus
*Manufacturers Hanover
Merck
*Neiman-Marcus
*Payless Cashways
Pitney Bowes
*Procter & Gamble
*Restaurant Enterprises Group
*Saks Fifth Avenue
*Salomon Brothers
Shearson Lehman Hutton
Syntex
*Time Inc.

NEW HAMPSHIRE

American Express
American Telephone & Telegraph
Avon Products
*Digital
Federal Express
General Mills
Hewlett-Packard
IBM
Levi Strauss
*Manufacturers Hanover
Merck
Pitney Bowes
Procter & Gamble
Shearson Lehman Hutton
Syntex

NEW JERSEY

American Express
*American Telephone & Telegraph
Avon Products
*Bidermann Industries
*CBS
*Conran Stores
Digital
*Federal Express
*Gannett
General Mills
Hewlett-Packard
IBM
Levi Strauss
*Manufacturers Hanover
**Merck
Pitney Bowes
*Procter & Gamble
*Restaurant Enterprises Group
*Saks Fifth Avenue
Shearson Lehman Hutton
*Syntex

NEW YORK

**American Express
**American Telephone & Telegraph
**Avon Products
**Bidermann Industries
**CBS
**Children's Television Workshop
**Conran Stores
Digital
**Drake Business Schools
Federal Express
*Gannett
General Mills
**Grey Advertising
**Hearst Trade Books
*Hewitt Associates
Hewlett-Packard
**Home Box Office

**IBM
Levi Strauss
*Lotus
**Manufacturers Hanover
Merck
*Neiman-Marcus
**PepsiCo
Pitney Bowes
*Procter & Gamble
*Recognition Equipment
*Restaurant Enterprises Group
**Rowland Company
**Saks Fifth Avenue
**Salomon Brothers
Shearson Lehman Hutton
Syntex
**Time Inc.

PENNSYLVANIA

American Express
American Telephone & Telegraph
Avon Products
*CBS
*Conran Stores
Digital
*Federal Express
*Fidelity Bank
*Gannett
General Mills
Hewitt Associates
*Hewlett-Packard
*Home Box Office

*Honeywell
IBM
Levi Strauss
*Lotus
*Manufacturers Hanover
*Merck
Pitney Bowes
*Procter & Gamble
*Restaurant Enterprises Group
*Saks Fifth Avenue
Shearson Lehman Hutton
Syntex
*Time Inc.

RHODE ISLAND

American Express
American Telephone & Telegraph
Avon Products
Digital
Federal Express
General Mills
Hewlett-Packard

IBM
Levi Strauss
Merck
Pitney Bowes
Procter & Gamble
*Restaurant Enterprises Group
Shearson Lehman Hutton
Syntex

VERMONT

American Express
American Telephone & Telegraph
Avon Products
*Digital .
Federal Express
*Gannett
General Mills

Hewlett-Packard
IBM
Levi Strauss
Merck
Pitney Bowes
Procter & Gamble
Shearson Lehman Hutton
Syntex

SOUTH

ALABAMA

American Express
American Telephone & Telegraph
Avon Products
Digital
Federal Express
General Mills
Hewlett-Packard
IBM

Levi Strauss
*Manufacturers Hanover
Merck
Pitney Bowes
Procter & Gamble
*Restaurant Enterprises Group
Shearson Lehman Hutton
Syntex

ARKANSAS

American Express
American Telephone & Telegraph
Avon Products

Digital
*Federal Express
General Mills

Hewlett-Packard
IBM
*Levi Strauss
Merck
Pitney Bowes

Procter & Gamble
*Restaurant Enterprise Group
Shearson Lehman Hutton
Syntex

DELAWARE

American Express
American Telephone & Telegraph
*Avon Products
Digital
Federal Express
*Fidelity Bank
*Gannett
General Mills

Hewlett-Packard
IBM
Levi Strauss
*Manufacturers Hanover
Merck
Pitney Bowes
Procter & Gamble
Shearson Lehman Hutton
Syntex

DISTRICT OF COLUMBIA

American Express
American Telephone & Telegraph
Avon Products
*Barrios Technology
*CBS
*Conran Stores
Digital
Federal Express
**Gannett
General Mills
Hewlett-Packard

*Honeywell
IBM
Levi Strauss
*Lotus
*Manufacturers Hanover
Merck
Pitney Bowes
Procter & Gamble
*Recognition Equipment
*Restaurant Enterprises Group
Shearson Lehman Hutton
*Time Inc.

FLORIDA

*American Express
American Telephone & Telegraph
Avon Products
Bidermann Industries

*CBS
Digital
*Federal Express
*Gannett

*General Mills
*GTE
 Hewitt Associates
 Hewlett-Packard
*Honeywell
 IBM
 Levi Strauss
*Manufacturers Hanover
 Merck

*Neiman-Marcus
*Pitney Bowes
 Procter & Gamble
*Restaurant Enterprises Group
*Saks Fifth Avenue
 Shearson Lehman Hutton
 Syntex
*Time Inc.

GEORGIA

*American Express
 American Telephone & Telegraph
*Avon Products
 CBS
**Citizens & Southern National
   Bank
 Digital
*Federal Express
**First Atlanta
*Gannett
 General Mills
*Herman Miller
*Hewitt Associates
 Hewlett-Packard

*IBM
 Levi Strauss
*Lotus
*Manufacturers Hanover
 Merck
*Neiman-Marcus
 Pitney Bowes
 Procter & Gamble
*Recognition Equipment
*Restaurant Enterprises Group
*Saks Fifth Avenue
*Salomon Brothers
 Shearson Lehman Hutton
 Syntex
*Time Inc.

KENTUCKY

 American Express
 American Telephone & Telegraph
 Avon Products
 Digital
 Federal Express
 General Mills
 Hewlett-Packard
 IBM

 Levi Strauss
*Manufacturers Hanover
 Merck
*Payless Cashways
 Pitney Bowes
*Procter & Gamble
*Restaurant Enterprises Group
 Shearson Lehman Hutton
 Syntex

LOUISIANA

American Express
American Telephone & Telegraph
Avon Products
Digital
Federal Express
*Gannett
General Mills
Hewlett-Packard
IBM

Levi Strauss
*Manufacturers Hanover
Merck
Pitney Bowes
*Procter & Gamble
*Restaurant Enterprises Group
*Saks Fifth Avenue
Shearson Lehman Hutton
Syntex

MARYLAND

American Express
American Telephone & Telegraph
Avon Products
*Conran Stores
Digital
*Federal Express
*Gannett
General Mills
Hewlett-Packard

IBM
Levi Strauss
*Manufacturers Hanover
Merck
Pitney Bowes
*Procter & Gamble
*Restaurant Enterprises Group
*Saks Fifth Avenue
Shearson Lehman Hutton
Syntex

MISSISSIPPI

American Express
American Telephone & Telegraph
Avon Products
Digital
Federal Express
*Gannett
General Mills
Hewlett-Packard

IBM
*Levi Strauss
*Manufacturers Hanover
Merck
Pitney Bowes
*Procter & Gamble
Shearson Lehman Hutton
Syntex

NORTH CAROLINA

American Express
American Telephone & Telegraph
Avon Products

Digital
Federal Express
*Gannett

General Mills
Hewlett-Packard
IBM
*Levi Strauss
*Manufacturers Hanover

Merck
Pitney Bowes
*Procter & Gamble
*Restaurant Enterprises Group
Shearson Lehman Hutton
Syntex

OKLAHOMA

American Express
American Telephone & Telegraph
Avon Products
Digital
Federal Express
*Gannett
General Mills
Hewlett-Packard
IBM

*Levi Strauss
*Manufacturers Hanover
Merck
*Payless Cashways
Pitney Bowes
Procter & Gamble
*Saks Fifth Avenue
Shearson Lehman Hutton
Syntex

SOUTH CAROLINA

American Express
American Telephone & Telegraph
Avon Products
*Citizens & Southern National
   Bank
*Digital
Federal Express
Hewlett-Packard

IBM
Levi Strauss
*Manufacturers Hanover
Merck
Pitney Bowes
*Procter & Gamble
Shearson Lehman Hutton
Syntex

TENNESSEE

American Express
American Telephone & Telegraph
Avon Products
Digital
*Federal Express
*Gannett
General Mills
Hewlett-Packard

IBM
*Levi Strauss
*Manufacturers Hanover
Merck
Pitney Bowes
*Procter & Gamble
Shearson Lehman Hutton
Syntex

TEXAS

American Express
American Telephone & Telegraph
Avon Products
**Barrios Technology
Bidermann Industries
*CBS
Digital
*Federal Express
*Gannett
General Mills
*GTE
*Herman Miller
*Hewitt Associates
Hewlett-Packard
*Home Box Office
IBM

*Levi Strauss
*Manufacturers Hanover
Merck
**Neiman-Marcus
*Payless Cashways
*PepsiCo
Pitney Bowes
*Procter & Gamble
**Recognition Equipment
*Restaurant Enterprises Group
*Saks Fifth Avenue
*Salomon Brothers
Shearson Lehman Hutton
Syntex
*Time Inc.

VIRGINIA

American Express
American Telephone & Telegraph
Avon Products
*Barrios Technology
*Conran Stores
Digital
Federal Express
*Gannett
General Mills

Hewlett-Packard
IBM
*Levi Strauss
*Manufacturers Hanover
Merck
Pitney Bowes
*Procter & Gamble
*Restaurant Enterprises Group
Shearson Lehman Hutton
Syntex

WEST VIRGINIA

American Express
American Telephone & Telegraph
Avon Products
Digital
Federal Express
*Gannett
General Mills

IBM
Levi Strauss
*Manufacturers Hanover
Merck
Pitney Bowes
Procter & Gamble
Shearson Lehman Hutton
Syntex

MIDWEST

ILLINOIS

*American Express
American Telephone & Telegraph
*Avon Products
Bidermann Industries
*CBS
Digital
*Federal Express
*Gannett
General Mills
*Grey Advertising
*GTE
**Hewitt Associates
Hewlett-Packard
*Home Box Office
*Honeywell

*IBM
*Levi Strauss
*Lotus
*Manufacturers Hanover
Merck
*Neiman-Marcus
*Payless Cashways
Pitney Bowes
*Procter & Gamble
*Recognition Equipment
*Saks Fifth Avenue
*Salomon Brothers
Shearson Lehman Hutton
Syntex
*Time Inc.

INDIANA

American Express
American Telephone & Telegraph
Avon Products
Digital
Federal Express
*Gannett
General Mills
Hewlett-Packard
IBM

Levi Strauss
*Manufacturers Hanover
Merck
*Payless Cashways
Pitney Bowes
*Procter & Gamble
*Restaurant Enterprises Group
Shearson Lehman Hutton
Syntex

IOWA

American Express
American Telephone & Telegraph
Avon Products
Digital
Federal Express
*Gannett

General Mills
Hewlett-Packard
IBM
Levi Strauss
*Manufacturers Hanover
Merck

*Payless Cashways
Pitney Bowes
*Procter & Gamble

*Restaurant Enterprises Group
Shearson Lehman Hutton
*Syntex

KANSAS

American Express
American Telephone & Telegraph
Avon Products
Digital
Federal Express
*Gannett
General Mills
Hewlett-Packard
IBM

Levi Strauss
*Manufacturers Hanover
Merck
*PepsiCo
*Pitney Bowes
*Procter & Gamble
*Restaurant Enterprises Group
Shearson Lehman Hutton
Syntex

MICHIGAN

American Express
American Telephone & Telegraph
Avon Products
*CBS
Digital
Federal Express
*Gannett
General Mills
**Herman Miller
Hewitt Associates
Hewlett-Packard

IBM
Levi Strauss
*Lotus
*Manufacturers Hanover
Merck
Pitney Bowes
*Procter & Gamble
*Restaurant Enterprises Group
*Saks Fifth Avenue
Shearson Lehman Hutton
Syntex
*Time Inc.

MINNESOTA

American Express
American Telephone & Telegraph
Avon Products
Digital
Federal Express
*Gannett
**General Mills
Hewitt Associates
Hewlett-Packard
**Honeywell
IBM

Levi Strauss
*Manufacturers Hanover
Merck
*Northwestern Bell
*Payless Cashways
Pitney Bowes
Procter & Gamble
*Restaurant Enterprises Group
Shearson Lehman Hutton
Syntex
*U.S. West Direct

MISSOURI

American Express
American Telephone & Telegraph
Avon Products
*CBS
Digital
*Federal Express
*Gannett
General Mills
**Hallmark
Hewitt Associates
Hewlett-Packard
*Home Box Office

IBM
Levi Strauss
*Lotus
*Manufacturers Hanover
Merck
*Neiman-Marcus
**Payless Cashways
Pitney Bowes
*Procter & Gamble
*Restaurant Enterprises Group
*Saks Fifth Avenue
Shearson Lehman Hutton
*Syntex

NEBRASKA

American Express
American Telephone & Telegraph
Avon Products
Digital
Federal Express
*Gannett
General Mills
Hewlett-Packard
IBM
Levi Strauss

*Manufacturers Hanover
Merck
**Northwestern Bell
*Payless Cashways
*Pitney Bowes
Procter & Gamble
*Restaurant Enterprises Group
Shearson Lehman Hutton
Syntex
*U.S. West Direct

NORTH DAKOTA

American Express
American Telephone & Telegraph
Avon Products
Digital
Federal Express
General Mills
Hewlett-Packard

IBM
Levi Strauss
Merck
*Northwestern Bell
Pitney Bowes
Procter & Gamble
Shearson Lehman Hutton
Syntex

OHIO

American Express
American Telephone & Telegraph
*Avon Products
Digital
*Federal Express
*Gannett
General Mills
*Herman Miller
Hewlett-Packard
IBM
Levi Strauss
*Lotus
*Manufacturers Hanover
Merck
*Mount Carmel Health
*Payless Cashways
*Pitney Bowes
*Procter & Gamble
*Restaurant Enterprises Group
*Saks Fifth Avenue
Shearson Lehman Hutton
Syntex

SOUTH DAKOTA

American Express
American Telephone & Telegraph
Avon Products
Digital
Federal Express
*Gannett
General Mills
Hewlett-Packard
IBM
Levi Strauss
*Manufacturers Hanover
Merck
*Northwestern Bell
Pitney Bowes
Procter & Gamble
Shearson Lehman Hutton
Syntex

WISCONSIN

American Express
American Telephone & Telegraph
Avon Products
Digital
Federal Express
*Gannett
General Mills
Hewitt Associates
Hewlett-Packard
IBM
Levi Strauss
*Manufacturers Hanover
Merck
*Pitney Bowes
Procter & Gamble
*Restaurant Enterprises Group
Shearson Lehman Hutton
Syntex

WEST

ALASKA

American Express
American Telephone & Telegraph
Avon Products
Digital
Federal Express
General Mills
Hewlett-Packard

IBM
Levi Strauss
Merck
Pitney Bowes
Procter & Gamble
Shearson Lehman Hutton

ARIZONA

*American Express
American Telephone & Telegraph
Avon Products
*Digital
*Federal Express
*Gannett
General Mills
Hewitt Associates
Hewlett-Packard
*Honeywell
IBM

Levi Strauss
*Manufacturers Hanover
Merck
*Mountain Bell
*Payless Cashways
Pitney Bowes
*Procter & Gamble
*Restaurant Enterprises Group
*Saks Fifth Avenue
Shearson Lehman Hutton
Syntex
*U.S. West Direct

CALIFORNIA

American Express
American Telephone & Telegraph
*Avon Products
Bidermann Industries
*CBS
*Conran Stores
*Digital
*Federal Express
*Gannett
General Mills
*Grey Advertising
*GTE

*Herman Miller
Hewitt Associates
*Hewlett-Packard
*Home Box Office
*Honeywell
IBM
**Levi Strauss
*Lotus
*Manufacturers Hanover
*Merck
*Neiman-Marcus
*Payless Cashways

*PepsiCo
Pitney Bowes
Procter & Gamble
*Recognition Equipment
**Restaurant Enterprises Group

*Saks Fifth Avenue
*Salomon Brothers
Shearson Lehman Hutton
**Syntex
*Time Inc.

COLORADO

American Express
American Telephone & Telegraph
Avon Products
*Denver Post
*Digital
Federal Express
*Gannett
General Mills
Hewitt Associates
*Hewlett-Packard
*Home Box Office
*Honeywell

IBM
Levi Strauss
*Manufacturers Hanover
Merck
**Mountain Bell
*Payless Cashways
Pitney Bowes
Procter & Gamble
*Restaurant Enterprises Group
Shearson Lehman Hutton
*Syntex
*U.S. West Direct

HAWAII

American Express
American Telephone & Telegraph
Avon Products
Digital
Federal Express
*Gannett
General Mills

Hewlett-Packard
IBM
Levi Strauss
Merck
Pitney Bowes
Procter & Gamble
Shearson Lehman Hutton
Syntex

IDAHO

American Express
American Telephone & Telegraph
Avon Products
Digital
Federal Express
*Gannett
General Mills
*Hewlett-Packard
IBM

Levi Strauss
Merck
*Mountain Bell
*Northwestern Bell
Pitney Bowes
Procter & Gamble
Shearson Lehman Hutton
Syntex
*U.S. West Direct

MONTANA

American Express
American Telephone & Telegraph
Avon Products
Digital
Federal Express
General Mills
Hewlett-Packard

IBM
Levi Strauss
Merck
*Mountain Bell
Pitney Bowes
Procter & Gamble
Shearson Lehman Hutton
Syntex

NEVADA

American Express
American Telephone & Telegraph
Avon Products
Digital
Federal Express
*Gannett
General Mills
Hewlett-Packard
IBM
*Levi Strauss

*Manufacturers Hanover
Merck
*Neiman-Marcus
*Payless Cashways
Pitney Bowes
Procter & Gamble
*Restaurant Enterprises Group
*Saks Fifth Avenue
Shearson Lehman Hutton
Syntex

NEW MEXICO

American Express
American Telephone & Telegraph
Avon Products
*Digital
Federal Express
*Gannett
General Mills
Hewlett-Packard
*Honeywell
IBM

*Levi Strauss
*Manufacturers Hanover
Merck
*Mountain Bell
*Payless Cashways
Pitney Bowes
Procter & Gamble
*Restaurant Enterprises Group
Shearson Lehman Hutton
Syntex

OREGON

American Express
American Telephone & Telegraph
Avon Products
Digital

Federal Express
*Gannett
General Mills
Hewlett-Packard

IBM
Levi Strauss
*Manufacturers Hanover
Merck
*Payless Cashways
Pitney Bowes

Procter & Gamble
*Restaurant Enterprises Group
Shearson Lehman Hutton
Syntex
*U.S. West Direct

UTAH

*American Express
American Telephone & Telegraph
Avon Products
Digital
Federal Express
General Mills
Hewlett-Packard
IBM

Levi Strauss
*Manufacturers Hanover
Merck
*Mountain Bell
Pitney Bowes
Procter & Gamble
Shearson Lehman Hutton
Syntex

WASHINGTON

American Express
American Telephone & Telegraph
Avon Products
Digital
Federal Express
*Gannett
General Mills
Hewitt Associates
*Hewlett-Packard
*Honeywell

IBM
Levi Strauss
*Lotus
*Manufacturers Hanover
Merck
Pitney Bowes
Procter & Gamble
*Restaurant Enterprises Group
Shearson Lehman Hutton
Syntex
*U.S. West Direct

WYOMING

American Express
American Telephone & Telegraph
Avon Products
Digital
Federal Express
General Mills
Hewlett-Packard

IBM
Levi Strauss
*Manufacturers Hanover
Merck
*Mountain Bell
Pitney Bowes
Procter & Gamble
Shearson Lehman Hutton

ACKNOWLEDGMENTS

Several people must be thanked for their contribution to this book, which at times seemed as if it would never be finished. We would like to thank Glenn Cowley for conceiving the idea; Al Lowman for bringing us together and standing by during the difficult times; Patricia Soliman for immediately grasping what we were trying to do; Fred Hills for shepherding the book through the final stages; and especially our families, not only for their patience, but also for their real and invaluable assistance: David and Chaim Zeitz, research assistants; Bill Zeitz for a most spectacular case of role reversal; and Anthony Brandt for his painstaking editing and suggestions throughout the process. We thank you all. Without your help this book never would have come to be.

We would also like to thank the executive recruiters, officers of professional organizations and others who responded to our first call for recommendations for good companies for women. Finally, we want to thank the hundreds of women—and dozens of men—who freely gave their time and expertise, who sat through interviews and countless callbacks to check facts, who filled out surveys and answered our requests for additional information. Without you, there would have been no book.

INDEX

ABOUT THE AUTHORS

Baila Zeitz, Ph.D., is former director of research at Catalyst, an organization supporting upward mobility for women, where she did large-scale research on two-career couples and the corporation. A business consultant, she lectures nationally on stress management, combining career and family, and sex-role stereotyping. Dr. Zeitz earned her doctorate at New York University, and is a psychologist with practices in New York City and Teaneck, New Jersey. She lives in New Jersey with her husband and is the mother of two grown sons.

Lorraine Dusky is an award-winning journalist and the author of *Birthmark*. She has worked in industry, for both a company that was good for women and one that was not. She is married and lives in Sag Harbor, New York.